♡   ♡

You   ♡   ♡

♡   me

FOR MY TOM,

A PASSION.

MARIA
                    .

September 2003

FOIE GRAS

A PASSION

MICHAEL A. GINOR

Mitchell Davis

Andrew Coe and Jane Ziegelman

Photographs by Gideon Lewin

Food Styling by Elizabeth Duffy

John Wiley & Sons, Inc.

New York • Chichester • Weinheim • Brisbane • Singapore • Toronto

Copyright © 1999 by John Wiley & Sons, Inc. All rights reserved.

Published simultaneously in Canada.

This publication is designed to provide accurate and authoritative information in regard to the subject matter covered. It is sold with the understanding that the publisher is not engaged in rendering professional services. If professional advice or other expert assistance is required, the services of a competent professional person should be sought.

Library of Congress Cataloging-in-Publication Data
Ginor, Michael.
    Foie gras : a passion / Michael Ginor, Mitchell Davis, Andrew Coe, Jane Ziegelman.
      p. cm.
    ISBN 0-471-29318-0 (cloth)
     1. Foie gras. 2. Cookery. I. Davis, Mitchell.   II. Coe, Andrew.
  III. Ziegelman, Jane.   IV. Title.
  TX750.G56   1999
  641.8'12—dc21   98-41794

Printed in the United States of America.
10 9 8 7 6 5 4 3

To my late father, Amos, for his inspiration and confidence;
my late mother, Zvia, for her guidance and devotion;
my wife, Laurie, for her clarity of mind and purity of spirit;
my children, Yonatan, Yarden, and Maya, who serve as my role models;
and to my partner, Izzy, who enabled me to achieve my dreams.

Contents

Recipe Contents

viii

Acknowledgments

This book is a reflection of the quality of the people involved. For their contributions special gratitude goes to:

LAURIE GINOR, my wife and an officer of Hudson Valley Foie Gras, for her tireless and relentless labor through every phase of this project from the moment of conception.

IZZY YANAY, my partner and friend, whose determination, tenacity, and resourcefulness gave birth to a foie gras industry in the United States and transformed the industry worldwide.

Gideon Lewin, a stable source of artistic illumination who brought the food on these pages to life through the lens of his camera.

Pam Chirls, my editor, for her invaluable support through the turbulent gestation of this book.

Elizabeth Duffy, food stylist, who meticulously translated the chefs' culinary creations into a striking and uniform body of work.

Kevin Zraly, a wine educator and authority whose comprehensive understanding of the interaction between food and wine increased the gastronomic breadth of the book.

Jane Miller, Lauren McGrath, and Yvette Fromer, who helped research, write, edit, test, and nurse the recipes and wine pairings to their final state.

Karen Hadley, who incubated the idea for this project and whose conviction turned it into a reality.

Dorothy Moylan, whose loyalty and dedication enabled me to be consumed by this project.

Izabela Wojcik, whose editing skill and sense of humor helped ease us through the final stages of production.

Zoltan Halasz for his assistance with research on the history of foie gras in Hungary, and Ike Shapiro for his help with its Jewish origins.

Peter Killelea, for his dedication and support in photographing the chef's creations.

Jean-Louis Palladin, for his thorough knowledge of, culinary expertise with, and inborn passion for foie gras.

Teresa Barrenechea, for her devotion to the cuisine of Spain and her relentless efforts in broadening the scope of this book.

Willa Morris and Emily Taitz, whose professionalism and wholehearted commitment helped us edit and bind this project together.

Barbara Kirshenblatt-Gimblett, Barbara Wheaton, Barbara Haber, and William Woys Weaver, for their expert elucidation of culinary history.

The chefs who contributed to this project and their colleagues throughout the world—the most passionate, creative, and industrious craftspeople I have had the honor to associate with.

Foie Gras . . . A Passion

THE LOVE STORY

Laurie and I tasted foie gras for the first time on a warm Thursday evening in September 1983. We were twenty years old at the time, and I remember the experience vividly. Ironically, it did not happen in France at a three-star Michelin restaurant, as one would assume, but in Israel at a Middle-Eastern grill. We were students participating in a study abroad college program at The Hebrew University in Jerusalem. At that time, my father, a former Boeing aircraft engineer who operated his own aircraft leasing corporation, happened to be traveling on business in Israel and visited us. That visit resulted in a series of events that would eventually change my life.

My father, a quiet, serious, and confident man, possessed a particular fondness for dining establishments whose names included the descriptions "barbecued" or "smoked," and he was comfortable selecting restaurants for their names or dining themes alone. A restaurant named "The Seven Seas," for example, was irresistible as it evoked travel through time and space. He was not a gourmand, but a "charred-meat and potato man," thus making us wary of his dining selections. Laurie and I, on the other hand, were both avid foodies. We always conspired with my mother to veto or undermine his culinary suggestions. This one particular meal, however, vindicated him.

After convening a large group of relatives and friends, my father insisted we venture to the Hatikva area of Tel Aviv, where the outdoor restaurants served "a kind of grilled liver." My mother loved it, he assured us. Laurie and I glanced at each other with suspicion. If we were about to be treated to a great meal, why should we have liver? Still, my father insisted and we hesitantly conceded.

The Hatikva area, located to the south of Tel Aviv, almost outside the city limit, is a dilapidated neighborhood known for its colorful, open-air market and all-night motorcycle and pedestrian traffic. Its main street is studded with pita bread bakeries, street peddlers, and inexpensive charcoal-grill restaurants serving simple Mediterranean fare. My father took us to the best of these restaurants, Avazi, and ordered *mezze*, a variety of Middle Eastern appetizers. Soon a parade of food arrived at our table, beginning with freshly baked Iraqi *laffa* flatbread, fragrant and exotically spiced salads and french fries, followed by a plethora of skewers of grilled meat and offal. Nestled among those skewers was the neighborhood's specialty, grilled *kaved avaz,* fattened goose liver. We took a reluctant taste.

The fattened goose liver was cubed, with five to six cubes (about three to four ounces) allotted per skewer. The liver was a perfect paradox of color and texture. It was well charred, with a crisp exterior and a creamy molten interior. It was a magical taste experience. As was the custom, we spread the accompanying warm *laffa* flatbread with hummus, nudged the cubes of charred liver on top, garnished it with french fries and a dab of fiery *harissa*, and rolled the *laffa* into a handful of sheer bliss.

Laurie and I exchanged looks of enchantment as she nibbled on another *laffa*. In light of her eating patterns, having seconds was a sure sign that this could be the single best food item she had ever tasted. It was at once sumptuous and completely overwhelming. We devoured skewer after skewer, and our love affair with foie gras was ignited.

Shortly after my father's visit, we began to make foie gras forays into Hatikva. Our friends were perplexed yet intrigued. Israelis would seldom travel from Jerusalem to Tel Aviv, a mere hour away by car yet a world apart philosophically. To make the journey simply for dinner in an open-air taverna in the unstylish Hatikva was unheard of. Yet we occasionally enticed friends to join us in our culinary escapades, and we introduced many people to foie gras that year.

At the end of our 12-month stay, Laurie and I returned to the United States and, except for some delicious memories, we left foie gras in Israel. We graduated from Brandeis University, married, and spent the next few years building our careers in the financial industry in New York City. In 1988 we returned to Israel where I served as an officer for the Israeli Defense Forces stationed in the Gaza Strip. Naturally, we resumed our regular visits to Hatikva to indulge our passion for grilled foie gras and, this time, we did not shy away from experimenting with cooking it either. We became quite bold in testing various preparations and spontaneously creating an abundant repertoire of accompaniments. We were mesmerized by the seemingly infinite versatility of this unique product.

Two years passed quickly and, once again, Laurie and I found ourselves back in New York. In December 1989, we dined at Café Rakel to celebrate the birth of our first son, Yoni. To our utter amazement there was a foie gras appetizer listed on the menu. Although it was very expensive, we were compelled to try it. When the dish arrived, the preparation was magnificent, but we were disappointed with the quality of the liver itself. It seemed that the foie gras in Israel was both less expensive and better. I questioned the waiter about the source of the product and he sent for the chef, Thomas Keller. From Chef Keller we learned that there was a single foie gras producer in the United States, but the supply was unstable and the quality and pricing inconsistent. I could taste the gap between supply and demand, and, for me, foie gras suddenly developed an entrepreneurial dimension.

THE PLAN

I became committed to supplying a fresh, high-quality product to the foie gras–deprived American public, and investigated the possibility of importing it. It was not long before I learned of an existing United States Department of Agriculture (USDA) ban on the importation of fresh poultry products. It seemed that my desire for an excellent foie gras would never again be satisfied within the United States. But I simply was not ready to settle for that and resolved to find some way to create a new source. There was only one producer in the United States, I reasoned, and he had a mediocre track record. There certainly had to be room in the marketplace for another.

THE PLAYERS

Fate must have intervened on my behalf. Just at this time, Gonzalo Armendariz, a childhood friend and now owner of a frozen-Mexican-food business, provided me with an important contact. Gonzalo had been renting his production facility at night to Ariane Daguin, of D'Artagnan, who was recreating traditional foie gras recipes from her native Gascony. She was hesitant to speak with me at first because issues of animal rights and controversy frequently surfaced in reference to foie gras. I think my unabashed enthusiasm must have seemed dubious; however, Ariane soon discovered that my interest was genuine and my motivation sincere. She put me in contact with Izzy Yanay.

Izzy was an Israeli foie gras expert whose achievements in the animal science field were well documented. He had recently left the only operative foie gras farm in the United States to pursue his dream of establishing his own production facility. Izzy and I connected instantly. He was forthcoming with information and full of enthusiasm. My strongest asset was marketing acumen, a skill that allowed me to be optimistic about the future growth and acceptance of foie gras in this culinarily emerging country. Our passions, skills, and similar Israeli backgrounds meshed perfectly. In Izzy I found not only a capable partner, but also my perfect counterpart. And the rest, as they say, is history.

THE HUDSON VALLEY STORY

In establishing the Hudson Valley Foie Gras label, we set out to create a reliable supply of high-quality, consistently priced foie gras, and to generate increasing future demand for the product. By 1990 we had incorporated as AGY Corporation and transformed an abandoned egg-laying chicken farm into our first operation. The initial stages of development proved to be exciting and full of anxiety. Twelve months later, between May 15 and June 15, 1991, Hudson Valley Foie Gras produced the first batch of 500 livers. During this same period, I was preparing for a master's degree in business administration from New York University. I took full advantage of the business theories and case studies I was learning and applied them to Hudson Valley's evolving business plan. By September, production levels had increased to 900 livers per week. Today, the Hudson Valley Foie Gras label represents an association of four farms working tirelessly to reach production levels of approximately 7000 livers per week. It is the largest single producer of the finest-quality foie gras in the world.

THE PHILOSOPHY

Few people would deny that foie gras is a somewhat unusual delicacy, not of the type typically embraced by the American palate. I believe that one of the reasons Hudson Valley Foie Gras has so successfully captivated the interest of both culinary professionals and the dining public is my obvious and genuine love for this product. My sensibility must be contagious. I have spent the last ten years consumed by this venture, spreading the "foie gras gospel," to anybody who will listen. I continue to travel extensively, educating myself through stages in some of the greatest kitchens of the world, and educating others in the proper handling, storing, and marketing of foie gras. I firmly believe that chefs, restaurateurs, and culinary educators ultimately dictate what the distributors will offer and what the dining public will appreciate. Therefore, I work closely with them, conducting tastings and classes to showcase our products.

Although delighting in foie gras is common in France, few people in the United States have tried it. For this reason, Hudson Valley Foie Gras has frequently initiated efforts to educate consumers by offering demonstrations in stores and cooking schools, as well as by introducing the public to foie gras through national culinary events and festivals.

THE BOOK

My culinary experiences and professional growth has led to this book. My objective was to produce an exhaustive manuscript that would reflect the historical significance of foie gras as well as the versatility and sensual pleasures that this extraordinary delicacy affords. *Foie Gras . . . A Passion* is at once a collection of preferences, fabulous recipes provided by renowned chefs, and a historical study of human expression at its culinary finest.

To provide a proper context for discussing foie gras as a part of contemporary cooking, we introduce it with a thorough account of the process by which this delicacy slowly made its way from the banquets of Egyptian pharaohs to the white tablecloth establishments of today. Foie gras is a unique food that has achieved both notoriety and high esteem among people of all social standing. *Foie Gras . . . A Passion* uncovers little-known facts about the crucial role Jewish culinary tradition has played in the evolution of foie gras. Surprisingly, Jewish cooking and culture is the thread that connects the historical tapestry of foie gras, weaving together its ancient origins with modern developments.

Additionally, no comprehensive foie gras book could forego the opportunity to include chapters on topics of nutrition and animal rights. The former has left many an anxious diner in the throes of fierce self-denial or proud self-indulgence, while the latter has been a source of heated debate and frequent controversy for generations.

The main body of this book defines the versatility of foie gras and the abundant personal creativity that it inspires through myriad cooking techniques and extraordinary accompaniments. As the world becomes a more unified marketplace, it is apparent that the exceptional qualities of foie gras can be incorporated into every type of cuisine. The innovative styles and unusual food pairings exhibited in this collection point to a thoroughly American ideology of embracing tradition while demonstrating a penchant for bold experimentation. The willingness we encountered from chefs around the world to participate in this culinary odyssey is a testament to the pervasive impact that foie gras has had on our culture.

At the conclusion of the book, the reader will find two glossaries. The first is a grouping of foie gras–related terms. The second is a general culinary glossary intended to inspire readers who might have a burgeoning culinary interest themselves. There is, finally, a selective list of sources for the ingredients mentioned throughout this book. It is my intention to provide the reader with as many options as possible to procure the recommended items; however, it is possible to substitute ingredients that are locally available and still get delicious results.

Nothing can compare to the initial taste experience of foie gras. Laurie and I can still enjoy foie gras. Sometimes I prefer an uncomplicated silken terrine garnished simply with freshly grilled toast points. Laurie likes a perfectly sautéed medallion of caramelized foie gras, embellished with flourishes of fruits and vegetables. But, most often, I crave a skewer of charcoal-grilled foie gras. Maybe at heart I, too, am a "charred-meat man" like my father. Whatever your preference, foie gras is a remarkably adaptable ingredient, and I am a devoted worshipper.

We invite you to share the passion!

Michael A. Ginor

HISTORY

ANCIENT ORIGINS

Geese and ducks were a mainstay of ancient Egyptian diet.
The Metropolitan Museum of Art, Rogers Fund, 1931. (31.6.8) Photograph © 1978 The Metropolitan Museum of Art.

The history of foie gras begins in ancient Egypt with the domestication of wild geese. Together with ducks and swans, the goose is a waterfowl belonging to the Anserinae family. In the Old World, geese migrate between summer nesting grounds in northern Europe and winter feeding areas around the Mediterranean basin. One of the richest wintering locations is the lush Nile delta with its abundant water and wealth of edible plants.

Perhaps it was in one of these watersheds that prehistoric hunters first began to trap live geese and stock them for breeding.

Egypt

The goose was highly esteemed by the ancient Egyptians, figuring prominently in their creation myths. The gods of Egyptian mythology could each assume a number of forms. Geb, the Egyptian earth god, was often portrayed with a goose on his head. Geb could also take the form of a gooselike being, and was known in this manifestation as Khenkenwer, the "Great Cackler."

According to Egyptian mythology, Khenkenwer gave birth to a cosmic egg out of which hatched the sun, thus filling the world with light. The birds came to be associated with fecundity (laying eggs) and strength (godly flight). Later, the goose became connected with the followers of Amon, the state god of Middle Kingdom Egypt. The priests of Amon raised geese for sacrificial offerings, tending to the birds in pools near their temples and also using them for food. Herodotus, the fifth-century B.C. Greek writer, noted with shock that these holy men would dine on the flesh of a bird they revered as sacred.

Ancient Egyptian farm laborers force-feed geese and other birds to produce extra fat.
Oriental Division
The New York Public Library
Astor, Lenox and Tilden
Foundations

From their numerous depictions in ancient art, we see that Egyptian geese were gray, possibly related to the greylag or white-fronted geese of today. Goose meat was available to both rich and poor in ancient Egypt and remains a traditional food in Egypt today. Aside from their culinary uses, geese were a common mortuary offering, and goose fat was an ingredient in many medicinal preparations. The center of the goose trade was in Chenoboscium or Chenoboscia, a town at the edge of the Upper Nile marshes whose name is believed to mean "place where geese are fattened."

2

A number of aristocratic tombs built around 2390 B.C. contain reliefs that show the deceased hunting geese on the marshes. In these scenes, the hunters, armed with bows and arrows, perch in boats or wait with traps and nets to capture the birds alive. Other panels depict poultry yards with geese, ducks, cranes, and other birds enclosed by large nets. At the necropolis of Saqqara next to Memphis, the Egyptian technique for fattening geese is shown. The tomb of Mereruka, an important royal official, contains a bas relief of an aviary scene in which servants grasp geese around the necks in order to push pellets down their throats. By their sides stand tables piled with more pellets, probably made from roast grain, and flasks for moistening the feed before giving it to the birds. The Saqqara reliefs, the earliest depictions of force-feeding, or *gavage,* yet found, suggest that this practice was favored by the aristocracy.

Hunting geese and ducks in the Nile marshes was a favorite sport of Egyptian aristocrats. Egyptian Expedition of The Metropolitan Museum of Art, Rogers Fund, 1930. (30.4.48) Photograph © 1992 The Metropolitan Museum of Art.

It is probable that the Egyptians practiced gavage for the purpose of producing a fattier bird. Nearly every culture through history (with the exception of the twentieth century affluent West) has treasured animal fats, as these are an important source of calories and vitamins. Fats are also an excellent high-temperature cooking medium and preservative. Goose fat is a particularly flavorful and versatile ingredient, and comes from a ritually "clean" animal, unlike lard, which comes from the pig, banned as food in ancient Egypt. Geese are easily transportable, are prolific breeders, and are inexpensive to raise. Capturing and fattening these birds, which flocked to the Nile delta, made both culinary and economic sense.

Greece

Over the two millennia that followed, the practice of goose-fattening spread from Egypt through the eastern Mediterranean. In the *Odyssey* the Greek poet Homer (possibly eighth century B.C.) has Penelope say, "I have twenty geese at home, eating wheat soaked in water."

After Homer, the earliest reference to fattened geese comes in the late fifth-century B.C. from the comic poet Cratinus, who wrote of "goose-fatteners, cow-tenders." Another poet, Epigenes (before 376 B.C.), states, "But supposing that someone took and stuffed him up for me like a fattened goose?" Nonetheless, Egypt maintained its reputation as a source for geese. When the Spartan king Agesilaus visited Egypt in 361 B.C., he was greeted with "fatted geese and calves," riches of the Egyptian farmers.

Most of what is known about ancient Greek gastronomy—including the above references to goose fattening—is preserved in a single Roman source. The *Deipnosophistae* (The Learned Banquet) is the account of a Roman symposium (a staged discussion) recorded by Athenaeus in the early third century A.D. Encyclopedic in scope, the *Deipnosophistae* covers a broad swath of human knowledge up to that time, including law and literature, and philosophy and medicine. It is significant that Athenaeus includes a discussion of culinary history and practice in the proceedings, as this knowledge was considered an integral part of a well-rounded intellect. Also telling is the setting of a banquet table, since the meal was the preferred context for learned debate in both ancient Greece and Rome.

The participants in the *Deipnosophistae* sought to outdo each other in their knowledge, citing from memory extended passages from literary and historical sources, most of them Greek (and most of them now lost). Athenaeus's most important source for Greek food customs is *The Life of Luxury,* Europe's oldest cookbook, written in the mid-fourth century B.C. by Archestratus, a resident of Syracuse, the Greek city in Sicily. Only one fragment on geese survives: "And dress the fatted young of a goose with it, roasting that also simply." What remains of *The Life of Luxury* adds up to the first written treatise on the aesthetics of food. The culinary vision painted by Archestratus is characterized by restraint; he believed in simple preparations that highlighted the intrinsic flavors of the ingredients. His recipes are sprinkled with advice on how these dishes should be enjoyed—in moderation and among small gatherings of friends. Read almost 2500 years later, his precepts sound distinctly modern.

Ironically, after Archestratus's death, *The Life of Luxury* became the culinary bible for a group of Greek gastronomes. The "people of Archestratus" scanned the book for its advice on where to find the best ingredients but ignored his moral message. These gourmets staged extravagant banquets, ate and drank copiously, and finished their evenings by auctioning off the servants as bedmates. The philosopher Plato (who believed the model citizen should dine temperately on bread, olives, cheese, vegetables, and fruit) condemned the permissiveness of "Syracusan" dinners, arguing that a keen interest in fine food signaled a weak moral character. This connection between the food one ate and the state of one's moral health has remained a persistent theme in food writing, one with particular relevance to foie gras. These ancient texts anticipate future debates in which foie gras is singled out as an emblem of moral degeneracy.

At the end of the *Deipnosophistae's* discussion of fattened geese, the narrator asks Ulpian, one of the discussants, "where among ancient writers is it thought worth while to mention those sumptuous goose livers?" Ulpian answers, "As for goose livers, which are excessively sought after in Rome, Eubulus [a Greek comic poet of the fourth century B.C.] mentions them in *The Wreathsellers,* saying, 'Unless you have the liver or mind of a goose.' "

In all the early references to geese, this is the only mention of goose liver. It is not until the Roman period that foie gras is clearly identified as a distinct food. Presumably, however, during millennia of fattening geese and eating their meat, the Egyptians and the Greeks must have known that the fattened liver was an especially tender and delectable object. They treasured the fat of the bird, and likely treasured the fat in the liver as well.

Rome

Under the Roman Empire, foie gras emerged from the body of the goose and for the first time became a delicacy in its own right. What before had been the by-product of goose cultivation was now the deliberate outcome of a systematic fattening process. And it was not until the Roman period that foie gras was given a name, *iecur ficatum.* This special designation distinguished it from other types of animal liver and fixed it in the culinary consciousness of Roman gourmets. The appearance of foie gras was concurrent with Rome's imperial expansion into new territorial and gastronomic realms. The historian Livy pointed to Rome's conquest of

From Homer's time onward, fattened geese were a Greek delicacy.
General Research Division
The New York Public Library
Astor, Lenox and Tilden
Foundations

formerly Greek domains in Turkey, Syria, and Egypt (culminating in the 186 B.C. defeat of Antiochus the Great) as the beginning of a new chapter in Roman culinary habits: "The army returning from Asia brought foreign luxury to Rome. It became a lengthy and costly business to prepare a meal. Cooks, who used to be regarded as slaves, began to demand high wages. That which had been toil became art."

We can trace the growing interest in foie gras through a survey of Roman literature. Descriptions of Roman goose-fattening methods appear in a long line of encyclopedic agricultural texts written by gentlemen farmers interested in maximizing the profits from their estates. In his *On Agriculture,* Cato (234–149 B.C.) includes the following: "To cram hens or geese: Shut up young hens which are beginning to lay; make pellets of moist flour or barley meal, soak in water, and push into the mouth. Increase the amount daily, judging from the appetite the amount that is sufficient. Cram twice a day, and give water at noon, but do not place water before them for more than one hour. Feed a goose the same way, except that you let it drink first, and give water and food twice a day."

Subsequent farming texts, including those by Varro and Columella, describe the process in greater detail, including how to house the birds and the age at which they are most receptive to fattening. Although goose liver does not receive special mention, these texts codified fattening methods, helping not only to spread the knowledge through the Roman world but to preserve it for the cultures that followed.

A Roman mosaic: plump ducks ready for the table.
The Metropolitan Museum of Art, Gift of Mrs. W. Bayard Cutting, 1932. (32.141)

The first explicit mention of foie gras appears in a different sort of encyclopedia, Pliny's *Natural History,* a record of all known about the natural world. Pliny wrote, "Our countrymen are wiser, who know the goose by the excellence of its liver. Stuffing the bird with food makes the liver grow to a great size, and also when it has been removed it is made larger by being soaked in milk sweetened with honey. Not without reason is it a matter of enquiry who was the discoverer of so great a boon—was it Scipio Metellus the consul [in 52 B.C. one of Rome's two chief magistrates], or his contemporary Marcus Seius, Knight of Rome?"

Elsewhere Pliny tells us that a Marcus Apicius (perhaps the same who gave his name to the cookbook discussed later) discovered "a method of treating the liver of sows as of geese," noting, "They are stuffed with dried fig." This feed of chopped dried figs instead of flour or barley was to become the preferred method of producing foie gras for the Roman banquet table. The Latin term for animal liver was *iecur,* but goose liver was called *ficatum* from the root *ficus* (fig). They also referred to it as *iecur ficatum*—"fig-stuffed liver." *Ficatum* was eventually so closely associated with animal liver that it became the root for *foie, higado,* and *fegato,* respectively the French, Spanish, and Italian words for "liver."

Foie gras' newfound popularity was one reflection of a growing obsession with the culinary arts. On the heels of imperial conquest, Rome, once a spartan culture devoted to war and agriculture, was awash in new wealth. Like the nouveaux riches of any era, Roman aristocrats devoted themselves to a life of conspicuous consumption, building mansions, soaking in thermal baths, and diverting themselves with sensory titillations including lavish banquets. The first and perhaps most ostentatious Roman gourmet was the general Lucullus (110–57 B.C.) who, after returning from victories in Asia Minor, built a series of magnificent palaces where he served feasts that amazed even Rome's wealthy. "The daily repasts of Lucullus were such as the newly rich affect," said Plutarch. "Not only with his dyed coverlets, and beakers set with precious stones, and choruses and dramatic recitations, but also with his arrays of all sorts of meats and daintily prepared dishes, did he make himself the envy of the vulgar."

In throwing a banquet, a Roman host's first objective was to display his infinite largesse. Lucullus boasted that at one of his many feast halls, the Apollo room, the meals were guaranteed to cost him 50,000 sesterces—an incredible sum for the era. The waste of food and money became so extreme that Augustus Caesar feared its effect on the Roman economy and instituted sumptuary laws demanding imperial agents be present at every feast to curb flagrant excess.

Ostentatious display was not the only point of a banquet, however. It also gave the host the opportunity to show off his refinement and cultural sophistication. Weeks of planning were spent organizing the event, both in the purchase of rare and marvelous ingredients and in decorating the room and hiring the musicians, dancers, and actors. The banquet was orchestrated to stimulate the palate along with the rest of one's senses. "See them, too, upon a heap of roses, gloating over their rich cookery," wrote Seneca, "while their ears are delighted by the sound of music, their eyes by spectacles, their palates by savours; soft and soothing stuffs caress with their warmth the length of their bodies, and, that the nostrils may not meanwhile be idle, the room itself, where sacrifice is being made to Luxury, reeks with varied perfumes."

The Roman appreciation for foie gras began with its presentation. The livers were customarily served whole to display their size and whiteness, then carved at the table. In this way, guests could watch as the carver's knife sliced into the soft flesh and the clear, slightly pink juices ran onto the platter. The flavor and feel of the meat was well suited to the Roman taste for luxury. When cooked to a bare minimum, foie gras has a delicate creamy texture; the hot flesh offers only the gentlest resistance to one's teeth; the meat's high percentage of fat causes it to flow down the throat like warm cream. This was the perfect dish for a host like the Emperor Heliogabulus, who, according to legend, on one occasion smothered his banquet guests to death beneath a mountain of rose petals! (In a gesture of utter decadence, he even served foie gras to his dogs.)

Foie gras also satisfied the Roman appetite for novelty foods. Many of the culinary elements comprising a Roman feast were imported from the farthest reaches of the Roman Empire and beyond; to eat them satisfied not only the body but also, symbolically, the imperial appetite to consume the known world. Seneca complained that Romans "want game that is caught beyond the Phasis to supply their pretentious kitchens, and from the Parthians, from whom Rome has not yet got vengeance, they do not blush to get—birds! From every quarter they gather together every known and unknown thing to tickle a fastidious palate." For the Roman connoisseur, foods had "biographies" that could render even local ingredients exotic. The host in Horace's *Satire* VIII (Book II) boasted, for example, that the evening's boar was caught "when a gentle south wind was blowing" (much as present-day menus might include information such as "line-caught Maine cod"). Even if geese were ordinary domestic animals, the cramming process and the special diet of figs required to produce foie gras elevated it to the realm of the extraordinary.

Finally, foie gras appealed to the Roman taste for artifice. The ability to transform ingredients beyond recognition was taken as a sign of the cook's mastery, and Roman banquets often featured transformed foods. Petronius pokes fun at this trend in the feast scene of *Satyricon,* when he describes a parade of dishes designed to fool the eye, if not the palate, such as a dessert of "pastry thrushes stuffed with raisins and nuts" and quinces "with thorns implanted in them to make them resemble sea-urchins." As Pliny makes clear, the Romans regarded foie gras as a human invention. The artificially enlarged liver signified man's control over the natural world. Moreover, it was a point of pride that a Roman had discovered the method for producing it. The epigrammist Martial exclaimed: "See how the liver is swollen bigger than a big goose! In wonder you will say: 'Where, I ask, did this grow?' "

Evidence from Rome's long tradition of satiric literature suggests that foie gras was accorded a place of honor at the Roman banquet. In Horace's *Satire* VIII, the grand finale begins when servants enter "bearing on a huge charger the limbs of a crane sprinkled with much salt and meal, and the liver of a white goose fattened on rich figs, and hare's limbs torn off, as being more dainty than if eaten with the loins." After lobster with asparagus, Corsican mullet, and Sicilian lamprey, the feast in Juvenal's *Satire* V culminates in three bloated dishes: "a huge goose's liver, a fattened fowl as big as a goose, and a boar, piping hot."

To the modern reader, these descriptions may sound mouth-watering, but to the satirists foie gras and other gourmet delicacies were emblems of aristocratic decadence. The virtuous narrator in Horace's *Satire* VIII chose to leave the foie gras untasted (although he did guzzle as much of the rare wine as possible). A banquet's true joy is found not in a fixation with food, says Statius in his *Silvae,* but in fellowship and conversation: "Unhappy they whose delight is to know how the bird of Phasis [pheasant] differs from a crane of wintry Rhodope, what kind of goose has the largest liver, why a Tuscan boar is richer than an Umbrian, on what seaweed the slippery shell-fish most comfortably recline. . . ."

Precise documentation for Roman foie gras preparations is sparse. Pliny tells us only that the livers were marinated in milk and honey, but gives no further instruction. The only extant foie gras recipes are preserved in *The Art of Cooking,* the single surviving cookbook from ancient Rome. Often attributed to Apicius, a famous gourmet of the first century A.D., *The Art of Cooking* is actually a fourth or fifth century compilation of somewhat older recipes. Of the two foie gras recipes it contains, the first is for a marinade made from pepper, thyme, lovage, a little wine, oil, and *liquamen.* Also called *garum, liquamen* was the Worcestershire sauce of ancient Rome, a condiment made from salted small fish and fish entrails left to rot in the sun for a few months. The second recipe is more complete: "Make incisions in the liver with a reed, steep in *liquamen,* pepper, lovage, and two laurel berries. Wrap in sausage-casing [probably pig's caul], grill and serve." Roman gourmets undoubtedly had many more methods of preparing foie gras. Nevertheless, these two types of marinades—in milk and in mixtures of spices, alcohol, and oil—would influence chefs for many centuries.

The appearance of *The Art of Cooking* was the last gasp of Roman gourmets. Northern tribesmen deposed the final Roman emperor in A.D. 476, and there followed centuries of silence on the pleasure of eating a fine meal.

EARLY EUROPEAN TRADITION

*A goose, from Rumpolt's
Kochbuch.*
Spencer Collection
The New York Public Library
Astor, Lenox and Tilden
Foundations

The long silence on foie gras following the Roman era coincided with a time of sustained political turmoil and cultural transformation. By the mid-fourth century, the once sprawling Roman economy had started to contract, Germanic tribes had pushed across the imperial borders, and well-to-do Romans were abandoning the cities for their country estates. Cosmopolitan culture was dying, and with it the era of Roman feasting. This period also saw the slow formation of a new kind of society. The manner of life in early medieval Europe was predominately agrarian, localized, and Christian. The monastery replaced the city as the center of art and learning, and the teachings of the Church echoed through the popular culture. Following in the footsteps of Plato, early Christians regarded the body with ambivalence; if the body was a temple, it was also the source of human corruption. The Christian ideal, epitomized by the monastic life, was to free the body—and the spirit—from the enticements of the material world. From within this framework, the pleasures of taste and texture were deeply suspect. At best they were distractions from spiritual matters; at worst they could lead the body to gluttony, one of the seven deadly sins. The purpose of food was to sustain the flesh for a life of work and prayer.

Despite the perils of fine food, Christian monks inadvertently preserved Rome's sybaritic culinary culture. In the monastic *scriptoria,* or writing workshops, monks copied and recopied the writing of Roman agriculturists, historians, and dramatists. The oldest extant manuscript of Apicius, dating to the ninth century, was produced in a monastery at Tours, France. Centuries later, when foie gras reemerged in the Renaissance, chefs turned to this body of literature for culinary inspiration. Still unknown are the exact historical conditions under which foie gras reappeared. After Rome's collapse, the art of making foie gras may have temporarily vanished from Europe, and Renaissance chefs may have relied solely on the classical texts to revive it. It is also possible that Roman foie gras techniques were perpetuated through the Middle Ages by scattered communities of European farmers. In the fifteenth cenutry, amidst growing interest in classical food, Renaissance cooks may have turned to these communities as a source for fattened livers along with knowledge about their production and preparation.

Following this second line of reasoning is one (French) theory that the Romans brought their knowledge of foie gras production to France, where it was imparted to the peasantry of present-day Languedoc, Gascony, and Périgord. According to legend, Gallic farmers guarded the tradition of making foie gras for many centuries, until it was rediscovered in the seventeenth century by chefs associated with the French court. Intent on creating a national cuisine, they made it one of the cornerstones of their art. Despite the powerful economic and nationalistic reasons for believing this story—foie gras is one of the glories of French cuisine and its production is an important industry—the evidence for it is lacking. It is known that the goose played a marginal role in the diet of medieval French peasantry and that the dominant source of meat was sheep and pork.

Ancient Jewish Cuisine

A more likely guardian of the foie gras-making arts were the Ashkenazi Jews of Western and Central Europe. First exposed to classical goose-cramming methods during their subjugation in Roman Palestine, the Jews carried this knowledge with them as they migrated north and west, eventually settling in the rich farmlands along the Rhine. A long trail of literary evidence linking the Jews to foie gras begins in the eleventh century with the earliest reference to fattened geese in medieval Europe.

Throughout their history, Jews have used food as a means of self-definition, and laws codified in biblical times still shape Jewish eating habits today. It was during the Exodus from Egypt, when Moses was trying to forge an unruly band of fugitive slaves into a unified tribe, that many dietary restrictions were first formulated. Some of the earliest laws defined which parts of the animal were available for human consumption and which were reserved for sacrificial offering. Animal blood was set aside for ritual use, along with most of the fat of the animal, which burned with a "sweet savor" pleasing to God. Mosaic law also stipulated which types of animals were fit for eating. Most limiting was the prohibition against pork, a staple of many world cuisines. Beef fat, unless marbled into the flesh or in the tail, was deemed unkosher. To further complicate matters, preparations combining meat and dairy were also prohibited.

Consistent with the Jewish impulse to question the divine, the early dietary laws were met with open scepticism. In fact, the followers of Moses rebelled against them repeatedly, at one point crying out:

> *Who shall give us flesh to eat? We remember the fish, which we did eat in Egypt freely; the cucumbers, and the melons, and the leeks, and the onions, and the garlick: but now our soul is dried away: there is nothing at all, beside this manna, before our eyes (Numbers 11:4–6).*

Medieval banquets featured sweet, highly-spiced dishes and elaborate roasts—but no organ meats.
The Metropolitan Museum of Art, Rogers Fund, 1919. (19.49.4)

It was only through threats, cajolery, and the timely appearance of wild quail that Moses was able to bring the Jews to the brink of the Holy Land.

The Jews conquered what became the kingdoms of Judah and Israel and built a capital in Jerusalem. Excavations show that during the First Temple period (1000–587 B.C.) grains and legumes were the mainstay of the Jewish diet, occasionally supplemented by meat from sheep and cattle. In 587 B.C., Jerusalem was captured by the Babylonians and the Jews were sent into exile. The Babylonian diaspora marked a shift in Jewish eating habits. It was imperative that the Jewish community in exile strike a delicate balance where food was concerned. While observance of dietary law insured spiritual survival, it was equally important that diaspora Jews adapt to the food resources of a new environment. This tension between conservatism and flexibility has remained a shaping force in the evolution of Jewish cuisine and, throughout the history of the diaspora, has played a key role in the Jewish foie gras story.

When Cyrus the Persian conquered Babylonia and allowed the Jews to return to Jerusalem in 539 B.C., Jewish consumption of beef had dropped to negligible quantities. The new meat staples were fowl, including chicken, goose, duck, dove, pheasant, and peacock, followed by sheep and goat. In 331 B.C., Alexander the Great conquered Persia and with it Judea; three centuries later the Roman army colonized the entire eastern Mediterranean and entered the Temple in Jerusalem.

The Greeks and Romans exerted a powerful influence over their Jewish subjects. Given a fair degree of freedom over their own affairs, the Jews appropriated many Greco-Roman cultural elements, investing them with new significance. This pattern is particularly evident in matters relating to food. By the close of the first century A.D., the Jewish Passover feast was remodeled to imitate the Greek symposium and the Roman banquet. The Passover custom of marking the meal's progress with a new glass of wine, the ritual spilling of wine, the mandate to recline at the Seder table, and the practice of pouring water over one's hands at the start and conclusion of the meal are all elements borrowed from the classical tradition. The Seder meal also incorporated Greco-Roman preparations, including an appetizer of boiled eggs and a sandwich made of unleavened bread and lettuce; another dish called *haroseth,* a sweet paste of chopped fruit and nuts, is also likely of classical origin.

Medieval German Jews used this pot to prepare cholent, a typical Sabbath dish, from beans (or barley), goose meat, and goose fat.
The Jewish Museum, NY /
Art Resource, NY

For the Jewish aristocracy in Palestine, the customs of the Roman elite set the standard for their own culinary practices, and it is possible that they encountered foie gras at this time. They also could have learned about fattened goose liver in Italy itself, where, by the first century A.D., an estimated 50,000 Jews had settled, most of them in and around Rome. We know that many Roman Jews operated their own butcher shops to ensure a reliable source of kosher meat. Perhaps they also sold *ficatum,* just as the kosher butchers of Renaissance Rome sold *fegato d'oche,* or foie gras, to the pope's private chef.

As Jews continued to move north and west, observance of dietary law, or *kashrut,* demanded constant culinary innovation. One of the most vexing challenges was the search for an acceptable source of cooking fat. Beef fat was forbidden, as was lard, and the use of butter as a cooking medium was largely off-limits due to the prohibition against mixing meat with dairy. For Mediterranean Jews, the answer had always been olive oil, and Babylonian Jews had turned to sesame oil, but neither were easily obtainable as the European Jews traveled further north. One remaining option was poultry fat, known in Yiddish (the language of the Ashkenazim) as *schmaltz,* and the way to produce abundant stores of it was through cramming. The easily transportable fattened goose became for the Jews a "walking larder": the meat was used for roasting or stewing; the deep-fried skin became *gribenes* (goose cracklings); the fat was rendered and used in soups, stews and baking; and, of course, the fattened liver was prized as the choicest morsel of all.

The fattened goose has figured in Jewish cuisine for well over a millennium. A delicious and versatile source of calories, it met the need for a source of fat consistent with dietary law;

however, it also created a broad range of new dilemmas that were to engage the most important rabbinic minds in Europe. The first glimmerings of the conflict over geese are found in a parable by Rabbah bar-bar Hannah, a third-century Babylonian mystic:

> *Said Rabbah bar-bar Hannah: Once upon a time we were traveling in the desert, and we saw those geese whose feathers had fallen out on account of their fatness and under whom flowed rivers of oil. I ventured to ask them: May we expect to have a share of you in the world to come? One of them lifted its wing and one lifted its thigh (leg) as one might lift a standard. And when I related this incident before Rabbi Eleazar, he remarked: The Israelites will eventually have to account for their conduct before Justice.*

While the full meaning of this cryptic tale remains opaque, for the last 1600 years rabbis have used it as a pretext for religious debate on goose fattening. On the one hand it evokes a vision of plenty, of endless supplies of savory oil in some heavenly future, and on the other hand it hints of corruption and divine retribution.

The Ashkenazi Tradition

The debate on goose fattening resumed in the region along the Rhine River in what is today northeast France and northwest Germany. This was the homeland of the Ashkenazi Jews who forged a distinct culture in the ninth and tenth centuries. It appears that the most famous Ashkenazi scholar, Rashi of Troyes (1040–1105), was also a dedicated gourmet; we know that he supplemented his income by managing a vineyard, while his writing betrays an appreciation for fine cooking. In this regard, it appears that Rashi was not alone. A weakness for fine food was a distinguishing trait of many medieval French rabbis. In fact, their German counterparts accused the French of studying Talmud "with their stomachs full of meat, vegetables, and wine."

In his massive Talmudic commentary, Rashi takes up the parable of Rabbah bar-bar Hannah, appending his own thoughts to the mysterious final line. Why would the Jews "have to account for their conduct before Justice"? Rashi says, "For having made the beasts [geese] suffer while fattening them." Rashi's commentary alludes to the principle of avoiding *Tza'ar Ba'alei Hayim,* the infliction of unnecessary cruelty on a living creature, a central tenet of Jewish belief. To fatten the goose, the farmer must stuff grain down its throat, and sometimes the sharp points of coarsely milled grain can puncture the walls of the esophagus. Moreover, when the throat is

A German-Jewish slaughter-house where cattle and geese were ritually killed for table.
The Dorot Jewish Division
The New York Public Library
Astor, Lenox and Tilden
Foundations

damaged a second dietary commandment is threatened—the prohibition against consuming "torn" flesh. Until the Jewish taste for goose meat and fat waned in the late nineteenth century, the issue of goose fattening and its possible cruelty would be one of the most debated topics in Jewish dietary law.

Further evidence of medieval goose fattening comes from the *responsa* literature, questions sent to and answered by rabbis. Rabbi Meir of Rothenburg, a thirteenth-century German scholar, was asked: "Is it obligatory to *take hallah* from coarse [dough] baked especially for fattening of geese, but which is also fit for human beings?" The significance of the question is technical. According to Jewish law, anyone baking bread was obliged to "take" or separate a piece of the dough and burn it in the oven as a symbol of the sacrifice once made by the High Priest in the ancient Temple. The Talmudic sources gave conflicting advice on this issue, so Rabbi Meir answered that it was necessary to take hallah as long as the dough being made was also fit for human consumption, as it apparently was. From a culinary point of view, this exchange suggests that medieval Jews fattened geese with the explicit intention of also fattening their livers. The aforementioned dough was almost certainly force-fed, the technique required to produce fattened livers, and nineteenth-century German Jews used similar doughs to produce their foie gras.

The earliest direct reference to the Jewish consumption of fattened liver is found in a fourteenth-century ethical will, a document of moral instruction given by a dying man to his descendants. In 1357, Eleazar of Mainz, a city along the Rhine, implored his children, "Now, my sons and daughters, eat and drink only what is necessary, as our good parents did, refraining from heavy meals, and holding the gross liver in detestation." If the fattened goose supplied poor country folk with a windfall of needed calories, well-to-do Jews like Eleazar could afford to look upon the enlarged liver with disdain. Unfortunately, the type of liver is not specified, but the broader implication is clear: fattened liver of any variety was emblematic of indulgent eating. A millennium after the fall of the Roman Empire, we see once again the association between fattened liver and excess.

Documents like the ethical will belie the savage times in which the Jews of France and Germany were living. In 1096, Christian mobs massacred Jews in Rouen, Metz, and other cities during the religious upheaval of the First Crusade. In the thirteenth and fourteenth centuries, Jews were ejected from England and France and forced eastward into Germany and Bohemia. There, violence and official edicts uprooted them again, and by 1500 large numbers had moved into Poland and Hungary. Wherever they moved, the evidence suggests, they carried with them the tradition of fattening geese.

Renaissance Europe

By the late Middle Ages, foie gras had crossed the divide between Jews and gentiles, appearing sporadically in the kitchens of the clergy. The asceticism of early Christianity had given way to a worldly Church flush with power. Medieval Church leaders lived in high style; the quality of their kitchens and the sumptuousness of their dinners rivaled those of the European courts, and their chefs produced some of the era's most important cookbooks.

The decadence of the clergy contributed to the erosion of its spiritual and intellectual authority. Across Europe, a class of priests who taught and studied at the great Church-operated universities of the day looked beyond Christian scholarship to a vast body of classical writing. They retrieved manuscripts by Pliny, Horace, and Columella from monastery storerooms and discovered others, such as the works of Athenaeus, which had been preserved in the libraries of the East. These readings encouraged the great cultural movement known as the Renaissance, which sought to build a new European civilization based on the classical past.

The appetite for Greco-Roman culture led humanist scholars to classical writings on food, where they found materials and preparations foreign to the medieval palate. During the High Middle Ages, European cookery had been modeled after Arab cuisine brought to Western Europe by the returning Crusaders. Medieval preparations were characterized by a generous use of sugar, spices, flower essences, and "golden" coloring (usually achieved with saffron). In classical literature, and particularly in Apicius, they discovered the Roman preference for sour and salty flavors (garum), the use of herbs rather than spices, and a long list of unfamiliar ingredients, including shellfish, olives, asparagus, artichokes, mushrooms, and organ meats, among them foie gras.

A model for the Renaissance scholar-priest was Platina (1421–1481), born Bartolomeo Sacchi, who studied the classical authors in Mantua, Florence, and Rome. In 1468, Pope Paul II threw him into prison on accusations of "paganizing." Platina had more congenial relations with Paul II's successor, Pope Sixtus IV, and rose to become the first Vatican librarian and a powerful personage in Roman affairs. Platina's most famous work, *De honesta voluptate* (On Right Pleasure), was the first intellectual study of food since the fall of the Roman Empire.

The chef to Renaissance popes and cardinals, Bartolomeo Scappi prepared foie gras in kitchens like this one (from his cookbook).
General Research Division
The New York Public Library
Astor, Lenox and Tilden
Foundations

In his book, Platina casts himself in the role of connoisseur, cataloging all the foods known to him and giving recipes for the best way to prepare them. His sources include Varro, Columella, Apicius, and, most of all, Pliny. Inspired by these Roman authors, he recommends numerous ingredients that had been shunned by medieval gourmets. Where medieval diners favored roasts, Platina expounds upon the culinary uses of offal, including the eyes, testicles, intestines, and livers. In his section on geese and ducks, which is heavily based on Pliny, he includes some thoughts on fattened goose liver: "The goose is of use to men . . . for its fat, with which many foods are seasoned; and for its liver, which is especially excellent if the bird has first drunk milk or mead." (An alternate translation reads: ". . . if first soaked in milk or wine sweetened with honey," which is closer to Pliny.)

Platina's reverence for classical food, however, was more theoretical than practical. The recipes included in his book, most borrowed from his friend Martino of Como's *Libro de arte coquinaria,* are steeped in the medieval tradition. The taste of the food is less important to him than its humoral properties, a medieval theory of food's effect on the body based on ancient Greek and later Arab medicine. For example, of goose he says that the flesh "has warmer force than duck." In the century after its appearance, Platina's *De honesta voluptate* was issued in almost 30 editions in Italy, Germany, and, especially, France.

By the second half of the sixteenth century, Renaissance gourmets finally dared to test their theoretical admiration for foie gras in a real kitchen. In France, the experiment was

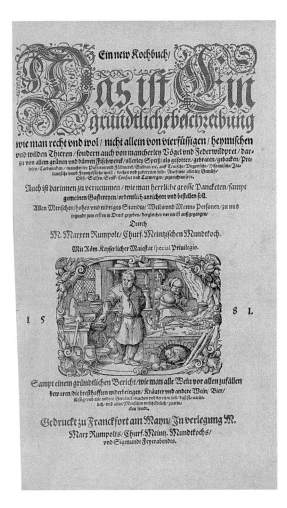

The title page from Kochbuch.
Spencer Collection
The New York Public Library
Astor, Lenox and Tilden
Foundations

apparently a failure; the court physician Bruyerin reported in 1560 that the French preferred the livers of fattened hens and cocks to that of geese. In Italy and Germany, however, chefs were willing to reach across religious, class, and cultural boundaries into the Jewish community of Western Europe, now tenuously resettled in Italy, France, and Germany. Foie gras was the meeting point for two disparate culinary cultures, the innovative cuisine of the European elites and the traditional cooking of Jewish farmers and townspeople.

Jewish suppliers were recognized as the principal sources of fattened goose liver in sixteenth-century Western Europe. In 1562, Hans Wilhelm Kirchhof of Kassel (a German city east of the Rhine) wrote that the Jews raise "good and fat geese" and particularly love its liver. Eight years later, Bartolomeo Scappi, chef to Pope Pius V, published his *Opera,* a sweeping cookbook combining medieval Italian dishes with more revolutionary recipes. In his section on poultry livers, he tell us that "the liver of the domestic goose raised by the Jews is of extreme size and weighs two and three pounds."

While Scappi felt no compunction about entering Rome's Jewish ghetto in search of exotic foodstuffs, his preparation for goose liver is distinctly un-Jewish. Like Pliny, he recommends soaking the goose livers in tepid milk for a day, which causes them to expand and become more tender when cooked. He also says they can be cooked in sheep's caul—a throwback to Apicius—or dipped in flour and fried in lard, turning them over once. After they are cooked, he advises squeezing Seville orange juice on them, sprinkling sugar on top, and serving them warm. This is the first documented example of a sweet and sour preparation for foie gras, a precursor to the fruit-based sauces favored by modern chefs.

Another court cook who frequented Jewish butchers was Marx Rumpolt, a resident of Mainz and a chef to various German nobles. Published in 1581, Marx Rumpolt's massive *Kochbuch,* the first great German-language cookery book, tells us that the Jews of Bohemia produced livers weighing over three pounds. Rumpolt recommends wrapping them in a calf's caul, roasting them, then serving them in a green or a brown broth—one "that is not sour." He also suggests making a mousse out of goose liver (the likely progenitor of pâté de foie gras), cooking it in pastry, or turning it into a goose liver wurst by blending it with ham, eggs, pepper, butter, and "tasty green cabbage."

By the end of the sixteenth century, fattened goose liver was still a rarity on aristocratic dinner tables. Both Rumpolt and Scappi include foie gras as a novelty—one of many in their exhaustive lists of foodstuffs—and their preparations seem mixtures of classical revivals and their own experiments. Neither the Germans nor the Italians made goose liver a regular feature of court cuisine. For that, it is necessary to look to France and the radical innovations of its royal chefs.

ORIGINS OF HAUTE CUISINE

Given the deeply French character of foie gras, as we think of it today, it would be reasonable to assume that French chefs created some of the earliest foie gras recipes in Renaissance Europe. This, however, was not the case. Sixteenth-century France produced no counterpart to Scappi or Rumpolt, scholar-cooks with a knowledge of classical cuisine and a zest for experimentation. The only original cookbook (as opposed to imports or reprints of Taillevent, the great medieval French chef) published during this century was Nostradamus's medicinal work on fruits and how to preserve them. Contemporary accounts of court festivals, which combined spectacular meals with music, dance, and drama, show the continuing influence of medieval cookery. The sixteenth-century feast was a form of theater in which the visual element took precedence over the food's flavor, aroma, and texture. The meal's highlights were whole roasted birds, including peacocks, swans, and herons, which the cook had artfully dressed in the birds' own colorful plumage. It mattered little to the assembled guests that the feathers were still attached to the birds' rotting skins. The spectacle was the point.

Early French Agricultural Texts

Modeling their work after such Roman authors as Pliny and Cato, French agronomists and naturalists of the period produced voluminous texts on local farming techniques and natural resources. These works provide a record of Renaissance goose-fattening techniques and show a growing interest in the bird's liver. In 1555, the naturalist Pierre Belon, who also wrote about fishes and trees, published *L'Histoire de la nature des oyseaux*. Of geese, he said, "The subjects of Francis I [1494–1547] greatly esteem a young goose that is well-fed, fat, and principally stuffed with dry feed." Jean Baptiste Bruyerin, physician to Henry II (1519–1559), makes reference in his 1560 *De re cibaria* to the Roman method of feeding geese with dried figs.

The first detailed account of French goose fattening, however, appears in Charles Estienne's 1564 *L'Agriculture et la maison rustique*:

> At four months, one chooses among the young geese and takes the finest and the largest and places them in a cellar or in some dark and warm place where the youngest stay 30 days and the oldest two months.
>
> One gives them three times a day barley flour and wheat soaked in water and honey: barley makes the meat white and the wheat fattens them and makes big livers.
>
> Some make a food for them out of fresh or dry figs with leavening and give them plenty to drink so they can fill themselves. Others pluck the feathers from the stomach and the thighs and the big feathers of the wings; also they dig out their eyes to fatten them: above all do not stint on food and drink because they are greedy and strongly love to drink. By these means they will be good and fat in less than two months.

*. . . Two-month-old geese are strongly recommended at springtime banquets for their deli-
cacy: just as, in autumn, the old ones stuffed with chestnuts [are recommended]: their liver also is
very pleasing for food and flavor.*

Estienne's reference to the use of figs for fattening is certainly learned from classical sources.
Entirely new, however, is the practice of blinding the geese, presumably an attempt to restrict
the animal's mobility. In 1600, Olivier de Serres repeats much of Estienne's information in his
monumental *Le Théâtre d'agriculture,* an encyclopedia of French farming, hunting, and food. To
this, he adds a paragraph on the goose-fattening techniques of Gascony in southwest France
(today a mecca of foie gras production). Serres also gives a picture of the culinary products
derived from a fattened goose:

*When the geese are fat enough, the farmers will kill them, pluck them, and skin them. The skin is
finely chopped and fried in a large pan (like people do for pig skin). The farmer adds a little bit
of salt and pours off the grease into clay jars; these jars are lined with glass. This way the grease
can be kept for a very long time and is the best for cooking meats. The grease never solidifies and
will always stay liquid like oil. The meat is salted (in the same way that fat bacon is) and will be
used all year round.*

To this list of goose products, Serres offhandedly adds that the liver is the most sought-after part
of the bird, but omits any details on its weight, color, flavor, or methods of preparation.

For modern goose farmers, most of the procedures described by Estienne and Serres are
eminently sensible. These old French techniques would certainly have fattened the geese. They
would not, however, have grown the foie gras that we know today; force-feeding is necessary for
that. The Renaissance livers would have been relatively small, dark-colored, and strongly flavored.
The one detail that gives modern farmers pause is the blinding of the geese, a practice that both
authors mention. As geese are extremely sensitive to stress, those that survived the procedure
would likely stop digesting, and, at the very least, stop eating. If this method was actually used, it
is a mystery to present-day veterinarians and farmers how the animals could have survived.

La Varenne: The First French Recipes

Recipes for the preparation of "foyes gras" are finally revealed in the mid-seventeenth century
with the publication of Pierre François de La Varenne's *Le Cuisinier françois* (1651), the first in a
sudden outpouring of French titles devoted to fine food and table etiquette. These books reflect
the developments in the food culture of the French elite during the previous hundred years. At
the same time, the transition from a predominately oral cooking tradition to one based on written recipes spurred developments that directed future trends.

The sudden reliance on cookbooks produced a methodical change in the manner in
which chefs approached their craft. Food is ephemeral, disappearing hours—or minutes—after
its creation in contrast to most other cultural arts. The written recipe gives food a form of per-
manence that differs from artistic representations or written descriptions of a dish. A recipe provides the chef with a template of ingredients and procedures, a neat encapsulation of ordered
steps, intelligible at a single glance. With the recipe as a guide, the chef could achieve new levels

of complexity. The use of recipes also tended to promote uniformity of results, and in time led to the institutionalization of both general kitchen techniques and individual dishes. At the same time, recipes encouraged experimentation, forming the bedrock upon which the chef could build and improvise. The distribution of seminal cookbooks such as those by Taillevent and Platina thus inspired culinary experimentation among a growing class of professional chefs throughout France and Europe.

La Varenne, the author of *Le Cuisinier françois,* achieved his fame as chef to the Marquis d'Uxelle, to whom the book is dedicated:

> *Although my humble birth does not make it possible for me to be capable of having a heroic heart, it does nevertheless give me enough true feeling not to forget my indebtedness. I have discovered in your household, during ten full years' employment, the secret of preparing foods delicately. I dare to say that I have practiced this profession with the great approbation of princes, marshals of France, and an infinity of persons of consequence.*

Frontispiece to La Varenne's revolutionary Le Cuisinier françois (from the English edition).
Rare Books Division
The New York Public Library
Astor, Lenox and Tilden
Foundations

La Varenne's dedication, wavering between humility and boastfulness, typifies the emerging relationship between patron and chef among the French nobility. As power became concentrated in the hands of the king, the social role of the aristocracy grew narrower, and manners, style, and taste became increasingly important markers of noble status. An educated palate was a sign of personal refinement, while possession of a great chef reflected one's membership in the highest social circles. From the chef's point of view, employment in a great household enhanced visibility and prestige. This mutually beneficial relationship served to propel French cuisine into a new era.

In *Le Cuisinier françois,* La Varenne's key innovation is a structured mode of cooking in which prepared elements (stocks, forcemeats, liaisons, herb mixtures, and so on) are combined in a single dish. Each element in the recipe serves a purpose—to thicken, bind, or flavor—but the soul of the new cuisine resided in the stock. La Varenne opens his book with a meat bouillon, the basic stock used in dozens of his recipes, including soups, ragoûts, and fricassees. This is the forerunner of the basic *fond,* brown stock, that was a key building block of French haute cuisine during the next 300 years. Though *Le Cuisinier françois* includes recipes and flavors typical of medieval cookery, the spirit of the work is modern.

The half dozen recipes for "foyes gras" in La Varenne are part of a broader seventeenth-century trend: the new desirability of organ meats and other delectable animal tidbits. *Le Cuisinier françois* gives recipes for head, tongue, calves' feet, tripe, cocks' combs, udders, and sweetbreads—animal parts that were already fashionable in Italian cooking. La Varenne's recipe for *foyes gras sur le grill* is reminiscent of Scappi: "Put it on the grill and sprinkle it with bread flour and salt; when it is roast, sprinkle lemon juice on top and serve." A second recipe, foie gras in the ashes, brings together the modern flavor of the bouquet garni with the medieval sweetness of cloves:

Wrap it in lard and season it well with salt, pepper, crushed clove, and a little bouquet of strong herbs; then envelop it in four or five sheets of paper, and put it to cook in the ashes like you do a quince. When it is cooked, be careful not to lose the sauce while removing it; lift off the paper on top and serve it with those beneath if you wish, or on a plate.

Another foie gras dish is prepared in a radical new style that swept the world of French court cooking. Here is La Varenne's recipe for *foyes gras en ragoust:*

Choose the fattest and the fairest [foie gras], clean them, and drop them in hot water to cleanse the bitterness, but remove them immediately. Wipe them, place them in a pan with butter or lard, and let them simmer with a bit of bouillon, parsley, and chive, and serve with a well-liaised sauce; you may add truffles, champignons, and asparagus.

59. *Foye gras en ragoust.*
Choififfez les plus gras & les plus blonds, nettoyez les, & iettez dans l'eau chaude pour ofter l'amertume, mais les retirez auffi-toft : Eftans effuyez, paffez les par la poëfle auec beure ou fain-doux, & faites mitonner auec peu de boüillon, perfil, & fiboule entiere; eftans cuits, oftez la fiboule, & feruez la fauce bien liée; vous y pouuez mettre trufles, champignons & afperges.

La Varenne's recipe for foie gras ragoût became the rage in the courts of Europe.
Rare Books Division
The New York Public Library
Astor, Lenox and Tilden
Foundations

This is the first recipe pairing foie gras with truffles, an enduring combination to the present day.

Ragoûts, conversely, have fallen out of vogue, but they were among the most popular dishes in the early days of haute cuisine. The word *ragoût* is derived from the verb *ragoûter,* "to revive the taste," and chefs served it to stimulate the appetites of their diners. Most ragoûts were prepared by browning or blanching the meat, then placing it in a pan with flour, lard, and bouillon; to this is added salt, pepper, a bouquet garni, mushrooms, and a selection of vegetables. The dish is then simmered until the sauce is thick and the meat well cooked. A ragoût could be served as a stand-alone dish or prepared as a gravy to be spooned over large cuts of meat, the ancestor of such classic French garnishes as the *financière* or the *impériale.*

To French diners bored with the endless parade of roasts, the ragoût came as a revelation. A craze for ragoûts spread through the courts of Europe, where the dish was recognized as a French invention (the English described the ragoût as "a high-seasoned dish after the French fashion") and helped to establish the reputation of French chefs abroad. In 1654, *Le Cuisinier françois* was translated into English with the following dedication to the Earl of Tannet (although it is not known if La Varenne ever entered the earl's employment):

My Lord, of all Cookes in the World, the French are esteem'd the best, and of all cooks that ever France bred up, this may very well challenge the first place, as the neatest and compleatest that ever did attend the French court and Armies. I have taught him to speak English to the end that he may be able to wait in your Lordships Kitchin, and furnish your Table with several sauces of haut goust, and with dainty ragousts, and sweetmeats, as yet hardly known in this Land.

Cuisine of the Enlightenment

Le Cuisinier françois set the high-water mark for refined cooking in the mid-seventeenth century, but within a generation a new group of chefs had declared it passé. Their reaction was a sign of the fever for novelty that consumed aristocratic palates. The newly minted idea of progress, an invention of the Enlightenment, had entered the French culinary world, and while it may not always be evident in their recipes, it certainly took hold of the rhetoric of chefs. In the introduction to his *L'Art de bien traiter* (1674), the cookbook writer known as L.S.R. heaps scorn on La Varenne:

> *I don't believe that you will find here the absurdities and revolting instructions which M. de Varenne dares to give, and with which he has for so long deluded and bemused the foolish and ignorant populace, passing off his concoctions as if they were eternal verities and his teachings in matters of cuisine as the most approved in the world. . . .*
>
> *Doesn't it already make you shudder to think of a teal soup* à l'hypocras, *or larks in sweet sauce? Can you contemplate without horror this pottage of shin of beef au talladin, or that vulgar broth? . . . Look at his shin of veal fried in breadcrumbs, his stuffed turkey with raspberries . . . and any number of other villainies that one would more willingly endure among the Arabs than in a gentler climate like ours, where refinement, delicacy, and good taste are our most zealous concern.*

By invoking the Arab culinary tradition, L.S.R. draws a distinction between the foreign-influenced medieval cookery and the more "enlightened" dishes of his own age.

Cooks such as L.S.R. continued to chip away at the medieval style. Nonetheless, the mingling of old and new is evident throughout their work and often manifest in very interesting ways. The organization of *Le Cuisinier* (1656) by Pierre de Lune and of L.S.R.'s *L'Art de bien traiter* shows that the grip of medieval thinking was still strong. Both books are divided into feast days and fast days, with the first section devoted to meat recipes and the second section to fish and vegetables. Well after the birth of French rationalism, cookbooks were still structured according to the Christian calendar, a paradigm so deeply accepted that it remained beyond question.

In the recipes as well, the movement toward a modern cuisine was halting, and chefs often circled back into the medieval past for ideas. For example, Pierre de Lune was one of the first chefs to use a roux for thickening sauces, but he also employed the medieval technique of adding crushed macaroons or bread crumbs to give body to soups. As in La Varenne, many late seventeenth-century recipes combined medieval and modern elements in a single preparation. Pierre de Lune's recipe for *boudin de foies gras et chapon* blends the new craze for organ meats with the old tradition of heavily spiced sausages:

The chef, an allegorical figure from eighteenth-century France.

> *Very finely slice a quarter pound of pork meat, chop a pound of foie gras with a pound of capon meat, season with fines herbes, chive, salt, pepper, nutmeg, ground clove, cinnamon, six raw egg yolks, two pots of cream. Put the preparation in a small intestine of pork or sheep or lamb and let it cook in milk with salt, green lemon, bay leaf, and then place it on a sheet of paper and lightly roast it. Serve with oranges.*

Often, innovation was a matter of perception. Old dishes were decreed new and only then were they accepted into the modern repertoire. Finely chopped or ground meats had been used in

European cookery for centuries but acquired new prestige when chefs discovered that Apicius included sausage and forcemeat recipes in his famous cookbook.

From 1661 to 1715, France was ruled by Louis XIV, an absolute monarch who was also the nation's leading gourmand. He presided over France from a series of country estates, most importantly Versailles, where the aristocracy was required to wait on his slightest whim. Court life consisted of elaborate ceremonies and entertainments organized to enhance the king's prestige and concentrate the attentions of the aristocracy on the minutiae of court life. In order to feed his courtiers, Louis built an enormous kitchen complex staffed by hundreds of professionals versed in the latest techniques. The meals they labored over were painstakingly choreographed affairs in which the seating arrangement, the configuration of dishes on the table, and the progression of courses all reinforced the notion of court hierarchy. Food became a prime topic of courtly discussion, and Versailles was periodically swept by fads for new dishes and new ingredients. Fruits and vegetables enjoyed a special vogue at the time, and Louis commissioned horticulturists to plant a huge indoor orange grove and a garden to produce out-of-season delicacies such as peas, a legume adored by Louis and his court.

An elaborate display of (probably cold) food for a seventeenth-century French banquet.
Rare Books Division
The New York Public Library
Astor, Lenox and Tilden
Foundations

One of the chefs who served at the Sun King's table was Massialot, author of *Le Cuisinier roïal et bourgeois* (1691). Although the second edition of his book was dedicated to Louis himself, Massialot's intended audience clearly extended beyond the world of the court. In urban areas such as Paris, a small but growing middle class—the *bourgeois* of his title—had started to emulate the eating habits of the nobility. In his preface to *Le Cuisinier roïal et bourgeois,* the first cookbook to recognize the culinary aspirations of the French middle class, Massialot addresses the reader's limited means:

> *Place and circumstance do not always permit the attainment of the very highest standards; one often has less than everything one needs, but nevertheless attempts to do the best one can. It is in this context that this book will be found not without utility in bourgeois households, where one is forced to limit oneself to a relatively few things. . . . Moreover, this book shows thousands of ways with quite ordinary things like chickens, pigeons, and even butcher's meat, which can give much satisfaction in everyday meals, especially in the country and in the provinces.*

Massialot's vision of a modest meal was skewed by the overblown scale at which he was accustomed to working in court kitchens. One of his model bourgeois menus begins with a quarter of a veal as the grand entrée, proceeds with two smaller entrées of chicken and *eclanche* (mutton shoulder) and ends with four separate hors d'oeuvres consisting of turkey, sweetbreads, partridges, and a filet of beef. An aristocratic dinner, meanwhile, could include over a hundred separate preparations, many garnished with truffles, wild birds, and foie gras—luxuries beyond the means of the bourgeois pocketbook.

By the time Massialot was writing, a core group of foie gras recipes had entered into the repertoire of elite chefs; there was foie gras ragoût, a roasted foie gras, and boudin of foie gras. Massialot's recipes for these foie gras perennials show few signs of innovation; he repeats Pierre de Lune's boudin of foie gras nearly word for word. To this trio of standards, however, Massialot adds a foie gras "tourte," or pie, a recipe that would be borrowed by many chefs in the decades to come:

> *Blanch the foies gras in hot water and lay them in a torte pan upon a fine pastry. Garnish them with chopped champignons, fines herbes, chives, and pounded lard and season with salt, pepper, nutmeg, cloves, and a bit of green lemon. Cover with the same pastry and after browning it let it cook for a good hour. Take one of the same livers, which you have set aside, and fry it in a pan with melted lard and flour. Then pound it and pass it through an étamine [sieve] with mutton stock and lemon juice, after having rubbed the bottom of the dish with a shallot. Then put all of this into your torte and serve.*

The *tourte de foie gras* is an updated version of the ubiquitous medieval meat pie. At the same time, it anticipates the future classic, *pâté de foie gras en croute*, into which the chef opens a hole and pours aspic or fat before chilling. For a more inventive foie gras dish, Massialot turns to chocolate, a New World ingredient only recently embraced by European elites:

> *Macreuse [scoter, a kind of northern diving duck] in ragoût with chocolate. After plucking and properly cleaning your* macreuse, *take out its insides and wash it. Broil it over coals and then put it in a pan and season it with salt, pepper, bay leaves, and a bouquet of herbs. Make a little chocolate as for drinking and pour it in the pan. At the same time, prepare a ragoût with the livers,* champignons, *morels,* mousserons *[a small mushroom], truffles, and a quarter pound of chestnuts. When the* macreuse *is cooked and arranged on the plate, you pour over your ragoût and serve it with a garnish of your choice.*

The novelty and expense of foie gras, chocolate, and a sea duck would have barred this dish from bourgeois tables. At the same moment that haute cuisine was trickling down to "commoners," chefs were creating new and elite preparations reserved exclusively for the nobility.

In 1746, a chef named Menon, author of a two-volume work on court cookery, published *La Cuisinière bourgeoise,* a book that continues Massialot's efforts to feed the middle class in style. From the feminization of its title, we know that it was intended for women chefs, the kind most likely to be employed by bourgeois households. *La Cuisinière bourgeoise* became one of the most popular French cookbooks and was reprinted frequently over the next century. The suggested menus in Menon are relatively extensive—16 dishes for a dinner serving 10, for example—but the preparations are fairly simple. The organization of *La Cuisinière bourgeoise* is clear, with chapters that follow the progression of a meal. Its content leans toward the practical; an opening recipe for basic bouillon, for example, is followed by advice on how to choose quality meat. In keeping with the budget of his audience, he includes far fewer luxury ingredients including only one foie gras recipe, a no-frills ragoût.

If Menon and Massialot were building a bridge to the bourgeois, Vincent La Chapelle, author of *The Modern Cook,* was building a wall to keep them out. He devised recipes that are impossible to prepare except in the largest kitchens; his instructions for *veau en tombeau d'epicure,* a baby calf stuffed with a huge assortment of delicacies, run for pages and call for a fortune in expensive ingredients, including foie gras. Although French, La Chapelle gained fame working in The Hague as chef to the British ambassador Lord Chesterfield. *The Modern Cook* was first published in London in 1733 and was then translated into French for editions in 1736 and 1742. Following his stint abroad, La Chapelle returned to France to cook for the Prince of Orange, Madame de Pompadour, and Louis XV.

In his preface to *The Modern Cook,* La Chapelle declares the dawn of a new culinary era. It is time to throw off the influence of Massialot's *Le Cuisinier roïal et bourgeois,* he says, and follow a new set of rules for cookery, those laid down in his book. (His attack on Massialot recently sparked an investigation in which researchers discovered that nearly a third of the recipes for the 1733 edition were "borrowed" from his predecessor.) To achieve a cleaner, more delicate presentation, La Chapelle expanded the repertoire of French cooking techniques. He advised, for instance, that coulis be degreased and that vegetables would retain their color if boiled with flour, salt, and butter. The emphasis on delicacy is evident in his recipe for a ragoût of foie gras, written in the precise style typical of La Chapelle's work:

> *Take the foie gras, remove the bitterness and blanch them; when they are done, place them in cold water. In a casserole put little* champignons, mousserons *[small mushrooms], truffles cut into slices and a bouquet [of herbs]; add some stock and let it simmer over a low fire. When it is half-cooked, add the foies and let them cook, taking care that the livers do not become overdone. Degrease the mixture well and thicken it with an essence or coulis, seeing that the ragoût has a good flavor and that it is cooked to a turn. Place the foies neatly on the serving plate, put the sauce and garnish on top and serve it warm as an* entremets. *Instead of letting the livers cook in a casserole, you may also cook them between strips of lard in an oven; when they are done, place them nicely on the serving plate with the same sauce as above, or better a* sauce à l'Espagnole.

The espagnole sauce was relatively new at the time; La Chapelle, and later, Carême, would refine it into a hallmark of French cuisine. In addition to the degreasing, La Chapelle pays careful attention to the meat's degree of doneness at each stage in the cooking process (to overcook foie gras is a sin), to the manner of serving, and to the neatness of presentation. His recipes spell out what previous cookbook writers left to the discretion of the chef.

By the middle of the eighteenth century, haute cuisine preparations had taken the form that they would keep for the next two centuries: meat or fish accompanied by a sauce and a

In eighteenth-century Europe, no banquets were as extravagant as those thrown by the French elites.
Culver Pictures

garnish. In the time of La Varenne, the sauce and garnish had been blended in the form of a ragoût and poured on the meat. Now the sauce was often prepared separately, and the garnish became a collection of delicacies such as artichoke bottoms, sweetbreads, mushrooms, whole pigeons, and foie gras, all to be arranged around the meat. When chefs created a new garnish, they bestowed a name that would associate it with wealth and power: *financière* (banker-style), *impériale, régence.* Almost 20 of the classic French garnishes included foie gras. The *Montglas,* invented in 1739 and named after a marquis, consisted of shredded tongue, champignons, truffles, and foie gras in a Madeira sauce. The Impériale was a garnish of truffles, foie gras, cocks' combs, and kidneys. A dish *à la Mancelle* meant that the meat was cooked *en salmi* (as a type of stew) and then garnished with foie gras. These garnishes became a mandatory part of a chef's education; their fame helped spread French haute cuisine—and foie gras—throughout Western Europe and beyond.

Despite an endless series of wars, the courts of seventeenth- and eighteenth-century Europe were closely linked by a web of marriages and other alliances, ensuring that any cultural development in one would quickly spread to all the rest. When foreign aristocrats first sampled the new French haute cuisine, they immediately wanted to bring its secrets home, preferably in the form of a French chef. La Chapelle was just one of many who built careers in England, Holland, and other countries. Foreign publishers reprinted French cookbooks in their original language or in translation. With the spread of French cookbooks and chefs, we can follow the dissemination of French methods for preparing fattened goose liver throughout Europe. In some countries, foie gras became a staple of aristocratic cuisine, and in others, such as England, it did not.

England

The English were among the most avid to sample the new French cookery. Aristocrats hired French chefs, English chefs traveled to France to learn the techniques, and publishers brought out English editions of French cookbooks as fast as they could translate them. *The French Cook,* the translation of La Varenne, was issued only two years after *Le Cuisinier françois.* In it, "foyes gras" becomes "fat liver," and we assume that the readers knew that it came from geese. The translations that follow La Varenne, however, such as the 1702 English version of Massialot, alter the recipes completely: "foies gras" becomes "capons-liver" or "fowl liver." The ingredient no longer comes from geese but some variety of chicken. It is quite likely that English farmers never developed a tradition of force-feeding, so chefs had to make substitutions. It is also possible that another agenda was at work. There is a hint of this in Patrick Brydone's 1770 *A Tour through Sicily and Malta,* in which he describes eating fattened livers at the table of a Sicilian bishop:

> *By a particular kind of management they make the livers of their fowls grow to a large size, and at the same time acquire a high and rich flavor. It is indeed a most incomparable dish; but the means of procuring it is so cruel, that I will not even trust it with you. Perhaps without any bad intention, you might mention it to some of your friends, they to others, 'till at last it might come into the hands of those that would be glad to try the experiment; and the whole race of poultry might ever have reason to curse me: let it suffice to say, that it occasions a painful and lingering death to the poor animal: that I know is enough to make you wish never to taste of it, whatever effect it may have upon others.*

Presumably the Sicilians had regaled him with the story that the birds—we are not told if they were geese—were blinded and their feet nailed to the floor. The English were among the first to pass laws punishing cruelty to animals, and this perception of cruelty may have kept them from producing foie gras themselves.

Italy and Germany

One of the great puzzles in the history of foie gras is the relative absence of it from Italian kitchens. From Brydone, we learn that the food served at the table of the Sicilian aristocracy was not based on local traditions but came from abroad:

> *The Sicilian cookery is a mixture of French and Spanish; and the Olio [Spanish meat stew] still presents its rank and dignity in the centre of the table, surrounded by a numerous train of fricassees, fricandeaus, ragoûts, and pot de loups; like a grave Spanish Don, amidst a number of little smart marquis.*

French cookery dominated Italian court kitchens, and elite chefs wrote cookbooks reproducing French preparations almost exactly. In eighteenth-century regional Italian cookbooks,

For the Jews of Northern Italy, fegato d'oca, or "fattened goose liver," was one of the special treats at the Passover table.
The Dorot Jewish Division
The New York Public Library
Astor, Lenox and Tilden
Foundation

however, recipes for foie gras are completely absent. The experimentalism of Scappi had disappeared, and even famous chefs such as Francesco Leonardi admitted that the evolution of Italian cookery lost its momentum. The only other Italians who were fattening geese were the Jews living in northern Italy along the Adriatic from Ancona to Venice. In the late eighteenth century, Casanova describes a "dîner à la juive" in Ancona that included goose liver and the company of the beautiful but elusive Lia, his companion. Italian Jews unfortunately did not begin to record their recipes until the nineteenth century, so we do not know what a dinner *à la juive* consisted of, or how their foie gras was prepared.

French cuisine also spread east into German-speaking lands, where it encountered a culinary culture already familiar with preparations of fattened goose liver. Eighteenth-century German cookbooks use many French terms, but the recipes more strongly reflect regional practices in the use of butter instead of lard and the preference for medieval flavorings. One of the most remarkable German cookery books is the 1739 *Nutzbares, galantes und curiöses Frauenzimmer Lexicon* (Useful, Gallant and Curious Lady's Dictionary), which combines recipes with short biographies of famous women, goddesses, and heroines. Of fowl liver it says, "The livers of birds are very strong and because of that hard to digest; of them, however, goose livers are an exception when they make them of a large size, so that they are a strangely delicate and healthy dish." Like Scappi and the Romans before him, the author recommends soaking the livers in milk for a day or two before cooking. What sets the recipes apart from the French is that most include seafood—a pie of goose livers and oysters, goose livers with mussels and, here, with anchovies:

Put a casserole with butter in it on the fire, drop in citron peels and muscat grape juice [verjus], add the already prepared goose livers and let it simmer for a while. Next take four anchovies, bone them, chop them up fine and pour them on the livers; sprinkle on bread crumbs, pour in a bit of wine and let it cook for a short time, but not too long so the livers do not become hard. If there is not enough broth, pour in some good bouillon, although this food should not be boiled for too long. When ready to serve, squeeze lots of citron juice on top and bring it out.

Other German cookbooks, perhaps aimed at the *bürgerlich* audience, dispense with the French trappings completely. Suzanna Egron's 1745 *Leipziger Koch-Buch* gives a goose liver recipe resembling a ragoût but flavored with a meat broth containing wine, pepper, clove, cardamom, and vinegar to which sliced citrons or lemons have been added—a highly medieval stew. Seasonings such as these would remain popular in German and German-Jewish cookery for the next 150 years.

Pâté de Strasbourg

By the second half of the eighteenth century, foie gras was an important ingredient in French haute cuisine, but no more than a host of others, including sweetbreads, morels, pigeons, artichoke bottoms, and woodcocks. It had yet to reach the status of an exquisite delicacy. Credit for that achievement, for propelling foie gras into the culinary stratosphere, has traditionally been given to Jean-Pierre Clause, a chef from Strasbourg. Born in 1756 or 1757, Clause entered the service of the marshall of Contades, the military governor of the area, at age 21. As the story is told, around 1780, the marshall of Contades, sick of Alsatian specialties like dumplings and rabbit with noodles, ordered the young Clause to prepare some "cuisine française" for his table. During a sleepless night, Clause came up with the idea of placing whole foie gras inside a pastry crust, filling it with a veal and lard forcemeat, and then covering and baking it. The marshall was delighted, and thus *pâté de foie gras de Strasbourg* was born.

The reality, of course, is somewhat more complicated. We have already seen goose liver made into pâté as early as Rumpolt's *Kochbuch*. In 1740, an anonymous chef (he may even have been the prince of Dombes to whom the book is dedicated) published *Le Cuisinier gascon* in Amsterdam. There is nothing of Gascon cuisine in the book; its eccentric recipes include "green monkey sauce," "chicken shaped like bats," and the first recipe for a pâté of foie gras with truffles:

You have the foies gras which you stick with truffles; you specially make a forcemeat of foie gras; you have the small pastries prepared, and you line the bottoms with the forcemeat, place a piece of foie gras on top and a truffle on each side, cover it with the forcemeat, finish it and brown the top, and put it to cook. When it is done, you open them up and pour a bit of essence inside and serve.

Portrait of Jean-Pierre Clause, the "inventor" of pâté de foie gras de Strasbourg. With permission from Cabinet des Estampes et des Dessins de Strasbourg

We do not have Clause's exact recipe for his pâté, originally called *pâté à la Contades,* only the semimythic description of its inception. In the early nineteenth century, Eduoard Nignon published an elaborate recipe for *pâté de foie gras de Strasbourg ou pâté de Clause,* calling for a forcemeat made of pork filet, lard, cooked ham, salt, spices, and foie gras. This forcemeat lined a pastry shell into which the chef placed two whole foie gras separated by truffles chopped in quarters and layers of forcemeat. After cooking, a Madeira aspic was poured into the pâté, which was aged 30 hours and served cold. Although it was named after Clause, the recipe probably reflects several generations of refinement by other hands.

If Clause did not actually invent pâté de foie gras de Strasbourg, he was responsible for its notoriety. In 1784, he left the marshall of Contades' service and married the widow of a local

Strasbourg *pâtissier*. In his new shop, he began to make his goose liver pâtés and did not stop until he died in 1827. In a very short time, gourmets were exclaiming over their heavenly flavor and texture. As early as 1782, the scholar Le Grand d'Aussy could write in his *Histoire de la vie privée des françois:* "Strasbourg, as one knows, makes with these livers the pâtés whose reputation is well known." Aside from their rich flavor, the pâtés had a special advantage over other goose liver dishes: cooked and sealed in lard, they would keep fresh for days and even weeks during the wintertime. Pâtés could be shipped all over Europe and tantalize palates as distant as the Americas.

To produce the elaborate garnishes and pâtés of the eighteenth century, French chefs needed a steady supply of foie gras. Given the era's lack of refrigeration and the vagaries of transport, the question is, where did the foie gras come from? Geese were a common feature of the French countryside in the seventeenth and eighteenth centuries, but goose fattening was a regional specialty. Most of it took place in Périgord and Gascony to the southwest or, on the opposite side of the country, in the area around Strasbourg and Metz in Alsace. Given the high perishability of fresh foie gras, trade between the southwest and Paris would have been

Early (top) and late (bottom) nineteenth-century Strasbourg foie gras labels. With permission from Cabinet des Estampes et des Dessins de Strasbourg

impractical. The trip would have taken a week or so, long enough for the meat to turn. The foie gras sold in the markets of Paris was probably supplied by Alsatian farmers, many of whom were Jewish.

Le Grand d'Aussy notes in his history that the Jews of Metz and Strasbourg possessed the same secret goose-fattening methods as the Romans and that this secret "made the Jews rich." It is unclear what Le Grand d'Aussy had in mind here, since goose farming methods had been well documented since Roman times. The impression of secrecy may reflect that the Jews of Strasbourg and Metz were particularly adept in their fattening efforts—their goose livers were plumper, firmer, and whiter than those of their competitors—and contemporaries were baffled as to why. The superiority of Jewish foie gras may be attributed to centuries of practice; Alsatian Jews had been fattening geese since the eleventh century.

By the early nineteenth century, the great popularity of pâtés de foie gras had inspired French farmers to develop more productive fattening methods. An 1805 appendix to a new edition of Olivier de Serres's *Le Théâtre d'agriculture* states that farmers have largely given up the old, cruel techniques of blinding the animals and nailing their feet: "Of a hundred fatteners, it is now difficult to find two who still do it, and even they only put out the eyes two or three days before killing. Also, the geese of Alsace are exempt from these practices and reach a prodigious girth and fatness."

The Alsatian farmers were apparently also the first to use a funnel for feeding, still standard practice in foie gras operations:

> One introduces grain into the crop of the animal with the help of an instrument: it is a funnel of tin, of which the pipe, 16 centimeters long and 20 millimeters in diameter, has the end cut into a beak fluted and rounded, forming a small rim smoothly welded to prevent any harmful chafing to the animal. This pipe has been fitted with a small stick to keep the grain flowing. The housewife, crouching on her knees, puts the instrument into the throat of the goose, which she holds with one hand, taking, with the other, some grain that is within reach, letting it flow slowly, and the stick little by little makes sure that it moves along. When she sees that the crop is almost full, she takes another goose. In between, she puts a bowl of fresh water under the beak of the [first] animal. In Alsace, people recommend that you throw a handful of fine gravel and some pulverized charcoal into the bottom of the bowl, believing that this drink contributes to the rapid fattening of the goose, by facilitating the passage of the corn and fattens the liver even more.

Before this time, the gender of the goose farmer was left unspecified, but from the nineteenth century forward it is certain that women were chiefly responsible for the delicate operation of cramming geese to produce foie gras. Eventually, as representations of the farm woman encircled by geese were reproduced in cookbooks, travel accounts, and on the labels of pâté terrines, this image came to symbolize the earthy glory of the French countryside.

LE GRAND CUISINE

In 1789, the French Revolution swept away the king, the aristocracy, and all the trappings of the *ancien régime*. Among the latter was the world of haute cuisine: the vast aristocratic kitchens, the armies of chefs and servants, and the courtiers who lived for the next splendid banquet.

The pastry cook specialized in pâté de foie gras and other delicate meat pies.
Print Collection
Miriam and Ira D. Wallach
Division of Art, Prints and
Photographs
The New York Public Library
Astor, Lenox and Tilden
Foundations

Replacing the old aristocracy were the bourgeois revolutionaries who, despite their contempt for privilege (and constant food shortages), became the new connoisseurs of fine French cooking. The French obsession with food ran too deep to eradicate. It was simply transferred to another social class and a new social setting: the restaurant.

The first restaurants arose in Paris in the years just before the Revolution. At that time, the word *restaurant* meant "restorative" or "fortifying" and was used to describe a class of strongly flavored bouillons. Later the word was applied to the establishments in which they were sold. Though diners could find cooked meals at inns, the food was unexceptional and generally prepared for travelers rather than gourmets. A more common source for cooked food was the culinary artisans—the bakers, pie makers, and meat roasters—who sold prepared food in their shops to be consumed at home. Alongside the specialists, were the *traiteurs* or caterers. If an eighteenth-century Parisian were interested in hosting a full-fledged banquet, he could order it from a traiteur—vendors who supplied everything from the entrée to the silverware. Each category of food vendor was organized into a guild that protected its selling privileges to particular types of dishes with traiteurs controlling selling rights to ragoûts and sauces.

The traiteur's monopoly was first challenged by a restaurateur named Boulanger, an early purveyor of "restaurants." In 1765, he introduced sheep's trotters in white sauce to his menu, a dish that could reasonably qualify as a ragoût. The traiteurs brought Boulanger to court and lost. He was allowed to continue serving the dish, which became the latest rage, and soon extended his menu to include other cooked meats. Boulanger's victory was symptomatic of the decline of the guild system. A 1786 decree allowed traiteurs and restaurateurs to serve meals in their own establishments, and a few years later the Revolutionary National Assembly disbanded the guilds.

In 1789, hundreds of chefs lost their aristocratic employers. With remarkable business acumen, this pool of highly skilled labor quickly identified a new opportunity: the Parisian restaurant business. In one step they went from employees dependent on their masters' wages (and whatever they could skim) to entrepreneurs selling their products for cash. The most famous of these restaurants were Méot, owned by a chef to the Prince de Condé, and the two establishments of Beauvilliers (ex-chef to the Count of Provence, the future Louis XVIII), first the Taverne de

28

Londres and then the eponymous Beauvilliers. Despite the turmoil outside their doors, Méot and Beauvilliers prepared the same elaborate dishes once cooked for the aristocracy, serving them in an atmosphere of unparalleled luxury. The Goncourt brothers, a pair of writers and gastronomes, later exclaimed over Méot's offerings, "Superlative wines, novel and exquisite refinements, a land of enchantment for the gourmet!"

The clientele at these restaurants represented a fairly broad swatch of the new Parisian society. Many were Revolutionary leaders and lesser members of the assembly. At the Revolutionary dinner table, heated discussions about food mixed with heated political debate. The Revolutionary factions attacked the greed and luxurious living of their enemies while sampling the finest food that France could provide. After the execution of Danton, the Revolutionary Tribunal retired to Méot for a hearty meal. The court that sentenced Marie Antoinette to death celebrated the event with a Méot feast of "béchamel with pinions [wing tips] and foie gras of goose, a roast chicken, quails and larks."

After the bloodbath of the Terror (1793–94), the Revolution lost its force and the populace turned from politics to pleasure. Dozens of new restaurants opened across Paris, the first visible effects of an emerging market economy on fine cuisine. Restaurant prices dropped due to increased competition, while, in some establishments, the selection of dishes rose to well over 100. The quality of the food improved as well. Unlike the old relationship between aristocratic patron and chef, the restaurant customer was fickle, and chefs could not afford to relax their standards.

The New Food Journalists

The multitude of eating options, along with the ephemerality of food trends, must have been daunting, and the new bourgeois diner needed guidance. On the scene appeared a new kind of specialist, the food critic, a self-appointed arbiter of fine cuisine. The most famous of these were Alexandre Grimod de la Reynière and Jean-Anthelme Brillat-Savarin, men of sharply different temperaments.

Grimod de la Reynière (1758–1837) was a bizarre character, trained in law but in love with theater. Not only did he write drama criticism, he conducted his life as if it were an outrageous entertainment. Legend has it that he was banished by his family to a monastery near Nancy following a particularly degrading (though unspecified) scandal. Here at the abbot's table he discovered the allure of fine cooking. On his return to Paris, he founded the Jury des Dégustateurs, a panel of taste-makers who met regularly to appraise the food supplied by restaurants and vendors, awarding the best with certificates of merit. The group was notoriously corrupt, but nevertheless Grimod de la Reynière went on to start a gastronomic periodical operating on the same premise, doling out endorsements in return for free samples. Published from 1804 to 1812, the *Almanach des gourmands,* a practical food guide to Paris, describes where foie gras was produced, how it was sold, and the best manner in which to enjoy it. During February, he wrote, "The wagons bend under the weight of truffled turkeys, of pâtés of foie gras, of terrines which, from the North, from the Midi, hurry to the capital to arrive before Lent. Nérac, Strasbourg, Troyes, Lyon, Cahors, Périgueux vie with each other in zeal and activity to shower us with delicacies." By Grimod's account, the weeks between New Year and Lent supplied a rare bounty of delights to the Parisian

Promenade Nutritive

gourmet. Supreme among them was waterfowl liver: "In this season, the pâtés of foies gras, either of geese from Strasbourg or of duck from Toulouse, are in all their goodness, because the livers have now acquired the completion of their *embonpoint* and the truffles of their perfume."

A winter menu suggested by Grimod includes a *grosse pièce* of foie gras to be served after the roast. His allusion to duck foie gras is among the first in French culinary literature and signals a turning point in the history of foie gras production. Until this point, chefs had focused solely on geese as their source for fattened livers. Although goose livers remained the prestige product, *foie gras de canard* became increasingly important, especially in areas that already specialized in duck farming. Also new is Grimod's emphasis on cold foie gras preparations. The ragoûts of the preceding century had lost ground to the pâté and the *grosse pièce,* a grand edible construction that reached its full glory under the great nineteenth-century chef Carême.

It is difficult to say whether Grimod established food trends or whether he simply reflected them. Though his palate was shaped by the time in which he lived, his preferences, more than those of the average gourmet, influenced scores of budding food enthusiasts. His special fondness for pâté de foie gras is thus an indication of existing tastes and a foreshadowing of the future. Grimod writes:

> *Nothing is better than an excellent pâté of foies gras: they have killed more gourmands than the plague. One knows it but nevertheless eyes them with abandon and eats them with delight, without contemplating how one will be able to digest them. To assist in their dissolution in the stomach, we advise chewing thoroughly, the intermediary of crusts of bread and most of all, adequate doses of rum or Swiss extract of absinthe, which are powerful digestives because they strongly stimulate the muscles and membranes of the stomach and accelerate the peristaltic movement.*

Grimod exercises poetic license when he attributes gourmand mortality to overzealous foie gras consumption. Nonetheless, he gives a sense of the food's popularity in the early part of the nineteenth century. Foie gras was the weakness of the gourmand in Grimod's Paris, a food so irresistible that it was worth the price of indigestion.

A counterpoint to Grimod de la Reynière was his contemporary Jean-Anthelme Brillat-Savarin (1755–1826). Where Grimod was practical and journalistic, Brillat-Savarin was rational and contemplative. Brillat-Savarin's classic work, *La Physiologie du goût,* is a hybrid creation combining food history, scientific discourse, philosophical reflection, and personal memoir. In writing this book, he hoped to found a new scientific discipline devoted to the study of food, which had so far escaped the attention of scientists and philosophers. He called the field "gastronomy," a term revived from ancient Greek, and defined it as "the reasoned comprehension of everything connected with the nourishment of man." The object of gastronomy, and the beauty of it as well, was the heightened pleasure that one could derive from enlightened eating. This was not knowledge for its own sake, but knowledge in the service of culinary enjoyment.

Brillat-Savarin believed that enjoying food was a kind of talent and, like other natural gifts, was distributed unequally among the populace. To identify the born gourmand, he devised a gastronomical test consisting of dishes so tempting "the mere sight of them must arouse all the gustatory powers of the properly constituted man." Passing his test required nothing more than the display of anticipatory delight, while those who show no "kindling of desire or glow of ecstasy can justly be marked down as unworthy of the honors of the occasion and the pleasures involved." Brillat-Savarin's most elaborate test, designed for the very rich, features eight courses of the finest delicacies, including a mammoth Strasbourg pâté de foie gras "in the shape of a bastion." This is one example of the newly desirable *grosse pièce,* in this case cold slices of goose liver pâté arranged on a castle-shaped structure that was probably inedible. At one dinner attended by the author, the presentation of "a Gibraltar rock of Strasbourg foie gras" stunned the guests into silence. "All conversation ceased, for hearts were full to overflowing; the skillful movements of the carvers held every eye; and when the loaded plates had been handed round, I saw successively imprinted on every face the glow of desire, the ecstasy of enjoyment, and the perfect calm of utter bliss." Despite Brillat-Savarin's emphasis on the rational study of food, he recognized that reason falters when the gourmand is presented with a dish so luscious as an excellent Strasbourg pâté.

BRILLAT-SAVARIN

Jean-Anthelme Brillat-Savarin was the foremost philosopher of gastronomy.
Culver Pictures

Nineteenth-Century Haute Cuisine

The culinary lives of both Grimod de la Reynière and Brillat-Savarin were essentially of the bourgeoisie, spent in restaurants and at comfortable if elaborate meals at home. Neither author habituated the highest levels of economic and political power—the sphere of the Rothschilds, of Talleyrand, and of the emperor Napoleon himself. In that world, the name on everybody's lips, the man whose fame spread as far as Vienna and the Winter Palace in St. Petersburg, was the chef Marie-Antoine Carême.

Born into utter poverty, Carême was abandoned to the streets of Paris at age ten and eventually became apprenticed to Bailly, one of the city's most famous pâtissiers. In his spare time, he studied architecture in the print room of the National Library. Here he became determined to wed haute cuisine with Beaux-Arts architecture and thus bring cookery into the world of the fine arts. Carême's skills attracted the attention of Bailly's distinguished customers. One of them, Talleyrand, the emperor's chief diplomat and political adviser, hired Carême to be his personal chef. The diplomat and the chef complemented each other perfectly: Talleyrand's immense resources meant that Carême could practice his art without economic limitations, while the chef's spectacular creations awed Talleyrand's guests, who included the most powerful men in Europe. He went on to work for the Prince Regent of England and Russia's Czar Alexander, among other distinguished patrons. Wherever he cooked, he reinforced the reputation of French cuisine as the finest in the Western World.

Carême was deeply aware of the long and glorious French culinary tradition that preceded him and at the same time was absolutely certain that he represented its brilliant apogee. Like his predecessors, Carême based his cuisine on stocks and other *fonds,* such as the roux, and used them as building blocks for his dishes. He based nearly all of his sauces, however, on just three basics—espagnole, béchamel, and velouté—and greatly reduced the number of delicacies, such as cock's combs, mushrooms, and artichoke hearts, used so copiously by earlier chefs. Carême's flavors were simplified, accentuating the distilled essence of the main ingredient—meat would taste like meat and fish like fish. This is not to say his recipes were easy to prepare; dozens of hours of labor by an entire team of chefs and assistants often culminated in a single dish.

Many of Carême's techniques are evident in his recipes for foie gras, most of them for ragoûts. His exacting instructions for *ragoût de foie gras à la financière* are a long way from the simplicity of La Varenne; days before the foie gras is even purchased, the chef must prepare a *grand bouillon,* Carême's basic stock, and from it produce a sauce espagnole. The quintessential haute cuisine sauce, the espagnole is prepared with greatly reduced meat bouillon, roux, herbs and other seasonings, and tomato purée. Then the chef prepares a ragoût of minced ham, herbs, spices, champignons, truffles, and Madeira and adds it to the espagnole to produce a *sauce à la financière.* Next he must buy the foie gras, because a few slices are needed to make a *ragoût à la financière,* which is not, however, the end product. Only now is the chef ready to prepare the dish:

> *After having soaked and blanched a small Strasbourg foie gras, you cook it in a mirepoix with a glass of Madeira. Let it cool; then you drain it and cut it in thin slices, rounding off the edges with the knife in order to trim them suitably. Place them to sauté in a small pan; pour on top of it the mirepoix, which you have degreased and passed through a silk sieve. A few minutes before serving, you warm it up for a moment by putting a low flame above and below. You then prepare a* ragoût à la financière, *which is demonstrated above. However, do not put in it more than a half-pound of truffles, and take out some of the cock's combs, kidneys and lamb sweetbreads. When it is ready to serve, you drain the slices and place half on the plate for the entrée plate and the rest in a hot saucière. Cover the foies with the financière [sauce]; place the entrée on top; around it add some blanched cock's combs and kidneys; pour the rest of the ragoût into the saucière and serve.*

The title page of Carême's L'Art de la cuisine française au XIX Siecle shows the names of his distinguished chef-predecessors wreathed in laurels.
General Research Division
The New York Public Library
Astor, Lenox and Tilden
Foundations

Unlike previous chefs, Carême uses the foie gras ragoût purely as garniture for chicken, game, or beef; from his time on, foie gras almost never appears as the main ingredient in a hot entrée.

Carême also stands apart from his predecessors in his emphasis on decoration. He constructed architectural models representing Roman ruins, Chinese temples, or the like out of nominally edible elements such as lard or spun sugar and marzipan then arranged the real food, such as slices of poached salmon covered with a sauce, around its base. Pâté de foie gras, which could be cut into such neat slices (perfect for arranging into geometric patters), was a natural building material for Carême's art. His recipe for *gros pâtés de foie gras aux truffes* is not so different from a Strasbourg pâté, but of course is far more complicated. Since chilled dishes were most appropriate for these presentations, Carême made the cold buffet the centerpiece of his banquets. Although the collection of fanciful building models must have appeared like examination time at Paris's École des Beaux-Arts, his guests were suitably flabbergasted by the spectacle.

After Carême's untimely death (it is believed that he inhaled too much coal fume while standing over the stove) in 1833, his pupil Jules Gouffé became the leading practitioner of haute cuisine. Gouffé made his fortune in his Paris restaurant, prepared banquets for Napoleon III, and in 1867 became the chef of Paris's elite Jockey Club. Here he wrote his most famous cookbook, *Le Livre de cuisine,* which is divided into two sections, domestic cookery and "grande cuisine." Like Carême, Gouffé drew a firm distinction between domestic and professional cook-ery. His recipes for the home are fairly detailed, while the haute cuisine preparations are given in shorthand. Only a professional chef would know how to fill in the blanks.

Not once does foie gras appear in his recipes for middle-class households. For Gouffé, foie gras was appropriate for elite tables only. His hot foie gras preparations include a ragoût, cro-quettes, and a variety of dishes to be served in small pastry cases or porcelain dishes. Each of these miniature portions, designed to accompany a more imposing entrée, call for truffles, sauce espag-nole, and the occasional addition of Madeira.

If Gouffé's hot dishes were diminutive, his cold ones were oversize. He gives recipes for foie gras pâté, a foie gras terrine, and a *pain de foie gras á la gelée,* an elaborate *grosse pièce* com-prising slices of foie gras and truffles on a base of goose liver purée that is then garnished with aspic. In Gouffé's era, aspic became a valuable asset to the French haute chef, neatly containing and preserving the dishes served at cold buffets, and adding a laquerlike finish that transformed flat-looking food into glimmering tableaux. For the rest of the century, Gouffé's repertoire of hot and cold foie gras preparations became fixtures of the haute cuisine table.

The emphasis on display was even more pronounced in the work of Gouffé's contempo-rary and rival. Urbain Dubois, who followed Carême's dictum that haute cuisine was a branch of the fine arts, built his reputation at some of Paris's finest restaurants, including the Café Anglais. He became chef to Prince Orloff of Russia and then Emperor Wilhelm I of Germany. Urbain Dubois's most important cookbooks were *Cuisine classique* and *Cuisine artistique,* works in which the visual element of a dish clearly takes precedence over taste, texture, and aroma. His *pain de foie gras á la régence* is actually an excuse for creating sculpture: A seated statue of Bellona, the Roman goddess of war, one foot on a cannon, is surrounded by flags and flanked by two eagles. Only the base, a purée of foie gras covered with a design resembling parquet flooring, is edible; the rest is constructed of cold fat. Urbain Dubois's recipe for this dish reads more like art criti-cism than culinary instruction:

> *Though this piece looks so simple, yet it is really very elegant; the effect of the whole being easy, and graceful. If the decoration of the* pain *is well managed; it is both striking, and agreeable to the eye; forming a pleasing contrast to the whiteness of the stand, and of the subject.*
>
> *The subject placed on the stand has also a pretty effect, without being difficult of execution. When the banners are nicely grouped, they enhance the subject considerably. The stand is light and airy, the friese is inclining, and the falling border very good. The imitation oak-leaves, if well mod-elled, and artistically grouped, are well suited to this sort of stand.*

The eagles on each side of the stand, serve as handles, and greatly contribute to the light appearance of the whole. In the way they are placed one on the top of the other, they cannot be otherwise than modelled: they, as well as the ball that supports them, ought to be modelled on the stand itself, on a piece of wood, firmly fixed to the friese of the stand.

Momentarily finished with his aesthetic musings, Urbain Dubois can now begin the actual recipe:

To make this pain, a purée of fat liver, or one of cooked chickens' livers, must be prepared; two-thirds of its volume of tepid chaufroix-sauce, reduced with Madeira wine, is to be mixed with it by degrees. When the preparation is smooth and cold, half its volume of very good butter, not melted, is introduced into it, but a little at a time, and beating the preparation up with a wooden spoon; by working it thus it becomes frothy. When all the butter is introduced, about a quarter of its volume of cooked fat-liver, cut up in dice, and a few cooked truffles cut up in the same shape, are mixed with the preparation. Previous to filling up the mold, its interior must be decorated, all round its sides, with lozenges of an equal size, cut out of some slices of pickled-tongue, slices of truffle, and slices of poached whites of eggs; thus a drawing, representing squares in relief, is achieved.

Dishes such as the pain de foie gras á la régence were served at banquets attended by kings, generals, and diplomats.

Through his travels, Urbain Dubois forged contacts with elite chefs from around the world. He collected many of their recipes in Cuisine de tous les pays (Cuisine of all nations), in which he described a cuisine universelle. That "universal cuisine" was French haute cuisine. Chefs in Paris, London, Frankfurt, Vienna, Berlin, Rome, Constantinople, St. Petersburg, New York, and Washington, D.C., all spoke the same language—French—underwent the same training, and prepared the same repertoire of dishes. Urbain Dubois's vision was not as rigid as that of Gouffé, however, and he had a greater sense of fun. His cookbook introduces a number of dishes that, while still based on haute cuisine methods, are clear departures from the classic repertoire:

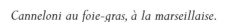

Canneloni au foie-gras, à la marseillaise.
This dish is a new creation of the southern school; it is not without merit.—Cook in salted water a dozen large canneloni; drain them, split them lengthwise, spread them on a cloth.
Separately, pound a cooked chicken stomach; add a quarter of its volume in chicken livers or foie gras, 4 spoonfuls of minced cooked ham, half a cooked calf brain, a ball of panade [a thickening paste made of flour, water, and butter] the size of an egg, and three egg yolks. Pass the mixture through a fine sieve; spread a small part in every canneloni. To see that they are garnished, roll them in paupiettes [thin slices of meat spread with forcemeat]; arrange them in a gratin plate; baste them with a bit of good gravy mixed with an equal portion of a liaised tomato sauce;

sprinkle them with grated parmesan; pour on a bit of butter; cover and cook under a low fire for a few minutes without letting them brown. Serve as soon as they are ready.

Urbain Dubois was also interested in what later became known as French regional cooking. Despite the many extant references to the excellence of the fattened duck livers from Toulouse, his *foie de canard à la mode de Toulouse* is one of the rare nineteenth-century recipes for this specialty:

Choose one or two foies-gras of duck, nicely firm and white and above all which have not been placed in water*; cut them in slices along their length and season them.

    Butter the bottom of a metal dish; sprinkle it with a pinch of shallots, a handful of chopped fresh mousseron [mushrooms]. On these fines-herbes arrange the slices of liver and between them slivers of lemons which have been skinned and seeded; sprinkle them with a pinch of parsley chopped with a small clove of garlic and mixed with a handful of panure *[a thickener made from bread soaked in milk]; brush on a bit of melted butter to moisten. Put them on a moderate heat and cook for 20 to 25 minutes, while they stew in their own juices. When they are well cooked, remove them and degrease; moisten with a bit of melted glaze mixed with the juice of a lemon. Place the dish on a platter and send it out.*

A marzipan dessert colored and shaped like a pâté de foie gras de Strasbourg.
General Research Division
The New York Public Library
Astor, Lenox and Tilden
Foundations

By the late nineteenth century, pâtés of Strasbourg foie gras were common on the tables of fine European restaurants. It was not enough, however, simply to buy a terrine, pop it open, and enjoy the contents. Urbain Dubois felt it necessary to give his readers precise instructions on the pâté's unmolding, dissection, and arrangement for the best possible display:

In every country, one can buy the terrines, the pâtés and the cans of foie-gras from Strasbourg; but, unless one finds oneself in a place where the foies-gras are abundant and good, it is better to buy the terrines than prepare them oneself. The only question is to chose one from a good source.

    A few hours before serving the terrine, surround it with ice, in order to firm up well the contents. Remove the layer of fat which covers the pâté, then cut into it, using a soup spoon made from thin iron, which you should take care to now and then dip into hot water: the pieces cut out should have the long concave form of the spoon; place them one by one on a plate. When the terrine is empty, half-fill it with a plug of ordinary bread and cover this with a layer of the fat which covered the terrine. Next stand the pieces of pâté in the terrine, forming them into a dome on top of a core made from the debris or from the smaller pieces. Place the terrine on a plate and send it out.

Strasbourg pâtés were so ubiquitous, in fact, that Urbain Dubois could make a visual pun on their glazed pastry shells and marbled interiors. The main ingredients of his *pâté de foie gras pour*

**The sellers of goose or duck livers, in order to increase the size and whiteness of their livers, soak them in hot water; this preparation is extremely prejudicial to the livers, because after absorbing the water they do not keep their form while cooking and melt into foam.*

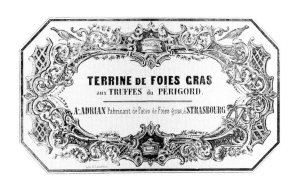

Mid-nineteenth-century
Strasbourg foie gras labels.
With permission from
Cabinet des Estampes et des
Dessins de Strasbourg

dessert are ground almonds mixed with vanilla-flavored sugar syrup. After pounding this into a paste, the chef divides it into four parts and colors each differently: "red veined with white, to imitate the ham; café au lait, to imitate the foie gras; black with chocolate and caramel, to imitate the truffles; and finally the color of cooked pastry." These pieces of colored dough are assembled in a foie gras terrine so they look like the Strasbourg product down to the hole in the pastry lid. Into this he pours sweet jelly, flavored with orange zest and liqueur instead of aspic. Then the chef unmolds the terrine and glazes the "pastry" sides with egg yolk and caramel. Before serving, he cuts a hole in the lid to expose the "pâté" within and surrounds the dish with chopped sweet "aspic." Urbain Dubois warns that this dish must only be served at dessert, because it looks too much like the real thing: "Presented to guests during the course of dinner, behind the main dishes, it is rare that it does not cause some misunderstanding."

The culture of French haute cuisine was spread by foreign visitors to France, by the assiduous international networking and self-promotion of chefs like Urbain Dubois, and by the export of the cuisine's emblematic delicacy: pâté de foie gras de Strasbourg. Before 1850, slow transport and traditional methods for sealing the terrines limited the distribution of Strasbourg pâtés to northern and central France (and neighboring Germany). By 1860, pâté manufacturers had begun to apply the methods of Nicolas Appert, a Frenchman who invented a way of using heat to seal and sterilize food. If kept in a cool place, pâtés which previously had a shelf life of a week or two could be kept for months, or even a year or more in the new steel cans. (The only doubter was Auguste Michel, pâté producer for celebrities and royalty, who claimed that all terrines older than four months turned bitter and moldy tasting.) At the same time, rapid trains and steam ships meant that any point in Western Europe was just days away, and a Strasbourg pâté could reach New York in less than a week. French foie gras had suddenly reached an international market that stretched from the palaces of St. Petersburg to the exclusive men's clubs of Washington, D.C.

The citizens of Strasbourg responded to this demand by opening more pâté firms. In 1860 alone, nine distinct pâté makers opened their doors, most located in the streets surrounding the cathedral. The 1870 capture of Alsace by Germany slowed business for only a year or two, and in 1874 six additional manufacturers opened for business. By the start of World War I there were 60 pâté manufacturers in the city with many others in the outlying towns. Most famous was the firm founded by Auguste Michel, who became identified as the king of Strasbourg pâtés. His pâtés were sold in elaborate ceramic terrines decorated with typical Alsatian themes. Pâté sizes ranged from small pots serving a modest dinner party to enormous terrines containing a quantity of foie gras large enough to feed a banquet of 50 or more. Wealthy and prominent gourmands, including Sarah Bernhardt, made pilgrimages to his business to sample his wares and receive his advice regarding pâté preparation.

In the first half of the nineteenth century, the Strasbourg pâté industry relied on small farmers in the surrounding countryside to provide them with their raw material. From early

December through March, the farmers would journey to the city carrying their livers, rarely more than a few dozen at a time, to sell to the pâté manufacturers. By 1870, however, the industry realized that demand was rapidly outstripping supply, and that local farmers were being lured by more lucrative work opportunities in the region's booming factories. The large pâté manufacturers developed contacts with goose farmers in Central Europe, principally Hungary, to supply livers grown to their specifications. Because pâté de foie gras was the supreme dish of France's glorious national cuisine, these contracts were kept discreet. The need to import Hungarian foie gras would have been perceived as a national disgrace.

These new sources of goose liver allowed manufacturers with connections in Central Europe to grow far more rapidly than others. The larger pâté companies began to acquire the small ones, and in the decades following World War I the small artisanal pâté shops began to disappear from the streets of Strasbourg. With the advent of industrialization, Strasbourg pâté slipped downward in the hierarchy of status foods. Its perishability, once so intrinsic to its appeal, was no longer a factor, and prices had fallen due to increased supply and decreased production costs. Fresh foie gras retained its exclusive cachet, but industrialization delivered Strasbourg pâté to a worldwide market of middle-class consumers.

Advertisement for Auguste Michel's famous pâté de foie gras factory, which was visited by the celebrities and gourmands of turn-of-the-century France.
With permission from Cabinet des Estampes et des Dessins de Strasbourg

Escoffier: The Climax of Haute Cuisine

In the late nineteenth century, the tradition of French haute cuisine, stretching all the way back to La Varenne, found its culmination in the career of Auguste Escoffier, one of the greatest chefs of all time. The son of a blacksmith, Escoffier was born in 1846 in a village in the south of France and at the age of 13 was apprenticed at his uncle's restaurant in Nice. Although his uncle served many local and classic French preparations, an important part of his clientele comprised Russian and German aristocrats who wanted the dishes of their native lands. Here Escoffier learned a crucial lesson: by catering to the highly mobile international rich (the era's equivalent of the jet-set), he could make his fortune. From Nice, Escoffier moved to Paris's Petit Moulin Rouge restaurant, known for both its fine cuisine and its facilities for discrete liaisons, where at the phenomenally early age of 27 he became head chef. In winter, he followed his clientele to the resorts of the south, where in 1884 he teamed up with César Ritz, manager of Monte Carlo's Grand Hôtel. For the next four decades, Escoffier spent his career designing and running the kitchens of the most famous hotels in the world, including London's Savoy and Carlton and New York's Ritz-Carlton. It was in these international hotel kitchens that Escoffier's art reached its highest point and where he developed the final and definitive repertoire of haute cuisine preparations for foie gras.

Although Escoffier was a great admirer of Carême and deeply devoted to the traditions of French cuisine, he was also a modernizer. He believed in using the latest technology and rational management techniques to reorganize every aspect of cooking from the raw ingredients to the table. His kitchens were the first to have adequate light and ventilation. He also streamlined the classic cooking processes that, since the days of La Varenne, had grown ever more elaborate. The chefs' stations were rationalized so that each corresponded to a stage of the cooking process. All of the classic *fonds*—the stocks, rouxs, and mirepoix—were still integral, but the latter stages of a dish's preparation were greatly simplified. If a chef were to start from scratch, it still would take days to prepare a saddle of veal Orloff. However, with the stocks and sauce espagnole simmering on the stove, he could prepare the dish in far less time than a chef in the age of Carême or Gouffé. Escoffier also radically simplified the garnitures. The main ingredient to his *garniture financière* was veal or chicken forcemeat quenelles; the old ragoût was replaced by reduced portions of mushrooms, cock's combs, kidneys, truffles, and olives (a new ingredient) in a sauce financière. Foie gras and sweetbreads, which are included in Carême's recipe, had disappeared. Last, Escoffier downplayed the visual display, particularly for the savories. Food should look like food, he said, and it is significant that, unlike many of his predecessors, he included few illustrations in his books.

Escoffier collected over 5000 of his recipes in his 1903 masterwork, *Le Guide culinaire*. Like all the great French cookbooks since La Varenne, the work opens with a recipe for the basic stock; the recipes run from the simplest to the most complicated, from scrambled eggs to elaborate banquet dishes. For each, Escoffier gives meticulous step-by-step instructions and measurements down to the gram—they are almost, but not quite, within the grasp of the home cook. In keeping with his international clientele, he includes many foreign dishes: osso buco, goulash, borscht, and clam chowder. Among his many foie gras preparations, however, he allows only one with a trace of outside influence, *foie gras au paprika*:

> Trim a nice raw foie gras, season it with salt and sprinkle with a teaspoon of paprika; sprinkle the bottom of a pan with 1 sliced large Spanish onion and a bayleaf and place the foie gras on top; cover and cook in a moderate oven for 30 minutes.
>
> Place the foie gras in an oval terrine, after carefully removing all of the onion and bayleaf, then strain the fat over it. Fill the terrine with melted jelly and allow to set.

(In German-speaking lands, similar preparations would have been served hot with the onion spread on top.) The rest of his dishes repeat the classic repertoire of chefs like Gouffé—foie gras caisses, croquettes, timbales, escalopes, and pains—with a few interesting exceptions. One of these is his *tourte de foie gras à l'ancienne,* a goose liver pie reminiscent of Massialot's 1691 recipe cited previously:

> Cut a raw foie gras into even-sized slices, season them and marinate in brandy together with an equal number of slices of truffle.
>
> Pass the trimmings of the foie gras through a sieve then mix it together with 100g chopped truffle and 600g good-quality sausage meat.
>
> Place half of this forcemeat mixture on a round sheet of Pie Paste leaving a 4cm wide space around the edge. Arrange the slices of foie gras and truffle on top, cover with the rest of the forcemeat and smooth the surface. Cover with a second sheet of the same paste.

Seal the edges together, moisten the top edge of the covering paste and surround with a band of puff paste. Knotch the edge of the paste to form a decoration, brush with beaten egg and bake for 45 minutes in a moderate oven.

On removing from the oven, detach the top layer of pie pastry by cutting round the inside edge of the puff pastry; coat the exposed filling of the Tourte with a little fairly thick Sauce Madère.

Of interest in these recipes is what is omitted—the fixation on the visual that marked Escoffier's nineteenth-century predecessors. Escoffier cared most of all about taste, and that concentration made *Le Guide culinaire* a bestseller and a classic of French cuisine that is still usable today.

When Escoffier died in 1935 at the age of 89, he was the world's most celebrated chef. Presiding over Europe's most renowned kitchens, he invented hundreds of dishes that had become elements of the permanent culinary repertoire. Escoffier had written the definitive haute cuisine cookbook and had been showered with honors by the French government and by people of high position, power, and wealth. Curiously, it was his success that helped lead to the downfall of French haute cuisine. Escoffier advanced the glorious tradition of French cookery to such a point that there was no room for another revolution without toppling the entire, elaborate structure.

BEYOND FRANCE:
NINETEENTH-CENTURY
JEWISH COOKING

*An Alsatian rabbi examines a
fattened goose.*
The Dorot Jewish Division
The New York Public Library
Astor, Lenox and Tilden
Foundations

The only culinary tradition to rival the French in its genius for cooking with foie gras belongs to the Ashkenazi Jews. Ashkenazi culture had originated in medieval France and Germany, radiating east to Poland, Hungary, Lithuania, and Ukraine during Jewish migrations in the fifteenth and sixteenth centuries. Ashkenazi cooking varied somewhat from region to region but overall was bound together by a unified cultural tradition. This included a common repertoire of dishes, Jewish dietary law, and a passion for good food.

The allures of foie gras made sense to the Ashkenazi palate. It possessed the same soft texture and earthy flavor as offal, a favorite of Ashkenazi Jews and usually the most affordable parts of the animal. Yet foie gras was set apart from other organ meats by virtue of its supremely fatty flesh. The modern distaste for animal fat is a relatively new culinary bias that would have confounded nineteenth-century Jewish diners. Jewish cookery embraced fat without reservation, both for the richness it imparted to other ingredients and for its life-sustaining attributes. Despite modern health fears concerning fat, the simple fact is that humans need fat to live, a point clearly recognized by Jewish homemakers in nineteenth-century Europe. The seasonality of foie gras also contributed to its value in the Jewish kitchen. Unlike most other organ meats, fattened goose liver was a winter delicacy most closely associated with the festival of Chanukah and the Passover meal. Like the Thanksgiving turkey or the Easter ham, foie gras was holiday food.

Jewish cooks grasped the possibilities of foie gras and incorporated it into varied preparations, as the main ingredient or as an enrichment to other meats. A few Jewish dishes closely resemble French creations, as if the two cuisines were moving along parallel lines in their understanding of foie gras cookery. A forcemeat of foie gras, ground veal, and chopped goose meat packed into the neck skin (i.e., stuffed goose neck) was very similar to the foie gras boudins prepared by Pierre de Lune and Massialot. And Jewish chopped liver, often made from foie gras, may well have sparked the invention of pâté de foie gras in Strasbourg.

Taking a broader view, however, the culinary culture of the Ashkenazi Jews was emphatically not French in several important respects. Jewish food traditions were based on the spoken word rather than the cookbook. Recipes were transmitted from mother to daughter, and for this reason Jewish cooking remained fairly stable through the generations. There was no counterpart in the Ashkenazi world to the professional French chefs and cookbook authors of the eighteenth and nineteenth centuries or to the competitive environment in which haute cuisine evolved. Jewish foie gras cookery developed in the hands of domestic cooks.

The Ashkenazi practice of fattening geese stretches back to at least the eleventh century, but documentation of Jewish goose-farming techniques is sparse until the mid-nineteenth

40

century, when a crop of Jewish cooking encyclopedias burst into print. One of the earliest, *Kochbuch für israelitischen Frauen* (1859) by Rebekka Wolf, contains the following instructions for goose fattening or "Gänse zu nudeln" (literally translated "to dumpling geese"):

> Start the geese in late autumn, first feeding them for a few weeks with oats and then putting them into a goose house, where they are seated one next to another. . . . Make dough from coarse meal and bran, adding a handful of salt, some beechwood ashes (if you have some) and water, so it forms a good ball in your hand, and make from it dumplings a half a short finger long and a fat finger thick and then dry them on a hot pan or at the baker. In the beginning a goose receives four pieces per serving, which is given four times a day, or 16 per day. Do this for three or four days and then for a few days give seven pieces per serving, then nine, then 11 and then at most 13 pieces, where you stay until the goose is fat, which is best felt on the bottom of the bird. Divide the feedings like this: mornings at seven o'clock, noon, afternoons at five and evenings at 10 o'clock. If you feel while doing this that not all the dumplings are being digested—feel along the throat to check—do not give any more but wait an hour. It is extremely important that in the trough that goes beside the goose house there is always lots of water, or else they quickly die. You must fatten the geese for four weeks, and in the last week they must be given fewer dumplings again. The dumplings should not be pointed on any side but should be round and completely smooth all over and must be dipped in water before you give them.

Herding geese in a nineteenth-century German village. Culver Pictures

Throughout the Ashkenazi world, goose farming was one of the few income-producing activities available to Jewish women.

The nineteenth-century Jewish cookbook, modeled after non-Jewish prototypes such as the *Praktische Kochbuch* by Henriette Davidis, marks a turning point in the history of Ashkenazi cooking and culture. The cookbook's newfound popularity is one expression of the desire among certain Jews to gain full membership in European society. Recipes in the cookbooks were drawn from diverse culinary traditions, not only Jewish but also German, Czech, Hungarian, and, most importantly, French, the continent's foremost cuisine. The "European-ness" of the cookbooks, however, was more than a matter of their content. The very idea of a comprehensive cooking manual embodied the Enlightenment impulse to amass large stores of knowledge and contain it in some organized form. Earlier in the century, German Jewish intellectuals had tried to reconcile their history and literature with modern science. Now it was time to bring the principles of science into the home. The women who used these cookbooks thought of themselves as Jewish, but Judaism was only one of their identities.

One form of guidance offered by the cooking encyclopedias concerned the observance of dietary laws, with special chapters on treating meat in a kosher fashion. Included in this material were guidelines for how to kosher foie gras. Liver was a special problem for the observant cook, since foie gras, like all liver, was plump with blood, which is prohibited under the dictates of *kashrut*. Before it could be incorporated into any dish, the foie gras has to be soaked for half an hour, salted, and allowed to stand. It is then roasted over coals for 15 minutes to release the remaining blood, after which it is ready to be "cooked."

One classic Ashkenazi foie gras dish follows the medieval style of sweetening meats with sugar. In her 1901 *Ausführliches Kochbuch* (Detailed Cookbook), Marie Elsasser, who lived in Karlsruhe not far from Strasbourg, gives a recipe for goose liver with apples, also known as "goose liver, old Jewish law":

> *Lightly salt a goose liver and place it in casserole with hot goose fat and put it over a fire. Peel a good apple, such as a Borsdorfer or a Goldreinetten, cut it into slices, and place it in the fat around the liver. Sprinkle a bit of sugar on top and cook the dish for half an hour. Serve on a hot plate with the apples laid on top.*

A second preparation with medieval overtones comes from Marie Kauders's *Vollständiges israelitisches Kochbuch* (1894), first published in Prague. Her recipe for a spiced foie gras dish called *besteckte* or "studded" goose liver simply reads: "The goose liver is studded with slivered sweet almonds, a small piece of cinnamon and cloves and roasted in the oven with a generous amount of fat."

Eastern and Central Europe was the land of the dumpling, so it is only fitting to find goose liver dumplings in the repertoire of regional foie gras dishes. Marie Elsasser offers the following version:

> *With this one use unattractive reddish goose liver. Cut the crust from 3–4 "water rolls," soak them in meat stock, and squeeze them out well. Mix them with chopped onions and parsley which has been cooked in goose fat and with 250–300 grams of finely chopped goose liver which has been passed through a sieve. Add salt, nutmeg, pepper, and ginger to the mixture and 3–4 eggs whose whites have been whipped into foam. If the dough is too soft, add grated breadcrumbs and maybe also work in some flour. With floured hands make dumplings, cook them in salt water, cover with onions cooked in goose fat, and then serve on sauerkraut.*

The dumplings could also be eaten plain or floating in a bowl of soup. During Passover, when leavened bread was prohibited, they could be made with matzoh meal.

Over the course of the nineteenth century, Jewish cookbooks, already hefty in size, tended to grow increasingly thicker. The range of dishes grew more international in scope, with an affinity for dishes in the French style. Elsasser's book, for example, offers a full complement of "French" foie gras dishes, including goose liver in truffle sauce, in Madeira sauce, *en gelée,* and cooked in timbales. She also gives two recipes for foie gras ragoût, one "plain" and one "fancy." Naturally, the French recipes have been revised in light of Jewish dietary law—all forego the use of dairy and pork products.

The women who wrote the cooking encyclopedias, along with the women who used them, were cosmopolitan in their culinary tastes. It would be safe to guess that they lived in culturally dynamic areas, cities or larger towns, where it was possible to sample foods from beyond the immediate region. They were certainly curious about French food, and if they did not prepare it at home, they may have sampled it in restaurants. In the 1920s, the eminent French physician and cookbook writer Edouard de Pomiane made a culinary tour of Jewish Poland. His account of the trip, *The Jews of Poland, Recollections and Recipes* (1928), confirms that the most fashionable Jewish restaurants in Warsaw were French-style eating emporiums. Of one Warsaw establishment, the Picadilly, de Pomiane says:

> *[It] has the air of a good Paris restaurant. . . . The room is clean and luxurious; the waiters are in dark suits; the public looks completely European. . . . Here the Jews have abandoned their oriental characteristics; they eat like everyone else; they tend to westernize themselves.*
>
> *Furthermore, the menu does not bear the three Hebrew signs which indicate that the food is prepared "according to ritual." These are replaced by four silhouettes of naked women squatting on cushions and admiring themselves in a mirror.*

Fashionable Warsaw at the time of de Pomiane's trip was under the thrall of Gallic culture. French was the language of the upper classes, and women of means paraded up and down the avenues in Parisian designs. As de Pomiane explains, the city's wealthier Jews, many intent on assimilation, enthusiastically adopted French culture and with it French cooking, the last word in culinary sophistication. Upon entering the Picadilly restaurant, patrons first stopped to admire the hors d'oeuvres displayed on the counter: slices of carp in aspic, a *macedoine* of cooked vegetables in mayonnaise, black and red caviar, and a mound of chopped goose liver. Local specialities—the goose liver—and French preparations combined to create a picture of Continental refinement.

To understand the role of foie gras in Jewish cookery, it is essential to grasp the full dietary significance of goose and its by-products. In describing a restaurant in Cracow, de Pomiane cites the menu in its entirety. Along with sautéed goose liver, he lists roast goose, green or unfattened goose, stuffed goose neck, stuffed goose gizzard, and goose giblets. Some part of the bird appears as a main ingredient in five of the 20 entrées, while the remainder almost certainly contained goose fat, the Jewish cooking medium of choice. Goose fat was used not only for frying on top of the stove and for roasting in the oven, but also to moisten vegetables, to enrich soups, and to prepare dumplings, puddings, and baked goods. And when slathered over a thick slice of bread, goose fat was a meal. "Good European food smells of butter," says de Pomiane. "Good Jewish cooking smells of goose fat." Foie gras and goose fat, products of the same farming method, can be seen as complementary elements in Jewish cuisine. Where goose fat was an everyday staple, foie gras was the exquisite culmination of the Jewish reliance on the goose in its entirety.

Restaurant food was for city dwellers, but foie gras also figured in the diet of Jewish townspeople and villagers. Here, in the Jewish world of the *shtetl,* it was closely linked with the celebration of the holidays. The succinctly titled story "Geese," by the Yiddish writer Sholom Aleichem (1859–1916), describes the labors of a Jewish goose farmer, a woman who structures her business according to the rhythms of the religious calendar. Birds are purchased at Sukot (the autumn harvest festival) and slaughtered at Chanukah in early winter; the rendered fat is set aside for use at Passover in early spring. The story's protagonist tells it this way:

Oh, me, what a business geese is! That is to say, it isn't such a bad business, and if God blesses the geese you can make a pretty ruble out of them. But what's the rub? That only happens once in ten years. More often you don't make a kopek from the geese. In fact, you end up in the red. You put so much work into the whole mess, that I swear it isn't worth the tumult. If so, you're liable to ask, if there's no profit in geese, why bother? Here's my answer—what else do you want me to do after working with geese all these years? Think of it! Tying up thirty geese, carrying them over to the slaughterer, coming home with thirty of them, plucking their feathers. Then salting, rinsing, and scalding them. Then separating the skin, the fat, the giblets, and the meat, turning everything into money, not letting a speck go to waste. And I do it all by myself. First of all, I fry the skin and the fat and make goose-fat out of it. I make Passover-fat every year, for my Passover-fat is considered the best and most kosher fat in the village. When I make kosher-for-Passover goose-fat, Passover steps into the house smack in the middle of Hanuka.

Sholom Aleichem's goose farmer ekes out just enough to support her family (the husband of the story spends his days studying Torah). Stray bits of goose meat are fed to the children: "a gizzard, a head, a foot, a drop of fat. The smell alone is enough for them." As de Pomiane suggests, the odor of Jewish cooking was so closely linked to goose fat that the merest whiff of it could conjure up an entire meal.

In addition to those who raised geese for profit, Jewish housewives might also raise a goose or two for family consumption. This practice, which continued until the eve of World War II, was especially common in smaller villages where it was impossible to buy all the necessary household provisions. Nat Sobel, former resident of a Polish shtetl called Luboml, remembers how his mother bought young birds in January, feeding them generously with seeds and grains (mostly corn) until they were brought to the *shochet,* the ritual slaughterer, in March or April. He still recalls the bountiful days after the geese were killed:

> *The women would divide up the meat. The goose fat would be melted and stored in glass containers. They would cook with that throughout the winter or we would spread it on bread with fried onions. Goose meat was saved for the Passover meal, but the liver was fried on hot coals and given to the children. Every kid got a piece. Ducks were for poor people, geese for the aristocracy!*

Meat was a scarce commodity in the shtetl diet, and generally reserved for the Sabbath meal, when its consumption was considered a *mitzvah,* a fulfillment of God's commandment. For people who lived on bread, potatoes, and noodles, goose liver was an invaluable source of energy-giving fat and vitamins. Regarded as a kind of health food, it was dutifully fed to growing children, who would benefit most from the additional calories. Nathan Eiger, another Luboml resident, now in his eighties, remembers his mother doling out Passover goose liver to the children in his family, certain that she never took any for herself.

If a Jewish family were fortunate enough to have a reasonable supply of meat, fish, and poultry, foie gras from the holiday goose could be used to prepare delectable appetizers and entrées. One utterly simple yet sumptuous recipe for cold goose liver was recorded by de Pomiane:

Take some very fat goose livers.

Heat some goose fat (about one tablespoonful of fat per liver) in a small saucepan and add the livers. Simmer for 20 minutes. Remove from the heat and arrange the livers on the dish. Pour the fat over them. Salt. Leave to cool and serve as they are.

A more intricate preparation that combines foie gras with other meats, de Pomiane's recipe for stuffed goose neck calls for:

1 goose neck

1 goose liver

About 8 ounces of ground veal

4 slices bread, crusts removed, soaked in water and squeezed

1 teaspoon salt

½ teaspoon pepper

½ teaspoon paprika

2 egg yolks

1 tablespoon goose fat

1 quart veal or chicken broth

Remove the skin from the goose neck by peeling it off, taking care not to tear it. Clean it and remove any membranes. Leave it right side out. Scrape the meat from the neck, chop it and mix it with an equal weight of goose liver. Weigh these meats and mix them with an equal weight of ground veal. Grind the mixture together and weigh again. Add to this mixture one third of its weight in squeezed bread. Season with salt, pepper and paprika. Bind the mixture with the egg yolks and goose fat.

Tie the neck at one end and fill it with the stuffing. Do not pack the stuffing in too tightly, or it will burst during cooking. Tie the other end with string. Prick the skin all over with the tines of a fork.

Put the sausage into a pot of cold broth. Gradually bring to the boil over low heat. Cover the pan and poach in barely trembling water for 1 hour.

Serve the sausage hot as it is. It can also be served cold, in which case, it should be allowed to cool pressed between two plates, with a 2½-pound weight on the top plate.

The slaughter of geese in Jewish Alsace was a time of heightened conviviality, an unofficial holiday before the real holiday of Passover began. In *La Vie juive* (1886), Leon Cahun describes the week preceding "Jewish Easter":

The last fattened geese of the season—poor beasts—are sacrificed. White and plump, how beautiful they are when, all plucked, one has them displayed triumphantly on the farmer's table. For eight days, there is nothing but comings and goings. . . . Each evening, everyone visits his neighbor to admire their Easter geese, the volume of their liver, the amplitude of their fat, the firmness of their skin, the delicacy of their giblets. A good smell of melting goose fat fills the Jewish houses of Hochfelden.

The art of goose fattening had thus become an occasion for neighborly competition among local connoisseurs.

Of all Europe's Ashkenazi communities, perhaps none consumed greater quantities of foie gras than the Jews of Hungary. It appears that geese occupied a central position in the Hungarian diet from a relatively early period. A reference to the bird is found in a document from 1292 enumerating the obligations of a serf to his feudal master. Among them is the presentation of two geese—one young, one old—every November 11th, St. Martin's Day. Born in Western Hungary in the fourth century, St. Martin of Tours traveled to France and helped bring Christianity to that region. He has long been considered the patron saint of geese because, like that bird, his life was characterized by migration. It also appears that geese were an early Hungarian export. A 1498 edict issued by King Ulaszlo decreed that all poultry destined for foreign lands, including geese, must pass through the "30th Customs Office."

The first Hungarian allusion to fattened goose liver is found in *A New Book About Cooking* (1680) by János Keszei, which the author, a court chef, dedicated to Anna Bornemisza, Princess of Transylvania. Keszei's material on goose liver is lifted almost directly from Marx Rumpolt's *Kochbuch* published in Germany a century earlier:

> *Envelop the goose liver in a calf's thin skin, bake it and prepare green or brown sauce to accompany it. I used goose liver fattened by Bohemian Jews, its weight was more than three pounds. You may also prepare a mush of it.*

Keszei's wording is so close to Rumpolt's that he must have known the German chef's work. It is understandable that Keszei would borrow lavishly from his predecessor as both were court cooks practicing within the same culinary tradition. Keszei may have procured goose liver from the same Jewish population that had supplied noble kitchens during Rumpolt's lifetime.

The Jewish presence in Hungary dates from the eleventh century, when Jews from Bohemia, Moravia, and Germany settled in the western part of the country. The medieval community of Hungarian Jews was relatively small and dissipated. It grew in size and importance during the fifteenth century, when towns such as Buda became a destination for Jews expelled from their homelands in Moravia and Austria. Eastern Hungary, settled mostly by Polish Jews, was culturally distinct from the west. By the mid-nineteenth century, the western communities were predominately orthodox, while eastern Hungary had become a bastion of Hasidism, a mystical Jewish sect founded in the previous century. The east was also where Jewish goose production was concentrated.

Typically, women were in charge of the raising, fattening, and marketing of geese. These entrepreneurs were known in Hungarian as *libásasszonyok* which, literally translated, means "geese women." In a curious passage from a late eighteenth-century housewife's manual called *The Good Housewife* (1796), the author, Mihály Veres, advises women to time their goose fattening efforts to the lunar cycle:

> *We know from experience that geese do not gain enough after a long fattening. The reason for this is the fat they gain while the Moon waxes disappears while the Moon wanes. If you want your geese to fatten quickly, close them in a narrow pen at the time of the new Moon and give them as much*

food as they are able to consume. The nourishment should be oats, wheat or corn soaked in water and yellow or wild carrots. You will see that at first they will eat well for a few days but after a time they will eat less. Nevertheless, there should always be some food available so that they can eat whenever they wish, and there should always be water. You will see them well-fattened after 14 days, and then you may kill them, because, with the Moon waning, they would only lose weight and there would be no point in keeping them further.

Included in *The Good Housewife* are instructions on how to prepare an especially heavy liver:

Crush antimony and rub it until it becomes soft; prepare a dough and make small cakes or little balls of dough. Each goose should get three pinches of antimony during the daily feedings. You may also feed the geese with dumplings or corn taking care not to overfeed them . . .

(French goose fatteners also used antimony, a whitish chemical element now known to be toxic, until health concerns caused the substance to be banned in the late nineteenth century.)

Jewish goose farms in the first half of the nineteenth century were modest operations accommodating 50 to 200 birds. The scale of production and of export expanded dramatically in the 1860s when the Jewish businessman Anton Hirschfeld founded the Anton Hirschfeld Erste Ungarisch-Österreichische Gänseleber Export-Gesellschaft (Anton Hirschfeld First Hungarian-Austrian Goose Liver Export Company). Hirschfeld's agents purchased their foie gras from independent farmers, then had their livers graded and shipped to branch offices in Budapest, Vienna, Strasbourg, and Paris. "First class" livers weighing between 750 and 1000 grams were reserved for the Strasbourg pâté manufacturers. The inauguration of the Orient Express in 1883, Europe's first continental railway, advanced the distribution of Hungarian foie gras; Hirschfeld arranged for a special "ice car" to be attached to the train specifically for the transport of his goose liver. Wrapped in parchment, then packed in wooden crates, the fresh, chilled livers could arrive in Paris within 72 hours. The new method of transport allowed for an increased volume of export. In the year prior to the opening of the railway, the Hungarians sold 23 metric tons of foie gras to France. By 1886, that figure had more than tripled. In 1938, on the eve of World War II, the Hungarians sold the French 497 metric tons of their choicest foie gras.

Goose was a popular ingredient in nineteenth-century Hungarian cooking, and foie gras was heartily consumed by the general population. The foundation of non-Jewish Hungarian cuisine, however, consisted of pork, bacon, and lard—all forbidden by kashrut. In their place, Jews turned to goose meat, goose crackling or *gribenes,* and goose fat, the core triad of Jewish-Hungarian food.

One signature goose dish from the Jewish-Hungarian kitchen was *cholent,* a Sabbath stew of legumes, grains, and meats, cooked overnight in a slow oven. Cholent was eaten by Jews across Europe, but the Hungarian version was made especially savory by the addition of fresh or smoked goose breast, leg, and feet. In a second preparation typical of the Jewish cook, goose *gribenes* were mashed together with hard-boiled eggs, goose fat, onion, and vinegar to form a kind of pâté. In both dishes, goose is used economically, as a concentrated source of flavor for less expensive ingredients.

Though nineteenth-century Hungarian cooks devised a broad array of foie gras dishes, many used lard or combined meat with dairy, often in the form of sour cream. Jewish foie gras cookery therefore developed along a somewhat independent line. One basic dish, a whole foie gras cooked and preserved in goose fat, was kept on hand in many Jewish households. On school days, mothers would place a slice of fat-marbled foie gras from the terrine inside a roll and pack it for their children's lunch. The Hungarian affection for goose found ample expression in a dish that combined *gribenes,* goose fat, and foie gras on a single plate. The *gribenes* were mashed with hard-cooked eggs, goose fat, and minced onions, then served atop fried slices of foie gras and sprinkled with paprika. Therese Lederer's *Koch-Buch für israelitische Frauen,* first published in 1876, gives a recipe for a kind of oversized foie gras dumpling in which the liver is passed through a sieve, combined with whole beaten eggs, soaked bread, whipped egg whites, and seasonings. The foie gras "dough" is then placed in a greased casserole, sprinkled with breadcrumbs, and baked until firm. The finished creation was sliced like a loaf of bread and served in soup.

The strength and the unity of Ashkenazi culture carried culinary traditions to communities far from the population centers of Alsace and Poland. Along Italy's Adriatic coast, Venice, Ancona, and other villages were home to small but vibrant Jewish communities. Here, Jews fattened geese for their own culinary uses and to sell to local gentiles for holiday meals. As in Alsace, the days before Passover were the most important for slaughter. In Ancona, the Jews who had no land for geese would buy birds and give them to local farmers for fattening. They did this only out of extreme necessity as birds were often treated so badly that the liver would be stained and the animal damaged enough to render it unkosher.

On the two feast nights of Passover, Ancona's Jews gave goose a place of honor on their Seder table. The menu for the first dinner included a special lasagne, *fegato d'oca e petisini* (goose liver and breast), peas, and artichokes and, for dessert, marzipan and candied quince. The goose liver was cut into pieces, seasoned with salt and pepper, and grilled over an open fire. Then it was transferred to a pan in which a good amount of goose fat was bubbling. The liver was cooked only for a few minutes and then the liver and fat were ladled into a small terrine that was allowed to cool. At the meal, the foie gras terrine was cut into slices and spread on matzoh. On the second night, dinner featured prosciutto and salami made from goose. Unfortunately, like almost all the Jewish communities of Europe, Ancona's was destroyed during World War II. The centuries-long Italian-Jewish tradition of fattening geese and eating *fegato d'oca* exists only in memory.

Germany

The Jews of Central and Eastern Europe had a profound influence on the (usually) German-speaking cultures in which they lived. This influence was felt not only in the realms of art, philosophy, and literature, but also in cuisine. From just east of Strasbourg all the way to the Russian border, Jews fattened geese, produced foie gras, and transmitted their love of that delicacy to the gentiles around them. In the eighteenth century, *gänseleber* (fattened goose liver) seems to have been confined to the area along the Rhine from Frankfurt south to the Swiss border; a century later, foie gras was considered a local specialty all the way to the border of the Ottoman Empire. The fine restaurants and banquet rooms of great cities such as Vienna and Berlin were claimed by Urbain Dubois as the territory of his "Cuisine Universelle." Nevertheless, the vast majority of the fattened goose liver was prepared in ways that had nothing to do with haute cuisine but reflected a blend of Jewish and local traditions of cookery. This included Strasbourg-style goose liver pâtés, which Germans saw as their own invention and which they prepared in recipes that diverged from the classic French repertoire.

We see the Jewish influence on German foie gras dishes most strongly in the simple preparations, such as a liver dredged in flour and then baked in its own fat. The region that is now Poland had one of the largest Jewish populations in Eastern Europe, and some of their recipes were transferred whole into the non-Jewish repertoire. Here is an example from *Neues allgemeines schlesisches Kochbuch für bürgerliche Haushaltungen* (New General Silesian Cookbook for Bourgeois Households), published in Breslau (now Wroclaw in Poland) in 1835:

> *To braise goose liver. Melt goosefat in a casserole and slowly cook the liver with an onion pricked with cloves over a low fire. Remove most of the fat, sprinkle the liver with flour, pour in three spoonfuls of meat broth and the same amount of wine, and let it braise. You can also roast the liver in fat with a peeled and quartered apple.*

Cooking the liver in its own fat and using the onion and apple are deeply rooted Jewish preparations for goose liver. As they moved away from Jewish influence, German chefs would substitute butter for goose fat and add anchovies, lard and ham for flavor.

In the first half of the nineteenth century, the most influential German cookbook was Frederike Löffler's *Neues Kochbuch,* first published in 1791. Löffler was actually a rare female chef, working as an official cook for the Dukedom of Württemberg (about 50 miles west of Strasbourg). Many of her recipes show a French influence (such as goose liver ragoût in truffle sauce) but the seasonings are far stronger than those found in haute cuisine preparations. For example, here is her recipe for a goose liver pâté:

A German goose market.
Culver Pictures

> *Finely chop two pounds of veal from the leg and a ½ pound of fresh bacon and add to this two ounces washed and sorted anchovies, two ounces capers, and the peel and flesh of one lemon, all also chopped fine. Put the forcemeat in a bowl with salt, pepper, clove, and nutmeg; add 3 to 4 tablespoons of vinegar. Prepare a good dough with a ½ pound of butter. Spread butter on the insides of a casserole or a deep baking tray, and sprinkle it with bread flour. Roll out the dough to the thickness of a strong knife blade, and stamp it with one of the Weinbaches molds, of which the heart is the most attractive. Line the bottom and the sides of the casserole with the decorated dough, spread on this a finger-thick layer of forcemeat, and lay on top a larded goose liver which has been seasoned with pepper and clove. Fill the casserole with the remaining forcemeat; make a lid from the rest of the dough and place it on top of the forcemeat. Make a small hole in the middle of the lid with the dough around it slightly raised. Cook in a moderate oven and then unmold it onto a sheet of paper. It may be served either cold or warm.*

Published just 11 years after Clause "invented" *pâté de foie gras de Strasbourg*, this recipe remakes the pâté to conform to the German taste for pungent flavor and strong spicing. Also typically German is the combination of foie gras with anchovies.

Löffler's successor as the top-selling German cookbook writer was Henriette Davidis, whose *Praktische Kochbuch*, first published in 1847, went through more than 60 editions. After Strasbourg (which always had a large German-speaking population) was captured by Prussia in 1870, she included four different Strasbourg pâtés in her book. Davidis credits the recipes to a lady of Strasbourg, who tells Davidis that the first of these is "the real recipe; experts have always found this Strasbourg pâté to be excellent and much better than most of those that you can buy":

Divide 6 large goose livers into halves, cutting them in two where they are joined. Remove the yellow spot where the gall bag was attached and wash the livers with sweet milk; water must not touch them. Peel some truffles, cut them into pieces about the length of the little finger and lard eight of the pieces of liver with them. Slice the remaining livers and pound very finely, season with a tablespoonful of finely sliced shallots stewed in butter, double this quantity of finely sliced truffles, fine salt, white pepper and nutmeg and pound all this very fine. During the pounding, add 2 pounds of fresh bacon which has previously been boiled for an hour and sliced and pounded after cooling; then pass the whole through a fine sieve. Line a goose liver terrine (you can buy this from a restaurant owner) with thin pork fat slices, then the forcemeat, after that the pieces of goose liver sprinkled with salt and white pepper, and then another layer of forcemeat, some more of the liver and so on until the terrine is filled; a layer of the forcemeat must be on top. Cover the top with pork fat slices and put the lid on the terrine; if it does not close tightly, seal it with strips of paper, using as a paste a little flour and water, put it into the oven and bake slowly for about two hours. For a smaller pie 1½ hours will perhaps be sufficient. As it sometimes happens that fat will drip from the terrine, it should at first be set on an old plate and afterwards on a low tripod.

Despite the "authenticity" of this recipe, Davidis tells us that most people prefer her next two pâtés, because they are "stronger, less fatty and less unhealthy." In addition to goose liver, they contain veal, anchovies, capers, lemon rind, and spices. They are, in fact, a lot more like Löffler than Clause.

The persistence of strong flavors and medieval spices in German foie gras cooking lasts well into the twentieth century. Here is a recipe for goose liver with anchovies from Lotti Richter's 1921 *Mein Kochbuch*:

After the goose liver has soaked in milk for 24 hours, dry it off, lightly salt it, sprinkle it with finely chopped anchovies and finely chopped slices of bacon and tie it in blanched cabbage leaves.

Now place in a casserole a piece of butter half the size of an egg, 1 small piece of onion, 1 parsley root, 1 stalk of celery, some thyme, a few peppercorns and cloves, a little bit of lemon rind, the juice of half a lemon, a half glass wine and one ladleful of soup. Before you pour in the soup and wine, let the rest cook a bit. Lastly put in the liver, which must steam for 1 hour, after which leave the cover on and let it cool. Then cut it into nice pieces, lay it on the dish, garnish with truffles and aspic and bring it to table.

Aside from the Frenchified garnish at the end, Richter's foie gras casserole could have easily appeared on the eighteenth-century German dinner table.

By the end of the nineteenth century, German-speaking cooks could no longer resist the siren call of haute cuisine. This was particularly true in Vienna, where the most popular cookbook of the late nineteenth and early twentieth centuries was Louise Seleskowitz's *Wiener Kochbuch*. Except for her *Würste von Gänseleber* (goose liver sausage), all of her foie gras recipes are given French titles, from *foie gras braisé au Madère* to *escalopes de foie gras aux truffes*. There remained a strong French influence on Viennese cooking until World War I, after which economic crisis precluded the ability to enjoy the luxurious fruits of haute cuisine.

Hungary, although part of the Austro-Hungarian Empire from 1711 to 1918, forged a culinary identity distinct from other German-speaking lands. Like them, however, its goose liver preparations were heavily influenced by its Jewish population. Except for the use of butter, this foie gras recipe from *The Little Book of the Cook Trade* (1742) is a copy of the classic Jewish goose liver and onions: "Soak the liver. Remove from pot, cut into slices, sprinkle with flour, and sauté in butter with sliced onion. Season with pepper. Garnish with the onions and serve hot." Hungarian chefs would later nationalize that dish with the addition of garlic and sliced green, red, and yellow peppers. The Jewish classic of chopped liver mixed with onions and eggs was also adopted by Hungarian cooks. In this pâté recipe from Sándor Csáky's collection of early twentieth-century dishes, Hungarian housewives have modified the classic chopped liver with the addition of French-influenced seasonings:

> *Clean two big goose livers. Sprinkle them with salt and ground pepper. Slice and sauté half an onion in oil. In a large pan, bake the goose livers in goose fat. When done, pass one of the livers through a sieve together with two boiled eggs and the cooked onion. Add two ounces tarragon-mustard, one tablespoon Madeira wine, one tablespoon cognac, and a few drops of Worcestershire sauce. Mix thoroughly. Spoon half the mixture into the bottom of a porcelain dish, place the remaining goose liver on top, and cover with the other half of the chopped liver. Allow to cool for two hours.*

Modern Hungarian goose foie gras.
Courtesy of Gundel, Budapest

In the nineteenth and twentieth centuries, Hungarian cuisine developed on two separate paths, peasant and urban cooking, with the latter being far more open to outside influences. In *The Cuisine of Hungary*, George Lang describes growing up on a farm and his mother preparing a special treat: "balloonlike bread, spread with paprika, goose fat, and thickly cut roast goose liver, not to mention the hot, fleshy, canary-yellow and green peppers." With paprika and peppers, this is a typical peasant dish.

The cooking of urban Hungarians was heavily influenced by Germany and France. In the mid-nineteenth century, German was the first language of most city-dwellers, particularly in Budapest, and German-style goose liver dishes, those soaked in milk, breaded and fried, for example, became common on bourgeois tables. In aristocratic kitchens, however, French haute cuisine was the dominant style. The main envoy of that imported tradition was Károly Gundel, who had apprenticed at one of César Ritz's hotels in Paris. In 1910, Gundel opened his famous Budapest restaurant, serving the repertoire of Escoffier to wealthy Hungarians. Over time, Gundel's chefs adapted the French dishes to local tastes, using sour cream instead of sweet cream and replacing the port wine with Tokaji Aszu.

Italy

This classic work by Pellegrino Artusi was one of the few Italian cookbooks to include recipes for foie gras.
General Research Division
The New York Public Library
Astor, Lenox and Tilden
Foundations

Like France and Germany, Italy had a local source for fresh foie gras: the geese raised by Italy's large Jewish population. Mysteriously, however, fattened goose liver never became a common element of Italian cuisine (unlike calf's liver, which was a staple). This was true even in the north, where there were strong influences from France and German-speaking lands. Here, *salame d'oca*—salami made of goose meat, pork pancetta, and seasoning—was a specialty, but local people still had no special love for the fattened liver. Giovanni Vialardi, the chef to Vittorio Emanuele II (1820–1878), includes only one goose liver dish in his 1854 *Trattato di Cucina pasticcera.* He calls it *fegato freddo d'oca in terrina* (pâté de foie gras), a clear imitation of Strasbourg pâtés.

Perhaps the most adventurous of nineteenth-century Italian cookbooks was also the most popular, *La Scienza in cucina e l'arte de mangiar bene,* first published in 1891. The author, Pellegrino Artusi, was willing to consider as edible many exotic meats, including peacock and frog. In his section on geese, he presents a good explanation for why the meat did not appear more often on Italian tables:

The domestic goose is larger than the wild varieties, and fatter too; indeed, it takes the place of pork among the Jews. I don't have much experience with it, for it is not available in the markets of Florence and is only rarely eaten in Tuscany. . . .

. . . In Germany geese are stuffed with apples and roasted, but this method isn't fit for Italians, who can't take liberties with greasy, heavy foods, as the following tale will show.

One of my tenant farmers, who observed Saint Anthony the Abbot's saint's day, decided one year to celebrate it to greater length, holding a banquet for his friends and inviting the supervisor as well.

All went well. However, one of the guests, a wealthy farmer who'd eaten and drunk his fill until his heart was swelled with joy, said, "For Saint Joseph's, the patron of my church, you're all invited to my home, and then we'll have some fun." The invitation was accepted, and nobody missed out on the occasion.

The high point of the party came when everybody sat down to eat: The meal began with goose broth, the fried dish was goose, there was boiled goose, the stew was goose, and the roast? Goose, of course! I don't know what fate overtook the others, but by evening my supervisor began to feel so odd that he skipped dinner, and during the night his insides rebelled in such a hurricane of thunder, wind, water, and hail that when people saw him the next day, pale and shaken, they wondered if he hadn't perchance turned into a goose, too.

Artusi goes on to tell us that one day he actually sampled a fattened liver:

I was given one from the Veneto region that weighed 1½ pounds and had the heart attached. The person who gave it to me told me to cook it by setting the fat, coarsely chopped, on the fire, then the heart, slivered, and finally the liver, cut into slices. It is then seasoned with just salt and pepper, the fat is drained away, then it is served with slices of lemon. It is, I must admit, a very delicate morsel.

The source for this liver may have been Jewish farmers, who were the main foie gras producers in the Veneto; the recipe is also highly reminiscent of Ashkenazi preparations. Despite Artusi's appreciation, however, goose meat's fatty and gassy reputation seems to have kept foie gras from entering the Italian mainstream. When it does appear, such as in the best-selling cookbooks of Ada Boni (Artusi's twentieth-century counterpart), it is always in French preparations. In her massive *Il Talismano della felicità,* foie gras appears three times, as terrines of goose liver in the style of Alsace, Périgord, and Strasbourg.

In Europe, countries that did not produce their own fattened goose liver relied solely on French recipes and Strasbourg pâtés. The consumption in these countries was limited to the aristocracy and the very rich. At a banquet in Madrid, King Alfonso XII was served *pâtés de foie-gras de Strasbourg* accompanied by Moët et Chandon champagne.

England

The British, as we have seen, had a long love affair with French haute cuisine. Whether English diner's embraced the consumption of fattened goose liver remains questionable, at least during the first half of the nineteenth century.

The ambiguity begins with Frederick Nutt's French-influenced *The Imperial and Royal Cook* (1809), which contains a recipe for "Fat livers in cases" but fails to specify if these are goose or chicken livers. Louis Eustache Ude was a French emigré who had cooked for Louis XVI and then for a number of English aristocrats. In his *The French Cook* (1828), he begins his recipe for *ragoût à la financière* with instructions to "procure cock's combs, cock's kidneys, fat livers, and a few fowl's eggs." He offers a long section on cleaning the cock's combs, but never explains where and how the fat livers should be cooked. Other chefs clearly state that chicken livers should be used (they may have been following the example of Beau-villiers, who used *foie de poularde* instead of *foie d'oie*). A recipe for *petits pâtés of chicken livers with truffles* appears in Robert Reynolds's 1829 *The New Professed Cook*. The vagueness of what constitutes a "fat liver" continues in the works of Charles Elmé Francatelli, who, despite his name, was a native Englishman. He claimed to have studied under Carême, then to have been Queen Victoria's chef and to have headed the kitchens at a number of private clubs, most famously the Reform Club. In his haute cuisine cookbook, *The Modern Cook* (1846), the fat livers may be "a light-colored calf's liver, or several fat livers of any kind of poultry." This kind of nonchalance

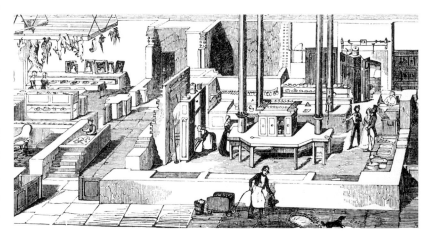

Alexis Soyer prepared foie gras in the elaborate kitchens of the Reform Club.
General Research Division
The New York Public Library
Astor, Lenox and Tilden
Foundations

would never have been allowed in France; chicken livers, Escoffier decreed, were suitable substitutes only for mutton kidneys.

A number of factors may explain the vagueness of the preceeding recipes. Chefs in Britain may have been less exacting in their adherence to classical standards than those in France. Supplies of foie gras and other French delicacies may have been cut off by the Napoleonic wars and subsequent conflicts, necessitating an attitude of flexibility on the part of Britain's chefs. And the animal rights issue and the conservatism of English palates may have scared them away from such exotic and morally suspect dishes as foie gras. Here the nineteenth-century gourmet William Jerrold records the reaction of an English family to the specialties at a top Paris restaurant:

> *I cannot recall the menu to mind at this moment: but Madame Manchester pushed the Marennes oysters from her with disgust, vowed she could not sit in the same room with the melon; and finally, when a* foie gras aux truffes, *perfectly cooked, was put upon the table, tasted, drew back from the table with an expression of uncontrollable disgust, saying, "Ugh! Whatever is that? I never tasted anything nastier in my life!"*

Not everyone had such parochial tastes. The iconoclastic Reverend Sydney Smith (1771–1845) announced, "My idea of heaven is, eating *foie gras* to the sound of trumpets." In 1846, Alexis Soyer, who succeeded Ude in the Reform Club kitchens, prepared a "first-rate" dinner that spared "no expense in procuring the most novel, luxurious, and rare edibles including, as a *releve,* a *chapon farce de foie gras à la Nelson.* The meal's supply of foie gras, as well as "some very fine fresh French truffles," was purchased locally at a London shop called Morel's, an indication of growing demand for the delicacy. After 1860, the numerous French cookbooks that appeared in English translations, including those by Gouffé and Urbain Dubois, contained definitive instructions for preparing goose foie gras dishes. By 1889, when Escoffier commanded the kitchens of London's Savoy Hotel, it was unthinkable that foie gras could have any other meaning than fattened goose liver.

The United States

When the Strasbourg pâtés began to arrive in the United States in the 1830s and 1840s, there already existed a strong, largely rural tradition of fattening geese to produce foie gras. It was practiced not by Jews but by German and Austrian immigrant farmers who brought with them the culinary skills of their homelands. For a time, haute cuisine chefs supplemented their imported pâtés with fresh livers from German-American farmers. This practice coincided

A banquet at Delmonico's in New York City featured the preparations of French haute cuisine.
Culver Pictures

with the golden age of classic French cuisine in this country. The years from 1860 to 1900 were a time when America's wealthiest citizens had the leisure and the means to travel regularly to Europe, and for whom sophistication became equated with the customs of European elites. The well-to-do no longer desired the bounty of local specialties such as turtle soup, shad, and corn on the cob. In New York, exclusive men's clubs and restaurants such as Delmonico's all employed French or French-trained chefs. In Washington, Abraham Lincoln sat down to state dinners whose menus were reproduced in Urbain Dubois's *Cuisine de tous les pays.*

The most famous of the American haute cuisine chefs was Charles Ranhofer, Delmonico's head chef from 1862 to 1895. His earliest menus included pâté de foie gras en Bellevue (glazed with aspic); in 1864 he served goose liver pâté at a dinner in honor of the admiral of the French fleet. Ranhofer's recipes were borrowed directly from the French. His great cookbook, *The Epicurean* (1900), is illustrated with hundreds of engravings taken from the works of Gouffé and Urbain Dubois. His pâté recipes closely replicate the repertoire of Gouffé, from the *petites caisses de foie gras* to the *foie gras à la financière.* His cold set pieces, such as his *aspic of foie-gras,* begin with phrases such as "Unmold a terrine of foies-gras," an indication that he was using the Strasbourg product. His hot dishes, however, clearly call for fresh livers, which must have been purchased from German-American farmers, presumably in Upstate New York or New Jersey. Here is his *fat livers à la Toulousaine:*

MENU

—

HUITRES

Potages

Consommé à l'impératrice   Tortue verte au clair

Hors d'oeuvre

Timbales, Talleyrand

Poisson

Bass rayée à l'italienne

Pommes de terre, duchesse

Relevé

Filet de boeuf à la financière

Haricots verts sautés

Entrees

Chapons farcis aux marrons

Petits pois à l'anglaise

Térrapène, Maryland

—

SORBET DALMATIE

—

Rots

Canvas-back   Cailles au cresson

Froid

Terrines de foie-gras à la gelée

Salade de laitue

Entremets de douceur

Poires à la Richelieu

Gelée aux cérises   Brisselets crème   Pièces montées

Glaces fantaisies   Fruit   Petits fours

Café

Le 19 Novembre, 1889.   DELMONICO'S.

A Delmonico's menu containing foie gras, probably imported from Strasbourg, for a dinner for the New York State Chamber of Commerce. General Research Division The New York Public Library Astor, Lenox and Tilden Foundations

Select a fine, raw, fresh and white fat liver that has not yet been put in water or milk; remove the gall, and stud each side with a row of raw truffles; season and butter over with a brush; wrap it first in thin bards of fat pork, then in a flat of pie paste, closing all the apertures carefully. Lay it on a baking sheet and cook for an hour and a quarter in a slack oven. After it has been removed, unwrap, take away the fat pork and dress the liver on a long dish, garnishing around with small molded quenelles, cocks' combs and mushrooms; serve at the same time an espagnole sauce reduced with Madeira and an infusion of Ceylon cinnamon.

Although the title of this preparation is similar to one by Urbain Dubois, Ranhofer's rendition is more like that of Gouffé.

Delmonico's most famous patron was the railway car magnate "Diamond Jim" Brady. A man of unsurpassed appetite, Brady was the epitome of an age in which men were admired for their ability to consume vast amounts of food, alcohol, and cigars. Nobody could consume more than Diamond Jim; when he died, doctors discovered that his stomach was three times larger than a normal man's. In 1896, he went to a railway car convention in Upstate New York to sell his products. In his biography *Diamond Jim,* Parker Morrell describes how, in order to impress the buyers, Brady laid out a spread containing the finest European delicacies as well as American specialties and rivers of booze:

Diamond Jim Brady, the greatest gourmet and gourmand in United States history.
Culver Pictures

Charles Ranhofer's terrine of foie gras in aspic.
General Research Division
The New York Public Library
Astor, Lenox and Tilden
Foundations

Brady hired three cottages at Saratoga and staffed them with twenty-seven Japanese boys. . . . He bought hundreds of bottles of beer, wines, ales and whiskies. He bought thousands of pounds of food, from imported caviar and paté de foie gras *with truffles, to mountain masses of American corned beef and cabbage. He scattered dozens of boxes of cigars through the rooms of the three cottages, and then paraded the convention, his pockets bulging with additional dozens of clear Havanas.*

The curious combination of these foods—foie gras *and* corned beef and cabbage—reflects the mixed audience for haute cuisine in turn of the century America. Alongside the expected old money patrons were the nouveau riche, local politicians, and even police officers who had lined their pockets with payoffs enjoying Delmonico's *terrine de foies-gras de Strasbourg.* New to French cuisine, this audience was less demanding than the old elite. After the reign of Ranhofer, it became harder and harder to find a restaurant adhering to the strict precepts of Gouffé or Urbain Dubois. Meals became smaller, menus shorter, and the haute cuisine market for fresh livers and Strasbourg pâtés gradually dwindled away.

Among the German-American community, however, there remained a strong demand for homegrown livers. In the eighteenth and nineteenth centuries, German speakers had settled in New Jersey, Pennsylvania, Indiana, and Wisconsin. Many of them were members of the Amish, Mennonite, and other religious groups fleeing persecution in the Rhine region of Germany—the homeland of foie gras. They built communities in areas such as Lancaster County, Pennsylvania, and practiced a lifestyle that rejected most temptations of the outside world. They were not, however, intent on rejecting the pleasures of good home cooking. Even today, these groups keep alive old culinary traditions that are elsewhere known only from books. One of these traditions is fattening geese, which, as in Europe, was a women's cottage industry. German-American cooks used every part of the goose. The fat was used not only as food but as medicine, an application that likely originated in German-Jewish folk remedies. They also sold the fat to Pennsylvania's large Jewish community, who, like their relatives in Europe, needed it for cooking.

According to the food historian William Woys Weaver, the most popular cookbook among the nineteenth-century Pennsylvania Dutch (the word "Dutch" comes from the German *Deutsch,* meaning "German") was Frederike Löffler's *Praktische Kochbuch.* Through Löffler's work, French culinary elements were transferred to German-American cookery. The following recipe for goose liver pie from *The Pennsylvania Dutch and their Cookery* (1935), by J. George Frederick, is complete with truffles and Madeira:

3 large goose livers	*2 tablespoons Madeira or red wine*
¾ pound fat pork	*salt*
¾ pound veal	*pepper*
6 truffles	*3 yolks of eggs*
1½ lemons	*1 teaspoon grated onion*
⅛ pound butter	*bacon slices to line the pan*
⅔ pint of bouillon	*4 tablespoons of flour*

Take two of the goose livers and lard with oblong slices of peeled truffles. Drip the juice from 1½ lemons on the livers and let stand for several hours.

Heat the butter and mix with the flour, salt and pepper and ¾ pt. of broth. Add the Madeira. Stir into the thick gravy the finely chopped or ground veal and pork. Chop one goose liver and fry 2 minutes in 2 tablespoonfuls of butter and the onion. Add salt and pepper and mix into the filling. Fill all this into a deep baking pan or mold lined with bacon slices so that it makes 2 or 3 layers of stuffing, alternating with slices of goose liver. Cover with slices of bacon, set in steamer over a kettle of boiling water and boil for 1½ hours or bake in oven for 1 hour. Serve with Madeira and truffle gravy.

This rather luxurious pie was a traditional Christmas dish. If they had an abundance of goose livers, the Pennsylvania Dutch would bake extras and sell them to wealthy gourmets in Philadelphia.

New York, Philadelphia, Baltimore, and Milwaukee also had large German populations who retained a great love for their native cuisine. German-language publishers issued a number of cookbooks that helped German-American women adapt their cookery to local ingredients. All of these, including a translation of Davidis's *Praktische Kochbuch,* contain recipes calling for fresh *Gansleber* (goose liver). The most popular of these were for *Gansleberpastete* using the "real Strasbourg recipe." The German-American cookbooks also copied without credit many of Löffler's recipes, including her goose liver with truffle sauce. Here is a recipe for *Gansleber mit Kastanien* (goose liver with chestnuts) from Charles Hellstern's 1891 *Deutsch-amerikanisches illustrirtes Kochbuch:*

Cut in slices a handsome, white and firm liver of a fattened goose, roll them in flour and bake them in butter until they are done to a beautiful yellow. Then sprinkle them with salt and pepper, squeeze a few drops of lemon juice on top, garnish them with glazed chestnuts and serve immediately.

To purchase goose livers, the reader had only to go to the local German butcher shop, which carried them during the Christmas season. They could also enjoy *Ganseleber* specialties in many German restaurants. In *Lüchow's German Cookbook* by Jan Mitchell, we learn that the famous New York restaurant purchased their geese and livers from Wisconsin: "They must be stall-fed, a special process well known to the German-Scandinavian population which inhabits that rich state. The liver from these geese, for which there is no substitute, is used for our homemade pâté de foie gras."

According to Stanley Lobel of Lobel's butcher shop in New York City, the German-American goose-fattening tradition lasted at least until the 1970s, when French producers began exporting semicooked, shrink-wrapped foie gras, which gourmet stores and many restaurants preferred due to the greater prestige of the French label. Fattened liver had always been at best a sideline of American farmers. Their goose-farming business continues, but the foie gras they produce is, unfortunately, kept for consumption on their own tables.

THE TWENTIETH CENTURY

In 1921, the same year that Escoffier retired, a pair of French food writers published an inexpensive booklet that began a new era in French cuisine, one made possible by the rise of the automobile. The authors were Curnonsky (the pen name of Maurice Sailland) and Marcel Rouff, two journalists whose influence equalled that of the nineteenth-century Grimod de la Reynière. The booklet was *Périgord,* the first guidebook in Curnonsky and Rouff's series *La France Gastronomique.* In it they explored the typical dishes, wines, and culinary traditions of the 32 provinces of France. Their audience was automobile tourists, who, freed from the restrictions of train and stagecoach travel, were now exploring the French countryside and discovering the delights of eating in small-town restaurants and country inns. To Curnonsky and Rouff, these regional dishes were a revelation, representing a tradition every bit as diverse and historic and carefully prepared as the finest haute cuisine.

Regional cuisine has its roots in the sixteenth century, if not earlier, drawing its traditions from local ingredients, festival dishes, and culinary practices (both medieval and haute) that had filtered down from aristocratic tables. As early as the late eighteenth century, Parisian gourmets had developed a taste for provincial specialties, eating bouillabaisse and *brandade de morue* (a purée of salt cod, olive oil, and milk) at Restaurant Les Trois Frères Provençaux, which opened in 1786. Following the guidance of Grimod de la Reynière, chefs and gastronomes began to seek out the finest provincial ingredients—butter from Isigny, chickens from Bresse, goose liver from Strasbourg—for their haute cuisine preparations.

The first French regional cookbook was the previously mentioned *Oberrheinisches Kochbuch,* originally published in 1815 and later translated into French as *La Cuisinère du Haut-Rhin.* In this popular cookbook, chefs could find all

A foie gras manufacturer from Southwestern France advertises its crème de foie gras.
Courtesy of Poster Photo Archives, Posters Please Inc., NYC

the Alsatian classics, including a *pâté de foie d'oie* that the anonymous author insisted was exactly the same as those made in Strasbourg. Other regional cookbooks followed, such as the *Cuisinier Durand* (1830), the first collection of recipes from Provence and other regions of southwest France. Despite a growing interest in the food of the provinces, it was still haute cuisine that most excited the tastebuds of Parisian gourmets; French provincial dishes rarely appeared on fine restaurant menus and were virtually unknown at the grand hotels over which Escoffier presided. This would all change as a result of the work of Curnonsky, Rouff, and a few other indefatigable food writers.

Traveling through the French provinces and tasting dishes previously unknown to them, Curnonsky and Rouff were the originators of culinary tourism. Their enthusiasm for adventurous eating lured a generation of tourists away from the Parisian temples of haute cuisine and into the small-town restaurants of provincial France. The fifth volume of *La France Gastronomique*, devoted to Alsace, consists mostly of restaurant reviews urging readers to explore new culinary terrain:

> *For those curious about peculiar cuisines, for those who hunt down useful things in this type of gastronomy, we mention the Restaurant-Hotêl Israélite Bloch [in Mulhouse] and generally advise while in Alsace not to neglect the manifestations of that peculiar cuisine that is Jewish cuisine. Admittedly, it is heavy, being made entirely with fat. Nevertheless, one can find there interesting and agreeable dishes, not to mention the famous* Carpe à la Juive *which has gone from the rabbis' table to the greatest Parisian restaurants. At the Restaurant Bloch, one first finds at every lunch a* pot-au-feu *such as one rarely eats elsewhere, perfectly done, succulent meat larded exactly as it should be and served in gigantic slices. . . . One also eats the original pudding that is the* Kugel, *the goose whose fat is the great resource of orthodox cooks because butter is forbidden, special beef sausages, salted meats, and more.*

The book also lists local specialties, among them sauerkraut and dumplings and 42 different kinds of pâté. Under Strasbourg, the authors list the best restaurants and their specialties, indicating where to sample foie gras of "the first order."

In 1928, Austin de Croze, one of Curnonsky's collaborators, published 1400 regional recipes in his remarkable *Les Plats régionaux de France*. These recipes came from local cookbooks, chefs in both the provinces and in Paris, and from a legion of amateurs—doctors, journalists, housewives. They constitute a repertoire as broad as Escoffier but with infinitely more variety. *Pâté de foie gras de Strasbourg,* which was perhaps the first French regional dish to gain wide acceptance, was included among many other dishes that were unknown outside the povinces. With their publication in this book and their replication on thousands of tables across France, they would soon be recognized as classics of French cuisine. An example is *Foie gras vigneronne* (lady wine-maker style), which de Croze credits to a M. Nabonne from Béarn, where the dish originated:

> *Take a foie gras weighing at least 700 grams and place it in a sauté pan with a small spoonful of goose fat. Cook it over a low fire for a half hour. Salt and pepper it and carefully turn it over. When the liver is almost cooked, remove almost all the fat except for a teaspoon or two. Add a glass of Portet or Jurançon [white wines from southwest France] and let it cook uncovered for a quarter hour. Ten minutes before serving, place in the sauce (after having washed them) 20 beautiful white grapes and as many red grapes. They should swell up but not burst. Then serve the foie gras with a wreath of these grapes.*

Some regional foie gras recipes include preparations that had gone out of style in haute cuisine. Both *foie d'oie ou de canard à la sauce Périgueux* and the following *ragoût de foie gras de Toulouse* are ragoûts of the type first introduced by La Varenne:

> *Place a beautiful foie gras or two small livers, trimmed and cleaned of the gall, in a small clay pot with a bit of water over a good flame. Add a whole clove of garlic, an onion cut in quarters, two*

branches of parsley, salt and pepper. When the liver is cooked, move it to the side of the stove and quickly make a light roux with the goose fat; add chopped shallots moistened with sweet or half-dry white wine and reduce. Arrange the livers on a hot plate and cover with the roux.

The flavors of this dish would be too pungent and too "unrefined" to appear in a top Paris restaurant. Other recipes echo culinary traditions predating La Varenne, but as the wheel of fashion has turned fully around, they appear completely modern. This sautéed foie gras from Alsace comes out of the Jewish tradition of sweet and sour preparations; only the addition of butter signals that it has been adapted by French chefs:

Choose beautiful Reinette apples, 3 or 4 per person; peel them and cut into thin slices. Sauté them in clarified butter and at the last minute sprinkle on powdered sugar. Seasoned, sliced and floured, the medallions of foie gras—two per person—should be sautéed in fresh butter. Place them on the apples, which have been basted with the foie gras juices, and serve very hot.

This dish of sautéed medallions of foie gras served on a fruit sauce would not be out of place on the menu of any upscale New York restaurant from the mid-1980s on. Before Curnonsky, Rouff, and de Croze, a recipe had to be "correct," that is, prepared in accordance with the reigning haute cuisine chef of the moment. Now a competing criterion emerged: a recipe had to be "authentic" or prepared in the traditional way of chefs in a particular region or country.

It should be remembered, however, that regional and haute cuisines did not encompass the whole of French cuisine. There was bourgeois cuisine, which found its bible in *Le Livre de cuisine de Madame Saint-Ange* (1927). There was also less celebrated peasant food cookery practiced by small farmers and townspeople. Though this was regionally based, its practitioners lacked the means to prepare the fairly elaborate dishes collected by de Croze. It is from this latter class that many of this century's greatest chefs have sprung. André Soltner, who made Lutèce a New York dining institution, was born in a small town in Alsace and recalls:

When I was a kid, my mother, like almost all our neighbors, kept two or three geese. There were no large farms like there are today. They would stuff them beginning in mid-November and slaughter them four, five or six weeks later. Then they would take the livers into town and sell them to restaurants. They would use the money to buy Christmas presents for their children. My mother kept her livers though, because my father was a gastronome. Every Christmas she made a foie gras terrine.

This was the simplest possible dish: seasoned goose livers baked in goose fat and then chilled. In the foothills of the Pyrenées at the opposite end of France, the mother of Alain Sailhac (long-time executive chef at Le Cirque and now dean of the French Culinary Institute) would also make foie gras terrines for the winter:

My earliest memory of foie gras—maybe I was four years old—is watching my mother making terrines from foie gras she bought from farmers at the market. They would bring the foie gras wrapped in napkins like something precious, and my mother would complain about the price. When

I was six, I had to go to the boucherie *to buy truffles for the terrine, but I didn't like the smell. She also would make preserved foie gras seasoned with a little salt, pepper, armagnac or eau de vie and then boiled and sealed. We would go on picnics down by the river and eat eggs, potatoes, preserved foie gras and bread.*

During the 1920s and 1930s, the exploration of regional cuisines was the most exciting development in French cookery. Haute cuisine had already begun its long slide into its current state as a historical curiosity. The culture that had supported stately banquets, long menus, and dishes swimming in fat- and flour-based sauces was quickly disappearing. International high society had been decimated by World War I; Germany was an economic ruin and Russia a Communist state. The middle class was ascendant, and its members lived a fast-paced commercial life that precluded the three-hour luncheons of another era. In the 1920s, girth fell out of fashion. Women wanted boyish figures and men were struggling to fit into the new styled sportswear. Regional cookery was a perfect fit for this modern culture. The meals had fewer courses, and their relatively quick preparation time meant that food could be readied with far fewer servants than in the old days.

During the 1930s and early 1940s, a series of events occurring far from restaurant kitchens had a devastating effect on European culinary life. Across Europe and around the world, the international economic depression closed restaurants and put chefs out of work. People could no longer afford to dine out. The rise of Nazism in Germany and, after 1938, the unleashing of the Holocaust almost obliterated European Jewish culture, and with it Jewish cuisine. This meant the disappearance of a great culinary tradition in which goose fat and goose meat played a central role. Finally, in 1945, after years of war, most of Eastern Europe became Communist; what remained of the region's cuisines was destroyed by party bureaucrats who publically proclaimed a deep distrust for fine food and everything it represented. After World War II, it would take over 30 years for chefs in Europe, Israel, and the United States to build a new tradition of fine cooking with foie gras.

The United States: Imported Delicacies

After the Delmonico's era, two great developments conspired to distract Americans from fine food. When Prohibition was enacted in the early 1920s, many of the best restaurants, deprived of profits from alcohol sales, were forced to close. They were replaced by speakeasies, where drinking and boisterous socializing took priority over culinary pursuits. When Prohibition was finally repealed in 1933, the nation was in the worst year of the Great Depression. Dining out, particularly at expensive European-style restaurants, was a luxury that few could afford.

The top New York City restaurant of the period was The Colony, an establishment that claimed to be French but actually served "Continental" dishes greatly simplified for its crowd of hard-drinking socialites and celebrities. According to one 1930s guidebook, the only "strictly French" restaurant was the Café Chambord at Third Avenue and Forty-ninth Street. Lawton Mackall's guidebook *Knife and Fork in New York* describes how its owner, Roger Chauveron, liked to take guests on a tour of his cellar, "pointing out piles of tins of imported pâté de foie gras, truffles from his native Périgord, and other costly rarities lavishly drawn upon, along with choice wines and aged Cognacs and Armagnacs, in preparing Chambord dishes." Those imported pâtés were a favorite of after-theater diners, who liked to enjoy the delicacy with a "bottle of a good red Bordeaux."

In 1939, the culinary map of New York and subsequently the entire nation was altered by the opening of the World's Fair that year at Flushing Meadows in Queens. Anxious to encourage American intervention in the war against the Nazis, many European nations spared no expense in outfitting their pavilions. The French and Belgian pavilions featured restaurants staffed with some of their finest chefs. Fairgoers were first shocked at the price—dinner for four at the Restaurant Français could cost a staggering $30—and then amazed at the quality of the dishes. They had never before experienced the refined flavors and preparations of the strictly à l'Escoffier menu of the French Pavilion. When the fair closed in 1940, the general manager at the Restaurant Français and the head chef at the Belgian Pavilion opened the two finest restaurants in New York, respectively Le Pavillon and the Brussels Restaurant. Both restaurants featured imported pâté de foie gras de Strasbourg. The Brussels Restaurant also included on its menu a capon breast stuffed with goose liver that was breaded, browned, and garnished with truffles.

Henri Soulé's Le Pavillon, which flourished until his death in 1966, instantly became the most fashionable restaurant in New York, upstaging The Colony as the place to be seen and to eat. From the kitchen to the coat-check room, the staff of Le Pavillon were nearly all French; Soulé began the transatlantic shuttle of French chefs and waiters seeking more lucrative work in the newly emerging territory of haute cuisine in the United States. This pool of classically trained chefs went on to open a string of restaurants—La Côte Basque (opened by Soulé for those not prominent enough to frequent Le Pavillon), La Caravelle, La Grenouille, Le Cygne, Lutèce—that cemented New York's reputation as the culinary capital of North America. The dishes were either

In the 1930s, Café Chambord was one of the few New York restaurants to feature imported foie gras.
General Research Division
The New York Public Library
Astor, Lenox and Tilden
Foundations

62

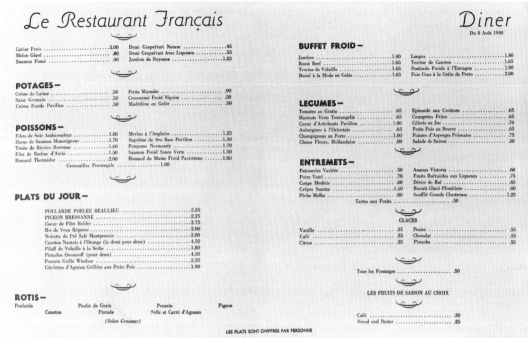

The Restaurant Français at the 1939 World's Fair introduced America to the best of French haute cuisine, including foie gras.
General Research Division
The New York Public Library
Astor, Lenox and Tilden
Foundations

strictly Escoffier—chateaubriand with sauce béarnaise, sweetbreads financière, peach melba—or, as at La Côte Basque, a mixture of haute cuisine with French regional cookery, such as cassoulet and rillettes.

For the expatriate chefs, one of the great disappointments of cooking in the United States was the impossibility of obtaining fresh foie gras. When Jacques Pépin came to Le Pavillon in 1959, the only available liver was canned, served either as slabs of cold pâté or sautéed for Tournedos Rossini. Jean-Jacques Rachou arrived in 1960, working first at The Colony and then at Lutèce. "We used to get in cans from Rougié [a major French pâté manufacturer]," he says. "We would slice it and coat it with aspic or maybe separate the slices with a piece of meat." The limitations of working with precooked foie gras were great, however, and chefs used it reluctantly.

Rougié is the largest manufacturer of foie gras products in the world.
Courtesy of Rougié, France

As international air travel became more economical, so did importing fresh foods from Europe. French poultry products, however, including foie gras, were illegal in the United States due to the existence of Exotic Newcastle Disease (END) in the regions that produced foie gras. (This disease is highly transmittable and could instantly wipe out entire flocks of birds.) Smuggling foie gras, therefore, became a favorite pastime among the younger chefs. For about ten years, beginning in the early 1970s, a group of French chefs ran a smuggling ring that shipped fresh foie gras as well as other forbidden delicacies. Jean Banchet, who in 1973 had opened his famous Le Français restaurant in the suburbs of Chicago, was willing to break the law to give his guests what no other restaurant could provide:

> I used to smuggle foie gras and I also brought in Bresse chickens. Every time I returned from France I would hide some in my suitcase. A few times I made the mistake of packing it in styrofoam boxes; when the inspector saw it, he knew that there was food inside. He would just throw the whole box of foie gras in the garbage, right in front of me.

Jean-Louis Palladin, former chef of Jean-Louis at the Watergate (Washington, D.C.), arrived in the United States in 1979 and quickly joined the ring of chef-traffickers:

> *I was smuggling foie gras in from France in boxes of fresh fish. Every time I ordered a case of fish, in the middle of it was a smaller case of foie gras. This went on for two years until one day they caught us. Luckily that was just about the time that Commonwealth [the first American duck foie gras farm] was starting to produce the first fresh domestic foie gras.*

Sometimes the smuggler was not the young and daring but the old and slightly naïve. Shortly after Lutèce opened, André Soltner remembers the arrival of an elderly French gentleman carrying a big suitcase:

> *He said, "I'm a chef and a restaurateur and yesterday I went to the market in [a town in south-west France] and bought you a lot of foie gras. I bring it to you as a gift." We opened it up and stared. It was filled with foie gras and also a few ortolans! "How the heck did you get this in?" we asked him. "What do you mean?" he said. He didn't know it was illegal and nobody stopped him. We called 20 or 25 of our chef friends and had a little party at Lutèce.*

In 1972, chefs began buying a new product that, while still not fresh, was an improvement over canned pâtés. Petrossian, the first family of luxury food products, began to import one kilo loaves of *mi-cuit* (half-cooked) whole livers that had been sealed in plastic. The foie gras had been cooked just enough to conform with USDA regulations though not enough to compromise its delicate texture and flavor. (This was the same goose liver that put German-American farmers out of business.) Since the *mi-cuit* was appropriate only for cold preparations, it provided only a partial solution.

Israel

The tradition of producing foie gras was brought to modern Israel shortly after World War II. In 1948, the year of Israel's independence, Moshe Friedmann, a survivor of the Holocaust, arrived in the new Jewish state. A third-generation goose farmer from the Hungarian town of Oradea (now in northwest Romania), Friedmann, and two other Hungarian-Jewish immigrants, decided to start raising geese and producing foie gras.

At the time, the young nation had almost no industry or agriculture and was desperate for foreign revenue. Friedmann tried to convince the Ministry of Agriculture that an enormous market existed for fattened goose liver in France, that he had sold to the French from Hungary, and that he could do it again from Israel. The officials had never heard of foie gras and had no knowledge of gourmet food; the idea was antithetical to the tough, self-sufficient culture of the early Israeli state. Nevertheless, Israel needed the money, so they allowed Friedmann to conduct a trial on a religious kibbutz. The experiment was a success; he sold a shipment of fattened goose livers to an Alsatian pâté manufacturer and foie gras became one of Israel's first export products.

Friedmann and his partners opened goose farms on the coastal agricultural strip north of Tel Aviv. The Israeli goose industry was organized as in France. Each stage of the operation—

hatchery, growing, feeding, slaughterhouse—was housed at a different location to avoid the spread of disease. Israeli farmers considered the rigid five-times-a-day feeding schedule too wearing for them so, as a result, many of the feeders were Arab farming families. The prices were strictly controlled by the export arm of the Israeli Ministry of Agriculture, which sought to find markets for other goose products, such as the meat, that were more difficult to sell abroad. In a moment of inspiration, it was realized that, properly smoked, goose meat tastes similar to bacon, which was prohibited under kosher law. Kosher goose "bacon" suddenly flooded Israeli stores (although real bacon remains extremely popular among secular Israelis).

Israel remains one of the most important producers of goose foie gras, most sold under the Carmel brand name.
Courtesy of Agrexco, Ltd.

Foie gras remained strictly an export product until the late 1970s. Moshe Friedmann's slaughterhouse was located by this time in a suburb of Tel Aviv. One of his customers was Yehuda Avazi (by coincidence, *avaz* is Hebrew for "goose"), who owned a casual neighborhood taverna—essentially a grill and a couple of tables—in Hatikvah, a blue-collar neighborhood on the outskirts of Tel Aviv. Most of Hatikvah's residents were Sephardic Jews from North Africa, where they had practiced a long tradition of grilling skewered meats over charcoal. This included beef, chicken, and lamb shish kebab as well as a variety of innards: brain, kidney, liver, heart, spleen, udder, testicles, spinal cord, and tongue. One day, Yehuda Avazi was in the slaughterhouse buying a selection of animal parts when he saw the goose livers for the first time. Yosi Lezha, Moshe Friedmann's son-in-law, offered Yehuda a foie gras to experiment with.

Tel Aviv's famous Yehuda Avazi restaurant features fattened goose liver and other grilled meats on its menu.
Courtesy of Yehuda Avazi restaurant

Today, Yehuda Avazi is one of the most popular restaurants in Tel Aviv. On the blue and white sign that stretches like a marquee across the facade floats the image of a goose, dispelling any doubt as to the specialty of the house. The restaurant walls are lined with signed photographs from celebrities and politicians. Other goose liver restaurants have opened along the street in downtown Tel Aviv, Jerusalem, and in other cities. Chefs grill skewered cubes of lower-grade liver (the higher grades are exported) over a line of charcoal braziers. This cooking method adds the sensation of texture, the crispy, charred edge contrasting with the warm, creamy interior of the foie gras cubes. The grilled livers are served with all the traditional accompaniments of Middle Eastern cuisine: pickles, large pita bread, hummus, chopped eggplant salad, carrot salad, pickled radish, spicy condiments, and french fries. If diners are too rushed to sit at a table, they can purchase a "sandwich" made from *laffa,* a taboon-baked flatbread the size of a small pizza that is rolled into a wrap and filled with grilled goose liver, hummus, and salads. These are purchased at the take-out window and eaten while walking. At several local markets and specialty meat markets, consumers can also purchase packages of skewered foie gras ready to prepare at home.

Foie gras's popularity in Israel signals the completion of two historical journeys. After thousands of years, the product has returned to the Middle East, only a few hundred miles from the Nile Delta where it originated. Also represented is the consummation of a cycle that began a thousand years ago with Rashi in the Ashkenazi heartland of northern France. Once the food of humble Jewish farmers and merchants, fattened goose liver became a key component of French haute cuisine. Now, in Tel Aviv, foie gras has become a delectable street food.

The American Cooking Renaissance

Behind the current popularity of foie gras in the United States are three decades of technological and culinary changes. The foie gras industry had long known that mulard ducks, sterile crossbreeds of moscovy and pekin ducks, stood up well to force-feeding and produced excellent livers. Chefs preferred the mulard liver to the goose liver, particularly for sautéeing, as it rendered off significantly less fat. The only problem was the sexual incompatability of the Muscovy and the Pekin ducks, rendering the production of mulards unpredictable. In the 1950s, changes in breeding occurred as scientists in Taiwan developed a method of artificial insemination. The Taiwanese bred a small type of mulard for its meat. For foie gras production, a larger strain of mulard was required, one that could offer both a large liver and an abundance of meat. In the 1960s, French agricultural experts began to use artificial insemination to produce a strain of mulard perfect for *gavage.* This laid the foundation for the large-scale duck farms that now dominate the French foie gras industry.

In 1959, André Daguin, chef of the famous regional restaurant Hôtel de France in Auch, the heart of Gascony's duck and corn country, popularized grilled magret, the French name given specifically to the breast meat of a foie gras duck, improving its commercial viability. Since the mulard duck is younger than goose when it is processed, it yields a breast that is tender enough to be eaten as a steak, rather than confited (slow-cooked and preserved in its own fat), as was traditionally the case. As Daguin recalls:

> *My grandfather [also a chef] used to tell me that if the duck is not too dirty it could be prepared undercooked like rare beef. I made sure that my ducks were raised in very clean conditions and*

started preparing "le magret grillée." I told my customers that it was "red meat" and they thought I meant that it was beef. It took ten years for people to really accept it, though.

In 1969, when Robert Dailey wrote an article for *The New York Times* extolling Daguin's magret, word filtered back to French chefs and within a few years they had all adopted the magret as their own. Farmers now had two highly prized items they could sell from foie gras ducks: livers and magret. A seasonal occupation of French peasants was becoming a profitable industry.

The increasing awareness and popularity of French food in the United States also readied Americans to experiment with foie gras. In 1951, Julia Child, a graduate of the Cordon Bleu cooking school who was then living in Paris, opened L'Ecole des Trois Gourmandes. It became a mecca for Americans seeking to learn the secrets of French cooking, but in classes tailored to their limited knowledge. When she moved back to the United States, she brought her vision of French cooking directly to the American public. At the time, American diners were in the midst of a love affair with processed and packaged convenience foods. The huge variety of seafood, wild game, and fresh fruits and vegetables that had graced nineteenth-century tables had largely disappeared. Foreign dishes were only eaten if thoroughly denatured—canned spaghetti with tomato sauce and chicken chow mein were among the period's ubiquitous grocery store items. With her wildly popular cooking show and her influential book *Mastering the Art of French Cooking* (1961), Julia Child ignited a revolution in American eating habits.

Child's cookbook, which she admitted "could well be titled 'French Cooking from the American Supermarket,' " presented a simplified Escoffier primer mixed with a few classics of bourgeois cuisine. Most shockingly to purists, she allowed her readers to substitute canned beef bouillon for homemade stock. One of her recipes, roast goose stuffed with prune and foie gras, appears to call for fresh goose liver, which is sautéed, mixed with canned foie gras, and stuffed into the prunes, but she does not tell her readers where to find these livers. All other recipes that use foie gras call for canned goose liver, including her tournedos Rossini, in which slices of foie gras are simmered in Madeira and stock (or canned bouillon).

Those seeking more authentic French recipes could turn to Elizabeth David's *French Provincial Cooking*, which was first published in the United States in 1962. An Englishwoman, David followed in the footsteps of Austin de Croze to produce this remarkable book filled with information about regional cuisine, local ingredients, and French culinary history. There were no shortcuts here; David loved to prepare imported foie gras with wine, but because fresh fattened livers were not available in England she included no recipes for them.

Another influential cookbook that emphasized authentic preparations was Richard Olney's *The French Menu Cookbook* (1970). Olney had been raised on an Iowa farm. In 1951, he moved to France, where he eventually had homes in Provence and a suburb of Paris. Within ten years he was considered—by the French—an expert on French cuisine, contributing articles to French gastronomic journals. His cookbook introduced American readers to Escoffier-style recipes with no shortcuts and with an emphasis on seasonality, absolutely fresh ingredients, and carefully arranged menus. In his discussion of foie gras for a winter menu, he tortures his readership with his description of a dish they could never produce at home: "Fresh *foie gras,* aside from the many hot preparations to which it lends itself, when served cold (poached, baked or braised, and kept pink throughout) is of a voluptuousness and subtlety undreamed of by those who know only the preserved variety." Of the canned livers, he recommends the *bloc de foie gras;* it "retains a delicate flavor and melts sensuously across the tongue like nothing else." The canned pâtés, purées, parfaits, and mousses, he concedes, "may, on their own terms, be perfectly respectable products."

Elizabeth David and Richard Olney became guiding spirits in the career of Alice Waters, one of the most influential American chefs in the second half of the twentieth century. Waters, who was raised in suburban New Jersey, had a culinary conversion experience when she spent a year studying in France. By the late 1960s, she was living in Berkeley, California, and cooking through every recipe in *French Provincial Cooking.* In her *Chez Panisse Menu Cookbook,* she describes how she and a group of friends decided to open "a place to sit down . . . and enjoy good food while discussing the politics of the day. . . . Chez Panisse began with our doing the very best we could do with French recipes and California products, and has evolved into what I like to think of as a celebration of the very finest of our regional food products."

Waters took from Elizabeth David the emphasis on simplicity and local ingredients and from Richard Olney, freshness and seasonality. She was uninterested, however, in slavish recreations of French regional cookery. Instead her style was what Curnonsky called *la cuisine impromptue,* "which you improvise in an instant from the chickens from the henhouse, the fish from the nearby river, the rabbit from the hutch, the vegetables from the garden, the fruits from the orchard." Here is Waters's own description of how she decides what preparation to use:

> When I cook, I usually stand at my kitchen table. I may pull a bunch of thyme from my pocket and lay it on the table; then I wander about the kitchen gathering up all the wonderfully fresh ingredients I can find. I look at each foodstuff carefully, examining it with a critical eye and concentrating in such a way that I begin to make associations. While this method may appear chaotic to others, I do think best while holding a tomato or a leg of lamb. Sometimes I wander through the garden looking for something appealing, absorbing the bouquet of the earth and the scent of the fresh herbs. Sometimes I butterfly my way through cookbooks, quickly flipping the pages and absorbing a myriad of ideas about a particular food or concept.

Following the example of Alice Waters, creativity became the watchword for a generation of young French-trained American chefs who were venturing to open restaurants of their own.

Alice Waters may have been unaware at the time, but her aesthetic coincided with revolutionary developments in the world of French cuisine. A pair of journalists decided that the 300-year-old tradition of haute cuisine had become moribund. The time had come to break free from the shackles of Escoffier. Henri Gault and Christian Millau had started a magazine and culinary guidebook in 1969 that was in direct competition with Michelin. They wanted to create names for themselves and saw an opportunity when *Time* magazine declared that the great restaurants of France were coasting on their reputations. Henri Gault had to agree, up to a point:

> Putting aside the claims in these articles that one ate as well in England and the United States— which is ridiculous—the reproaches that came to us from abroad were not that far from the truth: the Haute Cuisine Française was now no more than the sum of its parts. It was pompous, archaic,

heavy, without the least imagination, dishonest, and based on hundred-year-old recipes which were not in any way relevant to contemporary needs.

To fight this overbearing tradition, Gault and Millau saw:

the appearance of a new class of cooks: enterprising young men, filled with curiosity and above all much more free than their predecessors. They were free in their minds, with the memory of the spirit of revolt and even anarchy that had overtaken France in 1968.

The creativity of the new generation was in need of a mandate, and Gault and Millau took it upon themselves to provide one. In the October 1973 issue of their magazine, they issued their ten-point manifesto of "La Nouvelle Cuisine Française." Among their ten commandments are reduced cooking times, the use of fresh ingredients, the acceptance of modern technology (including freezers), the rejection of rich and heavy sauces ("these terrible brown sauces and white sauces, these espagnoles, périgueux, financières . . . that have assassinated so many livers"), the reduction of fat content, and the elimination of "deceitful" presentations. "Everything is permitted," declared Gault and Millau. Interestingly, though foie gras was identified with haute cuisine, it found a place in nouvelle cooking through preparations that closely resembled the simple Jewish recipes of the past: sautéed slices of liver with a sauce of apples and sugar.

The freedom of the *nouvelle cuisine* gave French chefs license to experiment with foreign influences, while chefs around the world were freed from the challenge of perfecting French dishes to assert their expertise. Instead, they could create a new style of cooking, regionalized because of the availability of ingredients, but international in scope. Foie gras was no longer confined to the classic French preparations. As a result, a taste and market for fresh foie gras was slowly developing outside of France. With strict import and export regulations in the United States, the procurement of fresh foie gras remained an obstacle.

American Foie Gras Reborn

I met Izzy Yanay at a fortuitous moment. I was looking to supply foie gras to the American public and he had recently ended his association with Commonwealth Enterprises, the farming operation he created and the first large-scale producer of foie gras in this country. Yanay graduated from the University of Rehovot's agriculture school in the late 1970s. He was working for Carmel Meat Products (now Silver Goose, one of the largest Israeli goose liver manufacturers), acting as a liaison between the slaughterhouse and the farmers they supplied with ducklings and feed. One day, Ramy Guoor, a friend of Yanay's from school, arrived at the slaughterhouse with a proposition for Yanay's boss. Guoor said that he had invented a way to crossbreed two types of ducks and produce mulards, which they could use for making fattened livers. Yanay's boss was interested. The Israeli government strictly controlled every phase of the goose liver industry, but ducks were beyond its jurisdiction. The mulard duck created a new, potentially profitable industry.

After two months of experimentation at a farm north of Tel Aviv, Guoor called the slaughterhouse to arrange a meeting. Yanay arrived early and walked into the back room, where, to his surprise, the farmer's son was clipping the nails of a little black and yellow duckling. (He was used to the far more delicate goslings, who might easily die if you clipped their nails.) Yanay held one of the ducklings, cradling it gently as if it were a gosling. Instead of cowering, the bird dug its tiny claws into his hand and jumped to the ground. Instinctively Yanay knew that the future of foie gras rested in the mulard.

During three years of experimentation with different feeding regimens, Yanay learned that the mulard's hardiness allowed for a dramatic change in the way the birds were raised. Due to the danger of disease, each stage of goose farming was housed at a separate facility. With mulards, a hardy, disease-resistant cross-breed, the entire operation could potentially be kept under one roof, greatly increasing efficiency and profitability. By 1981, his experiment was concentrated in the northern Israeli village of Bethlehem in the Galilee, an area known for turkey farming. Yanay convinced Yosi Nishry, an established local farmer, both to grow and to feed mulards. Other farmers soon followed.

Yanay decided to break away from Carmel Meat Products and, together with Nishry, build their own mulard duck foie gras farm. They met every night for six months, eventually devising a plan that encapsulated the knowledge and experience they had gained from their experimentation with the mulard breed. They received funding from an American real estate developer, Rubin Josephs, who agreed to invest on the condition that the farm be located in the United States.

Yanay arrived in the United States in August 1982 and Nishry joined shortly thereafter. The farm purchased by Josephs was in far worse condition than they had expected. Rather than take over a fully operative facility, they had to completely rebuild and convert a dilapidated chicken farm into a mulard duck operation. They learned next that, in order to process poultry under United States Department of Agriculture (USDA) guidelines, they would be required to erect their own USDA approved slaughterhouse, an unexpected and monumental expense. As costs skyrocketed, so did friction among the partners. Yanay and Nishry expected to launch the project, returning to Israel within a year or two. Instead, their families were uprooted to upstate New York. It took until the fall of 1984, two tumultuous years of arguments and near disaster, to achieve their goal.

The first several hundred foie gras were produced in the fall of 1983, with a production level of 2000 livers per week soon to follow. A single problem remained; they had no market. Yanay had warned Josephs of their production schedule, but Josephs had been unable to establish contacts with restaurants or meat distributors. One evening after work, Yanay and Nishry packed a cardboard box with shrink-wrapped livers and, still wearing work clothes and rubber boots, drove their pickup down to New York City to try to sell their fresh foie gras. Yanay began by visiting all the French restaurants that advertised in *New York* magazine:

> *I showed up at their doors around six in the evening—the wrong time to speak to chefs. They looked at me weirdly, in my dirty clothes and carrying a box of packaged foie gras. They thought I was a smuggler. Nobody bought any. Finally, by the time I got to Les Trois Petits Cochons [the New York pâté manufacturer] I had lost hope. Then Ariane Daguin came in and saw the livers and said, "Ah, foie gras!"*

Ariane Daguin, daughter of the Hôtel de France's André Daguin, had grown up surrounded by foie gras in all its forms and had helped prepare it for her father's restaurant. With plans to be a journalist, she attended Columbia University, but eventually found herself working at Les Trois Petits Cochons, a pâté manufacturer in lower Manhattan. The arrival of Yanay and Nishry with the box of livers was the turning point of her life:

> My first reaction was that they were smuggling. They said, "No, no, no, we have a farm with 50,000 livers in the works." It was all very well calculated, all except the sales. The foie gras was coming but they had no market, and they were starting to panic. But to me it was a very historic moment, the first fresh foie gras in America.

Ariane immediately understood that this represented an opportunity to transform the culinary culture of the United States. She negotiated with Rubin Josephs to grant Les Trois Petits Cochons exclusive distribution and processing rights for Commonwealth's foie gras, magret, and other duck products. During the drive to the farm to sign the deal, the directors of Les Trois Petits Cochons chose not to sign, believing that foie gras was too great a diversion from their core business, which was based in production, not distribution. Frustrated, Ariane quit her job. Determined to take a leading role in the development of the American foie gras industry, she (and a five-margarita lunch) convinced George Faison, a co-worker at Les Trois Petits Cochons, to join in her endeavor. Thus was born D'Artagnan, one of America's premier distributors of foie gras and specialty meats. "We were two young kids," says Ariane, "ambitious, crazy, and with nothing to lose."

At approximately the same time, Howard Josephs, Rubin's son, began to handle sales for Commonwealth. He contracted five New York wholesale meat packers to sell fresh foie gras. When approached by D'Artagnan, Howard claimed that he had too many distributors. To persuade him, Daguin and Faison pointed out that they had a superior knowledge and understanding of foie gras and would be able to advise chefs unfamiliar with the product on handling and preparation. Unlike any other distributor, they also had the technical knowledge and ability to process other parts of the duck, making pâtés, duck leg confits, mousses, and terrines (they later began smoking magrets in a portable barbecue in Ariane's home kitchen). Howard granted them distribution rights and the new partners canvassed the restaurants of New York, beginning with those run by French chefs.

"My first impression of the U.S. foie gras was that it was a good product," said André Soltner. "It changed a lot of our cooking: We started doing terrines, foie gras en brioche, and sautées with apples."

When George and Ariane visited Alain Sailhac at Le Cirque, he started buying immediately: "At the beginning, the foie gras was not bad at all, and within a year it was unbelievable. I took the best and started doing a foie gras appetizer sautéed with fruit every day—I had seen sautées when I was in Paris, with apples, figs, pears, cranberries, and cherries—and people liked it immediately."

Young American chefs, such as David Waltuck at Chanterelle and Patrick Clark at the Odeon, were also receptive to the new menu item. Ariane acted as a conduit of information, teaching chefs how to clean and cook the livers and passing along other chefs' preparations. The assistance of her father was crucial; in the preparation of foie gras, his expertise was unequaled.

*Izzy Yanay and Michael Ginor, owners of Hudson Valley
Foie Gras, revolutionized the foie gras industry
in the United States.*

Alfred Portale had prepared foie gras for Michel Guérard in France. When he returned
to New York to open Gotham Bar and Grill, he started purchasing from Commonwealth and
preparing the terrines and sautés as he had encountered them in France. The only barrier for these
young chefs was the price of foie gras. They hesitated to put too much on the menu, because,
unlike their French colleagues, they were new to the industry and feared the high prices would
limit their customer base.

The chefs saw that American customers, unlike those in France, preferred hot preparations to cold. They catered to their tastes, and sales rose dramatically. *The New York Times* ran an
article proclaiming "Foie Gras Goes American" and extolling the "richness and sweetness" of the
homegrown product. Barry Wine of the Quilted Giraffe contributed a recipe to that article for
sautéed foie gras with raspberry vinegar and currants. This style of preparation, foie gras sauté
with a sweet-sour fruit sauce, propelled Yanay's fresh foie gras into the luxurious realm of caviar
and lobster. With all their prejudices against variety meats, Americans, encouraged by a spate of
glowing articles in food magazines and newspapers across the country, enjoyed the creamy, freshly
cooked foie gras.

Two years after they started producing commercially, Commonwealth received its first
competition within the United States. In the early 1980s, Guillermo Gonzalez had attempted to
open a foie gras farm in his native El Salvador. This farm never achieved full operation, but he
became obsessed with the concept. He and his wife Junny sold their house and moved to Périgord
to study all aspects of foie gras production. After almost a year of study, and with strong
encouragement from a friend in the gourmet food business in San Francisco, Gonzalez bought a

facility in Sonoma Valley, directly in the heart of wine and food country. He named his new company Sonoma Foie Gras. At the same time, in a stroke of luck, Grimaud Farms, a large French duck- and goose-breeding company, was opening a major duck farm in the area. Gonzalez and Grimaud signed a deal whereby Grimaud would supply grown ducks to Sonoma Foie Gras who, in turn, would provide Grimaud with fattened livers to distribute. Grimaud's ducks were not mulards but Muscovies; before the arrival of the hybrids, Muscovies (*Barbaries* in French) had been the most popular ducks for force-feeding in France. Muscovy livers tend to be more mildly flavored than mulard livers and the Muscovies tend to render more quickly during high-heat cooking. Within a few years Sonoma Foie Gras controlled 30 percent of the market, selling mainly to restaurants and through mail order.

In the late 1980s, Commonwealth suffered from a series of setbacks that culminated in Izzy Yanay's departure from the company. In early 1990, Ariane Daguin introduced him to me. Izzy and I founded Hudson Valley Foie Gras. In late 1992, we acquired Commonwealth and merged operations. Since then, Hudson Valley has increased production to ten times the levels of the early 1990's, has sold the majority of the foie gras consumed in this country, and has been distributing worldwide. Once a rare and expensive delicacy, foie gras has begun its transformation into an ingredient that Americans are quickly learning is accessible and simple for the home chef to prepare.

Foie Gras: The Guilty Pleasure

At the end of the twentieth century, chefs in American restaurants have carved out a permanent place for foie gras on their menus. After three decades of experimentation, they have acquired the facility needed to use foie gras creatively in the culinary styles that now define American cooking. Bobby Flay's recipe for foie gras with barbecued duck, corn pancakes, and habanero chiles is one example of how foie gras has been combined with American regional flavors (see page 284). Another is David Burke's coffee-barbecued squab with foie gras, corn bread torte, and onion-pistachio marmalade (see page 292). Toni Robertson's recipe for foie gras rolled in slices of Kyoto Kobe beef served with tofu-skin millefeuille and ponzu sauce (see page 300) exemplifies the possibilities for foie gras in American fusion cooking. In this context, the dense richness of the foie gras provides an earthy counterpoint to the clear, often astringent flavors of classically Asian preparations.

One particularly playful trend in American foie gras cookery pairs typically high- and low-status foods in order to question the very nature of food and status. Anne Rosenzweig of The Lobster Club serves a foie gras club sandwich (see page 160), a dish representing the marriage of luxury dining and lunch-counter cookery. In a similar vein, a foie gras pizza has recently emerged from the kitchen of the Four Seasons. Both of these dishes, and dozens like them, can be viewed as an attempt to invert the associations people bring to the food they eat. On one level, the meeting of foie gras and pizza can be seen as an inducement to the intimidated consumer. The dish transforms foie gras into a familiar and accessible product. Taken a step further, the graphic pairing of high and low status foods offers a challenge to the relative values people generally assign to ingredients, whether plain or fancy, common or exquisite. On another level, the same pairing can reinforce our ideas about the values of foods, including our notions of foie gras as a world-class delicacy. The dishes capture our attention because of the contrasts they embody.

A 1997 *New York Times* article by food critic Ruth Reichl calls foie gras the "ultimate guilty pleasure," each bite "a little bit of sin." This sense of the forbidden is generally attributed to the health concerns posed by foie gras' fat and cholesterol content. Such trepidations arise even though foie gras is eaten in such small quantities that any potential health damage is, rationally speaking, almost negligible. Perhaps the guilt we manufacture when presented with a glistening slice of foie gras is merely another way to preserve the singularity of its voluptuous charms.

PRODUCTION

BETWEEN THE DUCK AND THE EGG

The method for producing foie gras has remained virtually unchanged for 4500 years. The technique illustrated on ancient Egyptian reliefs is the same seen on farms today: the force-feeding of ducks and geese. The most significant change has been in the animals' feed. The Egyptians fed the birds balls of moistened grain, while the Romans preferred using chopped dried figs as feed. In Western Europe, farmers stuffed them with ground wheat, barley, or millet, until they discovered in the late eighteenth century that corn, recently imported from the Americas, produced the largest and whitest livers. More recently, advances in artificial insemination, animal husbandry, and mechanical feeding techniques have greatly increased the quantity of foie gras produced worldwide and have made this delicacy much more affordable and popular.

Until 30 years ago, the main source of foie gras was geese. In the early nineteenth century, just as the pâté industry was beginning to flourish, the duck farmers of Auch and Toulouse in the southwest of France discovered that their birds could also produce fattened livers. Ducks remained a relatively minor part of foie gras production until the 1960s, when farmers realized that new breeding techniques could produce greatly increased numbers of mulard ducks that were much hardier than geese. The mulards, a hybrid of Pekin duck females and Muscovy duck males, had strong bodies with large esophagi and, unlike geese, were relatively resistant to disease. Goose farmers had to separate each stage of production to guard against epidemics, but with the hardier ducks, farmers could house the entire operation under one roof. As a result, raising mulards was significantly easier and less expensive, and the more cost-effective industrial-style production provided pâté manufacturers with a steady source of relatively inexpensive livers. Today, the vast majority of foie gras produced in the United States and throughout the world is mulard, not goose. Goose foie gras is still produced in Israel, Hungary, Czechoslovakia, France (on a small scale), and a few other countries, but fattened mulard liver has largely taken over the kitchens and tables of the world.

Eggs are placed in the climate-controlled setter of the hatchery (left), then candled to weed out infertile eggs and dead embryos (right).

Growing the Mulard

The word *mulard* originates from the French word for mule. Like a mule, the mulard duck—the product of a cross-breed—is sterile. At the Hudson Valley Foie Gras farm in upstate New York, the process of producing a fattened liver begins with the arrival of young Pekin females from European breeders. The Pekins are placed in breeding houses, and, although they are able to lay year-round, the lighting is adjusted to replicate the long spring days of their homelands. This subtle manipulation ensures that the birds will lay to their maximum potential.

After the Pekins are mature, have been laying eggs for a few weeks, and have reached the peak of their fertility, the females are artificially inseminated with the sperm of the Muscovy males. This procedure is necessary because these two types of duck are sexually incompatible. While the Muscovy males are large birds, the female Muscovies are very small. When the Muscovy attempts to mount the relatively large Pekin female, he often falls off her back. The Pekin instinctively believes she has been inseminated, refuses to let another male mate with her, and lays infertile eggs. To artificially inseminate, the farmer collects the sperm from the Muscovies and implants a portion of it in the female's cloaca. The Pekins lay fertile eggs, which are collected and placed into an egg cooler. It is imperative that the breeding barn be kept sterile and well organized—any form of stress (disease, disorder, bacteria) will cause the ducks to suddenly stop laying.

The black-and-yellow speckled ducklings do not quack.

Once a week, the eggs that have been collected in the cooler are brought into the hatchery, where strict climate (temperature and humidity) control ensures that they all will hatch within a specified twenty-four-hour period. All procedures at the farm run in one-week cycles, and each full series of cycles ends on the day of processing, roughly four months after hatching. Ducks hatched in August will deliver foie gras in December. The farmer making arrangements for the Christmas high season has to plan his breeding stock as well as his summer hatchings up to a year in advance. In France, where mechanical feeding shortens the production process, and a vast majority of the liver is destined to be canned pâté, timing is a slightly lesser concern.

The hatchery is a building housing the incubator and the setter. The incubator is a room-sized box that replicates the ideal climatic environment for duck eggs. Ducks usually lay in the spring and sit on the eggs during the beginning of the summer, so the incubator mimics these conditions closely. These conditions also make the hatchery a giant breeding ground for bacteria, so it must be kept absolutely sterile. Every Tuesday, the eggs are placed in a setter, on a giant rack that rotates them every hour, where they will remain for 28 days. They are sprayed twice a day with warm water and then aired; this makes the shell more fragile so the duckling will find it easier to break out. After a week in the incubator the eggs are candled (placed in front of a bright light to illuminate their contents) to weed out the infertile eggs and the dead embryos. On average, out of every four eggs, two are infertile, one becomes a mulard female and the other becomes a mulard male.

In order to remain healthy, the ducks need plenty of air and must be able to roam free.

The eggs hatch into little black-and-yellow speckled mulard ducklings. The ducks do not quack as one would expect, because they have inherited the whispery voices of their Muscovy fathers. The ducklings are sorted by sex in the hatchery. Females, which produce a small, poor quality foie gras, are not cost-effective to raise. They are usually sold to duck farmers that produce ducks for meat, not foie gras. The males are transported to the nursery. At nine days old, their nails are trimmed because the ducklings tend to be aggressive and can harm one another. The ducklings' four to five weeks in the nursery provide them with a solid healthy foundation. They are given high-protein feed, vitamins, and water, and the temperature is kept warm to encourage rapid, stress-free growth. The nursery is arranged as a line of large pens; each week's crop of mulard ducklings enters at one end and gradually moves down the line as the ducks grow larger. Once they reach the last pen, the now-adolescent ducks are transferred to the growing area.

During the two-month growing stage, the farmer wants the ducks to grow and remain strong. Although they spend most of their time on land, ducks are best adapted to living on water. In order to remain healthy, they must be allowed to exercise and strengthen their legs. They need plenty of fresh air and, ideally, a sloping, grassy yard in which they can walk. Any rocks, sticks, or bushes could cause them to trip and injure themselves. In addition to feed, the mulards are given hay for fiber; this aids digestion, keeps them busy, distracts them from fighting, and helps to expand the esophagus—a crucial preparation for gavage.

Foie Gras

Twelve to 14 weeks after hatching, the ducks are brought to the feeding barn, a long coop divided into lines of pens separated by walkways. The light is dim and numerous fans maintain a continu-

A plump foie gras sits inside the cavity of a duck and is removed after chilling.

ous warm breeze. Ten to 12 ducks are placed in each pen. The first day of feeding is the highest-stress stage of the process, largely due to the fact that the ducks have never before been in close contact with humans or fed by hand. Each employee takes care of 350 ducks. Many of the feeders are women, because the farmers have found that they are gentler and more patient with the ducks than are men. Once a feeder has been assigned to a group of ducks, absolutely no other person is allowed to handle them. Studies have shown that the birds recognize people by their faces and by the touch of their hands, and they become stressed if feeding is attempted by anyone other than their regular feeder.

On the first day the mulards are fed twice, at six A.M. and eight P.M. Every step of the feeding process must be executed in a calm and gentle manner. The feeder crouches on a small stool inside the pen and one by one brings the birds between her legs. Suspended on an elastic cord above the pen hangs a plastic funnel with a small electric motor attached. With one hand the feeder carefully opens the bird's beak, and with the other she checks along its throat to see if it is empty. Then she inserts the funnel tube into its esophagus (she brings the funnel to the bird, never the bird to the funnel). After the tube is gently moved down to the duck's crop, she pushes a switch on the side of the funnel, activating the electric motor. Then she pours the food inside the bowl; the motor turns a wire auger that impels the feed down the tube and into the crop. She then removes the tube and releases the bird, which immediately walks over to the water trough just outside the pen and takes a long drink. Each feeding takes about 30 seconds, then the feeder continues on.

The mulards are fed corn. Farmers have to be cautious as to the types of additives that are given to the birds, as even the smallest amounts can alter the liver. Trying to duplicate the Roman practice of stuffing the geese with dried figs, a farmer discovered that the supermarket-purchased figs had been treated with a trace of ascorbic acid as a preservative, imparting a bitter flavor to the livers. At the first few feedings, the mulards are given about an ounce of food, far less than their normal consumption. Amounts are then increased by carefully calibrated degrees. The greatest danger comes from overfeeding, as the excess would stress the bird, requiring its permanent removal from the feeding process.

After the birds become accustomed to this process, generally around the second day, the feedings are increased to three times a day. For the first two weeks, the bird accumulates body fat. The liver begins to whiten due to the corn, but has not yet begun its exponential expansion. Foie gras growth begins at day seventeen or eighteen and continues until the end of the feeding cycle. The changes in the liver might be likened to blowing up a brown balloon with a hole in it. As it expands, the color lightens—it becomes beige—but it also loses air due to the hole. If you stop blowing, it will deflate. The farmer has to decide what kind of livers he wants; if he needs a firm grade A, he has to keep feeding continuously, but if he wants a softer grade B, as it is simpler to devein for industrial production, further processing, and canning, he may stop the process a day before slaughter, to let the "air" out of the "balloon." By the twenty-fourth or twenty-fifth day, the first ducks are taken to the slaughterhouse and by the thirty-first day they all have been processed.

The leg and thigh of the foie gras duck.

In the processing plant—which is built to United States Department of Agriculture (USDA) specifications and is supervised by a USDA inspector whenever in operation—the ducks are killed, bled, and cleaned. The liver is too soft to remove immediately, so the carcass is chilled overnight. The next day it is taken to the eviscerating room, where the bird is checked for wholesomeness by the USDA inspector. The liver is eviscerated, graded, weighed, placed on ice to diffuse any remaining blood, and stored in a cooler at just above freezing. The remainder of the duck is then fabricated. The magret, legs, and thighs are packaged. The entire duck is utilized—skin, fat, bones, boned meat, and innards. The down is sold to pillow manufacturers and the feet and tongues are sold to Chinese markets. Within one to three days, the foie gras will be vacuum-packed, boxed, and rushed by express delivery to restaurants, distributors, and gourmet markets.

Industrialization of Foie Gras

The above describes the methods employed in the United States by producers of duck foie gras for the fine-restaurant and gourmet market. Over the last decade, French farmers have developed a mechanical feeding process allowing them to industrialize foie gras production. What was once an artisanal craft has in many regions become a highly profitable enterprise dominated by a few conglomerate agribusinesses. This change has greatly affected the overall quality of French livers. Currently, the vast majority of foie gras produced in France are industrial-quality duck livers used to produce canned foie gras products for the supermarket trade.

The magret, the breast of the foie gras duck.

The key innovation was the introduction of the mechanical feeder using a pneumatic pump, which pushes a computer-calibrated slurry of corn meal and water through a system of pipes and tubes. The birds are confined to individual cages slightly larger than the duck itself, greatly restricting their movement. Using the pneumatic feeder, one person can now tend to between 800 and 1000 birds, feeding the ducks two meals per day over a 14-day period. The feeder rapidly inserts the tube, presses a button to commence the automatic feed process, and moves on to the next bird. (The speed of this method allows each worker to relate to each bird about as much as a soda factory worker relates to a bottle.) The workers are not allocated time to determine if the bird has completely digested the previous meal, causing a higher mortality rate than with the traditional method. Additionally, the entire group of ducks are slaughtered on the same predetermined day rather than by the readiness of their individual livers. The resulting livers are smaller, weighing on average a pound (about two-thirds the size of those made by smaller boutique producers) and tend to be softer and contain more blood and other imperfections. These livers do not appear in fine restaurants. They are produced specifically for canned pâtés. Nevertheless, this system produces foie gras in only 12 to 14 days and with less labor and lower feed cost than the traditional method.

One of the reasons for ducks' ascendancy in popularity is that they are much easier to raise and feed than geese. Geese do not breed year-round. Farmers who produce goose foie gras throughout the year, must close the birds in a lightproof barn and closely regulate the timing of their "days" and "nights" in order to fool them into thinking it is laying season. Geese are much more delicate and disease-prone than ducks, so large numbers cannot be kept at one location. From a production standpoint, the single advantage geese have over the mulard is that they breed naturally, not requiring an artificial means of insemination. The greatest difficulty with geese occurs during the feeding process. Because their esophagi are very narrow and more delicate than the mulards', the geese must be given a generous amount of green grass, a process known as *pre-gavage,* to expand their esophagi prior to the onset of gavage. During feeding, the geese must be fattened very slowly with five feedings a day using narrow funnels to account for their fragile throats. Unlike the hardy mulards, any minor stress could kill an entire flock of geese. Due to their fragility, gavage requires 35 days, greatly increasing labor costs (with 175 feedings over that period versus 90 feedings over 30 days for ducks). Goose meat and other secondary products have a much smaller market than duck magret and other byproducts of the mulard duck. Fine quality goose foie gras, however, will weigh over two pounds and have a light beige hue. The taste is mild and the texture creamy and smooth.

The industrialization of foie gras is not necessarily the wave of the future. The French foie gras industry is learning that an educated public knows the difference between a quality product and one with less flavor and finesse. Currently in France, production of grade A duck and goose foie gras is extremely limited and nearly all these livers are sold to elite restaurants. Many French diners remember the taste and quality of foie gras from the days of their youth, and they long to be able to enjoy it again in a product that they can bring home for holiday feasts. The French are now developing the "Label" line of artisanal foie gras products. These livers come from birds that are fattened using traditional methods perfected by centuries of French peasants: the slow hand-feeding of corn for three weeks or more.

ANIMAL RIGHTS

The methods used in producing foie gras have concerned people since the eleventh century, when Rashi, the French rabbi, stated that the Jews would pay in the hereafter for making the fattened geese suffer. Since that time, farmers have constantly refined their techniques. In doing so, they have discovered that the way to decrease goose and duck mortality and increase the average weight of the livers is to treat the birds delicately. Nevertheless, animal rights groups continue to protest against the production of foie gras, both in Europe and the United States, campaigning against the farms and drawing attention to the issue from chefs and others in the food industry.

Foie gras farms operate in a tiny niche of the enormous United States poultry industry. From a strategic standpoint, they provide an easy target for animal rights activists: they are small and lack expensive lobbyists. Their main product is perceived as a luxury good, like fur, and many believe that, after extracting the liver, the rest of the bird is left unused. In reality, a greater portion of the foie gras duck is used than any other bird raised for human consumption. The breasts become magrets; the legs and wings are used in confits and to make rillettes; the fat is an excellent cooking medium; chefs use the carcasses to prepare stocks; and the tongues, feet, testicles, and intestines are sold to Asian markets. Feathers are sold for down.

The second issue that animal rights groups focus on is the method of feeding and the effect it has on the bird's liver. Waterfowl are not humans, however, and a practice that could cause us grave harm or death has little effect on a goose or duck. The birds' anatomy is fundamentally different from ours and reflects their natural environment and their twice-annual long-distance migrations. According to Dr. Tirath Sandhu of the International Duck Research Cooperative, an expert on water fowl with specialization in ducks, the birds must gorge, while preparing for their migrations, to amass the energy reserves of fat needed for the long flight. Ducks and geese and their relations possess livers that have specially evolved to become the main repository for this fat. If food is abundant, they will eat as much of it as possible as quickly as possible. This may include small fish, plants, and insects, some of them with spines and sharp legs (the tougher pieces are digested in the gizzard after passing through the stomach). Once they have gorged themselves, the birds must immediately drink water to prevent choking. In the feeding process, goose and duck farmers are taking advantage of the birds' natural eating habits and physiology.

The imagery of inserting a tube into the bird's esophagus can be perceived as cruel. A waterfowl throat, however, is not like the throat of a human. The lining of the duck and goose esophagus is keratinized. This means that it is composed of fibrous protein cells that resemble bristles or fingernails, allowing large pieces of food to pass safely. Because of this anatomical feature, the tube creates no discomfort for the ducks. Waterfowl gorging habits are also aided by the fact that their esophagi are extremely flexible. Near the bottom, their throats widen into a simple crop where the food is stored before being passed onto the stomach. During feeding, the smooth tube of the funnel is inserted into the bird's calcified esophagus and pushed down to the crop. The feed ends up here, and the bird is immediately released so it can waddle off to drink.

If feeding was indeed cruel, one would expect to see unhealthy birds on foie gras farms, perhaps refusing food, listless, and with a high rate of mortality. Scientists have discovered that ducks under stress have high levels of plasma corticosterone, a type of steroid produced in the brain. In 1996, French researchers with the National Institute of Agronomical Research published the results of a study on the corticosterone levels of ducks during feeding. They learned that the highest levels of stress were caused by handling—they were not accustomed to humans—and by moving the birds to new cages. Lower but still high corticosterone levels were recorded during the first feeding; stress levels returned to normal for all subsequent feedings. Once the birds become acclimatized to regular handling, the only reasons for a listless, unhappy bird are disease or other correctable problems, not the feeding.

After the food is digested, much of it is converted to fat; this is not burned for energy but stored on the animal's body, particularly in its skin and liver. Some critics of the foie gras industry claim that these fattened livers are diseased, that they are suffering from diabetes, cirrhosis, or a condition called "fatty liver" that occurs in some animals. According to Dr. Sandhu, however, diabetes does not occur in geese or ducks; cirrhosis can arise but is caused by passive heart congestion; and "fatty liver" is a disease of mammals, not waterfowl. The fattened liver caused by feeding is not diseased; it is simply fat, and if the bird stops overeating the liver will return to normal size.

One highly credible manner by which to measure the overall health and well-being of the foie gras duck is through the Jewish dietary laws of *kashrut*. One of the basic tennets of *kashrut* states that the animal must be healthy and maintain a damage-free esophagial tract. To comply with these laws, the esophagus of each animal is inspected for imperfection by the rabbi. This is of heightened importance in the case of the foie gras duck, where air is blown in to inflate the esophagus in order to verify that there are no punctures. The percentage of fattened ducks that fail kosher certification inspection is consistent with industry averages for other poultry. To further this point, kosher certification for foie gras has been granted through centuries of history, from the European Jews of France, Germany, and Hungary, to those in modern day Israel and the United States.

Due to the loud volume of critics, who often have excellent access to media outlets, farmers who produce foie gras are intensely aware of the issues surrounding its production. They are in frequent contact with experts in the field, and veterinarians normally visit their facilities once or twice a week. Many of these veterinarians are also involved in their local Society for the Prevention of Cruelty to Animals; if they encountered a problem on a foie gras farm, they would immediately take action. They have seen the process from breeding to marketing, and they are confident that cruelty is not inflicted on the animals. It should be noted that these veterinarians are specialists in poultry and other animals whose eventual destination is the dinner table; they are comfortable with the fact that these animals will be killed for food. Therein lies the heart of the foie gras and cruelty issue: One who can accept the idea that ducks or geese will be slaughtered to provide livers and meat for the table should have no objection to foie gras.

FOIE GRAS PRIMER

NUTRITION

Despite your preconceived notions, or what you may deduce from the media and your dining companions, a passion for foie gras is not synonymous with adverse health. The reality is that most people with a penchant for foie gras do not consume enough of it to have an effect on their health. As most nutritionists agree, moderation is the key to a healthful, balanced diet. But even if one's foie gras consumption were to rise above a moderate level, scientific facts detailing the composition of foie gras fat suggest the potential risk to one's nutritional well being is negligible. There is growing evidence suggesting that foie gras may aid the heart.

The common discourse regarding the sinfulness of foie gras, and by extrapolation the ill effects it is suspected of having on nutritional health, derives from the high fat content of this delicacy. Years ago, within the scientific community, discussions on cholesterol and fat consumption began with a focus on the quantity of fat consumed and its correlation to levels of blood serum cholesterol and incidence of heart disease. The conceptual leap from the quantity of fat in foie gras to its impact on heart disease seemed logical. But recent developments suggest that when linking fat consumption and serum cholesterol, the type of fat consumed is more important than the absolute quantity.

Fat has long been anathema to American nutritionists. Recently, however, a more nuanced picture of lipids has emerged in which fats are categorized as "good," "bad," or "neutral." Saturated fats are classified as "bad fats" because their consumption has been linked to increased serum cholesterol levels, which in turn has been shown to increase the risk of heart disease. Monounsaturated fats are classified as "good fats" because their consumption has been linked to a reduction in serum cholesterol levels. Polyunsaturated fats are considered neutral. Chemical analysis of foie gras indicates that it contains a higher proportion of monounsaturated fats (roughly two-thirds) than either saturated (roughly one-third) or polyunsaturated fats (present only in trace amounts). The monounsaturated fat is present in a form known as oleic acid, the main component of olive oil. Oleic acid is believed to be responsible for much of the nutritional benefit derived from the Mediterranean diet, an eating regimen that has been shown to lower serum cholesterol. Nutritionists suggest that any negative effects that might be caused by the saturated fat contained in foie gras (almost all of it in the form of palmitic acid) are counteracted by the oleic acid. The initial interest in the lipid composition of foie gras began with the release of the results of a 10-year epidemiological study conducted by French scientist Dr. Serge Renaud. Dr. Renaud, who is the director of research at the National Institute of Health and Medical Research in Lyons, surveyed the eating habits of the natives of the French departments of Gers and Lot, areas within Gascony, France's principal foie gras–producing region. Dr. Renaud found that the inhabitants of the region consumed far more saturated fat than any other population in the industrialized world. They not only consume foie gras twice a week on average, they utilize foie gras and duck fat as cooking oil and spread it on bread in place of butter. But the finding that shocked the world, he told Molly O'Neill of *The New York Times* in 1991, was that they also had "the lowest rate of death from cardiovascular disease in the country."

Dr. Renaud's findings were corroborated by the World Health Organization's Multinational Monitoring of Trends and Determinants in Cardiovascular Disease (MONICA), which undertook a study of eating habits, heart disease, and mortality based in Toulouse. Monica reported that out of 100,000 middle-aged French men, approximately 145 died of heart attacks. In Toulouse, the number was 80. In the United States, the number was 315. The discrepancy between these findings and the commonly held belief regarding the role animal fat was considered to play in the incidence of heart disease led world-wide media to report on the phenomenon as "The French Paradox." By the time the CBS news magazine *60 Minutes* broadcast an article in 1991, scientists were concurrently researching an explanation. Some pointed to the chemical constituents of red wine, also consumed in high quantities in those areas studied, while others focused on the composition of the foie gras fat itself.

The possibility that foie gras may promote health led a French diet impresario named Michel Montignac to develop a diet allowing foie gras, wine, and cheese. His Montignac Diet became a craze in France during the 1990's; French chef Paul Bocuse touted its success. On closer examination, however, it became evident that the foie gras and other "forbidden" foods recommended by Montignac were only permitted during a maintenance phase after several months under a stricter regime.

The amount of total fat (the combination of "good fat," "bad fat," and "neutral fat") consumed in a serving of foie gras depends to a large extent on the type of liver that is used and the manner in which it is prepared. Fat content is one of the principle benchmarks for determining grade—the higher the grade of liver, the more fat it contains. Fat content also varies between species and among individual birds. The degree to which the fat is rendered out of the liver during cooking will affect the fat content of the finished dish. Foie gras that is grilled over an open flame, for example, will lose more fat in the cooking process than foie gras that is cooked in a terrine.

Fat and iron are the nutrients present in foie gras with significant nutritional impact. A non-fattened duck liver contains 8.65 milligrams of iron per ounce. To calculate, an average non-fattened duck liver, weighing 3½ ounces becomes an average foie gras of 1½ pounds. An average portion size of 3 to 4 ounces would therefore contain approximately 4 to 5 milligrams of iron, roughly one-third of the daily requirement for women and one-half for men. A similar portion of white or dark meat chicken contains roughly 1.3 milligrams of iron, or only one-tenth of the daily requirement for women and one-seventh for men. Vitamin A is also present, but in quantities that render it only a nominally good source. To understand the relatively low level of other nutrients in the liver, it helps to recall that the original size of a non-fattened duck liver is not much larger than a chicken liver. The exaggerated size, attributable to the added fat that results after the process of gavage, dilutes the impact of the other nutrients found in liver. The notion that foie gras fat itself may be nutritionally beneficial beyond the scope of other animal fats presents some serious cause for celebration. Some people, including Chef Raymond Blanc, believe foie gras to hold an exalted status as a "superfood," an aliment he characterizes as one which influences good health. Foie gras fat, he claims, is the most concentrated source of energy found in a single food. In this argument, he returns to the theory of the French Paradox, where, for reasons not yet fully understood, foie gras has been connected with generally good health, including lower levels of serum cholesterol and heart disease.

PAIRING WINE WITH FOIE GRAS

by Kevin Zraly

Each recipe in this book is accompanied by a wine recommendation (or two) that was given either by the chef or the sommelier of the restaurant from which the dish originates. These pairings reflect a wide variety of approaches to matching foie gras with food. As you flip through the pages you will notice that about 75 percent of the wines suggested are dry, that red and white wines are split almost evenly, and that the wine selections tend toward lighter styles. This profile seems contrary to the foie-gras-with-Sauternes rule once held sacrosanct by wine aficionados. Were you to ask a different sommelier or chef for a wine suggestion for each dish, most likely you would get a completely different set of answers with a different profile. Even in this book we have provided you with some competing suggestions—some sommeliers suggested trying two completely different wines with the same dish, as if to say there are several directions you could take.

There is only one hard-and-fast rule when it comes to matching wine and food: The best wine to pair with your meal, whether it be foie gras or hamburgers, is a wine you like. Personally, when I think of foie gras, I automatically think of red wine—in particular, an aged Bordeaux. I am a red-wine drinker; my favorite wine is Bordeaux. This is a completely subjective opinion based on what I like to drink. That does not mean that red wine is always the best match for every foie gras dish—and it does not mean that red wine is what I would recommend to everybody. But if you start with a wine that you like, you are more than halfway toward a good match.

That said, you can't deny that there are certain wines that marry with certain foods better than others, pairings that make both the wine and the food taste better together than they do apart. I call this phenomenon "wine-and-food synergy," and when you are purposefully setting out to find a wine to match to a certain dish, this is the effect that you are always hoping for. The challenge arises with complicated dishes, like many in this book, for which you have to consider so many different components, such as the texture of the foie gras, the manner in which it is cooked, the sauce or accompaniments that are being served with it, and the serving temperature of the dish.

Beyond personal tastes, the most important consideration for choosing a wine to match a food is texture. The texture of food is easy to understand. Consider two pieces of fish—for instance, a fillet of Dover sole and a medallion of ahi tuna. Each has a distinct texture that in some ways requires different treatment. You wouldn't grill a delicate piece of sole or serve it with a hot-pepper salsa. Similarly, the same ingredients prepared in different ways will have different textures. A veal chop has a tougher, chewier, almost heavier texture than veal paillard. One of the most prized qualities of foie gras is its texture, which varies tremendously whether the liver is seared, poached, roasted, whipped, or molded into a terrine.

Wine also has texture, but it is often more difficult for people to comprehend. To describe the texture of wine, people use terms like "mouth-feel" and "weight." What they are referring to is literally the way the wine feels in your mouth—whether it coats your whole mouth with a lingering flavor, or just lightly settles on the tip of your tongue with a crisp, clean tap.

In general, there are three categories used to describe varying textures of wine: light, medium, and full-bodied. I think it helps to think of them with an analogy to dairy products, such as skim milk, whole milk, and heavy cream, respectively. The wines made from the six most important grapes can be divided into these categories of texture to help make wine pairing easier.

	White Wine Grape	**Red Wine Grape**
Light (skim milk)	Riesling	Pinot Noir
Medium (whole milk)	Sauvignon Blanc	Merlot
Full-Bodied (heavy cream)	Chardonnay	Cabernet Sauvignon

Of course there are other wines that don't fall into these specific categories. As a red wine, Zinfandel ranges from light to full-bodied, depending on the way it is vinified. Sauternes qualifies as a full-bodied white wine. And depending on the producer, Champagne can range from light to full-bodied. However, these categories do work for the majority of wines produced from these grapes.

Temperature is another characteristic that is closely tied to texture and that enters into the decision of pairing a wine with a dish. A chilled terrine of foie gras has a different temperature (and consequently, different texture) from a whole-roasted foie gras, served piping hot.

There is also a psychological component to wine pairing that cannot be ignored. When I look at the recommendations throughout this book, many seem predictable—a chef from Italy's Piedmont region picked a big Barbaresco, while a chef from Japan suggested a particularly flavorful sake. This phenomenon is due in part to the first rule I mentioned above: Pick a wine that you like to drink. But I also think that because of our psychological make-up, because of who we are, we pick wines that resonate well with us. When you are accustomed to a wine, it tastes good with a variety of foods.

Another consideration in wine pairing concerns the placement of the dish in the menu progression. As a rule, I like to move from lighter wines to fuller-bodied wines during the course of a meal. This is one of the reasons I do not always advise a Sauternes with foie gras, even though it is considered by many to be one of the great classic pairings. I find that at the start of a meal, a slab of rich terrine and a chilled glass of Sauternes is enough to stop you dead in your tracks. There is no where to go from there—winewise, that is. Now, if we are talking about an afternoon snack or an early evening meal, there is nothing more satisfying.

This book illustrates well the point that foie gras can be a very simple dish or it can be a very complicated one. This variation suggests a wide range of appropriate wines. Here are some other points to consider:

- Foie gras is often served with some sort of fruit, but some fruit is difficult to pair with wine because the acid in the fruit fights with the acid in wine. A wine must be chosen carefully. This is a situation in which Sauternes works perfectly because the sweetness in the Sauternes is higher than the acidity; the acidity in the fruit balances out the flavor of the Sauternes and matches well with the sweetness.

- Chardonnay is really a white wine masquerading as a red wine, and I would pair it with full-flavored, richly textured foods such as duck confit and seared foie gras.
- Champagne is good for rich, spicy foods, or those served with a cream sauce because it cuts through the richness and balances out the spice.
- Some ingredients, such as fennel, endive, and artichokes, are very difficult to match with wines. They have the effect of giving some wines an almost bitter, off taste that can be difficult to overcome. Again, the best advice here is to experiment with a wine that you like.

You will probably find that you consider some of the wine suggestions in this book to work well, and others not to work at all. There is no way around this sort of subjectivity when dealing with matters of taste. One interesting way to learn from it, however, is to serve two different types of wine with the same dish and see how people respond; you will not only enjoy a great gastronomic experience, but you will also learn something in the process. And who could ask for a more delicious scenario?

FOIE GRAS FACTS

The relatively high cost of foie gras can make preparing it intimidating. In actuality, foie gras is one of the simplest ingredients to use. The most important consideration when handling, cleaning, and cooking foie gras is to keep as little of the fat as possible from rendering. When cooking foie gras, all that is required is a quick cleaning to remove any blemishes, a simple seasoning with salt and pepper, and the application of the appropriate heat. As the recipes throughout this book indicate, most of the creativity and effort lie in the preparation of the sauces and accompaniments served with the foie gras.

Purchasing Foie Gras

Due to its perishability and cost, fresh foie gras is not readily available at retail outlets in North America. (Canned, or otherwise processed foie gras, is easier to find.) Only the most upscale gourmet or butcher shops in urban centers carry an inventory of fresh foie gras or can make arrangements to secure it. Most fresh foie gras in the United States is sold either directly from the producers, through specialty mail-order purveyors, or through a network of wholesale specialty restaurant distributors. To determine who carries it in your area, ask a local chef or refer to the list of producers and distributors on page 331.

The quantity of foie gras to purchase is dependent on the method of preparation. In general, one can figure approximately 3 to 4 ounces of raw liver per person for appetizer portions and 5 to 6 ounces of raw liver for main course servings. The richness and complexity of the accompaniments, however, is another factor in determining the portion size of foie gras. The yield of some recipes is constrained by the cooking technique. For instance, recipes for whole-roasted foie gras can be made only in increments of whole livers; their yields are affected only by the size of the original livers. Similarly, terrines can be made only as large or as small as the available terrine molds.

Because a considerable amount of fat will render out of the liver during cooking, the cooked weight will be significantly less than the raw weight. In general, expect a weight loss of approximately 15 to 20 percent when using mulard foie gras and 25 to 30 percent when using Moscovy. Goose liver loses approximately 35 to 45 percent of its weight, depending on how it is cooked. (This fact illustrates why goose liver is traditionally reserved for low-heat preparations such as terrines.) Practically speaking, a 3-ounce medallion of Grade A mulard foie gras, seared for 40 seconds per side, renders slightly more than a tablespoon of fat and weighs approximately 2¼ ounces when cooked. Purchases should be adjusted to accommodate these variables.

Grading

Foie gras is available in A, B, or C grades, determined by various physical properties of the liver (see table on page 90). In France, where tradition has produced a vast foie gras industry, the grading process is regulated by the government. In the United States, however, no such governmental regulation exists. Instead, grading criteria are imposed by the individual producers.

The factors considered when grading foie gras are size, shape, texture, and appearance. They may impact the flavor and fat loss during the cooking process. Size, the most important criterion, indicates the proportion of fat in the liver. Generally if a liver is too large, its flavor will be diluted and too much fat will be lost during cooking. If a liver is too small, the liver and mineral flavors will be more pronounced and the texture will be less creamy and luscious. In France, where the majority of foie gras is processed and consumed cold, smaller livers with more pronounced flavor and less fat are considered more desirable. In the United States, where the majority of livers are consumed fresh and in hot preparations, a larger liver is ideal. For preparations requiring low-heat cooking methods, such as baking, poaching, or steaming, which necessitate a relatively prolonged cooking time, the ideal size of the foie gras will vary from 1¼ to 1¾ pounds. For preparations requiring high-heat cooking methods, such as sautéing, grilling, broiling, and roasting, which necessitate a relatively short cooking time, the ideal size of the foie gras will vary from 1½ to 2¼ pounds. Goose foie gras are 25 to 30 percent larger than duck foie gras on average.

Shape is used as a grading criterion as it affects the portioning and, ultimately, the appearance and presentation of the final dish. The finest quality livers have a bulbous, fistlike shape. For low-heat preparations, rounded-shaped livers produce a richer, creamier interior. When portioning foie gras for high-heat preparations, rounded-shaped foie gras produce attractive, uniform medallions. Flatter livers are less desirable as they are not as rich and are more difficult to portion.

Texture is considered when grading foie gras as it indicates the proportion of fat present in the liver and, consequently, the consistency of the final preparation. Livers that are too small are low in fat, resulting in a final preparation that is not of the ideal richness. Livers that are too large are high in fat, and will render excessively. The finest foie gras will have a texture that is neither overly firm nor overly soft. Texture is tested by lightly pressing a thumb into the liver. Ideally, the liver should be moderately pliable and the imprint should slowly dissipate. A softer texture suggests the liver may have a damaged cellular structure and may disintegrate during cooking. A firmer texture indicates an elevated proportion of fat.

The appearance of the liver is judged by close visual inspection. The finest livers should be relatively free of any bruises or blemishes. Surface blood spots or a proliferation of small red pin dots indicate a breakdown of capillaries or an excessive number of veins that will affect the flavor and texture of the final preparation. In preparations requiring cleaning, an elevated quantity of veins will necessitate additional labor and increase the risk of damaging the integrity of the liver. In other preparations, the appearance of these veins is visually and texturally unappealing. The color of the liver depends largely on the feed used and is not an indication of quality.

Grade	Size	Shape	Texture	Appearance
A	1 to 3 pounds	Rounded, fistlike, bulbous	Firm to the touch; a thumbprint slowly returns to the surface	Creamy off-white, relatively free of blemishes, minimal number of veins
B	0.8 to 1.5 pounds	May be flatter or less compact	May be softer or harder, depending on proportion of fat	May be darker, have a blemish or two, more veins
C	Everything else			

Although it is desirable to always use the highest-grade liver, it is at times possible to substitute lower grades depending on the method of preparation. Factors to consider when deciding which grade to purchase are the visual impact of the finished dish and economic constraints. Because the integrity of the liver is important in a finished terrine, Grade A livers are preferred. Visual imperfections, such as excessive veins, render terrines unappetizing. While it is certainly possible to prepare a terrine with Grade B or Grade C livers, the amount of time and product lost to cleaning make the savings insignificant. Grade A livers are also essential when the foie gras is going to be kept whole, such as when it is roasted, poached, or steamed. Grade B livers are acceptable for searing, because the coloration that results from the high-heat cooking masks any minor imperfections. The high heat also causes the veins to shrink and release any residual blood. Grade C livers are acceptable for any preparation in which the integrity of the liver is inconsequential, such as sauces, mousses, or recipes in which the liver is whipped, melted, or otherwise broken down. Grade C livers provide the flavor of "gras" when the liver is going to be broken down or further refined.

Storage and Handling

Fresh foie gras is sold in individual vacuum packages. The livers should remain in these packages until they are to be used. Fresh foie gras will keep refrigerated in its vacuum pack for up to two weeks from the time it is harvested. Because it is difficult to ascertain exactly how much time the liver has spent in the distribution network before it arrives in your kitchen, plan to use fresh livers within one week of purchase. Once removed from the vacuum pack, the liver should be used immediately or wrapped tightly in plastic film and used within two days, as it oxidizes when it comes into contact with air. Any scraps that remain after cleaning and portioning should be wrapped similarly.

The ideal temperature for refrigeration is 33 degrees Fahrenheit, just above the freezing point of water. The warmer the storage temperature, the shorter the shelf life. If the liver is going to be kept longer than one week, it should be frozen. Frozen, foie gras can last up to one year. Be aware, however, that the quality of the defrosted liver is substantially diminished. During the freezing and defrosting processes, the cell walls within the foie gras disintegrate, allowing the moisture contained within the liver to evaporate, leaving the resulting dehydrated liver with a mealy, granular texture. Frozen foie gras should only be used for preparations in which the creamy texure of the liver is not essential, such as sauces or mousses. Terrines made from frozen foie gras suffer because the liver is difficult to clean and the finished texture is less silken. Producers are currently experimenting with advanced cryogenic technology to preserve the quality of foie gras during the freezing process. The extremely cold temperatures and the speed of freezing attained by the use of liquid nitrogen prevent the cellular breakdown that alters the texture of the liver. At the moment, however, the costs of this process are prohibitive.

Cleaning Foie Gras

After removing the foie gras from its vacuum package, it should be rinsed and patted dry with a clean cloth or paper towel. Traditional French recipes often call for the liver to be soaked for several hours in a salted milk bath. Historically, this step helped draw out residual blood left inside the veins of the liver. Because of modern processing techniques, which include resting the livers for several days on a bed of shaved ice to diffuse any residual blood, this step is no longer necessary from a hygienic standpoint. Still, some chefs continue to include a milk bath in contemporary recipes to preserve the tradition. Others do believe it still softens the texture of the foie gras.

The whole duck foie gras consists of two lobes: a larger, more rounded posterior lobe, which accounts for approximately two-thirds of the weight of the entire liver; and a smaller, flatter anterior lobe, which accounts for the remaining one-third. The larger goose foie gras has two lobes of nearly equal size. These lobes are connected by membranes, nerves, and veins. The bile sack is located in this area, between the two lobes. Any green discoloration between the lobes is bile. Bile spots should be removed with a sharp paring knife, as bile will give the liver a bitter taste.

The method of preparation dictates the manner in which to clean the foie gras. For recipes that require a whole foie gras fully intact, such as roasting, poaching, or steaming, the liver should be left whole. Do not separate the lobes. Simply remove any visible surface blemishes, such as blood spots or green spots, with a sharp paring knife. Some chefs recommend peeling the fine membrane off the whole liver, but this membrane is barely discernable once the liver is cooked, and it does help the foie gras to maintain its shape.

For recipes that require a foie gras separated into lobes, the manner in which to clean the foie gras depends on the type of heat that will be used to cook the foie gras. More specifically, high-heat cooking, such as searing or grilling, and low-heat cooking, such as poaching or baking, require different techniques of cleaning.

High-Heat Cooking

To cut the foie gras into medallions or other shapes for high-heat cooking, the lobes of the liver must be separated. For best results, work with a slightly chilled liver. Gently insert your hands between the lobes and, with one lobe in each hand, pull them apart. Use a sharp knife to cut the connective membranes and nerves between the lobes. Trim away any visible membranes, veins, or green bile. Rinse the liver and pat dry. Lay the lobes on the work surface with the rounded side facing up. Using a sharp slicing knife dipped in hot water, slice the liver on a diagonal into medallions of approximately ½- to ¾-inch thick. The size of the medallions will vary as the slices move along the lobe. The two factors to consider when slicing a liver into medallions are surface area and weight. As the surface area increases, medallions of uniform thickness will increase in weight. To maintain the same portion size, a thinner medallion can be cut, taking into account that thinner medallions will cook more rapidly. Avoid cutting medallions too thin, however, because they have a tendency to overcook and render all of their fat. Make adjustments while slicing the foie gras to ensure even portion size and consistent cooking time.

When sliced into medallions, an average Grade A liver of about 1½ pounds will yield approximately six 3½-ounce portions of uniform size and shape. Any scraps can be reserved for other preparations, such as mousses, stuffings, butters, or other dishes flavored with foie gras. Some chefs suggest using needle-nosed pliers to pull out visible segments of vein on the surface of the medallions. Such a maneuver, however, is usually difficult to accomplish without destroying the integrity of the medallion, causing holes in the surface of the liver. Moreover, if the liver is going to be seared, the veins will not be noticeable, as the high heat will diffuse the remaining blood and the sautéing of the medallion will create an attractive caramelized surface.

Medallions of foie gras should be arranged in layers separated by white butcher paper or parchment paper, wrapped airtight with plastic film, and stored in the refrigerator until ready to use. Such care is necessary to prevent the fat in the liver from oxidizing.

Low-Heat Cooking

To prepare a liver for a terrine or any low-heat preparation in which the liver will ultimately be sliced or served as a solid block requires careful cleaning and deveining. Care must be taken to remove any visible sign of veins, nerves, membranes, or discolorations from the flesh of the liver. These blemishes are not inedible, but they are unattractive and they may affect the flavor of the finished dish. Even a drop of residual blood renders an austere slice of chilled foie gras terrine unappetizing.

Interestingly, this aversion to any evidence of blood or veins in foie gras is recent. Until the middle of this century, most foie gras recipes did not call for cleaning the liver. The cleanliness of the liver was left to precautions taken during the production process and special treatments, such as the milk bath explained above, were designed to diffuse any residual blood from the interior of the liver. Regardless, diners today expect terrines to be free of any visual imperfections.

When cleaning foie gras for terrines it is important to keep the individual lobes intact as much as possible. You will need to work your fingertips or a small paring knife delicately into the flesh of the liver to remove the veins, being careful not to break the liver into too many separate pieces. The fewer the pieces, the greater the integrity of the finished terrine. It is easiest to clean the liver when it is at room temperature. To bring the liver to room temperature, remove the foie gras from the refrigerator and leave it in its vacuum package at room temperature for two and one-half to three hours. Alternately, to bring the liver to room temperature quickly, remove the foie gras from the vacuum package, rinse, and immerse it in a water bath of 95 degrees Fahrenheit. After soaking for one hour, the liver will be pliable enough to clean thoroughly.

Once the liver has come to room temperature, separate the two lobes. With the larger lobe lying wrong side up on the work surface, locate the area where the connecting membranes and veins are severed. Grasp the principal connecting membrane with your right hand. Gently tug the membrane to reveal the location of the central vein of the lobe. As you pull, use your other hand to gently peel back the flesh of the liver, tracing the location of the vein. Because of the temperature of the fat, the foie gras should have the consistency of soft clay. You should be able to clean the foie gras without having it break apart into pieces. The central vein extends roughly two thirds down the middle of the large lobe before it forks into two separate directions, forming an upside down Y. Continue tracing the path of the vein by gently tugging it, pushing aside the flesh to reveal the vein, and removing any evidence of coagulated blood, vein, or membrane you encounter. The point of a small paring knife may help lift out these imperfections. Be sure to cut away any green discoloration (evidence of bile) that will give the liver a bitter taste. Warm, moist paper towels help to clean any blood, fat, or membranes from your hands and your knife while you work. Use the same procedure to remove the central vein and any nerves or membranes from the smaller lobe.

When you are finished, you should be left with two flattened, somewhat misshaped lobes of liver that are largely intact, a few small scraps of liver that have broken off, and the membranes and veins. Discard the membranes and veins. Using the cleaned lobes and scraps, proceed with the recipe.

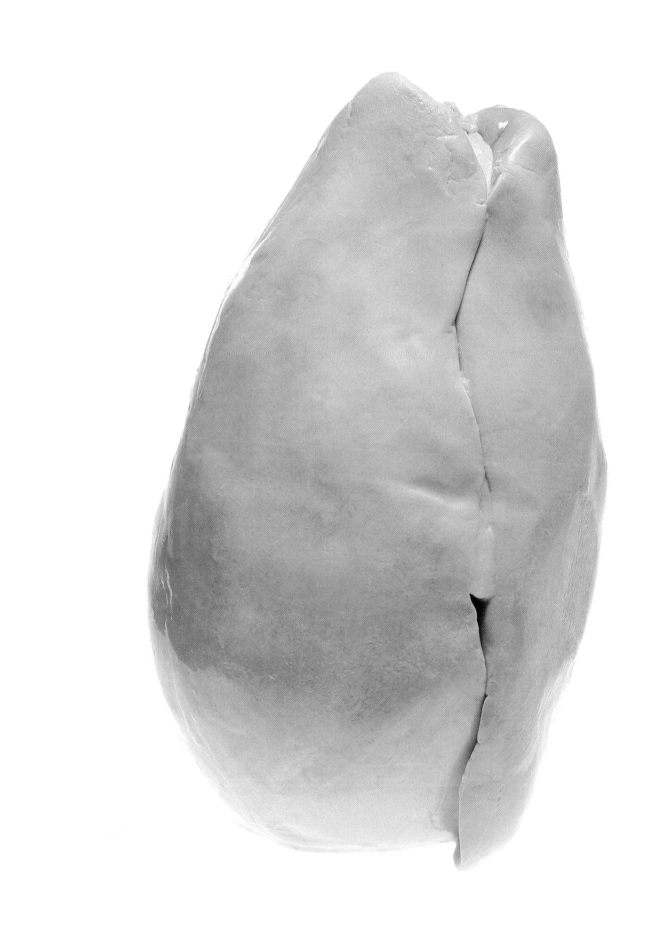

RECIPES

Cromesquis

Michelin three-star chef Marc Meneau has made this mystifying hors d'oeuvre one of his signatures. The technique of using gelatin to solidify a liquid in order to seal it in a package, only to melt it later through cooking, echoes the preparation of the famous soup dumplings of Shanghai. For the cromesquis, named for a Polish gourmand, Meneau makes a filling of foie gras, truffles, port, and cream, which he envelopes in a classic breading. Because of the molten center, it is important to cool the cromesquis slightly before serving so that guests can pop them into their mouths whole, thereby avoiding a potentially messy situation while fully experiencing the sensual flavor and texture.

Filling

1¾ ounces gelatin, about 24 leaves
   or 5 packages

2 cups Port

¾ pound foie gras, diced

3 cups heavy cream

¼ cup black truffle juice

Coarse salt

Black pepper, freshly ground

1 ounce black truffle, finely chopped

Breading

Flour for dredging

6 eggs

6 egg yolks

4 cups fine white bread crumbs

Grapeseed or vegetable oil for frying

Wine Recommendation

Bollinger Brut Grand Année 1989 (Champagne), or another dry vintage Champagne.

Filling

Whether using leaves or powder, dissolve the gelatin in enough cold water to cover. In a large saucepan set over high heat, reduce the port by slightly more than half, about 20 to 30 minutes. Meanwhile, in a very hot sauté pan, cook the diced foie gras for about 1 minute. Set aside. Add the cream to the reduced port and bring the mixture to a boil. Add the truffle juice and return the mixture to a boil once again. Stir in the dissolved gelatin, salt, and pepper and return the mixture to a boil. Remove from the heat and add the foie gras, along with any fat that may have rendered out. Transfer to the bowl of a food processor and process for several minutes until smooth. Pass through a fine chinois to strain.

Sprinkle the chopped truffle over the bottom of a half hotel pan or 2-quart baking dish, then pour in the cromesquis mixture. Refrigerate for about 12 hours, until set. Cut the chilled mixture into 1-inch squares.

Breading

Dredge the squares in flour and refrigerate for 8 hours. Beat together the eggs and the egg yolks. Dip the floured squares in the egg mixture and coat thoroughly in the bread crumbs. Refrigerate for at least 2 hours. Repeat the breading procedure (egg and bread crumbs) and return the cromesquis to the refrigerator until service.

Service

Preheat the oven to 400 degrees. In a large, deep sauté pan or pot, heat the oil to 350 degrees. Quickly deep fry the cromesquis until golden brown, drain, transfer to a rack set on a sheet pan, and finish in the oven for 3 or 4 minutes until heated through. Change the oil frequently as the bread crumbs will burn. Handle the cromesquis very gently, as the filling will have completely liquefied. Allow to cool slightly before serving. Expect that several of the cromequis will break during the cooking process and will not be usable.

FoieReos

Foie gras can be used as a flavorful substitute for other fats. Michel Richard's original inspiration for this recipe was economic—he wanted a way to use foie gras scraps left over from other preparations. Richard's extensive experience as a pastry chef led him to create this fanciful, savory cookie modeled after the Oreo. This cookie has the distinct flavor and the texture of traditional English shortbread. The bite-sized cookies can be served alone as hors d'oeuvres or as a garnish for other preparations of foie gras.

Cookie
8 ounces foie gras scraps, mousse, or terrine

4 ounces pastry flour

½ teaspoon baking powder

½ teaspoon sugar

1 teaspoon balsamic vinegar

⅛ teaspoon coarse salt

⅛ teaspoon black pepper, freshly ground

2 egg yolks, lightly beaten

Sea salt

Filling
3 to 5 ounces foie gras mousse (see page 114)

Special Equipment
1½-inch round cookie cutter

Wine Recommendation
Taittinger Brut Blanc de Blancs Comtes de Champagne 1989 (Champagne), or another dry vintage Champagne.

Cookie
Place the foie gras scraps, mousse, or terrine in the bowl of a food processor and process until smooth. Add the pastry flour, baking powder, sugar, balsamic vinegar, salt, and pepper. Process until the ingredients are combined, being careful not to overmix. The dough should be soft. Wrap the dough in plastic wrap and refrigerate for at least 2 hours. Preheat the oven to 325 degrees. On a floured surface, gently roll out the soft dough to ¼-inch thickness. Shape the cookies using a 1½-inch round cookie cutter. Reroll the scraps once only. Carefully place the cookies on a parchment-lined sheet pan.

Score the top with the back of a small paring knife to decorate as shown. Brush lightly with the beaten egg yolks and sprinkle with the sea salt. Bake for approximately 20 minutes, until light golden brown. Let the cookies cool on a rack. Spread the foie gras mousse on the bottom of half of the cookies and form sandwiches with the remaining cookies.

Chef Notes
The cookies are best if baked fresh. The dough can be stored in the refrigerator for up to one week and in the freezer for up to one month. Fill the cookies just before serving.

Foie Gras and Smoked Salmon Beggar's Purse

The most familiar beggar's purse is filled with beluga caviar and crème fraîche. Wayne Nish's version of this luxurious amuse-bouche conveys the same sense of indulgence by combining foie gras and smoked salmon. The purses must be kept small so that you can fully experience the concentration of flavors and the contrast in textures in a single, sumptuous bite.

YIELD: ABOUT 80 BEGGAR'S PURSES

Crêpes
8 extra-large eggs
2 cups plus 2 tablespoons all-purpose
 flour
3 cups whole milk
Pinch coarse salt
1 cup clarified butter, melted and
 cooled

Filling
2 cups foie gras mousse (see page 114)
2 cups finely chopped smoked salmon

Garnish
80 to 100 long chives
Salmon roe

Special Equipment
8-inch nonstick pan or seasoned
 crêpe pan
4¾-inch round cutter
Microwave oven
1-ounce ice cream scoop

Wine Recommendation
Emilio Lustau Jerez Dry Oloroso
Single Cask (Spain), or another oloroso
sherry. Or for a different effect, Krug
Clos de Mésnil 1985 (Champagne), or
another full-bodied vintage
Champagne.

Crêpes
In a large mixing bowl, whisk together the eggs, flour, milk, and salt until well blended. Pass the mixture through a fine chinois. Cover and let rest for ½ hour. Stir ¼ cup of the clarified butter into the batter. Place the nonstick pan over medium-high heat. Using a clean cloth dipped in the remaining clarified butter, swab the preheated pan. Pour 1 ounce, about 2 tablespoons, of batter into the pan and swirl immediately to cover the full bottom of the pan. The crêpes should be almost transparent. Cook on one side only for about 30 seconds. Remove the crêpe to a clean plate and repeat the process, stacking the finished crêpes on top of one another, until all the batter is used. If the crêpes are to be reserved for later use, cover with a piece of plastic wrap. They can be refrigerated for up to two days if tightly wrapped.

Filling
In a large mixing bowl, combine the foie gras mousse and chopped smoked salmon. Using

a wooden spoon or rubber spatula, mix until well integrated, or use an electric mixer fitted with a paddle attachment. Cover and set in the refrigerator until ready to use.

Service and Garnish
Wrap the chives in a damp paper towel and place in the microwave oven for 10 seconds on high power. Using the cutter, carefully cut the crêpes into 4¾-inch circles. Turn the crêpes cooked side up. Place a 1-ounce scoop of the foie gras mixture in the center of each crêpe. Gather the edges into pleats to form a small purse and tie each with a blanched chive. Trim the chive and set aside. Serve at room temperature or slightly chilled. The purses can be assembled up to one day in advance, covered in plastic wrap, and refrigerated until ready to serve.

Chef Notes
It is best to have all the elements ready, the crêpes and the filling, and assemble the purses as close to service as possible.

Caraway-Infused Corn Custard
with Honey-Glazed Foie Gras

Corn Custard

12 jumbo brown eggs (see Chef Notes)
1 pint heavy cream
1 cup corn kernels, fresh or frozen
1 tablespoon caraway seeds, toasted
1 tablespoon coarse salt
Black pepper, freshly ground

Honey-Glazed Foie Gras

¼ pound foie gras, cubed
Coarse salt
Black pepper, freshly ground
½ cup corn kernels, fresh or frozen
3 tablespoons red wine vinegar
2 tablespoons red or other dark honey
¼ cup chopped chives

Garnish

4½ ounces foie gras, cut into 3 slices,
  each about 1½ ounces and ¼-inch
  thick
Coarse salt
Black pepper, freshly ground
1 tablespoon finely sliced chives

Special Equipment

Cardboard egg carton
Egg scissors or sharp serrated knife

Wine Recommendation

Merryvale Merlot 1994 (Napa). Or for
a different approach, Domaine
Trimbach Cuvée Frédéric Emile
Riesling 1996 (Alsace), or any
medium-bodied wine with pronounced
fruit to complement the richness of
the custard.

Served in fanciful egg cups, this corn custard baked in an egg shell is one of David Burke's playful signature appetizers. Over the years he has paired it with a variety of garnishes, but when served with foie gras, David says, the dish becomes downright sexy. The texture is ethereal—soft, juicy, and rich. The sweet and sour glaze on the foie gras helps offset some of the richness of the custard and the liver. The only disappointment is that the portion is limited by the size of the shells. Duck eggs, which are slightly larger and richer than chicken eggs, can be substituted for an even creamier result.

Corn Custard

Remove the top of the eggs with egg scissors or a sharp serrated knife. Empty 3 of the eggs into a large mixing bowl and reserve for the custard. Empty the remaining eggs into a container and save for another use. Rinse the inside of the shells and remove any loose shell with your fingertips. Place the 12 cleaned eggshells back into the original cardboard carton and set the carton in a baking dish. Preheat the oven to 350 degrees. Simmer the heavy cream with the corn and caraway seeds for 7 minutes. Purée in a food processor and strain through a fine-mesh sieve. Whisk the 3 reserved eggs, and slowly beat in the strained cream mixture. Season with salt and pepper. Fill the eggshells two-thirds full with the custard mixture. Pour about 1 inch of water into the baking dish holding the egg carton with the filled eggshells, cover the pan with aluminum foil, and carefully set in the preheated oven. Bake for 45 to 50 minutes, or until the custard is set. Carefully remove the egg carton from the baking pan and set aside.

Honey-Glazed Foie Gras

While the custard is cooking, season the foie gras cubes with salt and pepper. In a small sauté pan, sear the foie gras over high heat for 1 minute. Reduce the heat, add the corn to the pan, and cook for an additional 30 seconds. Deglaze the pan with the vinegar, add the honey, and heat for 30 seconds. Stir in the chives and adjust the seasoning with salt and pepper.

Garnish

Season the foie gras slices with salt and pepper. Heat a small sauté pan over high heat. Add the foie gras and sear on each side for 30 seconds. Remove from the pan, place on paper towel, and keep warm.

Service

Top each custard with a generous spoonful of the honey-glazed foie gras mixture. Cut the seared foie gras into strips and position inside the egg shell. Sprinkle with sliced chives and serve in decorative egg cups with espresso spoons.

Chef Notes

For a richer custard, duck eggs can be substituted for chicken eggs. To compensate for the larger yolks, add 3 tablespoons heavy cream to the custard mixture.

Curls of Salt-Cured Foie Gras on Toasted Country Bread

In Gascony, the southwestern region of France famous for foie gras, the liver is sometimes served raw and unadorned. Laurent Manrique, a Gascon native, prepares this interpretation of his favorite childhood snack. Seasoned with nothing but granules of briny sea salt and cracked black pepper, the thin curls of cured foie gras melt deliciously into warm toasted country bread. Because the foie gras is buried in sea salt, which draws out the moisture, the liver is in effect "cooked" in the same manner in which gravlax is prepared.

Salt-Cured Foie Gras
1 foie gras, about 1½ pounds, cleaned for low-heat cooking (see page 93), at room temperature
2 pounds sel gris

Garnish
Toasted country bread
Black pepper, freshly cracked

Special Equipment
Cheesecloth
Butcher's twine
Sharp cheese knife

Wine Recommendation
Château Jolys Vendage Tardive 1995 (Jurançon), or another off-dry Jurançon.

Salt-Cured Foie Gras
Lay out a double rectangular layer of cheesecloth on the counter. Arrange the cleaned foie gras along one of the long edges. Tightly roll up the foie gras in the cheesecloth to make a sausage-shaped cylinder about 2 inches in diameter. Be sure to tighten and tuck under the cheesecloth after each turn to make a compact roll. Tie the ends tightly with butcher's twine like a bonbon.

Place half the salt in a baking dish or roasting pan large enough to hold the foie gras "sausage." Position the foie gras on top and cover with the remaining sel gris. Use more sel gris if necessary to ensure the foie gras is completely buried. Refrigerate for 16 hours.

Remove the cured foie gras from the refrigerator and brush off the sel gris. Keep refrigerated until 1 hour before service.

Service and Garnish
One hour before service, place the cured foie gras in the freezer. To serve, carefully remove the cheesecloth from the foie gras. Using a sharp cheese knife, thinly slice the liver into curls and place the curls directly onto warm toast. The heat of the toast will cause the fat of the liver to melt into the bread. Sprinkle with cracked pepper and serve.

Chef Notes
The cured foie gras should be used within 24 hours of being prepared. Keep refrigerated until served.

Foie Gras Entier en Bocal

Whole foie gras preserved in a jar is a specialty of Gascony, France's principle foie gras-producing region. Nicole Manrique, a native of the region, remembers feeding her own birds to make foie gras every year during the holiday season. When the livers were small, they were roasted and eaten right away. But the largest, most beautiful livers were preserved "en bocal" so they could be enjoyed throughout the year. In effect, the lengthy cooking process conserves the liver for long-term storage. According to Nicole, the entier is best after it has aged, unopened, in a cool, dark place for two years. If protected from light during storage, the liver will keep up to ten years—the flavor changing and maturing as time passes. Once opened, the liver should be consumed within one week.

YIELD: 8 TO 10 APPETIZER SERVINGS

Foie Gras

¼ cup Armagnac

1 whole foie gras, about 1½ pounds, cleaned of any visible surface imperfections

Sel gris

Black pepper, freshly cracked

Garnish

Toast

Sel gris

Black pepper, freshly cracked

Special Equipment

1 large canning jar with seal, just large enough to hold the foie gras tightly

Tongs

Wine Recommendation

Château Montus Pacherenc du Vic-Bilh Sec 1995, or another wine from Southwest France.

Foie Gras

Thoroughly wash the jar with soap and water. Bring a large pot of water, big enough to completely immerse the jar, to a boil. Boil the jar for a minimum of 5 minutes to sterilize. Reduce the heat to a simmer. Thoroughly rinse out the jar with the Armagnac. Be sure to rinse the lid and the seal as well. Season the foie gras with sel gris and freshly cracked black pepper. Stuff the foie gras into the jar and pack tightly. The jar should be almost too small to hold the liver, but able to accommodate it with the application of a little pressure. Don't be afraid to break the liver. Seal the jar.

Place the sealed jar in the simmering water and cook for 1½ hours. Some of the foie gras fat will rise to the top of the jar and some juice will collect at the bottom. With tongs, remove the jar from the simmering water and let cool to room temperature.

Store in a cool, dark place (a wine cellar is perfect) until ready to serve.

Service and Garnish

When ready to serve, open the jar. Remove the top layer of fat and reserve. Unmold the liver into a dish, reserve any liquid. Remove any white coating that has formed. Thinly slice the liver and place on warm toast. Sprinkle with sel gris and freshly cracked black pepper. Serve with the fat and juice for dipping.

Chef Notes

While you can serve this dish as soon as it is canned, the liver is best after it has aged for one to two years. As it matures, it develops a buttery, nutty flavor. Be sure the jar is protected from any light while stored.

Confit of Whole Foie Gras

Duck, goose, and other tough meats were traditionally confited—slowly simmered and stored in their own fat—as a means of tenderization and preservation before the advent of household refrigeration. Traditionally, the spice mix quatre-épices *was used for both its flavor and antiseptic qualities. Alain Sailhac, a native of France whose mother often prepared foie gras confit, developed this particular recipe by combining various Gascon techniques. Instead of the traditional spice mix, he uses white pepper and allspice. While many chefs choose to pair foie gras with sweet wines, Sailhac remembers his father enjoying this particular dish with the vigorous, tannic red wines of the region.*

YIELD: 6 APPETIZER SERVINGS

Confit

½ teaspoon white pepper

Dash allspice

2 teaspoons fine salt

½ teaspoon granulated sugar

1 whole foie gras, about 1½ pounds

3 pounds fresh duck fat (with skin) or 2 quarts rendered fat

⅓ cup coarse salt

1 rib celery

Garnish

1 knob celeriac, peeled and cut into julienne

1 head endive, cut into julienne

1 head radicchio, cut into julienne

1 Granny Smith apple, peeled and cut into julienne

Walnut oil

Fresh lemon juice

Mâche

Sliced raisin-walnut bread

Special Equipment

Deep ceramic container

Ceramic terrine

Wine Recommendation

Château Lagrezette, Cuvée Dame Honneur 1984 (Cahors), or another heady red wine from the region.

Foie Gras Preparation

Mix together the white pepper, allspice, fine salt, and sugar. Rub the foie gras with the spice mixture and wrap in plastic wrap. Refrigerate for 24 hours.

Fat Clarification

Place half the duck fat in a deep ceramic container. Cover with a layer of coarse salt. Add another layer of duck fat and cover with another layer of salt. Let sit for 24 hours in the refrigerator. Remove the fat and salt from the container and soak in a large pot of cold water for 10 minutes. Remove the fat from the water and chop into very small pieces. In a pot, combine the chopped duck fat, celery stalk, and ½ cup of water. Melt the fat slowly over low heat until the fat is clear. When the fat is clarified, it will sit in a layer on top of the water. Pour off the fat through a fine chinois and reserve.

Foie Gras Confit

In a saucepan large enough to hold the foie gras, heat the fat until it reaches 185 degrees. Place the foie gras in the duck fat and cook for 7 minutes; turn the foie gras upside down and cook for 3 more minutes. Remove the saucepan from the heat and let sit until the fat reaches 160 degrees. Remove the foie gras from the duck fat and set on a rack until cool. Place the cooled foie gras in a ceramic terrine and cover completely with the cooled, but still liquid, duck fat. Refrigerate the confit for 15 days before serving.

Service and Garnish

To serve, cut the confit into six slices with a knife that has been dipped in warm water. Place a slice of confit on each of six plates. Combine the celeriac, endive, and apple and toss with the walnut oil and lemon juice, to taste. Garnish the plates with this salad and the mâche; serve with several slices of raisin-walnut bread.

Chef Notes

Clarified duck fat is available in many specialty food stores and can be used to prepare the confit. To preserve the leftover terrine, cover any exposed confit with duck fat and cover with waxed paper. Wrap the entire terrine in plastic wrap. The confit will keep for several weeks.

Terrine of Foie Gras with Cognac Aspic

This terrine by Jacques Pépin combines the techniques of a classic terrine and a torchon. By wrapping the liver in a dish towel, or torchon *in French, before placing it in the terrine, Jacques is able to remove some of the fat that renders once it has cooked without altering the shape or texture of the finished product. A classic dish requires classic accompaniments, such as Cognac aspic, fresh brioche, truffles, and a glass of Sauternes.*

Terrine

1½ teaspoons coarse salt

1 teaspoon sugar

½ teaspoon white pepper, freshly ground

2 teaspoons unflavored gelatin powder

¼ teaspoon saltpeter (optional)

1 foie gras, about 1½ pounds, cleaned for low-heat cooking (see page 93)

3 tablespoons Cognac

Cognac Aspic

2 leeks, greens only, coarsely chopped

2 stalks celery, coarsely chopped

1 small carrot, coarsely chopped

½ cup fresh chervil, loosely packed

2 large sprigs fresh tarragon

¼ teaspoon black pepper, freshly ground

1½ teaspoons coarse salt

4 envelopes unflavored gelatin, about 3 tablespoons

2 egg whites

1 cup dry white wine

4 cups chicken or beef stock, or a combination

3 tablespoons Cognac

Garnish

Fresh chervil

1 small black truffle, chopped (optional)

Brioche

Special Equipment

Butcher's twine

Terrine with cover

Wood block to fit terrine

1 pound weight

Cheesecloth

Wine Recommendations

Château d'Yquem 1989 (Sauternes), or another sweet Sauternes.

Terrine

In a small bowl, combine all of the ingredients except the foie gras and Cognac. Sprinkle the foie gras with this mixture. Place the large lobe of foie gras on a clean kitchen towel and arrange the smaller lobe and any scraps that broke off during cleaning on top. Wrap the towel carefully around the foie gras to compact it into a tight mass. Tie the ends of the towel tightly with butcher's twine—wrapping the string around the foie gras to help maintain its shape—and place in a terrine mold. Pour the Cognac on top.

Preheat the oven to 225 degrees. Cover the terrine with a lid and cover the entire terrine tightly with aluminum foil, securing the foil around the edges. Place the terrine in a roasting pan and fill the pan with tepid water so that it comes at least two-thirds of the way up the outside of the terrine. Set in the preheated oven and bake for 1 hour. The inside of the foie gras should reach approximately 130 degrees. Remove from the oven.

Remove the foil and the lid and set the wood block on top of the liver. Place the weight on top of the wood and refrigerate overnight. The following day, remove the wood and scrape off the surface fat. Run a knife around the towel-encased foie gras to release it. Pull on the towel to unmold; if it doesn't unmold easily, warm the terrine slightly by immersing it in hot water. Unwrap the foie gras and clean away any visible fat by wiping with a paper towel. Refrigerate.

Cognac Aspic

In a small saucepan, combine the leeks, celery, carrots, chervil, tarragon, pepper, salt, and gelatin. Add the egg whites and stir in the wine. In a separate saucepan, bring the stock to a boil and add while hot to the gelatin mixture, stirring to combine. Cook this mixture over a medium-high flame, stirring until it comes to a strong boil. Stop stirring, remove from the heat, and set aside for about 15 minutes. Do not stir. Strain the aspic into a saucepan through a cloth towel or several layers of cheesecloth. There should be about 2 cups. Let cool for a few minutes and add the Cognac. Pour the aspic into a bowl and refrigerate until firm.

Service and Garnish

Slice the foie gras into eight to ten slices and arrange on the serving plates. Cut the aspic into rough cubes and sprinkle around the foie gras. Garnish with sprigs of fresh chervil and chopped truffle. Serve with brioche.

Chef Notes

If the foie gras is to be kept longer than three days, it should be wiped clean with a paper towel to remove any juice or liquid, placed back in the terrine, and covered with clear fat—preferably duck or goose fat—or butter, so the liver is completely immersed in the fat and air cannot get to it. Packed this way it can keep for several weeks under refrigeration.

Terrine

1 foie gras, about 1 pound 2 ounces,
    cleaned for low-heat cooking (see
    page 93)

1 teaspoon salt

Pinch white pepper

Pinch sugar

¼ cup Sauternes

Sauternes-Onion Marmalade

2 medium onions

2 ounces butter, cut into small cubes

½ teaspoon coarse salt

¼ cup Sauternes

Vinaigrette

2 tablespoons sherry vinegar

1 teaspoon mustard

Coarse salt

Black pepper, freshly ground

¼ cup hazelnut oil

Black-Eyed Pea Salad

1 cup cooked black-eyed peas

1 small shallot, minced

1 tablespoon chives, chopped

Vinaigrette (from above)

Coarse salt

Black pepper, freshly ground

1 ounce baby greens

Garnish

¼ cup hazelnuts, toasted, peeled, and
    finely chopped

1 teaspoon chives, chopped

Special Equipment

Ceramic terrine mold

Mandoline

Wine Recommendation

Disznókő Tokaji Aszú 5 Puttonoyos
1993 (Hungary), or a similar sweet
wine.

Foie Gras Terrine with Sauternes-Onion Marmalade, Black-Eyed Pea Salad, and Hazelnuts

The more I enjoy foie gras, the more I appreciate a simple, elegant terrine. If I had to eat foie gras everyday, I would save the seared medallions for special occasions and reach for a classic terrine de foie gras au Sauternes, such as this one by Bill Telepan. One of the secrets to the succulence of Bill's terrine is that he only cooks the foie gras to an internal temperature of 100 degrees. Although the terrine continues to cook somewhat once it is removed from the oven, the gentle heat gives it a delicate texture and a delicious, rich flavor. Bill's creativity is evident in the accompaniments, which highlight the dish's strong, earthy tones.

Terrine

Season the foie gras with the salt, pepper, and sugar. Line a shallow bowl with plastic wrap. Drizzle half the Sauternes in the bowl, add the foie gras, and drizzle with the remaining Sauternes. Refrigerate overnight.

Preheat the oven to 275 degrees. Let the foie gras stand at room temperature for 15 minutes. Pack the foie gras into the terrine mold, pressing well to make sure there are no air pockets. Wrap the entire mold in two layers of plastic wrap and place in a larger baking dish. Fill the dish with warm water to come two-thirds up the sides of the terrine. Cook the terrine in the oven, in the water bath, until the internal temperature reaches 100 degrees, about 30 to 40 minutes.

Remove the plastic wrap from the terrine. Carefully pour off the fat from the top of the terrine, reserving it in a separate container. Cut a piece of cardboard that will fit exactly into the inside of the mold. Wrap the cardboard in plastic wrap and place on top of the terrine. Press gently to remove all the air bubbles. Set a wood block or second terrine on top to weigh down the liver. Pour off any excess fat. Pour some of the reserved fat over the terrine; use just enough to seal the foie gras completely so that no liver is exposed to air. Let sit for 24 to 48 hours before serving.

Sauternes-Onion Marmalade

Slice the onions paper thin using a mando-

line. Melt the butter in a saucepan set over low heat. Add the onions and salt and cover the pan. Cook until very tender, 1 to 1½ hours, stirring occasionally. Strain the onions through a chinois, pressing firmly to remove all excess butter. Place the strained onions back in the pan, add the Sauternes, and simmer until the onions are a syrupy consistency. Add more salt if necessary.

Vinaigrette

In a small bowl, whisk together the vinegar, mustard, salt, and pepper. Slowly whisk in the hazelnut oil to create an emulsion. Adjust the seasoning if necessary and set aside.

Black-Eyed Pea Salad

Warm the black-eyed peas slightly. In a bowl, combine the peas, shallots, chives, and 1 tablespoon of the vinaigrette. Season with salt and pepper. Place the baby greens in a separate bowl, add the remaining vinaigrette, and toss to coat. Season with salt and pepper.

Service and Garnish

Slice the terrine into six or twelve slices; place one or two slices in the center of each of six plates. Place a spoonful of marmalade to the right of the terrine, a spoonful of peas to the left, and the baby greens above. Sprinkle the plates with the hazelnuts and chives.

ABC Terrine

A classic terrine is a solid block of foie gras, slow cooked at low temperature to ensure that a minimum of fat is lost, pressed to compact the shape, and chilled to guarantee a smooth, creamy texture. This version by Christopher Gross is actually three traditional foie gras preparations in one—terrine, mousse, and pan-seared medallions—assembled in the shape of a terrine. The result is a study in foie gras, as each preparation offers a distinct flavor and texture. From a professional chef's perspective, this terrine has the added benefit of utilizing three different grades of liver—A, B, and C—each best suited to one of the preparations, thereby minimizing the overall food cost of the dish.

YIELD: 10 TO 12 APPETIZER SERVINGS

Foie Gras Mousse

2 whole foie gras (Grade C), about 1½ pounds total, cleaned for low-heat cooking (see page 93)

2 tablespoons Armagnac

1 tablespoon white truffle oil

Sea salt

White pepper, freshly ground

Terrine

1 whole foie gras (Grade A), about 1½ pounds, cleaned for low-heat cooking (see page 93)

2 tablespoons Armagnac

1 tablespoon white truffle oil

Sea salt

White pepper, freshly ground

1 whole foie gras (Grade B), about 1 pound, cleaned for low-heat cooking (see page 93)

Foie Gras Mousse

Place the two cleaned Grade C foie gras in a resealable plastic bag. Add the Armagnac and the truffle oil. Season with salt and white pepper. Close the bag and refrigerate for at least 4 hours. Using either a commercial steamer or a large pot of boiling water, cook the foie gras in the sealed bag for 7 minutes. Open the bag and drain off the fat, reserving it at room temperature. Reseal the bag and set in the refrigerator to chill.

Remove the foie gras from the refrigerator and take it out of the bag. Clean off and discard any congealed fat from around the liver. Allow the liver to come to room temperature. Pass the cooked liver through a vegetable mill fitted with a fine disk or through a fine mesh strainer (using a spatula) to form a mousse. Whip the mousse with a wire whisk to lighten and beat in about half the reserved fat, adding more as needed to achieve desired consistency. The finished mousse should have the consistency of stiff icing. Refrigerate the mousse until ready to assemble the foie gras, but be sure to allow enough time to bring it back to room temperature.

Terrine

Place the cleaned Grade A foie gras in a bowl and splash with half the Armagnac and 1 tablespoon of the truffle oil. Season with salt and pepper, cover, and let marinate, refrigerated, for 6 hours. Remove from the refrigerator and let sit at room temperature for 20 minutes. Pack the marinated liver into the bottom of the ceramic terrine and cover with plastic wrap. Preheat the oven to 210 degrees. Fill a roasting pan halfway with simmering water and set the terrine in the warm bath. Place in the oven and bake for 20 minutes. Remove the terrine from the water bath, place the block of wood and weight on top of the liver, and let cool for 20 minutes. Set in the refrigerator for 6 hours. The fat will rise to the top and congeal; it can be removed and saved for another use.

Preheat the oven to 350 degrees. To prepare the Grade B foie gras, cut the large lobe into four equal pieces and the smaller lobe into two. Gently pound so each piece is 2½ to 3 inches thick. Heat a sauté pan over high heat. Sear the foie gras on both sides, about 30 seconds per side, and finish in the preheated oven until cooked through, about 5 to 8 minutes. Cool. Slice the liver into pieces that will fit nicely into the terrine.

To assemble the finished terrine, unmold the grade A foie gras and trim it with a sharp knife so its thickness will occupy one-third of the final terrine. Clean the mold and replace the trimmed layer of foie gras terrine inside. Arrange the slices of seared Grade B foie gras on top to make an even layer, occupying the second third of the terrine. Spread the mousse of Grade C foie gras on top of the

Tuiles

2 teaspoons shallot, finely minced

2 tablespoons water

¼ pound unsalted butter, melted and cooled

½ tablespoon potato starch

2 tablespoons sugar

2 egg whites

Pinch salt

¾ cup Wondra flour

1 ounce Parmigiano-Reggiano cheese, finely grated

Date Purée

½ pound whole pitted dates

Madeira Glaze

1½ cups Madeira

Salad

2 tablespoons extra-virgin olive oil

4 tablespoons sherry vinegar

½ pound mixed baby greens

Sea salt

Black pepper, freshly ground

seared B foie gras to even out the terrine and fill the mold. Reserve any leftover mousse to smooth out the sides of the finished terrine after unmolding. Cover with plastic wrap and refrigerate until firm, about 6 hours. Unmold by inserting an offset spatula around the circumference of the terrine. Invert onto a plate. Smooth out the sides with the reserved mousse. Cover with plastic wrap and refrigerate until ready to serve.

Tuiles

In a small saucepan, combine the shallot with the water and butter. Bring to a simmer and cook until the shallots are tender, about 5 to 10 minutes. Combine the shallot mixture with the remaining ingredients in the bowl of a food processor and purée. The batter should be thick enough to spread. Preheat the oven to 350 degrees.

Line a sheet pan with parchment paper and spread a thin layer of batter over the parchment. Set in the preheated oven and bake for about 10 minutes, until set. The dough will give off a lot of butter as it bakes. Remove from the oven, cut into duck shapes using the cookie cutter, and return to the oven to continue baking for another 5 minutes, until golden brown. When cool, transfer to an airtight container.

Date Purée

Blanch the dates in boiling water for 5 minutes. Remove from the water and cool. Peel the skin off the dates and discard. Pass the date flesh through a fine mesh strainer to form a purée.

Madeira Glace

Pour the Madeira into a small, nonreactive saucepan. Set over medium-high heat and reduce to form a syrupy glaze, 35 to 40 minutes, or until about ¼ cup remains.

Salad

Just before service, in a small mixing bowl, combine the olive oil and sherry vinegar. Add the greens, season with salt and pepper, and toss until the greens are dressed.

Service and Garnish

Remove the terrine from the refrigerator. Using a thin, sharp knife that has been dipped in boiling water, slice the terrine into slices about ⅓-inch thick. Arrange the slices on chilled serving plates. Arrange the dressed greens around the terrine and drizzle the Madeira glaze on the plate. Using a teaspoon, form a mound of the date purée on the plate and stand one of the duck-shaped tuiles in it. Sprinkle the plate lightly with coarse sea salt and cracked white pepper. Serve with freshly toasted brioche.

Garnish

Coarse sea salt
White peppercorns, cracked
Toasted brioche

Special Equipment

1 ceramic terrine with 1½-quart
    capacity
Block of wood, wrapped in plastic
    wrap or foil, to fit terrine
1-pound weight
Resealable plastic bag
Vegetable mill, fine mesh strainer,
    or tamis
Parchment paper
Duck-shaped cookie cutter

Wine Recommendation

Far Niente Dolce or another late-harvest wine from California.

Apple Terrine

4 ounces foie gras (in one piece),
    cleaned for low-heat cooking
    (see page 93)

½ teaspoon salt

⅛ teaspoon saltpeter

Pinch white pepper

Pinch sugar

Pinch nutmeg

1 large apple (see Chef Notes)

Blackberry Sauce

½ cup plus 1 tablespoon sugar

½ cup rendered foie gras fat, melted
    and strained

½ cup balsamic vinegar

½ pint blackberries

Apple Charlotte

6 slices brioche, crusts removed and
    cut into ½-inch strips of equal
    length, plus four 1¼-inch rounds

5 Granny Smith apples, peeled, cored,
    and diced

½ pound butter, softened

1 teaspoon cinnamon

1 tablespoon sugar

½ teaspoon clove

Rendered foie gras fat to taste

Garnish

1 Granny Smith apple, cut into fine
    julienne

½ pint fresh blackberries

1 bunch upland cress (see Chef Notes)

Special Equipment

Melon baller

4 ring molds, 2½ inches in diameter

Wine Recommendation

Kent Rassmussen Late-Harvest
Sauvignon Blanc 1993 (Napa), or
another late-harvest wine from
California.

Apple Terrine of Foie Gras with Apple Brioche Charlotte, Fresh Blackberry Sauce, and Upland Cress

Although Michael Mina is known for his inventive fish and seafood preparations, his San Francisco restaurant actually serves more foie gras than almost any other establishment in the country. Michael's background as a pastry chef influenced the creation of this particular dish, a play on a traditional apple charlotte. The foie gras is served chilled alongside a charlotte of warm apples, creating an interesting composition of contrasting temperatures.

Apple Terrine

To increase the surface area of the foie gras, gently flatten it by applying pressure with your hand. Combine the salt, saltpeter, pepper, sugar, and nutmeg, and coat the foie gras with this mixture to cure. Wrap in plastic and refrigerate for 12 hours.

Preheat the oven to 325 degrees. With an even slice, cut off the top of the apple, about ¼ inch from the crown, and carefully remove the core without breaking through the bottom. Using a melon baller, hollow out a deep, wide cavity inside the apple. Fill the apple with the cured foie gras, packing firmly, and replace the apple top. Place the apple in a baking pan filled with ¼ inch of water, cover with foil, and bake for 10 to 15 minutes, until a knife pierced into the center comes out warm. Carefully remove the apple from the water, wrap in plastic, and chill for several hours.

Blackberry Sauce

In a saucepan set over a low flame, combine the sugar and foie gras fat, stirring to form a thick mixture. Continue heating and stirring until most of the sugar is absorbed. Whisk in the balsamic vinegar and bring to a boil, watching closely because this mixture has a tendency to boil over. Remove from the heat. Mash the blackberries into the sauce by pressing them with the back of a spoon against the side of the pot. Strain and set aside.

Apple Charlotte

Preheat the oven to 300 degrees. Lay the strips and rounds of brioche on a sheet pan and toast until lightly colored. In a baking dish, combine the apples, butter, cinnamon, sugar, and clove, and cook until tender, 30 to 40 minutes. Purée the apple mixture in a food processor, adding foie gras fat to taste.

Service and Garnish

Line the insides of the ring molds with the strips of toasted brioche arranged vertically as shown in the photograph. Place a disk of brioche on the bottom of each. Spoon the apple purée into the charlotte molds, using the purée to hold the strips of brioche together, and gently warm in the oven. Unmold the charlottes on each of four plates. Top with some julienned apple. Gently heat the blackberry sauce and add the fresh blackberries. Spoon the sauce around the charlotte. Slice the apple terrine into quarters and place one slice on each plate. Garnish with upland cress or other baby greens.

Chef Notes

Use a tart, firm apple such as Golden Delicious, Gala, Braeburn, or similar variety. Upland cress is a wild, peppery relative of watercress that grows in California. If unavailable, substitute any similar cress.

Foie Gras in Pumpkins with Banyuls

A terrine of foie gras is named for the ceramic or enameled cast iron vessel in which the liver is cooked. For this autumnal variation, Gascony native Ariane Daguin substitutes a large pumpkin for the traditional mold—a technique first perfected by her father, Gascon chef André Daguin. While providing a dramatic presentation, the effect of the pumpkin is to seal in the natural flavors of the liver as it cooks. Once the terrine is consumed, the pumpkin flesh can be transformed into a delicious soup redolent of the flavor of foie gras. Ariane also uses a hollowed-out miniature pumpkin to enhance the presentation of a classic foie gras mousse.

Terrine

1 foie gras, about 1½ pounds, cleaned
    for low-heat cooking (see page 93),
    at room temperature
Salt
White pepper, freshly ground
1 pumpkin, 3 to 4 pounds
½ cup Banyuls (see Chef Notes)

Mousse

4 baby pumpkins
Salt
White pepper, freshly ground
4 tablespoons Banyuls (see Chef Notes)
2 cups foie gras mousse, about 1 pound
    (see page 114)

Wine Recommendation

Domaine de la Rectorie Cuvée
Elisabeth Banyuls (NV), or another
fortified red Banyuls or tawny port.

Terrine

Preheat the oven to 250 degrees. Generously season the foie gras with salt and pepper. Cut off the pumpkin top and remove the seeds and membrane from the cavity, being careful not to pierce the skin. Pour the Banyuls into the cavity and sprinkle with salt and pepper. Pack the foie gras into the pumpkin, placing the large lobe underneath the small lobe. Place the top back on the pumpkin and wrap in aluminum foil. Place the pumpkin on a sheet pan lined with aluminum foil. Bake for 1½ to 2 hours or until the internal temperature of the liver reaches 115 degrees. Remove the pumpkin from the oven and cool to room temperature. Refrigerate for 12 hours before serving. Unwrap the pumpkin and remove the top. Trim the sides of the pumpkin until they are even with the top of the liver. If desired, also remove some of the fat that has coagulated on top to expose the foie gras.

Mousse

Preheat the oven to 350 degrees. Cut off the pumpkin tops and hollow out the insides, being careful not pierce the skin. Season each with salt, pepper, and a tablespoon of Banyuls. Cover and bake 30 to 40 minutes, until tender but firm. Pour out the wine and cool. Fill the cooked pumpkin shells with mousse and cover with the tops. Refrigerate at least 1 hour.

Service

Remove both dishes from the refrigerator 1 hour before service.

Chef Notes

Banyuls is a sweet red wine from the Languedoc-Roussillon region of France.

Torchon

1 whole foie gras, about 1½ pounds, cleaned for low-heat cooking (see page 93), at room temperature

Coarse salt

1 tablespoon black pepper, freshly cracked

1 bottle full-bodied dry red wine

4 shallots, chopped

1 bay leaf

1 sprig thyme

Poached Pear

2 cups dry red wine

1¼ cups sugar

One 2-inch strip lemon zest

Juice of ½ fresh lemon

1 bay leaf

1 clove

5 firm, ripe Bosc pears, peeled and cored, but left whole with stems

Pear-Shallot Jam

1 tablespoon butter

½ cup finely diced shallots

½ cup diced Bosc pear

½ cup red wine

2 tablespoons sugar

Garnish

Black pepper, freshly cracked

Sel gris

Assorted baby greens

Special Equipment

Ceramic terrine

Butcher's twine

Wine Recommendation

Veuve Clicquot Brut Rosé Réserve 1988 (Champagne), or another dry sparkling rosé.

Red Wine–Poached Torchon of Foie Gras with Poached Bosc Pear and Pear-Shallot Jam

Shortly after Israel was founded in 1948, foie gras production evolved as part of a national agricultural initiative. Today foie gras has become an important cottage industry, with over 300 producers exporting some of the highest-quality foie gras in the world. Israel Aharoni, one of the leading chefs in the country, has several foie gras offerings on his menu. To prepare this variation of a classic torchon, Aharoni alters the traditional technique slightly. Instead of wrapping the marinated foie gras in a towel, shaping it like a sausage, and poaching it, he heats the marinade and pours it over the liver to gently cook it. When the liver has cooled, Aharoni forms the torchon into the classic shape.

Torchon

Season the foie gras with salt and pepper. Place the seasoned lobes in the terrine, without pressing them down, and set aside. In a saucepan, combine the wine, shallots, bay leaf, thyme, and cracked pepper. Bring the mixture to a boil and cook for 15 minutes. Remove the mixture from the heat and strain. Bring the mixture back to a boil and immediately pour over the foie gras. Let stand for one hour at room temperature, then refrigerate overnight.

Bring the foie gras back to room temperature. Spread a clean towel on a work surface and place the lobes side by side along one edge of the towel. Roll the foie gras in the towel, tightening as you go to create an even log, 2 to 2½ inches in diameter. Tie the towel securely with butcher's twine and refrigerate the torchon overnight.

Poached Pear

In a saucepan large enough to hold the 5 pears, combine all of the ingredients except the pears. Set over medium-high heat and bring to a boil. Reduce the heat and simmer for 5 minutes, or until the sugar has dissolved. Add the pears to the simmering liquid and poach for 10 to 15 minutes until the pears are tender. Be careful not to overcook; the pears should retain their shape. Remove

the saucepan from the heat and cool to room temperature. Lift the pears out of the cooking liquid with a slotted spoon and place in a bowl or storage container. Strain the liquid into a clean saucepan. Set over medium-high heat, bring to a boil, and reduce by half, about 15 minutes. Bring this syrup back to room temperature, pour over the poached pears, cover, and refrigerate until service.

Pear-Shallot Jam

Melt the butter in a saucepan. Add the shallots and sauté until they are translucent. Add the pear and sauté until translucent. Add the wine and sugar and cook until the mixture has a jamlike, syrupy consistency.

Service and Garnish

Remove the torchon from the refrigerator 15 minutes before service. Unwrap the torchon, and using a sharp knife dipped in hot water, slice the liver into 20 ½-inch slices. On chilled serving plates, arrange two slices of the liver. Top with a pinch of cracked black peppercorns and sel gris. Remove the pears from their poaching liquid. Cut the pears in half, thinly slice each half without cutting all the way through, and fan out on the serving plates. Garnish with assorted baby greens and quenelles of pear-shallot jam. Dab the plates with some of the poaching liquid.

Foie Gras Terrine with Savoy Cabbage and Winter Fruits

Prunes macerated in Cognac and simmered chestnuts situate this terrine by legendary French chef Roger Vergé in the late fall, high season both for foie gras production and consumption. The visual effect of layering the pieces of foie gras with the winter fruits gives an attractive mosaic pattern to the slices of terrine. Other ingredients—cooked mushrooms, fresh figs, dried apricots—can be layered in the same way to produce different flavors and visual effects.

YIELD: 6 APPETIZER SERVINGS

Terrine

1 whole foie gras, about 1½ pounds, cleaned for low-heat cooking (see page 93)

Coarse salt

Black pepper, freshly ground

3 tablespoons port

1 pinch sel rose

½ pound whole, unpeeled chestnuts, or 3½ ounces peeled

1 cup water

1 cup milk

1 rib celery, chopped

1 tablespoon butter

Pinch sugar

3½ ounces prunes, pitted and halved

3 tablespoons Cognac

8 green Savoy cabbage leaves

Special Equipment

Ceramic terrine mold with a 2- to 3-cup capacity

Block of wood cut to fit the terrine

Wine Recommendation

Château Léoville-Barton St.-Julien 1995 (Bordeaux), or another medium to full-bodied, earthy red wine.

Terrine

Season the foie gras with salt and pepper. Combine the port and sel rose, and marinate the foie gras in this mixture for 12 hours. Score the chestnuts, blanch in boiling water for 2 to 3 minutes, and peel. In a saucepan heat the water and milk. Add the chestnuts, celery, butter, sugar, and a pinch of salt. Cook for 30 to 35 minutes, until the chestnuts are tender. Remove the chestnuts from the cooking liquid and break them into large pieces. Soak the prunes in Cognac for 1 hour. Remove the prunes from the Cognac and combine with the chestnuts. Remove the ribs from the cabbage leaves. Bring a pot of salted water to a boil and cook the cabbage leaves for 2 minutes. Remove from the water and carefully pat dry. Preheat the oven to 220 degrees. Remove the foie gras from the marinade and cut into 3 large pieces to fit the terrine. Line the terrine with 6 of the blanched cabbage leaves. Place one piece of foie gras into the terrine and pack down.

Cover with half the prunes and chestnuts. Place another piece of foie gras into the terrine and cover with the remaining fruit. Top with the last piece of foie gras and cover the whole terrine with the remaining cabbage leaves so that the entire terrine is wrapped in the cabbage. Place the terrine in a water bath and cook for 45 to 55 minutes, until the internal temperature of the terrine reaches 125 degrees. Remove the terrine from the oven and let rest at room temperature for 1 hour. Cover the terrine with plastic wrap, place the weight on top, and refrigerate for two to three days before serving.

Service

To serve, remove the weight from the terrine and scrape off any fat that has coagulated at the surface. Run a thin knife along the sides of the terrine to loosen and invert onto a cutting board. Slice the terrine into ½-inch thick slices and serve chilled.

Lemongrass-Infused Thai Spiced Terrine

Terrine

1 whole foie gras, about 1½ pounds, cleaned for low-heat cooking (see page 93)

1 tablespoon galangal, minced

2 tablespoons lemongrass, sliced

2 tablespoons cilantro, minced

½ teaspoon salt

½ teaspoon pepper

Chili Sauce

1 red bell pepper, seeded and minced

1 red hot pepper, seeded and minced

2 garlic cloves, minced

1 shallot, minced

1 cup water

¼ cup sugar

1 teaspoon salt

2 tablespoons Thai fish sauce

Sticky Rice

1 cup Thai sticky rice

1 cup coconut milk

½ teaspoon salt

1 tablespoon sugar

½ teaspoon turmeric powder

Garnish

1 seedless cucumber, cut into 36 thin rounds

¼ cup mint leaves, 6 sprigs left whole, the rest cut into thin strips

12 hot peppers

6 fresh cilantro sprigs

Special Equipment

12 ramekins, 2½ inches in diameter

1 cardboard circle, 2½ inches in diameter, cut to fit inside the ramekins

3-inch ring mold, lightly greased

Wine Recommendation

Le Gallais Riesling Auslese Gold Cap Mosel-Saar-Ruwer Wiltinger Braune Kupp 1996 (Germany), or another sweet, crisp white wine.

The fragrant spices and complex flavors of Thai cuisine are surprisingly well-suited to foie gras. Lemongrass, kaffir lime, galangal, and chilies provide the foil for the richness of these individual terrines, prepared by Arun Sampathavivat. Coconut sticky rice completes the Thai allusion.

Terrine

Place the foie gras in a medium bowl, coat evenly with the remaining ingredients, cover and marinate, refrigerated, for at least 12 hours. Preheat the oven to 225 degrees. Cut the foie gras into the largest pieces that will fit into the ramekins. Divide the foie gras among 6 of the ramekins. Wrap the cardboard circle in plastic and place it on top of one of the foie gras-filled ramekins. Using your fingertips, press down on the cardboard circle to compact the foie gras into the ramekin. Repeat with the remaining 5 ramekins. Place the ramekins in a baking pan and add enough warm water to come up two-thirds of the sides of the ramekins. Place the pan in the preheated oven and bake for 20 to 25 minutes, until the foie gras reaches an internal temperature of between 125 and 130 degrees.

Remove the ramekins from the water bath and let cool slightly. Wrap the bottoms and sides of the remaining empty ramekins in plastic wrap, fill with water, beans, or other weighty matter, and set on top of the terrines to weigh them down. Refrigerate the weighted terrines for at least 3 hours.

Chili Sauce

Combine all ingredients in a saucepan set over medium-high heat. Bring the mixture to a boil, reduce the heat slightly, and continue cooking until the mixture is reduced by two-thirds, about 15 minutes.

Sticky Rice

Rinse the rice in cold water several times until the water runs clear without any starchy residue. Place the rice in a bowl, add enough water to cover, and let soak for at least 4 hours. Combine the soaked rice with the remaining ingredients in a saucepan. Bring to a boil, reduce the temperature to a gentle simmer, and cook until the rice is sticky and tender, about 25 additional minutes. Keep warm until service.

Service and Garnish

Place the 3-inch ring mold in the center of one of six serving plates. Fill with sticky rice, making sure the rice is pressed down, and unmold the rice onto the plate. Arrange six cucumber slices in a circle over the bed of rice, with the cucumber slightly hanging over the edges of the rice. Unmold a foie gras terrine on top of the cucumbers. Drizzle chili sauce around the bottom of the rice mold, and sprinkle the chopped mint around the plate. Repeat for five more serving plates. Place two hot peppers, a sprig of cilantro and a sprig of mint on top of each foie gras terrine.

Caramelized Torte of Foie Gras, Smoked Eel, Spring Onion, and Apple

The foie gras in this elegant, multilayered torte by Spanish chef Martin Berasategui is actually cooked before it is sliced paper thin and layered with smoked eel and apples. The caramelization of the top layer of apples adds a finishing hint of sweetness—a gentle complement to the smokey flavor of the eel and the tang of the apples.

YIELD: 8 APPETIZER SERVINGS

Torte
1 whole foie gras, about 1½ pounds
1 quart chicken stock
1 pound scallions
½ pound unsalted butter
2 smoked eels, about 1½ pounds
2 Granny Smith apples, peeled and
    cored

Spring Onion Sauce
1 pound scallions
½ pound unsalted butter
Coarse salt

Garnish
3 tablespoons sugar

Special Equipment
Electric slicer or mandoline
Loaf pan
Blow torch
Block of wood
1-pound weight

Wine Recommendation
Bodegas Vega Sicilia Ribera del Duero Unico Gran Riserve 1986 (Spain), or another mature Spanish red wine with complex tannins.

Torte
Place the foie gras and the chicken stock in a medium saucepan. If necessary, add more stock to cover the liver. Bring to a gentle simmer and let cook for 6 minutes, making sure the stock does not come to a boil. Turn the foie gras over and simmer for another 6 minutes. Drain the foie gras and refrigerate for several hours until very cold.

Cut the white part of the scallions into very fine julienne. Melt the butter in a saucepan set over low heat, and add the scallions and enough water to cover. Cook until the scallions are very soft, about 30 minutes. Strain the scallions well and wring in a cloth to remove any excess moisture. Keep refrigerated.

Carefully remove the skin and bones from the eels and cut them lengthwise into fine strips. Keep refrigerated.

Using a slicer or mandoline, slice the apples very thin. Reassemble the apple slices into their original shapes and wrap in plastic wrap to prevent oxidation. Keep refrigerated.

Remove the foie gras from the refrigerator and, using a slicer, slice into very thin slices. Carefully wrap the slices in plastic wrap and refrigerate.

To assemble the torte, arrange a layer of apples on the bottom of the loaf pan, making sure to cover the bottom with one thin, even layer. Top with a layer of foie gras slices. Put another layer of apples over the foie gras and top the apples with a layer of smoked eel. Place another layer of apples over the eel and top with a layer of scallions. Continue to layer the ingredients in this order, making sure that apples are between all of the other ingredients and that they form the top layer. When the torte is complete you should have 18 to 20 layers. Cover the torte with plastic wrap and using the block of wood, evenly weight the top to press and compact the torte. Refrigerate for several hours.

Spring Onion Sauce
Chop the white part of the scallions, discard the greens. Melt the butter in a saucepan, add the scallions and just enough water to cover. Poach the scallions until very soft, about 30 minutes. Add salt to taste. Purée the scallion mixture in a food processor and strain.

Service and Garnish
Flip the loaf pan upside-down to unmold the torte, and cut into eight 2-inch-squares. Place one piece on each of eight serving plates and garnish with a line of sauce. Sprinkle the top layer with the sugar and, using a blow torch, caramelize until golden brown.

Sake-Marinated Torchon of Foie Gras in Dashi with Sea Urchin and Fresh Wasabe

Japanese cuisine is as much about texture and tradition as it is about taste. This inspired creation by Hiro Sone combines many traditional elements of Japanese cooking—dashi, uni (sea urchin), and wasabe—with foie gras. Foie gras is actually similar in taste and texture to the Japanese delicacy akimo, (monkfish liver). Although the combination of elements is innovative, the overall effect of this appetizer is thoroughly Japanese in character.

Dashi

2 ounces dried kombu seaweed

2½ quarts water

6 cups bonito flakes, about 1½ ounces

Torchon

1 whole foie gras, about 1½ pounds, cleaned as for low-heat cooking (see page 93), at room temperature

2 tablespoons sake

Coarse salt

Black pepper, freshly ground

Garnish

20 pieces fresh sea urchin

1 ounce fresh wasabe, finely grated

Special Equipment

Cheesecloth

Butcher's twine

10 martini glasses

Wine Recommendation

Chalone Chardonnay 1996 (California), or another smooth Chardonnay with balanced acidity.

Dashi

Break the kombu into large pieces and place in a large saucepan. Cover with the water, set over medium heat, and bring to a gentle simmer. Lift the kombu out with a slotted spoon and discard. Turn up the heat and bring the kombu broth to a boil. Add the bonito flakes and remove from the heat. Let steep for 1 minute. Strain through a fine chinois or a sieve lined with cheesecloth. Refrigerate until needed.

Torchon

Dampen a clean dish towel with cold water and lay it on the work surface. Arrange the cleaned foie gras along one end of the towel. Sprinkle the liver with the sake and season with salt and pepper. Tightly roll up the towel, shaping the foie gras into an even sausage about 2 inches in diameter. Twist the ends of the towel in opposite directions like a candy to compact and shape the liver. Securely tie the towel at both ends with butcher's twine. Wrap the twine along the length of the foie gras to hold its shape. Refrigerate overnight.

The following day bring 2 quarts of the dashi to a gentle simmer (about 180 degrees) in a saucepan large enough to hold the foie gras torchon. Submerge the torchon in the simmering dashi and cook for 10 minutes, without allowing the broth to come to a boil. Immediately remove the torchon from the broth and chill.

Service and Garnish

Allow the torchon to sit at room temperature for 15 minutes. Untie and unwrap the torchon, and, with a sharp knife dipped in hot water, slice into rounds approximately ½-inch thick. Heat the remaining dashi to a gentle simmer. Arrange slices of the foie gras in martini glasses. Carefully pour the warm dashi around the slices of foie gras. Top with pieces of sea urchin and garnish with freshly grated wasabe.

Foie Gras and Chicken in Aspic

The effect of wrapping the foie gras in chicken to poach it in Eberhard Mueller's elegant terrine simulates the preparation of a classic torchon. Eberhard encases this foie gras and chicken roll in a flavorful aspic, attractively decorated with vegetables, to produce this elegant chilled appetizer.

YIELD: 10 APPETIZER SERVINGS

Chicken Stock

2 medium onions, cut in half

6 pounds chicken bones

2 medium carrots

2 celery stalks, diced

2 medium leeks, julienned

Bouquet garni

20 black peppercorns

Coarse salt

Black pepper, freshly ground

Foie Gras and Chicken Roll

1 chicken, about 3 pounds

Coarse salt

Black pepper, freshly ground

1 whole foie gras, about 1½ pounds, cleaned for low-heat cooking (see page 93)

1 bunch chervil

1 bunch tarragon

1 gallon chicken stock (from above)

3 large carrots

2 bulbs celeriac

10 pieces asparagus

1 head Savoy cabbage

Chicken Stock

Set a heavy cast iron pan over high heat. Place the onions cut side down in the pan and sear until darkly browned. Rinse the chicken bones in cold water. Bring 1 gallon of water to a boil. Add the chicken bones and bring back to a boil. Cook for 2 minutes. Drain and rinse the chicken bones again under cold water. Refill the stockpot with 1½ gallons of cold water and add the chicken bones. Bring to a slow boil and skim frequently. Simmer for 1½ hours, then add the vegetables (including the browned onions), bouquet garni, and peppercorns. Simmer for another 1½ hours. Skim off whatever fat or scum rises to the top during cooking. Remove the bones and vegetables and discard. Strain the stock through several layers of fine cheesecloth. Adjust the seasoning with salt and pepper.

Foie Gras and Chicken Roll

Cut the chicken into pieces, removing the wings and reserving them for another use. Remove the legs and thighs and reserve. Remove the two breast halves from the carcass. Skin and flatten the breasts to a ¼-inch thickness between two layers of plastic wrap. You should obtain two chicken scallops, approximately 4 by 6 inches. Season with salt and pepper.

Season the lobes of foie gras with salt and pepper. Reassemble the lobes and trim slightly, squaring off the edges so the liver will fit into the terrine with the other ingredients. Wrap the two chicken scallops around the foie gras, place the roll into a layer of cheesecloth, and tie the ends with butcher's twine. In a saucepan large enough to hold the chicken stock and the chicken and foie gras roll, bring the stock to a boil. Season with salt and pepper and add the chervil and tarragon. Place the roll into the boiling stock and reduce heat. Simmer 20 to 30 minutes until the roll is cooked through and the internal temperature of the chicken reaches 160 degrees (the foie gras temperature should not exceed 125 degrees; if it does, remove it from the stock). Remove the roll from the stock; chill the roll and the stock separately.

Peel and cut the carrots and the celeriac into long ¼-inch batônnets, reserving the trimmings for the consommé. Cook in boiling salted water until very tender, refresh in ice water, and drain well. Trim and peel the asparagus and cook in boiling salted water until very tender, refresh in ice water, and drain. Remove the outer leaves of the cabbage. Remove 6 to 8 tender leaves—enough to wrap the foie gras and chicken roll—blanch them in boiling salted water, and refresh in ice water. Dry the leaves well on paper towels.

Remove the strings from the chicken and foie gras roll and wrap tightly in the blanched cabbage leaves, pressing the leaves with a kitchen towel to ensure that they stay in place.

Aspic

Meat from 2 chicken legs and thighs
  (from above)
Vegetable trimmings (from above)
1 small onion, peeled and quartered
1 small leek, trimmed, sliced, and
  washed
4 egg whites
2 to 3 ice cubes
15 black peppercorns
Chicken stock (from above)
10 to 15 leaves gelatin

Aspic

To clarify the consommé for the aspic, use a "raft." Place the reserved boned leg and thigh meat from the chicken along with the carrot and celeriac trimmings, onion, leek, and egg whites into the bowl of a food processor. Run the food processor for 2 to 3 minutes, keeping the mixture chilled by periodically adding an ice cube. Add the peppercorns and a pinch of salt. Remove the stock from the refrigerator and skim off any fat that has coagulated on the surface. Transfer the stock to a large saucepan or small stock pot. Mix the ground raft mixture into the chicken stock and set the pot over medium heat. Bring the stock slowly to a soft boil. Stir often so that the egg whites do not settle on the bottom of the pan and burn. The proteins in the mixture will start to coagulate and float in one big cake on top of the stock. Simmer for 30 minutes, carefully pull back the "raft," and strain the consommé through several layers of cheesecloth into a clean pan.

Bring the consommé back to a slow boil and reduce by one-fourth. You should now have 2¼ quarts of consommé. Remove from the heat. Soften 10 gelatin leaves in cold water, squeeze dry, and add to the consommé. Check the seasoning—the mixture needs to be heavily seasoned or the aspic will be bland when chilled. Check the firmness of the aspic by pouring a small amount onto a chilled plate. Refrigerate for 5 to 10 minutes. The aspic should be quite firm. If not, add a few more leaves of gelatin to the consommé, repeating the above procedure. Chill the aspic to just below room temperature.

Assembling the Terrine

To assemble the terrine, make sure the chicken aspic is of the proper consistency—

pourable, yet able to stick to the mold and vegetables. Adjust the consistency by slightly warming or cooling the aspic as needed.

Ladle enough aspic into the terrine to cover the bottom with about ¼ inch, swirling so that it sticks to the mold. Pour the excess aspic off into a separate container. Refrigerate the terrine for a few minutes so that the first layer of aspic can solidify. Pour 2 or 3 cups of aspic into a separate container and submerge the carrot and celeriac sticks. Remove the terrine from the refrigerator and begin lining the terrine by alternating carrot and celeriac sticks on the bottom and sides. Move the terrine in and out of the refrigerator as the consistency of the aspic changes. When the sides and bottom are lined with the vegetables, pour ⅛ inch of aspic into the terrine and let it set in the refrigerator. Place some of the asparagus in the mold, pour more aspic in, and let it set. Place the chicken

and foie gras roll in the center of the terrine. Fill with more aspic to the top of the roll and let set again. Place more asparagus in the terrine and top with more aspic. Finish with a last layer of carrots and celeriac, and pour the remaining aspic to the top of the terrine. Refrigerate for at least 24 hours.

Service

To unmold the terrine, run warm water over the outside and bottom of the mold. Place a cutting board over the top of the terrine and invert the terrine onto the cutting board. To slice the terrine, run hot water over a long, thin, sharp knife and carefully cut ½-inch slices.

Chef Notes

All the vegetables need to be very tender so that the finished terrine will be easy to slice.

Special Equipment

Cheesecloth

Butcher's twine

1 terrine mold, chilled in the refrigerator

Wine Recommendation

Schloss Johannisberg Riesling Auslese Rheingau 1996 (Germany), or another medium-bodied white wine with a hint of sweetness.

Ballotine

1 whole foie gras, about 1½ pounds,
   cleaned for low-heat cooking
   (see page 93)

2 teaspoons coarse salt

Pinch sel rose

Black pepper, freshly ground

3 tablespoons Port

1 teaspoon Cognac or Armagnac

1 teaspoon sugar

Pinch nutmeg

Duck Skin

1 cup sugar

1 cup honey

1 cup cider vinegar

1 gallon water

3 tablespoons cornstarch

2 duck skins (see Chef Notes)

Pickled Lemons

2 quarts water

1 teaspoon coriander seeds

1 teaspoon white peppercorns

4 whole allspice berries

1 cinnamon stick, 1-inch long

¼ teaspoon ground turmeric

4 bay leaves

Pinch red pepper flakes

2 ounces coarse salt

1 teaspoon sugar

10 lemons

Tangerine Glaze

2 cups orange juice, freshly squeezed

1 cup rice wine vinegar

½ cup mirin

3 stalks lemongrass, about 5 ounces,
   coarsely chopped

1 piece ginger, 4-inches long, peeled
   and chopped

1 ounce dried tangerine peels

¼ cup honey

Pinch salt

Ballotine of Foie Gras with Pan-Seared Quail, Crisped Duck Skin, Mirin Aspic, and Tangerine Glaze

The sources of inspiration for this complex dish by Gray Kunz are vast and varied—the crisped duck-skin garnish evokes the waferlike skin of Peking duck; the tangerine glaze and mirin aspic enhance the allusion to China; the preserved lemons suggest the Magreb; the Sauternes aspic tastes of France's foie gras country. The result of these seemingly disparate elements is the sort of exhilarating gastronomic harmony that has become Gray's signature.

Ballotine

In a medium bowl, season the cleaned pieces of foie gras with salt and combine with the remaining ingredients. Cover and marinate, refrigerated, for 12 hours, turning every 3 to 4 hours to evenly distribute the marinade. Bring to room temperature. Pat the livers dry with paper towel and place into an oval terrine—arranging the large lobe pieces cut side up on the bottom, filling in the gaps with smaller pieces, and then placing the smaller lobe pieces cut side down on top. Press the foie gras into the terrine with fingertips, and refrigerate for at least 1 hour before cooking.

Preheat the oven to 180 degrees. Place the terrine in a roasting pan and fill with 110-degree water up to about ¾ inch below the top of the terrine to form a bain marie. Set in the preheated oven and cook for 35 to 45 minutes, until the liver reaches an internal temperature of between 125 and 130 degrees. Remove the terrine from the oven and allow it to sit at room temperature for 3 hours. After the terrine has cooled to room temperature, cover it with plastic wrap and weigh it down with a piece of wood, collecting any excess fat that spills over. Clarify this fat by passing through a cheesecloth-lined chinois, and use later to reseal the terrine for storage. Refrigerate until service.

Duck Skin

In a large saucepan, combine all ingredients except the cornstarch and duck skin. Set over medium-high heat and bring to a boil. Dilute the cornstarch in enough cold water to form a mixture with the consistency of heavy cream. Add this mixture to the pan. Boil for 1 minute more, stirring out any lumps. Remove from the heat and cool. Transfer to a hotel pan.

Spread the duck skins out flat and, using a trussing needle and some butcher's twine, sew the skin flat and taut onto the roasting racks. Fill the hotel pans with about 1 inch of water and set over medium-low flames to simmer. Set the racks, with the skin attached, on top of the hotel pans, cover with aluminum foil, and steam the skins for 2½ minutes. Let the skin cool, then dunk into the marinade mixture twice, for about 10 seconds each time. Discard the marinade and let the duck skin dry out in the refrigerator, on the racks, standing up, for two days.

Preheat the oven to 200 degrees. Roast the duck skin on the racks for about 1 hour, checking occasionally, until there is no more fat dripping and the skins begin to look glossy and dry. Cool on the racks. Using sharp scissors cut the skin off the racks and cut into sixteen 4-inch triangles. Reserve.

Garnish

½ cup vegetable oil

1 piece ginger, 4-inches long, cut into
    julienne

2 tablespoons clarified butter

1 slice brioche, ¼-inch thick, cut into
    8 lengths of 2-inches

1 tablespoon pink peppercorns

8 celery leaves

Mirin Aspic

½ cup chicken consommé

2 sheets gelatin, softened for 3 minutes
    in cool water

3 tablespoons mirin

3 tablespoons Sauternes

5 tablespoons rice wine vinegar

1 piece lemongrass, 4-inches long,
    coarsely chopped

1 piece ginger, 2-inches long, peeled
    and coarsely chopped

1 piece orange zest, about 1-inch long

Tangerine glaze (from above)

Fried ginger (from above)

Zest from 1 orange in long, thin
    strands

Sauternes Aspic

1 cup Sauternes

2 sheets gelatin, softened for 3 minutes
    in cool water

Fresh Fig Sauce

8 fresh figs, quartered

2 cups Sauternes

1 pound dried figs

2 tablespoons honey

2 tablespoons lemon juice

1 teaspoon ras el hanout

Coarse salt

Pickled Lemons

In a small stockpot, combine all ingredients and bring to a boil. Remove from the heat and allow the lemons to cool in the liquid. Store the lemons in the liquid, refrigerated, until needed. To use, julienne the outer rind only, discarding the interior.

Tangerine Glaze

In a large saucepan, combine all ingredients, set over medium-high heat, and reduce to the consistency of a glaze, about 1 hour. Set aside.

Garnish

In a medium sauté pan, heat the vegetable oil until hot. Fry the julienned ginger briefly in the oil, just until the pieces are a pale golden color and crispy. Drain on a paper towel and set aside.

In a small sauté pan, heat the clarified butter and fry the brioche croutons until they are crispy and lightly browned. Drain on a paper towel and set aside.

Place the pink peppercorns into a small sieve over a bowl and rub them around gently to remove the flaked skin. Set the skins aside, discarding the peppercorns.

Reserve the celery leaves until service.

Mirin Aspic

In a small saucepan, heat the consommé to a simmer (do not boil) and add the softened gelatin leaves. Add the mirin, Sauternes, and rice wine vinegar. Add the lemongrass, ginger, and piece of orange zest, and let steep for about 10 minutes to cool but not gel. Strain. In the bottom of eight very small bowls or ramekins, place a drop of the tangerine glaze,

and some strands of the fried ginger, reserving some for the final garnish, and orange zest. Spoon in about 2 tablespoons of the aspic and refrigerate.

Sauternes Aspic

Place half of the Sauternes in a small saucepan and set over a low flame. Add the gelatin and stir until dissolved. Add the remaining Sauternes. Pour 2 tablespoons of this aspic into the center of each serving plate. Chill the plates until service.

Fresh Fig Sauce

In a medium saucepan, combine the fresh figs, Sauternes, and dried figs. Bring this mixture to a simmer and let cook for about 15 minutes, until the dried figs are soft but still hold their shape. Strain, reserving the figs for use in the salpicon recipe. Reduce the liquid until it coats the back of a spoon, about 5 to 6 minutes. Cool in a bowl over ice, and, when cold, add the honey and lemon juice. Finish by adding the ras el hanout. Adjust the seasoning to taste with salt and pepper.

Salpicon

In a small sauté pan set over a medium flame, heat the butter. Add the almonds and toast until they turn light brown. Strain, chop, and set aside for the quail topping. Reserve the butter in the saucepan. Add the confit, lentils, figs, and duck stock and heat through. Adjust the seasoning with salt and pepper and set aside to cool. Chop coarsely. Reserve the chives until service.

Quail Breast

In a small sauté pan, heat the vegetable oil until hot. Season the quail breast with salt and pepper and sauté, skin side down, until nicely browned. Flip, lower the heat, and cook until done, 3 to 4 minutes. Set aside in a warm place until service. Reserve the pan to prepare the topping. In another sauté pan, heat the corn oil and fry the lentils until lightly colored. Drain on a paper towel and reserve. Set the quail pan over medium-high heat and add the chopped almonds, fried lentils, pickled lemon, and chives. Season to taste with salt and pepper. Bind with 2 or 3 tablespoons of the fig sauce and beat in the butter. Keep warm until service.

Service and Garnish

Garnish the ramekins of mirin aspic with the celery leaves, additional fried ginger, the pink peppercorn skins, and the fried brioche. Unmold the foie gras ballotine from the terrine and cut the oval into two semicircular pieces. Slice on the bias to produce a total of 16 slices. Reheat the salpicon and toss in the chives.

Remove the plates with the Sauternes aspic from the refrigerator and let them come to room temperature. Place a few drops of the tangerine glaze on top of the aspic. Place two upright slices each of the ballotine and the duck skin, alternating the two. Spoon some of the salpicon alongside the foie gras and lay the quail breast on top, skin side up. Carefully spoon some of the topping onto the quail breast. Serve with a ramekin of mirin aspic on the side.

Chef Notes

When removing the duck skin from the whole duck, it is important to keep it as intact as possible. To do so, cut a line down the back and gently work your hand under the skin to loosen it from the flesh. The components of this dish can be made separately in advance and stored until service.

Salpicon

4 tablespoons butter
2 ounces blanched almonds
3 ounces quail and duck leg meat confit (see page 276)
1 ounce cooked pink lentils
2 tablespoons diced cooked fig, reserved from above
⅓ cup duck stock
Coarse salt
Black pepper, freshly ground
Pinch chopped chives

Quail Breast

Vegetable oil for sautéing
8 quail breasts, boned
Coarse salt
Black pepper, freshly ground
4 ounces corn oil
1½ ounces pink lentils, blanched
2 ounces almonds, reserved from above
¼ pickled lemon (from above), rind only, cut into julienne
Pinch chopped chives
5 tablespoons fig sauce (from above)
1 tablespoon cold butter

Special Equipment

16-inch oval ceramic terrine fitted with a block of wood
Trussing needle
Butcher's twine
2 large roasting racks

Wine Recommendation

Robert Chevillon Nuits-St.-George Le Vaucrains 1991 (Burgundy), or another spicy, full-bodied Pinot Noir.

Terrine of Whole Roasted Foie Gras, Squab, Sweetbreads, and Wild Mushrooms with Wild Mushroom Emulsion

Dramatic, towering terrines are a signature of Jean-Louis Palladin's interpretive style of cooking. He hails from the heart of France's foie gras country, but his cooking in America spans the globe. Instead of a simple traditional terrine of foie gras, Jean-Louis offers this elegant construction, for which the individual components—foie gras, squab, sweetbreads, and wild mushrooms—are cooked separately before being "suspended in space" with the aid of a flavorful aspic. The result is an intriguing combination of flavors and textures.

YIELD: 15 TO 18 APPETIZER SERVINGS

Terrine

4 pounds sweetbreads

2 quarts beef consommé
(see page 324)

8 leaves gelatin

2 whole foie gras, about 1½ pounds each

Coarse salt

Black pepper, freshly ground

¼ cup rendered duck fat
(see page 108)

5 cloves garlic, finely chopped

4 pounds wild mushrooms, such as a mixture of porcini, chanterelles, shiitake, and black trumpets

1 sprig fresh thyme

10 squab breasts, boned

Mushroom Emulsion

Sautéed mushrooms and cooking liquid
(from above)

5 tablespoons beef consommé
(from above)

2 tablespoons vinegar

5 tablespoons grapeseed oil

Garnish

1 bunch fresh chervil

Special Equipment

2 ceramic terrine molds, 13 inches by 4 inches by 4 inches

Wine Recommendation

Château Palmer-Margaux 1995 (Médoc), or another silken red Bordeaux with subtle tannins.

Terrine

Place the sweetbreads in a large, shallow bowl with enough water to cover. Let soak, refrigerated, for 2 hours, changing the water twice (the sweetbreads should lose their pinkness and turn milky white). Bring the consommé to a simmer, add the sweetbreads, and cook for 20 minutes. Drain the sweetbreads on paper towels and strain the consommé through several layers of cheesecloth. Set aside 5 tablespoons of consommé for the mushroom emulsion. Soften the gelatin leaves in cold water for 5 minutes, add to the hot consommé, and stir to dissolve and combine.

Preheat the oven to 300 degrees. Season the foie gras with salt and pepper. Place a large sauté pan over medium-high heat and sear the whole foie gras on all sides until the surface is golden brown, about 5 minutes. Place the pan in the oven and roast the foie gras for 12 minutes, until it is firm and cooked through. Remove the foie gras from the pan and drain on paper towels. Strain the fat that has accumulated in the pan through a chinois and reserve.

Heat the duck fat in a large sauté pan set over medium heat. Add the garlic and cook for 1 minute. Add the mushrooms, thyme, and salt and pepper to taste, and cook for about 8 minutes until the mushrooms have released most of their liquid. Remove the mushrooms from the pan with a slotted spoon and drain on paper towels. Reserve the liquid.

Season the squab breasts with salt and pepper. Place the reserved foie gras fat in a sauté pan set over medium-high heat. Cook the squab breasts for 3 to 4 minutes on each side, until they are cooked through. Set aside.

To prepare the terrine, cut the sweetbreads, foie gras, and squab breasts into 1½-inch chunks, and combine with three quarters of the mushrooms. Reserve the remaining mushrooms for the emulsion. Fill the terrine mold with the mixture. Pour the gelatinous consommé over the mixture, adding as much as the terrine will hold. Place the second terrine over the filled terrine and weight it just enough so that the consommé begins to spill over the sides. Place the weighted terrine in the refrigerator for 24 hours.

Mushroom Emulsion

Place the reserved mushrooms and cooking liquid, consommé, vinegar, and grapeseed oil in a blender, pureé, and strain through a chinois.

Service and Garnish

Unmold the terrine and cut into 15 to 18 slices. Place a slice of terrine on each serving plate with 2 tablespoons of the emulsion. Garnish each slice with a sprig or two of fresh chervil.

Sautéed Belgian Endive
with Melted Foie Gras
and Champagne-Poached Black Truffle

Snowy white endive is so common these days, it is easy to forget that it originates from Belgium. The small Benelux country is also home to Roger Souvereyns, whose elegant restaurant offers sophisticated cuisine in a pastoral country setting. This recipe evokes the Gascon tradition of eating foie gras raw, although in this dish the heat of the freshly sautéed endive and the poached truffle actually melts the thin slices of liver.

YIELD: 4 APPETIZER SERVINGS

Poached Truffle

4 fresh black truffles of equal size,
   about 1 ounce each
1 cup dry Champagne
1 cup beef consommé (see page 324)
1 bay leaf
4 drops high-quality 100-year-old
   balsamic vinegar
Pinch black pepper, freshly ground

Belgian Endive

1 tablespoon butter
1 tablespoon olive oil
3 Belgian endives, cut into thin strips
Coarse salt
Pinch black pepper, freshly ground
½ teaspoon nutmeg, freshly grated
1 teaspoon sugar
½ teaspoon sherry vinegar
½ ounce black truffle, cut into julienne

Foie Gras

½ pound foie gras, sliced on the bias,
   as thinly as possible, not more than
   ⅛-inch thick

Garnish

Allspice, freshly grated

Wine Recommendation

Moët & Chandon Brut Champagne
Cuvée Dom Pérignon 1988
(Champagne), or another vintage brut
Champagne.

Poached Truffle

Combine all of the ingredients in a nonreactive saucepan, set over medium heat, and bring to a simmer. Cook for 4 minutes. Remove from the heat and keep warm.

Belgian Endive

Heat the butter and olive oil in a sauté pan. Add the endive and cook over high heat for 2 minutes. Add the salt, pepper, nutmeg, and sugar, and lightly caramelize the endive for about 3 minutes. Deglaze the pan with the vinegar. Add the julienned truffle and let macerate for about 10 seconds.

Service and Garnish

Spoon the hot endive into the middle of four serving plates. Place a poached truffle in the center of each. Top the endive with the thin slices of raw foie gras. The heat will gently melt the liver. Sprinkle each plate with freshly ground allspice.

Foie Gras Escabeche

Julian Serrano's Spanish heritage inspired this dish, an adaptation of a classic escabeche. Traditionally, small whole fish are fried and marinated in a spicy vinegar-based dressing. In this version, Julian replaces the fish with foie gras, cooking the lobe in an aromatic liquid that he reduces to produce a sauce.

YIELD: 8 APPETIZER SERVINGS

Escabeche
Olive oil
16 baby leeks, cleaned and drained
8 cipolline onions, peeled
3 tablespoons sugar
⅓ cup sherry vinegar
1 quart duck stock (see page 328)
1 large lobe foie gras, about ¼ to
    1 pound
2 cloves garlic, minced
10 sprigs thyme
8 bay leaves
10 black peppercorns
24 baby carrots, peeled and blanched

Garnish
Crystalized salt
Fresh thyme
Fresh bay leaves

Wine Recommendation
Domaine du Clos Naudin Foreau Vouvray Demi-Sec 1996 (Loire), or another young, lively Vouvray with some sweetness.

Escabeche
Set a large sauté pan over high heat, add enough olive oil to cover the bottom of the pan, and cook the leeks and onions until they begin to color. Set aside.

Set another large saucepan over high heat, add the sugar, and cook until it is caramelized. Add the sherry vinegar, stock, foie gras, garlic, thyme, bay leaves, peppercorns, and reserved onions and leeks. Cook for 10 minutes. Add the carrots and cook for 5 minutes more. Remove the foie gras from the pot with a slotted spoon and set aside. Remove the vegetables from the pot and set aside. Reduce the liquid in the pot for about 5 minutes, until it coats the back of a spoon. Strain the reduced sauce, reserving the bay leaves for garnish.

Service and Garnish
Slice the foie gras while still warm into eight portions, each approximately ½-inch thick. Place a slice at the top of each of eight plates. Place 3 carrots, 2 leeks, and 1 onion on each plate. Sprinkle the foie gras with crystalized salt and garnish with the reserved bay leaves and fresh thyme. Drizzle the sauce around the foie gras.

Foie Gras Poached in Russian Tea with Fava Beans, Watermelon, Papaya, Pine Nuts, and Beaufort Cheese

Fava Bean Mélange

½ pound fresh fava beans, shelled
(about 2 pounds in the shell)

1 small very ripe papaya

6 tablespoons maple syrup

3 tablespoons balsamic vinegar

½ pound fresh watermelon, seeded and
cut into small dice

1 teaspoon fresh coriander, minced

2 ounces pine nuts, toasted

Fleur de sel

Black pepper, freshly cracked

Foie Gras

2 cups Russian tea, well steeped with
a lime rind (see Chef Notes)

1 pound foie gras, cut into 4 slices,
4 ounces each

Fleur de sel

Black pepper, freshly cracked

Garnish

4½ ounces beets, steamed and sliced
into fine strips

1 tablespoon lemon juice

Coarse salt

Fresh herbs

4 slices black bread, cut into triangles

4 slices Beaufort cheese, cut into
triangles (see Chef Notes)

Wine Recommendation

Château Sociando-Mallet Haut-Médoc
1995 (Bordeaux), or another big red
wine with serious tannin and
prominent fruit flavors.

Fava Bean Mélange

Plunge the fava beans into rapidly boiling salted water. Blanch for 1 minute, then shock in ice water. Cut open the papaya, remove the seeds, and scoop out the pulp. Cut the pulp into small dice. In a sauté pan combine the diced papaya, maple syrup, and vinegar, and simmer for 30 minutes. Remove from the heat and chill the mixture. Add the fava beans, watermelon, coriander, and pine nuts. Season with fleur de sel and cracked black pepper.

Foie Gras

Place the tea in a saucepan and heat to 140 degrees. Add the foie gras slices and poach for 10 minutes. Remove the foie gras and set aside. Skim the fat from the tea and add the fat to the fava bean mélange. Season the tea with fleur de sel and cracked black pepper.

Service and Garnish

Toss the beets with the lemon juice and salt. Divide the papaya mixture evenly among four warm serving bowls. Top with a slice of foie gras and garnish with the beets and fresh herbs. Divide the tea among four cups. Serve each bowl with a cup of tea on the side and triangles of black bread topped with triangles of Beaufort cheese.

Chef Notes

Russian tea is a blend of black teas with a hint of smokiness. Beaufort is a firm, creamy, full-flavored cheese from the Savoie region of France. If Beaufort is unavailable, a good Comté or Gruyère can be substituted.

Steamed Foie Gras with Rhubarb-Orange Compote

Waldy Malouf believes that steaming foie gras is an excellent way to capture the juices and fats of the liver, thereby preserving its richness. The result is a lighter, more subtle-tasting foie gras than either roasting or poaching affords. Waldy steams the liver over aromatics—oranges, rhubarb, and star anise— to infuse it with the flavors that will ultimately enhance the finished dish.

Foie Gras and Compote

¾ cup dry white wine

¼ cup brandy

2 pieces star anise

1 large lobe foie gras, about 1 pound

Coarse salt

Black pepper, freshly ground

2 stalks rhubarb, thinly sliced, about 1½ cups

2 tablespoons sugar

1-inch piece orange zest, cut into fine julienne

3 tablespoons fresh orange juice

Garnish

Orange segments from 1 navel orange

Additional rhubarb (from above)

Star anise

6 to 8 sprigs chervil

Special Equipment

Stove-top steamer with basket and tight-fitting lid

Wine Recommendation

Rivendell Vineyards and Winery "Tear of the Clouds Late Harvest" (New York) or another late-harvest Riesling.

Foie Gras and Compote

In the bottom of the steamer, bring the wine, brandy, and star anise to a boil. Season the foie gras generously with salt and pepper on both sides and place in the steamer basket. Place the basket inside the steamer, cover, and steam the liver for 7 minutes. Without turning off the burner, remove the steamer basket and set aside. Add the rhubarb, sugar, orange zest, and orange juice to the steaming liquid. Return the basket containing the foie gras to the steamer and cover. Steam the liver for an additional 5 minutes, or until it reaches an internal temperature of 115 to 120 degrees. Line a plate with several layers of paper towel and lay the steamed foie gras on it. Remove the star anise from the steaming liquid along with a few slices of cooked rhubarb to use as a garnish. Stir the steaming liquid to break apart the remaining cooked rhubarb.

Service and Garnish

Warm six serving plates. Cut the foie gras into ½-inch-thick slices. Place 1 tablespoon of the rhubarb-orange compote in the center of the warmed plates and set a slice of foie gras on top. Place the orange sections on top of the foie gras and garnish with the additional rhubarb, star anise, and chervil.

Côteaux du Layon–Poached Foie Gras with Simmered Fennel and Cracked Black Pepper Caramel

YIELD: 2 MAIN COURSE SERVINGS

Fennel

1 medium bulb fennel, cored, trimmed, and thinly sliced, feathery stalks reserved for garnish

1 tablespoon unsalted butter

Pinch coarse salt

Poached Foie Gras

3 cups Côteaux du Layon or other sweet wine, such as Sauternes or Gewürztraminer

1 small lobe foie gras, about 8 ounces

Caramel

2 tablespoons sugar

1 teaspoon black pepper, freshly cracked

¼ cup foie gras poaching liquid (reserved from above)

1 tablespoon fresh lemon juice

Coarse salt

Garnish

Feathery stalks of fennel (reserved from above), blanched

Fennel seeds, toasted

Wine Recommendation

Josmeyer Tokay Pinot Gris L'Exception 1995 (Alsace), or a similar dry Alsatian wine with full body and rich fruit flavors.

Jean-Georges Vongerichten strives for simplicity in his preparations, relying on the natural complexity of flavors to build his sophisticated style of cooking. By simply poaching the foie gras in a sweet wine from his native Alsace, one of the great foie gras regions of France, and pairing it with fresh fennel and a savory caramel sauce accented with lemon and black pepper, he creates a dish that tastes clean and familiar, but that is at the same time uniquely Jean-Georges.

Fennel

Place the fennel slices in a saucepan and add just enough water to cover. Add the butter and salt and cook over medium heat until the fennel is tender, about 8 minutes. If there is any water remaining, pour it off. Set aside, covered, to keep warm.

Poached Foie Gras

Place the wine in a small saucepan. Bring to a gentle simmer and poach the foie gras for about 5 minutes on each side. The foie gras should feel firm to the touch and should retain most of its fat. Using a slotted spoon, remove the foie gras from the saucepan and cover to keep warm. Reserve ¼ cup of the poaching liquid for the caramel.

Caramel

Place the sugar and cracked black pepper in a small nonstick sauté pan. Cook over medium heat until the sugar dissolves and begins to caramelize, 2½ to 3 minutes. Swirl the pan periodically to prevent the caramel from burning and to encourage the sugar to brown evenly. Deglaze the pan with the reserved poaching liquid. Continue to cook over medium heat, reducing the mixture until it has the consistency of a light syrup, an additional 5 or 6 minutes. Season to taste with lemon juice and salt.

Service and Garnish

The foie gras may be presented whole and carved tableside or sliced and plated in the kitchen. Either way, place the cooked fennel in the middle of the serving plate(s) and top with the foie gras. Drizzle with the cracked black pepper caramel and garnish with the blanched fennel tops and toasted fennel seeds.

Miso-Marinated Foie Gras
with Fried Shiso

Umami is a Japanese word used to describe what experts believe may be a fifth basic flavor—in addition to sweet, sour, salty, and bitter—that derives from the presence of glutamate in an ingredient or dish. The distinctive earthy flavor of miso typifies umami, and Nobu Matsuhisa uses it masterfully in this inspired dish. By marinating in a sweet miso sauce for two days, the liver itself takes on the illusive umami flavor. Interestingly, the flavor and texture of the foie gras is similar to the Japanese monkfish liver delicacy, akimo, *which Nobu often pairs with miso as well.*

YIELD: 6 APPETIZER SERVINGS

Sweet Miso Sauce
1 cup mirin
1 cup sake
1 pound white miso
1 pound sugar

Foie Gras
1½ pounds foie gras, cut into 12 slices, each about 2 ounces and ½-inch thick
2 cups sweet miso sauce (from above)

Fried Shiso
2 cups vegetable oil
12 fresh shiso leaves

Garnish
6 bamboo leaves
1 seedless cucumber, sliced very thin
6 large radicchio leaves
12 edible flowers

Wine Recommendation
Hokusetzu Dai Ginjo sake, or another Dai Ginjo sake that has a clean, fruity flavor and aroma.

Sweet Miso Sauce
In a medium saucepan, combine the mirin and sake. Heat over a low flame until the mixture is warmed through. Turn off the heat and remove the pan from the stove. Light a match and pass it over the warm liquid to flambé the mixture. Return the pan to the heat and cook until the flame dies. Stir in the miso and sugar and continue heating until it almost reaches the boiling point. Pour the sauce into a glass container and cool completely before proceeding to marinate the foie gras.

Foie Gras
Marinate the slices of foie gras by immersing them completely in 2 cups of the sweet miso sauce for two days in the refrigerator. Remove the foie gras slices and reserve the marinade.

Fried Shiso
In a small saucepan, heat the vegetable oil to 180 degrees. Drop in the shiso leaves and remove them as soon as the bubbles in the oil disappear, less than a minute. Drain well on paper towels.

Service and Garnish
Preheat the broiler. Lay one bamboo leaf diagonally across each of six serving plates. Create a circle of thinly sliced cucumber and lay a radicchio leaf in the center of each circle. Transfer the foie gras slices to a broiling pan and broil until caramelized on each side, taking care to work quickly since the marinated foie gras burns easily, about 1 minute per side. Place 2 slices of broiled foie gras on top of each radicchio leaf. Garnish each plate with 2 fried shiso leaves and 2 edible flowers.

Kalua Pig

4 pounds pork butt

2 tablespoons salt

1 tablespoon liquid smoke

1 to 2 fresh banana leaves

4 ti leaves, ribs removed

Tomato Soups

3 small chilies (see Chef Notes)

2 tablespoons water

3 ripe red tomatoes, about 1 pound,
quartered

3 teaspoons minced garlic, separated,
1 teaspoon for each soup

1 cup olive oil, separated, ⅓ cup for
each soup

Salt

Black pepper, freshly ground

3 ripe green tomatoes, about 1 pound,
quartered (see Chef Notes)

3 ripe yellow tomatoes, about
1 pound, quartered

Sandwiches

1¼ pounds foie gras, cut into 10 slices,
each about 2 ounces and ½-inch
thick

Coarse salt

Black pepper, freshly ground

¼ cup flour

1 teaspoon vegetable oil

Butter

1 French bread, cut into 20 slices, each
¼-inch thick

10 slices mozzarella cheese

10 ounces kalua pig (see Chef Notes)

Special Equipment

Butcher's twine

Cheesecloth

10 champagne flutes

Wine Recommendation

Arrowood Viognier Russian River Valley
Saralee Vineyards 1995 (California), or
another fruity, rich white wine.

Kalua Pig and Foie Gras Sandwich with a Trio of Chilled Tomato Soups

Kalua pig is a celebratory Hawaiian dish typically served at a luau. A whole pig is cooked in an imu—
*a rock-lined, underground oven lined with banana and ti leaves—producing a tender, succulent
roasted pork with a distinctive smoky flavor. Alan Wong, known for his Pacific Rim cuisine and playful
presentations, reinterprets a typical "soup and sandwich" lunch, combining foie gras and kalua pig in
a sandwich, and balancing it over three intermingling tomato soups, artfully presented in a champagne
flute. The flavor of the kalua pig is simulated by wrapping pork butt in banana and ti leaves and
roasting it in a conventional oven.*

Kalua Pig

Score the pork butt on all sides and rub the salt and liquid smoke into the meat. Wrap the pork in the banana leaf, wrap the ti leaves over the banana leaf, and tie the parcel securely with butcher's twine. Wrap the parcel in aluminum foil and refrigerate overnight.

Preheat the oven to 350 degrees. Place the parcel in a roasting pan filled with ½ inch of water. Roast for 4 hours. Remove the package from the roasting pan and open. The meat should be fork tender.

Tomato Soups

In the bowl of a food processor, combine the chilies and water and purée. Pass this purée through several layers of cheesecloth, reserving the water that is given off. Discard the chile pulp. In a blender, purée the red tomatoes, 1 teaspoon of garlic, and 2 teaspoons of chili water. Add the olive oil and purée for 1 second more. Add salt and pepper to taste and set aside. Repeat this process with the green tomatoes and the yellow tomatoes, washing the blender between each batch. Chill the three tomato soups in separate containers.

Sandwiches

Season the foie gras slices with salt and pepper and dredge lightly with flour. Set a medium sauté pan over high heat. Add the oil and sear the foie gras for about 30 seconds per side, until golden brown. Cool slightly. Butter both sides of all 20 bread slices. To assemble the sandwiches, lay out 10 slices of the buttered bread. Top each with a slice of cheese, some kalua pig, a slice of seared foie gras, and another slice of bread. In a hot sauté pan, cook the sandwiches on both sides until golden brown, as though preparing a traditional grilled cheese sandwich.

Service

Transfer the tomato soups to three separate pitchers, stirring each to incorporate all the ingredients. With the aid of another person, simultaneously pour the three tomato soups into a champagne flute, creating a tricolored swirl of soup. Place a sandwich over the top of each flute.

Chef Notes

Use jalapeño or serrano chilies for the tomato soup. Pulled, roasted, or smoked pork can be substituted for the kalua pig. Green tomatoes are a variety of sweet tomato available in specialty produce stores. Do not use tomatillos or unripe red tomatoes.

Almond-Crusted Croquette of Foie Gras with Truffled Scallop Mousse, Carrot-Ginger Marmalade, Tomato-Fennel Seed Confit, and Crab Bisque

Hong Kong–born, French-trained chef Susur Lee artfully combines Asian ingredients and French techniques to create his unique style of cooking. His extravagant presentations unfold with surprises. In this dish, built around a molten croquette of foie gras, elements of land and sea converge to produce an ethereally delicious appetizer.

YIELD: 6 APPETIZER SERVINGS

Carrot-Ginger Marmalade

4 medium carrots, peeled and grated

2 cups fresh carrot juice

1 bay leaf

1 piece fresh ginger, ½-inch long, peeled and cut into fine julienne

1 cup sugar

2 tablespoons white vinegar

¼ teaspoon coarse salt

1 teaspoon orange zest, grated

Tomato-Fennel Seed Confit

3 large tomatoes, peeled, seeded, and chopped

1 tablespoon olive oil

¼ cup sugar

½ teaspoon coarse salt

¼ teaspoon fennel seeds, toasted

Crab Bisque

¼ cup olive oil

10 blue crabs, cleaned and cut into pieces

2 small carrots, chopped, about 1 cup

1 large onion, chopped, about 1 cup

2 ribs celery, chopped, about 1 cup

5 heads garlic, peeled

1 bay leaf

2 cups white wine

3½ quarts chicken stock

⅓ cup heavy cream

Carrot-Ginger Marmalade

In a saucepan, combine all of the ingredients except the orange zest and set over high heat. Bring to a boil, reduce the heat, and cook until the mixture thickens to a jamlike consistency, about 1 hour. Remove the bay leaf and stir in the orange zest.

Tomato-Fennel Seed Confit

Combine all of the ingredients in a small saucepan and set over medium heat. Bring to a simmer and cook for 45 minutes, until the mixture thickens to a jamlike consistency.

Crab Bisque

Heat the oil in a large saucepan, add the crab pieces, and sauté until cooked through. Add the carrots, onion, celery, and garlic, and cook until the vegetables are tender. Break the crab into smaller pieces and add the bay leaf, wine, and stock. Cook over a low heat until the mixture is reduced to about 2 cups. Strain through a fine sieve. Reserve about ½ cup and add the cream to the remaining mixture. Keep warm.

Carrot-Crab Sauce

Combine all of the ingredients except the butter in a small saucepan and set over medium-high heat. Bring to a boil, lower the heat, and reduce until only ⅓ cup remains,

about 25 minutes. Whisk in the butter and set aside.

Crisp Duck Skin

Preheat the oven to 400 degrees. Bake the duck skin until most of the fat is rendered and the skin has begun to brown, about 10 to 15 minutes. Remove the skin from the fat and cut into strips. Combine the honey, soy sauce and five-spice powder. Toss the duck skin strips in the honey mixture to glaze. Return the strips to the oven and continue cooking until very crisp, about 5 additional minutes.

Scallop Mousse and Nori Roll

Place the scallops in the bowl of a food processor and process to the consistency of a thick paste. Add the ice cube and process to combine. Add the egg white, salt, and pepper and process until the mixture reaches a mousselike consistency. Lay a large square of aluminum foil on the work surface. On top of the foil lay a piece of plastic wrap. Place the nori on the plastic wrap. Spread a ½-inch-thick layer of the scallop mousse evenly over the nori, leaving a clean ½-inch lip along one end of the seaweed. Place the truffle slices in a line in the center of the scallop mousse parallel to the clean lip of the nori. Moisten the lip with a damp cloth. Carefully roll up the nori like a sushi roll around the

Carrot-Crab Sauce

¼ cup carrot juice, about 3 carrots
   juiced

½ cup crab stock, from above

Juice of ½ lemon

2 tablespoons white wine

1 tablespoon minced shallot

1 tablespoon butter

Crisp Duck Skin

1 duck skin, 8-inch piece, about
   1 breast

1 tablespoon honey

1 tablespoon soy sauce

¼ teaspoon Chinese five-spice powder

Scallop Mousse and Nori Roll

¾ pound fresh sea scallops

1 ice cube

3 tablespoons egg white

½ teaspoon coarse salt

¼ teaspoon black pepper, freshly
   ground

1 piece toasted nori seaweed, 8-inch
   square

½ ounce black truffle, sliced

scallop mixture, bringing the clean lip of nori up and over to the opposite side to seal. Wrap the roll in the plastic wrap, twisting the ends to form a tight sausage. Tightly wrap in aluminum foil to support the shape. Bring a large pot of water to a boil. Place the roll in the water and turn off the heat. Let the roll poach in the water for a half hour, then remove.

Croquette of Foie Gras

Trim the crêpes into rectangles. Season the foie gras with salt and pepper and divide evenly among the crêpes, gathering it in the center. Wrap the crêpes around the foie gras to form six croquettes. Combine the ground almonds and panko crumbs in a small bowl. Dust the croquettes with the flour, dip in the egg, and roll in the almond mixture to coat. Preheat the oven to 375 degrees. On the stove, heat the oil to 350 degrees. Deep fry the croquettes until golden brown, about 1 minute per side. Remove from the oil, drain, and finish in the oven for 2 minutes.

Service and Garnish

Spoon a half cup of the crab bisque into each of six shallow bowls. Place a dollop of carrot-ginger marmalade in the center of each bowl. Cut the croquettes in half, and place two halves in the bowl, securing them in place with the marmalade. Remove the nori roll from the foil and plastic wrap and slice into six rounds with a sharp serrated knife. Balance a slice vertically on top of each croquette. Place a quenelle of tomato-fennel seed confit on the nori roll. Spoon the carrot-crab sauce around the plate and garnish with the crisp duck skin and coriander seedlings.

Croquette of Foie Gras

6 crêpes, 7-inch diameter each
    (see page 100)
6 ounces foie gras, cut into small dice
Coarse salt
Black pepper, freshly ground
1 cup ground white almonds
1 cup panko crumbs
1 cup flour
2 eggs, beaten
Oil for deep frying

Garnish

Coriander seedlings

Wine Recommendation

Kurt Darting Durkheimer Nonnengarten Rieslaner Auslese 1994 (Germany), or another rich, off-dry white wine.

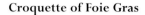

Foie Gras Club

Perhaps the culinary irony of transforming an ordinary diner club sandwich into an elegant upscale entrée is among the reasons why Anne Rosenzweig's creative sandwiches have become one of her signature dishes. Her lobster club was so popular she even named a restaurant after it. In this decadent version of a triple-decker, Anne layers foie gras mousse and seared foie gras between thick rounds of toasted brioche. Crunchy duck cracklings serve as bacon, mousse of foie gras as mayonnaise, and fresh pea shoots as lettuce.

Tomato Jam

½ cup sugar

½ cup balsamic vinegar

½ large onion, minced, about ½ cup

1 piece ginger, 1 inch long, minced

4 tomatoes, peeled, seeded, juiced, and
　chopped

2 teaspoons black pepper, freshly
　ground

1 teaspoon cardamom

1 teaspoon coriander seeds, toasted
　and ground

Duck Crackling

1 pound duck skin

Coarse salt

Black pepper, freshly ground

3 cups rendered duck fat or
　vegetable oil

Foie Gras

1½ pounds foie gras, cut into 12 slices,
　each about 2 ounces and ⅓-inch
　thick

Coarse salt

Black pepper, freshly ground

Garnish

1½ cups foie gras mousse
　(see page 114)

18 slices brioche, cut into rounds

Pea shoots

Mustard oil

Wine Recommendation

Lenswood Chardonnay 1995
(Australia), or another white wine with
honey and spice flavors.

Tomato Jam

Combine the sugar and balsamic vinegar in a small saucepan and bring to a boil. Let the mixture simmer until it thickens and caramelizes, about 10 minutes, being careful not to let the mixture burn. Add the remaining ingredients and cook until the mixture thickens to a jamlike consistency, 50 to 60 minutes. Cool. Adjust the seasoning to taste.

Duck Crackling

Season the duck skin with salt and pepper. Heat the duck fat or oil in a sauté pan to 375 degrees and fry the skin until crispy, from 10 to 20 minutes depending on the thickness and fattiness of the skin. Remove the skin with a slotted spoon, drain on paper towels, and allow to cool. Cut the crisp skin into bacon-shaped strips, and season again with salt and pepper to taste.

Foie Gras

Season the foie gras slices with salt and pepper. Heat a sauté pan over high heat and, in batches, sear the foie gras for about 30 seconds on each side, and drain on paper towels.

Service and Garnish

To prepare the sandwich, spread 2 tablespoons of foie gras mousse on each of two brioche rounds. Spread 1 tablespoon of jam over the mousse on each of the rounds. Place a small handfull of pea shoots over the jam-covered rounds. Top each with a slice of duck crackling, and a piece of seared foie gras. Stack one round on top of the other and place a plain brioche slice on top.

　Repeat to make six sandwiches. Garnish with mustard oil.

Millionaire's Salad of Wilted Greens with Foie Gras, Lobster, and Papaya

Because of the high price of foie gras, it is often used in conjunction with other luxury items, such as truffles or Sauternes. Jasper White pairs lobster with foie gras to create a rich appetizer that belies its origins as a salad. Although Jasper, a New England chef, is known for his seafood preparations, foie gras is a staple on his menus. He believes that when diners eat seafood, they are more inclined to splurge on indulgences such as foie gras and dessert.

YIELD: 4 APPETIZER SERVINGS

Lobster
¼ cup coarse salt
2 chicken lobsters, about 1 pound each

Salad
⅓ cup peanut oil
Black pepper, freshly ground
½ small red onion, about 2 ounces, thinly sliced
3 tablespoons aged sherry vinegar
Zest of 1 lemon, cut into thin strands
2 sprigs fresh basil, leaves only, chopped
Coarse salt

Foie Gras
8 ounces foie gras, cut into 4 slices about ½-inch thick
Coarse salt
Black pepper, freshly ground

Garnish
½ pound mixed hearty lettuces, such as frisée, radicchio, mizuna, and/or endive, washed and dried
1 large, ripe papaya, peeled, seeded, and cut into 1-inch cubes

Wine Recommendation
Pedro Domecq Amontillado Jerez 51-1a Non-Vintage (Spain), or another chilled sherry, either amontillado or fino.

Lobster
Fill a 10- or 12-quart pot with water about two-thirds full. Add the salt and bring the water to a rolling boil. With your hand on the carapace, or central part of the body, place the lobsters in the pot and cook, uncovered, for exactly 3½ minutes. Using a pair of tongs, remove the lobsters from the pot and allow them to cool to room temperature. Remove the meat from the claws and knuckles, keeping the meat as intact as possible. Break the carcass off the tail and reserve for another purpose. Using a sharp knife or cleaver, split the tail in half lengthwise and remove the meat. Remove the dark "vein." Cut each half-tail in half again. Cover and refrigerate.

Salad
Set a 12-inch sauté pan over medium heat and add the peanut oil. Lightly season the lobster pieces with pepper and add to the hot oil along with the red onion. Cook the lobster and the onion for about 3 minutes, turning and moving the lobster pieces with tongs so they cook evenly. Remove the lobster to a plate and let it sit while you finish the salad. Leave the onions in the pan and remove the pan from the heat. Add the vinegar, lemon zest, and basil; season with salt and pepper. Also add any liquid that accumulates on the plate with the lobster meat. Set aside, leaving the dressing in the pan.

Foie Gras
Score the slices of foie gras and season with salt and pepper. Place the slices directly into a hot, dry 10-inch sauté pan. Sear for about 30 seconds on each side, until a nice brown crust has formed. Remove the foie gras immediately and keep warm. Reserve the fat.

Service and Garnish
Return the 12-inch sauté pan with the dressing to the heat. Add the mixed lettuces to the pan. Using a pair of tongs, toss the lettuce over the heat until the greens are slightly warmed, but not cooked, about 1 minute of continuous tossing. When the greens are warm, lift them out of the pan and divide evenly among four serving plates. Work very quickly. Place the foie gras on top of the salad and lean the lobster claw meat against it. Garnish the salad with the remaining chunks of lobster and the ripe papaya. Spoon the remaining dressing over the salad and sprinkle with a few drops of the foie gras fat.

Tripe Salad with Foie Gras and Fava Beans

Tripe

1 pound tripe, honeycomb, or blanket tripe, rinsed three times in cold water

1 teaspoon coarse salt, plus additional for seasoning

2 bay leaves

2 cups white wine

1 onion, coarsely chopped

1 carrot, coarsely chopped

1 stalk celery, coarsely chopped

1 clove garlic

Black pepper, freshly ground

1 sprig thyme

2 eggs, lightly beaten

10 ounces bread crumbs

Fava Beans

10 ounces fresh fava beans, about 2½ pounds in the shell

Vinaigrette

1 shallot, minced

1 tablespoon strong dijon mustard

1 tablespoon country mustard

2 tablespoons white wine vinegar

1 tablespoon balsamic vinegar

2 tablespoons tripe cooking liquid (from above)

6 tablespoons olive oil

Foie Gras

6 tablespoons peanut oil

8 ounces foie gras, cut into 4 slices, each about 2 ounces and ½-inch thick, and scored

Garnish

4 cups baby lettuces

4 quail eggs

4 sprigs chervil

Wine Recommendation

Zind-Humbrecht Pinot Gris Clos Windsbuhl Hunawihr 1995 (Alsace), or another rich, intensely fruity white wine with honey overtones.

Though Americans aren't accustomed to eating tripe, the stomach lining of a cow or pig, other cultures prepare it in a variety of tempting ways—sausages, soups, stews, and even salads. Alsatian chef Marc Haeberlin, whose restaurant in one of France's principle foie gras regions is a destination for culinary pilgrims, breads and fries strips of tripe to toss with fresh fava beans and seared foie gras. Though it is difficult to think of foie gras as offal, in fact, technically speaking, it falls into the same category as tripe. However, this elegant dish doesn't qualify as anything but a delicacy.

Tripe

Place the tripe in a saucepan, cover with cold water, and set over high heat. Add the teaspoon of salt and one of the bay leaves. When the water comes to a boil, lower the heat and simmer for about 1 hour, until the tripe feels tender when pricked with a fork. Remove the tripe from the cooking liquid and let cool to room temperature.

Cut the cooked tripe into strips, about ½-inch wide by 1- to 2-inches long. Place half of the tripe strips into a saucepan with the wine, onion, carrot, celery, garlic, additional salt, pepper, thyme, and the remaining bay leaf. Simmer for 30 minutes. Strain the tripe, reserving the cooking liquid. Dip the remaining tripe strips into the beaten egg and coat thickly with the bread crumbs. Set aside.

Fava Beans

Plunge the fava beans into rapidly boiling water and blanch for 1 minute. Shock the beans in ice water, peel, and set aside.

Vinaigrette

Beat together the shallot, mustards, vinegars, and tripe cooking liquid. Slowly beat in the olive oil until the dressing emulsifies. Set aside.

Foie Gras and Garnish

Heat the peanut oil in a sauté pan. Sear the foie gras for 30 seconds per side. Set aside. In the same pan, fry the breaded tripe for 1 minute on each side or until browned. Set aside.

Gently heat the vinaigrette. Add the fava beans and poached tripe. Divide the baby greens among four serving plates. Place two slices of poached tripe and some fava beans in the center of each mound of salad. Place two pieces of fried tripe next to the salad and a slice of foie gras on top. Quickly fry the quail eggs sunny side up. Trim the eggs to make them round and top each piece of foie gras with a quail egg and a sprig of chervil.

Duck Quartet Salad
with Roasted Shallot Cane Vinaigrette

*Like variations on a theme, this quartet of duck preparations by Jamie Shannon highlights the versatility
of duck and foie gras. The resulting salad offers intriguing contrasts among the textures and flavors
of the sweet, supple prosciutto, the browned, crisp cracklings, the salty, dense smoked breast,
and the earthy, silken foie gras.*

Duck Prosciutto

1 cup dark brown sugar

1 cup coarse salt

3 juniper berries

1 duck breast

Marinated Smoked Duck Breast

3 cups water

½ cup coarse salt

⅓ cup sugar

1 clove

1 star anise

1-inch piece cinnamon stick

1 duck breast

½ cup orange juice

¼ cup Jack Daniel's

¼ cup brown sugar

2 tablespoons coarse salt

Vinaigrette

5 shallots, peeled

1 tablespoon vegetable oil

1 tablespoon Dijon mustard

3 ounces cane vinegar (see Chef Notes)

1 cup olive oil

Duck Prosciutto

In a small mixing bowl, combine the brown sugar, salt, and juniper berries. Pack the duck breast in the mixture and refrigerate for 6 to 8 days. When done, the breasts should be firm to the touch, with a completely cooked texture and no evidence of raw meat. Wipe off the seasoning completely, wrap in plastic, and refrigerate.

Marinated Smoked Duck Breast

In a large saucepan, combine the water, salt, sugar, clove, star anise, and cinnamon, and bring to a simmer. Remove from the heat and cool to room temperature. Transfer this solution to a clean container and submerge the duck breast in it. Allow the duck breast to cure, refrigerated, for up to 12 hours. Remove from the curing solution and rinse. Set up a cold smoker and heat to 85 degrees. Place the duck breast in the smoker and smoke for 2 hours. Chill.

In a small mixing bowl, combine the orange juice, Jack Daniel's, brown sugar, and

salt. Marinate the smoked duck breast in this mixture overnight. Remove the breast from the marinade and discard the marinade. Score the duck skin into a diamond pattern, cutting three-fourths of the way into the skin. Heat a small sauté pan over medium heat and cook the duck breast slowly, rendering as much fat as possible without burning the skin. Turn the breast over and cook to medium rare. Remove from the pan and set aside until service.

Vinaigrette

Preheat the oven to 400 degrees. Coat the shallots lightly with the vegetable oil and roast them in a small pan for 30 minutes or until soft. In the bowl of a food processor, combine the roasted shallots, mustard, and vinegar. With the motor on, add the olive oil in a slow, steady stream to form an emulsion. Set aside until service.

Duck Cracklings

Skin of 1 duck breast, cut into ¼-inch
    strips

½ cup water

Cane Vinegar Reduction

4 cups cane vinegar

Salad

¼ pound mesclun greens

1 orange, sectioned

2 ounces fresh peas

Foie Gras

8 ounces foie gras cut into 4 slices,
    each 2 ounces and ½-inch thick,
    scored

Coarse salt

Black pepper, freshly ground

Duck Cracklings

Place the strips of duck skin in a small saucepan with water and cook over medium heat until all the fat is rendered and the skin becomes crisp. Strain, set the cracklings aside, and reserve the fat for another use.

Cane Vinegar Reduction

In a small saucepan set over medium-high heat, reduce the vinegar until only ¼ cup remains, about 1½ hours. Set aside.

Salad, Foie Gras, and Garnish

Using a meat slicer or a very sharp knife, slice the duck prosciutto into thin strips, being careful to keep the fat attached to the meat. Slice the smoked duck breast thinly, on the bias. In a large mixing bowl, place the mesclun greens, duck prosciutto, smoked duck, orange segments, and peas. Toss with the roasted shallot vinaigrette. Divide the salad evenly among the four serving plates. Heat a large sauté pan over high heat until hot. Season the foie gras slices with salt and pepper and sear for 20 seconds per side. Place each slice atop a salad. In a small non-stick sauté pan over medium heat, fry the quail eggs sunny side up. Place one on top of each piece of foie gras. Garnish each plate with a few duck cracklings and drizzle the vinegar reduction over the top.

Chef Notes

Cane vinegar, a Louisiana specialty, is a by-product of sugar production. One of the most popular brands is Steens. If you cannot smoke your own duck breast, you can usu-ally purchase it, as well as duck prosciutto, from specialty meat purveyors.

Garnish

4 quail eggs

Special Equipment

Cold smoker

Wine Recommendation

Ridge Zinfandel Sonoma Valley Pagani Ranch 1994 (Sonoma), or any spicy, full-bodied red wine.

Pan-Roasted Duck and Foie Gras Salad
with Fuyu Persimmons
and Walnut-Sherry Vinaigrette

Traci Des Jardins is known for her interpretive California bistro cooking. In this salad, an update of the classic frisée salad with lardons, Traci replaces the traditional bacon with the crisped skin of the confit, another bistro staple. She adds foie gras, which she combines with a vinaigrette composed of walnut oil and sherry vinegar. The nutty flavor of the dressing brings out similar qualities in the foie gras, lending the salad an intriguing depth of flavor. The Fuyu persimmons add a tart sweetness, and serve to balance the richness of the foie gras.

YIELD: 4 APPETIZER SERVINGS

Pan-Roasted Duck

4 small duck legs

1 tablespoon duck fat or vegetable oil

Salad and Vinaigrette

4 Fuyu persimmons (see Chef Notes)

3 tablespoons aged sherry vinegar

4 tablespoons walnut oil

Coarse salt

Black pepper, freshly ground

1 head baby frisée, washed, green
    outer leaves discarded

1 bunch small arugula, washed, stems
    removed

1 bunch watercress, washed, stems
    removed

1 shallot, peeled and diced

2 tablespoons chives, chopped

Foie Gras

4 ounces foie gras, cut into ¾-inch dice

Wine Recommendation

Iron Horse Cabernet Sauvignon
Alexander Valley Cuvée Joy 1994
(Napa), or another California Cabernet
Sauvignon.

Pan-Roasted Duck

Preheat the oven to 450 degrees. Remove the thigh bone and drumstick from the duck legs by twisting the bones and pulling them out, making sure to keep the skin and meat intact. In an ovenproof sauté pan set over a medium-high flame, heat the duck fat or vegetable oil. Place the duck, skin side down, into the pan, reduce the heat slightly, and cook until the skin is crisp, about 4 to 6 minutes. Place the pan in the oven and cook until the duck meat has warmed through, 5 to 8 minutes. Place the duck, skin side down, on a cutting board. Carefully remove the meat from the skin, making sure to keep the skin in one piece. Using your fingers, break the duck meat into large chunks and set aside for the salad. Cut the skin into julienne and set aside for garnish.

Salad and Vinaigrette

Slice three persimmons into twenty ⅛-inch-thick rounds. Cut the remaining persimmon into 2-inch-long matchsticks. Marinate the persimmon slices and matchsticks in 1 tablespoon of the sherry vinegar. Place the remaining 2 tablespoons of sherry vinegar in

a mixing bowl, slowly whisk in the walnut oil, and season to taste with salt and pepper. Place the frisée, arugula, and watercress in a bowl with half the diced shallots and half the chopped chives. Add the duck meat, persimmon matchsticks, and half the vinaigrette. Season with salt and pepper to taste and toss the salad. Add the remaining shallots and chives to the remaining vinaigrette and set aside.

Foie Gras and Service

Arrange 5 persimmon slices in a circular pattern on each of four serving plates and season with salt and pepper. Gently top the persimmon with the tossed salad. In a very hot sauté pan, sear the diced foie gras for 45 seconds to 1 minute, just until browned around the edges. Remove the foie gras from the pan and add to the remaining vinaigrette. Spoon the foie gras mixture over the salad. Garnish with the julienne of crisped duck skin.

Chef Notes

Fuyu persimmons are the most widely available variety. For this recipe you can use any variety of sweet, ripe persimmon.

Foie Gras-Stuffed Duck Legs

6 duck legs of uniform size

5 ounces foie gras, sliced into 4
    medallions

1 tablespoon ketjap manis or dark soy
    sauce (see Chef Notes)

½ teaspoon garlic, finely minced

½ teaspoon fresh ginger, finely minced

1 tablespoon coarse salt

1 tablespoon light brown sugar

2 tablespoons Chinese five-spice powder

Fresh Plum Sauce

1 teaspoon olive oil

½ medium yellow onion, cut into
    small dice

1 teaspoon minced ginger

3 ripe plums, skins on, cut into
    small dice

Juice of 2 limes

¼ cup Hoisin sauce

Foie gras fat (from above)

Duck jus (from above)

Coarse salt

Black pepper, freshly ground

Spicy Salad Dressing

2 tablespoons rice wine vinegar

2 tablespoons lime juice

2 tablespoons honey

1 teaspoon sambal oelek (see Chef Notes)

3 tablespoons canola oil

Asian Salad

3 scallions, cut into julienne

¼ head Napa cabbage, shredded

1 cup mizuna (see Chef Notes)

1 cup tatsoi (see Chef Notes)

¼ cup sunflower sprouts

1 carrot, peeled and cut into fine julienne

½ cup sliced cucumber, peeled and
    seeded

2 tablespoons cilantro, roughly
    chopped

Wine Recommendation

Hugel Gewürztraminer Jubilée Réserve
Personnelle 1995 (Alsace), or another
dry Alsatian Gewürztraminer or
Riesling.

Foie Gras–Stuffed Five Spice Duck Leg with Fresh Plum Sauce and Asian Salad

Although most people think of using duck legs only for confit, New Orleans chef Susan Spicer bones, stuffs, and roast the legs for this Asian-flavored appetizer. As the leg roasts, the rendered fat bastes the meat making it tender and juicy. Chunks of seared foie gras enrich the stuffing, and a tart fresh plum sauce and spicy salad dressing make this a perfect way to start a meal.

Foie Gras-Stuffed Duck Leg

Debone 4 of the duck legs and trim off all excess fat, silverskin, and tendons. Pound the duck legs between two sheets of plastic wrap to an even width. Debone the remaining two duck legs, trim off all skin and fat, and finely chop the meat. In a very hot sauté pan, quickly sear the foie gras for 30 seconds on each side. Remove the foie gras from the pan and let cool, reserving any fat for the plum sauce. Cut the cooled foie gras into ¼-inch dice. Combine the chopped duck meat, diced foie gras, ketjap manis or soy sauce, garlic, ginger, and 1 teaspoon of the salt. Divide the foie gras stuffing among the pounded duck legs. Roll the legs around the stuffing and tie them securely with butcher's twine. Combine the remaining salt with the brown sugar and the five-spice powder. Coat the rolled duck legs with this mixture and let stand for at least 1 hour or refrigerate overnight. Preheat the oven to 375 degrees. Wipe the excess seasoning from the stuffed duck legs and pat dry. In a very hot sauté pan, sear the rolls until browned. Finish the duck legs in the oven for 15 to 20 minutes, depending on the size of the legs, until just cooked through. Reserve the juices in the sauté pan. Let the meat rest for 5 to 10 minutes before serving.

Fresh Plum Sauce

Heat the olive oil in a sauté pan set over high heat. Sauté the onion and the ginger until translucent. Add the plums and continue to cook for 2 minutes; the plums should remain firm. In the bowl of a food processor, combine the plum mixture with the remaining ingredients. Process until smooth and strain.

Spicy Salad Dressing

In a bowl, combine the vinegar, lime juice, honey, and sambal oelek. Whisk in the canola oil in a slow, steady stream to create a temporary emulsion.

Asian Salad

In a bowl, gently combine all ingredients. Toss with the spicy salad dressing.

Service

Untie the duck leg rolls and slice into six rounds each. Place the rounds on each of four plates. Place a handful of salad, in a mound, on top of the duck leg slices. Place eight dollops of plum sauce around each plate.

Chef Notes

Ketjap manis, or kecap manis, is a thick, syrupy, sweet Indonesian sauce, similar in flavor to soy sauce. It can be found in Asian markets. Dark Chinese soy sauce can be substituted. For the salad, greens other than mizuna and tatsoi can be substituted based on preference and availability. Sambal oelek, a combination of chilies, brown sugar, and salt, is a condiment most commonly used in Malaysian, Indonesian, and southern Indian cuisines. It is available in Asian markets.

Pain au Foie Gras with Arugula and Braised Onions

The buttery layers of croissant dough provide the medium for Nancy Silverton's elegant pastry creation. A play on the traditional French pain au chocolat, this savory variation sandwiches marinated foie gras between layers of fresh arugula, accents it with sweet onions braised slowly in red wine, and wraps the whole package in a tender, rich envelope of pastry. The side salad of bitter greens turns the pain au foie gras into a hearty appetizer or a perfect luncheon entrée.

Croissant Dough

1¼ pounds unbleached white bread flour, plus extra for dusting

1⅓ cups whole milk

2¼ cakes compressed fresh yeast or 1½ tablespoons dry yeast

1½ teaspoons coarse salt

3 tablespoons light brown sugar, packed

1½ cups unsalted butter, chilled

Braised Onions

3 tablespoons red wine vinegar

3 cups red wine, plus extra if needed

2 large onions, peeled, trimmed, and cut into ½-inch dice

Bouquet garni of thyme, bay leaf, and parsley

Coarse salt

2 tablespoons unsalted butter

Black pepper, freshly ground

Croissant Dough

In the bowl of an electric mixer fitted with a dough hook, place the flour, milk, yeast, salt, and brown sugar. Mix on low speed until the dough is smooth, about 8 minutes. Remove the dough from the bowl and knead by hand for about 5 minutes, until smooth. Press the dough into a rectangle, about 1½ inches thick. Wrap the dough tightly in plastic wrap and refrigerate for 1 hour. Meanwhile, place the cold butter between two linen towels or two pieces of plastic wrap and, beating it with a rolling pin, flatten the butter into a rectangle measuring about 5 by 8 inches. Refrigerate for 30 minutes.

Remove the dough from the refrigerator and unwrap. On a lightly floured surface, roll out the dough to an 8-by-10-inch rectangle, making sure the short end of the dough is parallel to the edge of the work surface. Remove the butter from the refrigerator and remove the wrapping. The butter should be the same temperature as the dough. Place the butter on the upper two-thirds of the dough rectangle. Fold the dough like a business letter, folding the bottom third of the dough over the buttered dough and then folding the top of the buttered dough over the first fold. Rotate the dough 180 degrees and roll out again, maintaining its rectangular shape, until it is ½-inch thick. Fold the dough again like a letter, this time folding the left side of the dough into the middle and the right side of the dough over the left. Wrap the folded dough tightly in plastic wrap and refrigerate for 1 hour. This completes the first "turn" of the dough. You will need to complete three more turns of the dough, making sure the open seam of the dough is always to the right, and refrigerating the dough between each turn for at least 30 minutes. After the fourth turn, tightly wrap the dough in plastic wrap and refrigerate for 3 hours.

Braised Onions

In a medium saucepan over medium-high heat, combine the vinegar and wine and bring to a boil. Add the onions, bouquet garni, and a pinch of salt. Bring back to the boil, cover the saucepan with a tight-fitting lid, and continue to cook for 3 to 5 minutes. Remove a tablespoon of the onions and set aside for garnish. Reduce the heat to very low and continue to cook the remaining onions for about 3 hours, checking every 30 minutes to make sure there is enough liquid to cover the onions. If the onions start to dry out, add more wine. When the onions are very soft, increase the heat to high and bring the mixture to a rapid boil. Boil the mixture for about 10 minutes, until thickened, stirring frequently to prevent burning. Remove from the heat and take out the bouquet garni. Stir in the butter and season with salt and pepper to taste. Reserve.

Marinade

¾ cup port

½ cup black currants

½ teaspoon nutmeg, freshly grated

Pain au Foie Gras

1 large lobe foie gras, about 1 pound

Croissant dough (from above)

1 bunch arugula

Braised onions (from above)

Coarse salt

Black pepper, freshly ground

Arugula and Endive Salad

4 tablespoons sherry wine vinegar

2 large shallots, peeled, trimmed, and
  minced

4 teaspoons fresh lemon juice

½ teaspoon coarse salt

1 teaspoon black pepper, freshly
  ground

6 tablespoons hazelnut oil

6 tablespoons almond oil

4 heads Belgian endive

1 bunch arugula, cleaned and well
  dried

½ cup black currants (from Marinade)

Marinade

Combine the port, black currants, and nutmeg in a small saucepan and bring to a simmer. Remove from the heat and let cool. Strain the currants from the marinade and reserve them for the salad. Set aside the marinade.

Pain au Foie Gras

From the large end of the foie gras lobe, cut 8 square portions, about 1½ ounce each. Reserve the trimmings. Place the foie gras squares in the cooled marinade and marinate for at least 30 minutes, turning frequently to coat all sides. In a sauté pan set over medium heat, cook the remaining foie gras and trimmings to render all the fat. Reserve the fat and keep warm.

Preheat the oven to 425 degrees. On a lightly floured work surface, roll out the croissant dough to 1/16-inch thickness. Cut out sixteen 3-inch squares of dough. Wrap and freeze any remaining dough and save for another use. Carefully mark the centers of eight of the squares of dough with a 2½-inch round pastry mold. Reserve the remaining eight squares. Brush the center circles with the rendered foie gras fat. Place a few leaves of arugula in each circle, followed by a tablespoon of the braised onions. Remove the foie gras squares from the marinade and season with salt and pepper. Place a square of foie gras over the onions and cover with a few more arugula leaves. Carefully place a reserved square of dough over each of the first eight squares. Gently seal the two pieces of dough together using the 2½-inch cookie cutter, being very careful not to cut through the dough. Using a 3-inch round fluted cookie cutter, cut out the dough to form circular, ravioli-shaped "croissants." Allow the croissants to proof for 20 to 30 minutes. Lower the oven to 400 degrees. Place the croissants on a sheet pan lined with parchment paper and bake for 15 to 20 minutes, until golden brown. Keep warm.

Arugula and Endive Salad

In a medium bowl combine the vinegar, shallots, lemon juice, salt, and pepper. Slowly whisk in the hazelnut and almond oils until well combined. Slice the endive on the bias into ½-inch pieces. Gently toss the arugula, endive, reserved onions, and black currants with the vinaigrette.

Service

Place a croissant in the middle of each of eight serving plates. Arrange the salad in a ring around each croissant.

Special Equipment

2½-inch round cookie cutter
3-inch round fluted cookie cutter

Wine Recommendation

Steel Pinot Noir Mendocino DuPratt Vineyard 1995 (Mendocino/Lake), or another complex, spicy Pinot Noir from California.

Foie Gras and Shiitake Pot-Stickers with Steamed Asian Pear and Port Sauce

Susanna Foo incorporates European ingredients and techniques into the dishes of her Chinese culinary heritage. An exemplary Chinese dumpling is hot, juicy, and crunchy. In this version, the aromatic juices of the foie gras and mushrooms are sealed within the steaming dumpling, creating a sensory explosion of taste and aroma.

YIELD: 4 APPETIZER SERVINGS

Pot-Stickers

8 ounces foie gras cut into 4 slices, each about 2 ounces and ½-inch thick

Coarse salt

Black pepper, freshly ground

6 ounces fresh shiitake mushrooms, stems removed, cut into ½-inch dice, or 1½ ounces dried shiitakes, rehydrated and cut into ½-inch dice

3 shallots, finely chopped

2 tablespoons tarragon, finely chopped

1 tablespoon ginger, freshly grated

1 tablespoon soy sauce

12 Chinese dumpling wrappers (see Chef Notes)

Asian Pears

2 medium Asian pears

Port Sauce

2 tablespoons corn oil

3 shallots, finely minced

6 tablespoons balsamic vinegar

1 cup port

Garnish

1 tablespoon corn oil

3 fresh shiitake mushrooms, stems removed, sliced

1 cup mixed baby greens, including chrysanthemums, sunflower sprouts, and mâche

Special Equipment

Steamer

Wine Recommendation

Simi Winery Chardonnay Reserve 1990 (Sonoma), or another Sonoma Chardonnay with buttery notes.

Pot-Stickers

Heat a heavy sauté pan until very hot. Season the foie gras slices with salt and pepper. Place the slices in the hot pan and sear on each side for 30 seconds. Remove the seared foie gras to a cutting board. Pour the rendered foie gras fat into a small bowl and reserve. When the foie gras is cool, cut into ½-inch dice. In a large mixing bowl, combine the mushrooms, shallots, tarragon, ginger, soy sauce, and 2 tablespoons of the reserved foie gras fat. Mix well. Add the diced foie gras, and season with salt and pepper. Place about 1 tablespoon of foie gras stuffing in the center of one of the dumpling wrappers. Moisten the inner edge of the wrapper with a dab of cold water, then fold the wrapper over the filling to form a half-moon shape. Pinch the edges together with your fingers to seal. Repeat to make a total of 12 dumplings. Set aside until service.

Asian Pears

Bring water in a steamer to a simmer. Peel, halve, and core the pears. Dunk them in cold water, pat dry, and steam until tender, about 10 to 15 minutes. Remove and keep warm.

Port Sauce

In a small saucepan, heat the corn oil. Add the shallots and cook over medium heat until soft. Lower the heat and add the balsamic vinegar and port. Reduce by three-fourths, about 45 minutes. Turn off the heat. Strain. There should be approximately ½ cup of sauce.

Service and Garnish

Heat the tablespoon of corn oil in a large nonstick sauté pan and place the dumplings inside in a single layer. Pour ¼ cup cold water into the pan. Cover the pan and cook over low heat until the water has evaporated and the dumplings are golden and crisp on the bottom, about 15 to 20 minutes. Remove the dumplings to a large plate, and quickly sauté the sliced mushrooms in the same pan until heated through. To assemble, place a pear half in the center of each of four serving plates. Surround each pear with 3 dumplings. Drizzle the sauce around the plate, and garnish with sautéed mushrooms and baby greens.

Chef Notes

Chinese dumpling wrappers are easy to find in Chinatown markets. Gourmet specialty stores also carry them. They are available either natural or with a slight yellow tint. Either is fine for this recipe.

Truffled Flan of Foie Gras with Wild Mushroom Fricassee and Mâche

This flan from Todd English is perhaps the richest foie gras preparation I have encountered. By puréeing the foie gras and adding egg yolks and heavy cream, the texture of the finished flan approximates that of the creamy interior of seared foie gras. The earthy flavor of the truffles and the meaty texture of the mushrooms complements the rich flavor and consistency of the flan.

YIELD: 4 APPETIZER OR SIDE-DISH
SERVINGS

Flan

2 cups heavy cream

¼ pound foie gras, finely chopped

1 ounce black truffle, finely chopped

5 egg yolks

1 teaspoon coarse salt

1 teaspoon black pepper, freshly
    ground

1 teaspoon truffle oil (optional)

Fricassee

2 tablespoons unsalted butter

1 medium shallot, diced

⅔ pound assorted wild mushrooms,
    trimmed and wiped clean

3 tablespoons ruby port

1 cup chicken or duck stock

1 teaspoon fresh thyme leaves

½ teaspoon coarse salt

¼ teaspoon black pepper, freshly
    ground

Garnish

4 bunches mâche, washed

Shavings of black truffle

Special Equipment

4 flan, ramekin, or soufflé molds,
    ¾-cup each, buttered

Wine Recommendation

Château La Fleur de Gay 1995
(Pomerol), or another earthy red wine
with intense flavor.

Flan

Preheat the oven to 325 degrees. Place ½ cup of the cream and the chopped foie gras in a blender or food processor. Process until smooth. Pass the mixture through a fine strainer into a large stainless steel bowl. Discard any foie gras pieces left in the strainer. Clean out the work bowl of the blender or processor. Place a second ½ cup of the cream and the chopped truffles in the work bowl and process briefly. Combine with the foie gras mixture. Add the remaining 1 cup of cream, the egg yolks, salt, pepper, and truffle oil, if using. Gently whisk until well incorporated. Place the buttered molds into a 2-inch-deep roasting pan. Pour the flan mixture into the molds until each is three-fourths full. Fill the roasting pan with enough warm water to come halfway up the sides of the molds, creating a bain marie. Bake for 60 to 75 minutes, or until the flans are set and firm to the touch. The tops will brown and appear bubbly. Carefully remove the flans from the roasting pan and let cool at room temperature for 10 to 15 minutes.

Fricassee

Begin the fricassee when the flans are out of the oven. Melt the butter in a large sauté pan over medium heat. Add the shallot to soften, then add the mushrooms and cook until tender, about 10 minutes. Deglaze the pan with the port and scrape the browned bits from the bottom of the pan. Add the stock, thyme, salt, and pepper, and simmer until reduced to a sauce consistency, about 10 minutes.

Service and Garnish

To serve, carefully unmold a flan into the center of each of four serving plates by first running a small knife around the circumference of the flan, inverting the mold onto the plate, and then gently tapping the bottom of the mold. Spoon the fricassee around the perimeter of the flan and garnish each plate with mâche and truffle shavings. Serve warm.

Chef Notes

The flans can be made several hours ahead of time and gently reheated just before serving in a 300-degree oven for 5 to 10 minutes.

Foie Gras "Hamburger"

Christian Delouvrier's signature foie gras "hamburger" is a thick "patty" of seared foie gras sandwiched between a "bun" of caramelized fruit, either Granny Smith apples or, as in this version, sweet white peaches. The peaches are poached in a syrup of Sauternes, which is further reduced to produce the sauce. Surprisingly simple, the combination of the generously thick cut of foie gras and the sweet, tender peaches is exceedingly luscious.

YIELD: 6 APPETIZER SERVINGS

White Peaches
½ cup water
½ cup sugar
½ cup dry white wine
4 cups Sauternes
6 white peaches

Foie Gras and Garnish
3 tablespoons unsalted butter
2 tablespoons sugar
¼ cup fresh raspberries
12 ounces foie gras, cut into 6 slices, each about 2 ounces and 1½-inch thick
Coarse salt
White pepper, freshly ground

Wine Recommendation
Château Guiraud 1991 (Sauternes), or another sweet wine from Sauternes or Barsac.

White Peaches
In a nonreactive saucepan, combine the water and sugar and set over medium-high heat. Bring to a boil, turn down the heat, and simmer for 10 minutes to produce a simple syrup. Add the white wine and Sauternes, bring back to a boil, and cook for an additional 30 minutes, or until the mixture takes on a syrupy consistency; the bubbles will get larger and will slowly rise to the surface. Cut the peaches in half and remove the pits. Trim the flesh to shape the peaches uniformly and place any trimmings in the simmering Sauternes mixture. Add the peach halves to the Sauternes mixture and bring back to a boil. Poach the peach halves, covered in the syrup, for about 1 to 2 minutes, or until the flesh is tender and the skin begins to shrink away from the flesh. Remove from the syrup and let cool. Peel the poached peaches and add the peelings to the simmering syrup. Continue gently simmering until the mixture is the consistency of a thick syrup, about 45 minutes. To test if the syrup is finished, pour a spoonful onto a cold plate. If it doesn't run, it is done. Pass the syrup through a fine sieve and reserve in a warm place.

Foie Gras, Service, and Garnish
In a nonstick sauté pan, heat 2 tablespoons of the butter with the sugar. Add the peaches, cut side down, and sauté until they have caramelized to a golden brown, about 10 minutes. Reserve. In another small sauté pan, heat the remaining butter. Add the raspberries and crush with the tines of a fork to make a chunky purée. Cook for an additional 2 minutes and set aside.

Preheat the oven to 400 degrees. Heat a large nonstick ovenproof sauté pan over high heat. Season the foie gras slices with the salt. Add the foie gras slices and sear until brown, about 30 seconds per side. Season the foie gras with the white pepper. Place the pan in the oven for about 2 minutes to finish cooking. Remove the foie gras from the pan and pat dry on paper towel. Place half a peach in the center of each of six serving plates, cut side up, and spoon the raspberry purée into the peach hollow. Position the seared foie gras on top and crown with another peach half, cut side down. Drizzle the reduced Sauternes poaching liquid on top of the peach.

Crisped Sautéed Foie Gras with Buttered Golden Delicious Apples and Melfor Vinegar

Apples and foie gras are often paired in Alsace, where André Soltner was raised. André dredges the foie gras slices in flour and then sautés them in sweet butter. This technique is typical of the region, where goose foie gras is predominant. When heated, goose liver releases its fat more readily than duck liver, and the flour crust helps lessen the amount of fat lost in the pan. The crust also adds a pleasant textural element to the finished dish. Though most chefs sear Moulard foie gras without flour or butter, André retains the technique to enhance the authentic character of the dish.

Buttered Apples

4 Golden Delicious apples, peeled and cored (see Chef Notes)

1 tablespoon unsalted butter

Foie Gras

1½ pounds foie gras, cut into 12 slices, each about 2 ounces and ½-inch thick

All-purpose flour for dredging

Coarse salt

Black pepper, freshly ground

3 tablespoons unsalted butter

2 tablespoons Melfor vinegar (see Chef Notes)

½ cup veal stock or duck stock

Wine Recommendation

Pierre Sparr Tokay Pinot Gris Grand Cru Mambourg 1993 (Alsace), or another Tokay Pinot Gris.

Buttered Apples

Cut each apple into 8 slices. In a large sauté pan, heat the butter and add the apple slices. Sauté over medium heat about 3 minutes on each side, until the apples become slightly caramelized. Remove the apple slices from the pan and keep warm. Reserve the pan to cook the foie gras.

Foie Gras and Service

Dredge the slices of foie gras in the flour and season with salt and pepper. Melt 1 tablespoon of the butter in the pan used to cook the apples and sauté the foie gras slices over medium heat for 1 to 2 minutes on each side. The liver should be nicely browned on the outside, and slightly pink inside. On six warm plates, arrange 4 or 5 apple slices and 2 pieces of foie gras. Pour off all of the fat from the pan. Over high heat, briefly deglaze the pan with the vinegar, then add the stock and reduce by half. Lower the temperature and whisk in the remaining 2 tablespoons of butter. Cook for another 2 minutes, making sure the sauce does not boil or separate. Pour the sauce over the foie gras and the apples and serve.

Chef Notes

Depending on what is in season, you may substitute other cooking apples for the Golden Delicious. Melfor vinegar is a honey vinegar that is common in Alsace. Apple cider vinegar makes an acceptable substitution.

Seared Foie Gras with Apricot-Ginger Compote and Apricot Sorbet

Though juicy, ripe apricots can be difficult to find, when they are in season in June and July, they provide a unique tangy taste of summer. German native Joachim Splichal—whose restaurants span California, the state in which roughly 95 percent of the apricots in the United States are grown— uses apricots in this appetizer to counter the richness of the foie gras. The startling combination of a medallion of hot seared foie gras with a scoop of frozen sorbet makes this a dish à la mode for a hot, sunny day.

YIELD: 6 APPETIZER PORTIONS

Compote

1-ounce piece fresh ginger, peeled and cut into julienne

2 pounds ripe apricots

⅓ cup sugar

Sorbet

1 pound ripe apricots

1 cup sugar, plus extra for apricot cups

1 cup water

Juice of 1 lemon

Garnish

Apricot peels (reserved from compote above)

2 tablespoons sugar

6 brioche rounds, each 3 by ¼ inches

1 cup roast chicken jus or rich, dark chicken glace

Foie Gras

1 pound foie gras, cut into 6 slices, each about 2½ ounces and ½-inch thick

Special Equipment

Ice-cream machine

Wine Recommendation

Château Coutet 1989 (Barsac), or another sweet white wine from Barsac or Sauternes.

Compote

Blanch the julienned ginger in boiling water for 1 minute, remove, and shock immediately in ice water. Repeat the blanching and shocking process two more times. Set aside the ginger. Cut the apricots in quarters, and carefully peel off the skin. Reserve the peels for the garnish and dice the quartered apricots. In a saucepan, combine the blanched ginger, diced apricots, and sugar. Cook over low heat for 1 to 1½ hours, until the compote reaches a jamlike consistency. If the mixtures becomes too dry, add a tablespoon or two of water and continue cooking. Reserve and keep warm.

Sorbet

Select the three nicest apricots and set aside to use as sorbet cups. In a saucepan, combine 1 cup of the sugar and water, bring to a boil, and cool immediately. Purée the apricots with the lemon juice and strain into a deep bowl. Slowly add the cool syrup, checking the sugar density against the recommendations of the ice-cream machine manufacturer, until the desired density is reached. Freeze in the ice cream machine according to the manufacturer's instructions. Keep frozen until service.

To prepare the sorbet cups, preheat the oven to 300 degrees. Cut the reserved apricots in half and carefully peel the halves. Cut the bottom of each half to flatten, so the cups will easily stand on a plate. Sprinkle the cups with sugar and place on a parchment-lined baking sheet. Bake until the cups are soft and slightly shrunken, about 20 minutes.

Garnish

Preheat the oven to 300 degrees. Place the reserved apricot peels on a parchment-lined baking sheet. Sprinkle with the sugar and cook for 10 minutes, until they are dried. Set aside for service. Toast the brioche circles. Reserve the chicken jus until service.

Foie Gras

Preheat the oven to 350 degrees. In a very hot pan, sear the foie gras for about 30 seconds on each side. Finish the foie gras in the oven until just warmed through.

Service

Gently heat the chicken jus. Spread the toasted brioche circles with the apricot compote. Place a brioche circle on each of six serving plates, along with one apricot cup. Top each brioche circle with a slice of foie gras and fill each apricot cup with a scoop of sorbet. Pour 2 to 3 tablespoons of the chicken jus over each slice of foie gras and garnish the plates with the dried apricot skins.

Pan-Roasted Foie Gras with Golden Raisins, Celery, and Dry Jerez

YIELD: 4 APPETIZER SERVINGS

Dried Apple Skins

1 Red Delicious apple

1 Granny Smith apple

Coarse salt

1 tablespoon dry sherry

Golden Raisins and Celery

1½ cups dry Jerez (sherry)

2 ounces golden raisins

1 tablespoon honey

4 cups water

4 ribs celery, trimmed and peeled to eliminate fibers, and cut into 2-inch pieces

Coarse salt

Foie Gras

14 ounces foie gras, cut into 4 slices, each about 3½ ounces and ¼-inch thick

Coarse salt

Black pepper, freshly ground

2 tablespoons panko crumbs

1½ tablespoons butter

Garnish

1 tablespoon celery seed, toasted

Celery leaves

Wine Recommendation

Jean-Claude Thévenet Mâcon-Pierreclos 1996 (Burgundy), or another full-bodied Chardonnay.

According to Alain Rondelli, food should be about pleasure and excess. He particularly appreciates the sensual character of foie gras, which he complements in this dish with the sweet flavor of raisins and the mild grassiness of celery. The Jerez (Spanish sherry) brings both sweetness and acidity to this satisfying and whimsical appetizer.

Dried Apple Skins

Peel the skin of both apples into strips, 2 inches long by ½-inch wide. Place the strips in a bowl and sprinkle lightly with salt. Add the sherry and mix gently. Spread the apple skins on a parchment-lined half sheet pan, place in an oven with a pilot light, and let dry overnight.

Golden Raisins and Celery

Place the Jerez in a small saucepan set over high heat. When the Jerez begins to boil, place a lit match over the Jerez and let the alcohol burn for 2 to 3 minutes. Add the golden raisins, honey, and water and bring to a boil. Simmer for 7 minutes, cool, cover, and refrigerate overnight. Strain the raisins from the liquid and set aside. Place the liquid in a saucepan and add the celery sticks. Simmer for 10 to 12 minutes over medium heat. Remove the celery from the liquid and set aside. Reduce the liquid, over medium high heat, to about 3 tablespoons, about 1 hour. Season with salt, to taste. Add the reserved celery and golden raisins.

Foie Gras

Season the foie gras slices with salt and pepper and coat lightly with the panko crumbs. In a very hot sauté pan, sear the foie gras slices for about 40 seconds on each side, until golden brown. Add the butter to the pan and cook for an additional minute, using the butter to baste the foie gras. Remove from the pan and drain on paper towels.

Service and Garnish

Divide the sauce, along with the raisins and celery, among four serving plates. Place a slice of foie gras over the sauce. Garnish with the dried apple skins, celery seed, and celery leaves.

Hatikva Charcoal-Grilled Foie Gras with Duck-Prosciutto-Fig-Cardamom Jam and Pomegranate Glaze

Having spent my childhood years in Israel, one of the largest foie gras producers and exporters in the world, I was exposed to this delicacy at an early age. Though most of the Israeli-produced livers were exported, the lower grades were consumed by locals in outdoor tavernas in the Hatikva neighborhood of Tel Aviv, where foie gras was cubed, skewered, and charcoal-grilled. Pomegranate and figs, indigenous to the region, provide the sweet acidity necessary to balance the richness of the foie gras. Furthermore, ancient Egyptians fattened geese with plump figs, framing the preparation in a historical context. Duck prosciutto, a natural complement to figs, adds depth and nuttiness. Incorporating cardamom and ginger into the fig jam infuses the dish with an exotic Middle Eastern essence.

Fig Jam

1 pound fresh figs or ¼ pound dried, diced

½ red onion, finely chopped

½ tablespoon ginger, peeled and minced

10 cardamom pods, lightly cracked and tied into a cheesecloth sachet

2 cups port

Juice of 2 lemons

4 ounces duck prosciutto, finely diced (see page 166 and Chef Notes)

Pomegranate Glaze

Juice of 3 pomegranates (see Chef Notes)

3 tablespoons sugar

Grilled Foie Gras

1 pound foie gras, cut into 6 slices, each about 2½ ounces and ¼-inch thick

Coarse salt

Black pepper, freshly ground

Grilled Pita

1 pita bread

Duck or foie gras fat

3 cardamom pods, toasted and ground

Coarse salt

Black pepper, freshly ground

Garnish

3 fresh figs, quartered

Duck or foie gras fat

6 long chives

Sea salt

Black pepper, freshly cracked

Pomegranate seeds

Special Equipment

2-inch ring mold

Charcoal grill

Wine Recommendation

M. Chapoutier Crozes-Hermitage Les Varonniers 1994 (Rhone), or another full-bodied red wine.

Fig Jam

In a small saucepan combine the figs, red onion, ginger, cardamom, and port and set over medium-high heat. Bring to a boil, reduce the heat, and simmer for 20 to 30 minutes, stirring frequently to prevent burning, until the mixture acquires the consistency of a thick jam. Remove from the heat and stir in the lemon juice. After the mixture has cooled slightly, discard the cardamom sachet. Stir in the cubed duck prosciutto and set aside.

Pomegranate Glaze

In a small saucepan, combine the pomegranate juice and sugar and reduce the mixture to a glaze, about 20 minutes. Remove from heat and set aside.

Grilled Foie Gras

Score the foie gras and season with salt and pepper. Grill over charcoal, turning once, cooking the medallions for a scant minute per side, depending on the temperature of the grill. Be prepared to control flare-ups with a water-filled squirt bottle.

Grilled Pita

Brush the pita on both sides with the duck or foie gras fat and season with the cardamom, salt, and pepper. Cut the pita into six triangles and grill on both sides.

Service and Garnish

Brush half the figs with fat and grill lightly. To serve, set a ring mold in the center of one of six serving plates, spoon in one-sixth of the fig jam, and remove the mold. Place a grilled pita wedge on top of the jam. Balance a grilled foie gras medallion on top of the pita, and place both a grilled and a fresh piece of fig on top of the foie gras. Spoon some of the pomegranate glaze over the foie gras and around the plate. Drizzle some of the rendered fat around each plate. Garnish with chives, a sprinkle of sea salt, cracked black pepper, and pomegranate seeds.

Chef Notes

If you do not wish to make your own duck prosciutto, cured Chinese duck legs (available at Chinese grocers), smoked duck breast, or pork prosciutto may be substituted. Pomegranate syrup, purchased at Middle Eastern specialty stores, may be substituted for the pomegranate glaze. Bring to a boil, but do not reduce before serving. If a charcoal grill is not available, seared foie gras may be substituted.

Foie Gras Millefeuille with Toasted Almond, Caramelized Onion, Dried Blueberry Sauce, and Pineapple Brûlée

Almond Phyllo Pastry

2 rectangular sheets phyllo dough, 12 by 16 inches (see Chef Notes)

¾ cup unsalted butter, melted and cooled

½ cup crushed almonds

Dried Blueberry Sauce

¼ cup dried blueberries

2 tablespoons Armagnac

1 teaspoon rendered duck fat

½ yellow onion, cut into fine dice

2 cups rich duck stock

¼ teaspoon coarse salt

⅛ teaspoon black pepper, freshly ground

1 teaspoon rice vinegar, unseasoned

1 teaspoon honey

Caramelized Onions

1 tablespoon clarified butter

1 small yellow onion, finely sliced

Seared Foie Gras

10 ounces foie gras, cut into 4 slices, each about 2½ ounces and ½-inch thick

¼ teaspoon coarse salt

Pineapple Brûlée

2 rings fresh, ripe pineapple, cut in half to form 4 semicircles

2 tablespoons sugar

Special Equipment

Flat-top grill or grill pan

Propane torch

Wine Recommendation

Domaine Weinbach Cuvée Theo Riesling 1995 (Alsace), or another fragrant, crisp, dry Riesling.

Phyllo is a paper-thin Middle Eastern pastry traditionally used in both savory and sweet preparations. Frank Brigtsen straddles the line in this dish, using multilayered almond phyllo squares to add a textural component to the foie gras and to enhance the natural nuttiness of the liver. The dried blueberry sauce and pineapple brûlée add sweet and sour notes that complement and offset the richness of the liver.

Almond Phyllo Pastry

Preheat the oven to 350 degrees. Lay out one sheet of phyllo dough on a clean, dry cutting board. Cut lengthwise into four 3-inch-wide strips. Cover with a damp cloth to prevent from drying out. Repeat with the second sheet of phyllo dough. Brush each phyllo strip with melted butter. Scatter 1 tablespoon of crushed almonds on each phyllo strip, leaving 3 inches from one end clean. Fold the short end of the phyllo over the almonds and brush the top with melted butter. Continue to fold the phyllo, brushing each layer with melted butter, to form a 3-inch square. Repeat with the remaining phyllo strips. Place the eight pastry squares on a half sheet pan lined with parchment paper. Top with another sheet of parchment and another half sheet pan to keep the pastries flat while baking. Bake for 25 to 35 minutes, until light golden brown. Transfer the pastries to another sheet pan to cool.

Dried Blueberry Sauce

In a small bowl, combine the dried blueberries and the Armagnac, and let sit for 15 minutes, or longer if time permits. Heat the duck fat in a small saucepan over medium heat. Add the diced onions and cook, stirring constantly, until the onions are just beginning to brown, 3 to 4 minutes. Remove from the heat and add the blueberries and Armagnac. Return to the heat, add the stock, salt, and pepper. Bring the mixture to a boil, reduce the heat, and simmer, stirring occasionally, until the liquid has reduced to 1 cup, about 20 minutes. Add the rice vinegar and honey. Pureé the mixture in a blender and strain through a fine sieve. Keep warm.

Caramelized Onions

In a sauté pan set over a medium-high flame, heat the clarified butter. Add the onions and cook, stirring constantly, for 10 to 15 minutes, until the onions become dark brown. Set aside and keep warm.

Seared Foie Gras

Season the foie gras slices with the salt. Heat a flat-top grill or grill pan until very hot and grill the foie gras about 30 seconds on each side, making sure the liver remains pink inside.

Pineapple Brûlée

Place the pineapple slices on a heatproof pan. Sprinkle each slice with about 1 teaspoon of sugar and caramelize the sugar using a propane torch. Sprinkle additional sugar while torching the slices to ensure an even coating.

Service

Place a phyllo square in the center of each of four serving plates. Top with a slice of grilled foie gras and a second phyllo square. Top the pastry with a slice of pineapple brûlée and a spoonful of the caramelized onions. Drizzle the blueberry sauce around each plate.

Foie Gras Sauté on Polenta Cake with Country Ham and Blackberries

At his glorious country inn in Virginia, Patrick O'Connell incorporates Southern ingredients into his French-inspired cooking. The blackberries, cornmeal, and country ham in this dish evoke some of the traditional flavors of the South. Although foie gras is not a Southern staple, the combination of flavors and textures produces a sophisticated appetizer redolent of Southern hospitality.

Blackberry Sauce

1 tablespoon unsalted butter

1 small shallot, finely chopped

½ bay leaf

1½ pints fresh blackberries

½ cup water

½ cup cassis liqueur

2 tablespoons currant jelly

2 tablespoons chicken stock

½ teaspoon fresh thyme leaves, finely chopped

Black pepper, freshly ground

Polenta

2 tablespoons unsalted butter

¼ cup olive oil

1 small clove garlic, chopped

1 bay leaf

1 cup water

1 cup milk

1 cup heavy cream

½ cup yellow cornmeal

⅓ cup grated Parmigiano-Reggiano or Asiago cheese

Coarse salt

Cayenne pepper

Foie Gras

1½ pounds foie gras, cut into 8 slices, each about 3 ounces and ½-inch thick

Coarse salt

Black pepper, freshly ground

Garnish

2 cups mixed colorful baby lettuces or greens

¼ cup extra-virgin olive oil

Coarse salt

Black pepper, freshly ground

8 very thin slices country ham, trimmed of fat (see Chef Notes)

Fresh chives

Wine Recommendation

Domaine Henri Gouges Nuits-St.-Georges Clos de Porrets 1990 (Burgundy), or another full-bodied Pinot Noir.

Blackberry Sauce

In a 2-quart saucepan, melt the butter. Add the shallots, bay leaf, and ½ pint of the blackberries. Sweat over low heat for 3 minutes. Add the water, cassis, currant jelly, and stock. Simmer over medium heat for 30 minutes or until the sauce is the consistency of a light syrup. Remove from the heat, add the thyme leaves and fresh pepper, and set aside, off the heat, for 10 minutes. When cool, strain the sauce. Reserve.

Polenta

In a 4-quart saucepan, melt the butter. Add 1 tablespoon of the olive oil, the garlic, and bay leaf, and sweat over low heat for 30 seconds. Add the water, milk, and cream, and bring to a simmer. Remove the bay leaf. Whisking constantly, slowly add the cornmeal in a steady stream. Simmer for 10 minutes, until the polenta begins to thicken. Whisk in the cheese and season with salt and cayenne pepper. Line a half sheet pan with plastic wrap and pour the polenta onto the pan. Cover the polenta with plastic wrap and flatten to a thickness of about ½ inch. Refrigerate for 1 hour, then remove and cut into 2-inch squares. Heat the remaining olive oil in a sauté pan and cook the squares of polenta until both sides are golden brown. Reserve and keep warm.

Foie Gras

Season each slice of foie gras with salt and pepper. Heat a sauté pan over high heat and sear the foie gras for about 30 seconds on each side, or just until a brown crust forms. Remove the slices from the pan and blot on paper towels. Pour off excess fat from the pan and deglaze with ½ cup of the blackberry sauce. Stir this mixture back into the sauce, and gently add the remaining pint of blackberries.

Service and Garnish

Toss the greens in a mixing bowl with the olive oil, salt, and pepper. Place a small bouquet of dressed greens in the center of each of eight warmed serving plates. On top of the greens, place two squares of the crispy polenta. On top of the polenta place a slice of the country ham. On top of the ham, place a piece of seared foie gras. Spoon the sauce and the blackberries over the foie gras, and garnish with chives.

Orange Sauce

4 teaspoons water

4 tablespoons sugar, plus
    2 tablespoons, if necessary

3 cups orange juice

¼ cup lime juice

1 cup reduced chicken stock

1 tablespoon orange rind, grated

1 teaspoon lime rind, grated

2 tablespoons butter

2 tablespoons tequila

Pinch coarse salt

Pinch black pepper, freshly ground

2 tablespoons chili chipotle adobo
    sauce, canned

Lemon juice

Ancho Chilies

1 large ancho chili, seeded and
    deveined

½ small onion, minced, about ⅓ cup

2 large cloves garlic, crushed

¼ cup extra-virgin olive oil

¼ cup white wine vinegar

¼ cup Grand Marnier

¼ cup orange juice

½ tablespoon orange zest

1 tablespoon sugar

Pinch coarse salt

Pinch black pepper, freshly ground

1 tablespoon dried oregano

Oranges

2 blood oranges, segmented

2 oranges, segmented

1½ tablespoons sugar

2 teaspoons tequila

Foie Gras

1 tablespoon all-purpose flour

12 ounces foie gras, cut into 4 slices,
    each about 3 ounces and ½-inch
    thick

Wine Recommendation

Joh. Jos. Prüm Riesling Auslese Mosel-Saar-Ruwer Wehlener Sonnenuhr 1995 (Germany), or another wine with citrus notes and medium sweetness.

Sautéed Foie Gras with Blood-Orange Sauce and Ancho Chilies

The bold flavors of Mexican cooking provide the backbone for this intriguing appetizer, prepared by the doyenne of Mexican cookbook authors, Patricia Quintana. Chipotle peppers—actually dried and smoked jalapeños—in adobo sauce and marinated anchos add piquancy to the dulcet orange flavors.

Orange Sauce

In a saucepan set over medium heat, combine the water and sugar and heat until the sugar is completely dissolved. Increase the heat to high and bring the mixture to a boil. Cook until the syrup is golden brown, approximately 5 minutes. Gradually add the orange juice, stirring constantly, then add the lime juice. Slowly add the stock and cook for 15 minutes. Add the orange and lime rinds and continue to cook until the sauce is the consistency of a light syrup, about 10 minutes. Remove the sauce from the heat and swirl in the butter, stirring until it is completely absorbed. Stir in the tequila, salt, pepper, chipotle adobo sauce, and lemon juice to taste. If desired, add the extra 2 tablespoons of sugar to intensify the flavor of the sauce.

Ancho Chilies

Preheat the oven to 450 degrees. Place the chili in the oven and roast for 10 minutes. Remove from the oven and cut into julienned strips. Place the chili strips in a bowl and add the remaining ingredients. Let marinate for 2 hours.

Oranges

Place the orange sections in a bowl. Sprinkle with the sugar and the tequila. Set aside.

Foie Gras

Preheat the oven to 400 degrees. Sprinkle the flour on each foie gras slice and shake off the excess. Place a sauté pan over high heat. When the pan is extremely hot, add the foie gras and sear for 30 seconds on each side, until browned and crisp. Place the foie gras in a roasting pan and cook in the oven for 1 to 2 minutes. The foie gras should be medium rare and soft to the touch.

Service

Arrange the oranges in a fan pattern around each of four serving plates. Place a slice of foie gras on top. Add a teaspoon of foie gras fat from the pan to the orange sauce and swirl to incorporate. Spoon the orange sauce over the foie gras and garnish with the ancho chilies.

Hazelnut-Crusted Foie Gras with Plums and Sunflower Honey

YIELD: 4 APPETIZER SERVINGS

Sautéed Plums

2 tablespoons butter

4 red plums, cut into ¼-inch wedges

2 tablespoons sunflower honey, or
    another flowery honey

2 teaspoons lemon juice

⅛ teaspoon allspice

Coarse salt

Black pepper, freshly ground

Foie Gras

8 ounces foie gras, cut into 4 slices,
    each about 2 ounces and ½-inch
    thick

Coarse salt

Black pepper, freshly ground

¼ cup hazelnuts, roasted, skins
    removed, and chopped

Garnish

2 tablespoons plum sauce
    (see page 172 and Chef Notes)

Small handful baby greens

4 slices raisin nut bread, cut into
    triangles and toasted

Wine Recommendation

Calera Viognier 1995 (San Benito), or
another full-bodied white wine with
honey fragrances. Or else, Fonseca
Vintage Port 1968, or another
full-bodied vintage port.

Matthew Kenny's fresh, light style of cooking is greatly influenced by the Mediterranean. The red plums and sunflower honey in this recipe evoke the sun-drenched flavors of Morocco and accent the foie gras. The hazelnut crust complements the nuttiness of the liver and adds a contrasting texture to the dish.

Sautéed Plums

Melt the butter in a sauté pan set over medium-high heat. Add the plums, honey, lemon juice, and allspice. Sauté until the plums have softened and released their juices, 7 to 10 minutes. Season to taste with salt and pepper. Set aside.

Foie Gras

Preheat the oven to 500 degrees. Wrap each piece of foie gras in plastic wrap and lightly pound the slices to ⅓-inch thick. Unwrap, score each side lightly with a sharp knife, and season generously with salt and pepper. Set an ovenproof sauté pan over high heat. Add the foie gras and sear quickly, about 30 seconds. Turn over the slices and sprinkle with the chopped hazelnuts. Place the pan in the oven and cook the foie gras until medium-rare, about 30 seconds.

Service and Garnish

Warm the plum sauce slightly. Divide the baby greens evenly among four serving plates and top with the sautéed plums. Place the foie gras on top of the plums, with the hazelnut-crusted side up. Drizzle the plum sauce decoratively over the foie gras, and place two wedges of toasted raisin nut bread on each plate.

Chef Notes

If you prefer not to prepare your own plum sauce, you can purchase a high-quality Chinese one.

Duck Jus

1 pound duck bones

1 clove garlic, peeled

1 shallot, coarsely chopped

½ medium onion, diced

½ carrot, diced

½ celery stalk, diced

½ cup white port

½ cup white wine

2 tablespoons tamarind paste

Green Papaya Compote

2 cups white port

3 tablespoons lemon juice

2 tablespoons sugar

4 fresh bay leaves

1 medium green papaya, skinned,
    seeds removed

Tamarind Sauce

¼ cup plus 2 tablespoons water

2 tablespoons tamarind paste

2 teaspoons sugar

1 tablespoon olive oil

Foie Gras

1 pound 2 ounces foie gras, cut into
    6 slices, each about 3 ounces
    and ¼-inch thick

Coarse salt

Black pepper, freshly ground

Garnish

4 ounces unsalted pistachios, shelled

6 chives, cut into 1-inch spears

6 tablespoons pistachio oil

Special Equipment

Mandoline or vegetable peeler

Cast-iron skillet

Wine Recommendation

Lucien Thomas Sancerre 1996 (Loire),
or another fruity white wine with
some sweetness, such as an off-dry
Gewürztraminer or a late-harvest
Chenin Blanc.

200

Seared Foie Gras with Green Papaya Compote, Tamarind Sauce, and Pistachio

In its pure state foie gras has a natural nutty flavor likened to pistachios. In this preparation from Rocco DiSpirito, these nutty undertones are accentuated by toasted pistachios and pistachio oil. Rocco also invokes the flavors of Southeast Asia, incorporating into the dish the fresh, flavorful crispness of unripened green papaya and the tartness of tamarind. This combination of sweet and sour provides a counterbalance for the rich creaminess of the foie gras.

Duck Jus

Preheat the oven to 500 degrees. Place the duck bones in a roasting pan and roast for 20 minutes until browned. Add the garlic, shallot, onion, carrot, and celery, and roast for an additional 10 to 15 minutes. Deglaze the roasting pan over a high flame with the port and wine. Transfer everything to a small stockpot and add enough water to cover the ingredients. Stir in the tamarind paste. Bring to a boil, lower the heat to a simmer, and reduce by half, 1½ to 2 hours. Strain and reserve the jus.

Green Papaya Compote

In a medium saucepan, combine the port, lemon juice, sugar, and bay leaves, and cook over medium-high heat until the liquid reduces by half, 12 to 15 minutes. Using a mandoline or a sharp vegetable peeler, cut the papaya into long, thin ribbons, less than ⅛-inch thick. Add the green papaya ribbons to the saucepan and cook until al dente, about 2 minutes. Remove from the heat so the papaya maintains its crunch. Remove the bay leaves. Keep warm.

Tamarind Sauce

Reconstitute the tamarind paste by combining ¼ cup water and the tamarind paste in a saucepan. Simmer the mixture until it forms a thick concentrate, and strain through a fine sieve. In a small sauté pan, cook the sugar over medium heat until it caramelizes to a golden brown. Stir frequently to be sure it does not burn. Whisk in 2 tablespoons of the tamarind concentrate, the olive oil, and the remaining 2 tablespoons of water, and heat through. Remove from the heat.

Foie Gras and Garnish

Season the foie gras slices with salt and pepper. Heat a cast-iron skillet over high heat and sear the foie gras for about 30 seconds on each side. Remove to a warmed platter. In the foie gras fat, sauté the pistachios and chives for 30 seconds. Season with salt and pepper.

Service and Garnish

Evenly divide the warm green papaya compote onto the center of each of six serving plates. Place a piece of seared foie gras on top, and garnish with a spoonful of the sautéed pistachios and the chives. Top the foie gras with a tablespoon of warm duck jus and circle the dish with a drizzle of tamarind sauce and a swirl of pistachio oil.

Down Island Brioche French Toast with Curaçao-Marinated Foie Gras, Savory Citrus Caramel Sauce, and Exotic Fruit Salsa

Norman Van Aken puts a New World spin on brioche and foie gras in this savory, tropical version of French toast. Norman relies on a melange of exotic fruits and a tart citrus caramel sauce to add the sweetness and acidity required to balance the richness of the foie gras. He marinates the foie gras in the same flavorings he uses to make the French toast batter so that the seared foie gras and sautéed French toast have a strikingly similar flavor. The custardy textures of both elements complement each other well.

YIELD: 4 APPETIZER SERVINGS

Foie Gras

1 cup Curaçao
½ Tahitian vanilla bean, cut in half lengthwise
½ teaspoon ground mace
½ teaspoon ground cinnamon
Zest of 1 orange
1 pound foie gras, cut into 8 medallions, about 2 ounces each, scored on both sides

French Toast

5 eggs, slightly beaten
½ Tahitian vanilla bean, cut in half lengthwise
2 cups half-and-half
½ teaspoon ground mace
½ teaspoon ground cinnamon
6 slices fresh brioche, about ½-inch thick, cut in half diagonally

Foie Gras

Pour the Curaçao into a large bowl. With the tip of a knife, scrape the seeds of the vanilla bean into the liqueur; reserve the pod for another use. Add the mace, cinnamon, and orange zest, and whisk until blended. Place the foie gras into this marinade and cover with plastic wrap. Make sure the liver is completely coated with the marinade. Refrigerate for at least 2 hours and up to 12 hours before service, occasionally turning the foie gras over in the marinade.

French Toast

Place the eggs in a medium bowl. With the tip of a knife, scrape the seeds of the vanilla bean into the eggs. Reserve the pod for another use. Add the half-and-half, mace, and cinnamon and beat until well blended. Place the slices of brioche into this mixture. Cover with plastic wrap and refrigerate until the brioche has absorbed the mixture, 10

minutes to 1 hour, depending on how dry the brioche is. The brioche should be soaked through when you are ready to cook it.

Savory Citrus Caramel Sauce

In a heavy, shallow saucepan, combine the stock, juice, and sugar. Set over high heat and cook until the mixture begins to turn a dark caramel color, 20 to 30 minutes, depending on the size and conductivity of the pan. Look for wisps of steam rising from the pan to be sure the sugar is caramelizing. Carefully whisk in the heavy cream, little by little. Bring to a boil, whisking continuously. When the sauce has turned a dark caramel color and has large, lazy bubbles, about 4 minutes, add the soy sauce. Stir and pass through a fine mesh strainer. Reserve.

Exotic Fruit Salsa

In a small bowl, combine all the ingredients. Reserve.

Savory Citrus Caramel Sauce

1¾ cups chicken stock

¾ cup fresh grapefruit juice or other
    fresh acidic fruit juice

⅓ cup sugar

2 cups heavy cream

2 or 3 drops soy sauce

Exotic Fruit Salsa

½ cup chopped fresh pineapple

½ cup chopped fresh papaya

½ cup chopped fresh mango

2 to 3 tablespoons fresh pineapple juice

Service and Garnish

Remove the foie gras from the marinade. Discard the marinade. Carefully remove the brioche slices from the egg mixture and set them on a plate. Heat a cast-iron skillet over medium-high heat. Add some of the clarified butter and lay the brioche into the hot pan. Cook as for French toast, until golden brown on both sides. Remove from the pan and keep warm. Repeat until all pieces are cooked.

Heat a clean pan over high heat. Sear the foie gras on both sides until caramelized, about 30 seconds per side. Drain off the fat. Ladle some of the warm caramel sauce in the center of each of four warm serving plates. Place a piece of French toast on the sauce. Top with a piece of seared foie gras and another slice of French toast. Place another piece of seared foie gras on top, and finish with a third slice of French toast. Spoon additional sauce around the plate. Sprinkle the exotic fruit salsa around the French toast and garnish with the candied zests, ginger, and kumquats. Serve immediately.

Chef Notes
The savory citrus caramel recipe will yield about 1½ cups. Leftovers can be refrigerated for up to two weeks and reheated at another time. Any combination of ripe exotic fruits can be used to prepare the salsa. The candied zests, ginger, and kumquats used for garnish can be purchased in specialty candy stores or made by blanching the ingredients in several changes of boiling water and simmering in simple syrup until tender.

Garnish
2 tablespoons clarified butter
Candied zests of orange, lemon, and
    lime, cut into julienne
Candied ginger, cut into julienne
Candied kumquats, sliced

Special Equipment
Cast-iron skillet

Wine Recommendation
Dienhart Riesling Beerenauslese
Mosel-Saar-Ruwer Bernkasteler
Doctor 1995 (Germany), or any sweet
wine with good acidity and fruit.

Jerk Foie Gras with Roasted Sweet Potato, Coconut, Lime, and Scotch Bonnet

Jerk is a barbecue technique from Jamaica that involves rubbing a fiery dry spice mixture on meat and cooking it over hot coals, often in oil drums on the side of the road. Allen Susser adapts the jerk method to prepare a spicy grilled foie gras. The roasted sweet potato, pineapple, and coconut add another Caribbean element to the dish, as well as a contrast of flavors and textures.

YIELD: 8 MAIN COURSE SERVINGS

Jerk Foie Gras

4 whole scallions

1 cup red wine

3 cloves garlic, chopped

1 tablespoon fresh cilantro, minced

1 tablespoon olive oil

¼ cup ground allspice

4 teaspoons ground cinnamon

1 teaspoon tamarind pulp

1 teaspoon coarse salt

1 teaspoon minced Scotch Bonnet pepper

½ teaspoon nutmeg, freshly grated

1½ pounds foie gras, cut into 8 slices, each about 3 ounces and ¼-inch thick

Roasted Sweet Potato

3 cups sweet potato, cut into 1-inch cubes

2 cups fresh pineapple, cut into 1-inch cubes

4 tablespoons olive oil

1 tablespoon diced serrano chili, seeds removed

2 cups coconut milk

2 tablespoons fresh lime juice

1 teaspoon coarse salt

½ teaspoon black pepper, freshly ground

Garnish

Fresh lemon thyme

Wine Recommendation

Château Roumieu 1995 (Barsac), or another medium-sweet, somewhat spicy white wine.

Jerk Foie Gras

In a large ceramic bowl, combine all the ingredients except the foie gras. Toss the foie gras slices with this seasoning mixture, cover, and refrigerate for at least 2 hours.

Roasted Sweet Potato

Preheat the oven to 400 degrees. In a small roasting pan, combine the sweet potato, pineapple, and 3 tablespoons of the olive oil. Roast for 20 minutes, until the potato starts to soften. Remove a quarter of the roasted ingredients, reserve, and continue to roast the remaining ingredients for an additional 20 minutes or until slightly caramelized to golden brown. In a medium sauté pan, sauté the serrano chili in the remaining tablespoon of olive oil. Add the reserved potato and pineapple mixture, the coconut milk, lime juice, salt, and pepper. Over medium heat, reduce this mixture by half. Purée the reduced mixture in a food processor until smooth. Set aside both the purée and the roasted potato and pineapple mixture, and keep warm.

Service and Garnish

Preheat a grill or grill pan until very hot. Grill each piece of foie gras for 30 seconds on each side, charring the outside while leaving the inside medium rare. Spoon a pool of purée onto each of eight serving plates. Top with the roasted sweet potato and pineapple mixture and finish with a medallion of grilled foie gras. Garnish with a sprig of fresh lemon thyme.

Anise-Braised Duck and Foie Gras Empanadas

Taking familiar dishes and techniques from traditional Latin American cuisines and adding contemporary elements is the signature of Douglas Rodriguez's "Nuevo Latino" style of cooking. This foie gras empanada typifies how Douglas can be whimsical without sacrificing flavor or tradition. In this instance, the foie gras intensifies and enriches the flavorful filling. The flaky pastry can be used for other empanadas or savory fried pockets.

YIELD: 10 APPETIZER SERVINGS

Orange Curls
20 oranges

Dough
2½ cups all-purpose flour
½ cup vegetable oil
½ cup water
1 teaspoon salt
1 teaspoon fennel seeds, toasted

Filling
1 duck breast, about 10 ounces, fat removed
½ cup orange juice, freshly squeezed
Zest of 1 orange
3 pieces star anise
1 tablespoon black peppercorns
1 sprig rosemary
2 cups cold water
Coarse salt
Black pepper, freshly ground
1 tablespoon achiote oil
1 small red pepper, seeded and diced
1 teaspoon garlic, minced
1 red onion, diced

Orange Curls
To make the orange curls, use a channel cutter or sharp paring knife to peel each orange in one long, thin strand. To be sure the strip of peel is as long and thin as possible, cut around the circumference of the orange in one motion. Reserve the oranges for another use. Tuck one end of the peel into a drinking straw and secure with a piece of tape. Tightly wrap the strip of peel around the straw. Tuck the second end into the opposite end of the straw and tape. Repeat with the remaining peels. Place the straws in a food dehydrator or in a gas oven with the pilot light on overnight until dried and crisp. Remove the tape and uncoil the peels. Carefully remove the curls from the straws.

Dough
Place 2 cups of the flour in the bowl of an electric mixer fitted with a dough hook. Add the oil and water and slowly mix on low speed. Add the remaining ½ cup of flour, the salt, and fennel seeds. The dough will crumble and then, after about 10 minutes of mixing, it will come together again to form a ball around the hook. Increase the speed to medium and continue mixing until the dough is elastic. It will feel silky and pull away from the sides of the bowl. Remove the dough from the mixing bowl, wrap in plastic, and refrigerate for 1 hour. Reserve the frying oil until ready to prepare the empanadas.

Filling
In a medium saucepan, combine the duck breast, orange juice and zest, star anise, peppercorns, rosemary, water, salt, and pepper. Set the saucepan over medium-high heat and bring to a boil, reduce to a simmer, and let the duck breast poach gently for 1 hour, or until the meat is tender. Remove the pan from the heat and let the duck cool in the poaching liquid. When cool, remove the duck breast and shred the meat. Discard the liquid.

In a sauté pan set over high heat, heat the achiote oil. Add the red pepper, garlic, onion, and the shredded duck breast. Sauté for about 3 minutes, remove from the heat, and set aside.

Foie Gras

1 pound foie gras, sliced into
    5 medallions, about 3 ounces each

Course salt

Black pepper, freshly ground

4 ounces flat-leaf spinach leaves,
    washed, stemmed, and blanched

Empanadas

Dough (from above)

Filling (from above)

Foie Gras (from above)

1 to 2 tablespoons cold water

Vegetable oil for frying

Salad

1 red onion, unpeeled

2 red bell peppers

1 tablespoon mustard oil

1 pound flat-leaf spinach, washed and
    destemmed

2 tablespoons sherry vinegar

Coarse salt

Black pepper, freshly ground

Foie Gras

Season the foie gras generously with salt and pepper. Heat a sauté pan over high heat. Add the foie gras and sear for about 30 seconds on each side. Remove the foie gras from the pan and let cool. Cut the medallions into ten even pieces and wrap each piece in spinach to form a tight package. Reserve until ready to prepare the empanada.

Empanadas

Place the rested dough on a well-floured surface and roll out to a thickness of less than ⅛ inch. Cut out 20 circles using a 3-inch round pastry cutter. Place 1 tablespoon of the duck filling in the center of each of the pastry rounds and pat down with the back of a spoon to flatten. Be sure to leave about ¼-inch rim around the circumference of the circle in order to seal the empanada later. Set a piece of the spinach-wrapped foie gras on top of each of ten rounds. Top the foie gras with another tablespoon of filling. Lightly dab the edges of the remaining ten rounds of dough with water. Gently flip these on top and seal the edges by squeezing the two circles of dough together with your fingertips or with the tines of a fork to form little round packets. Repeat until you have ten empanadas.

Pour the vegetable oil into a cast-iron skillet to a depth of about 2 inches. Heat the oil to 350 degrees and fry the empanadas for about 4 minutes per side, until they rise to the surface of the oil and turn a deep golden brown.

Salad

Preheat the oven to 425 degrees. Place the red onion into the oven and roast until tender, 45 minutes to 1 hour. Cool to room temperature, remove the peel, and cut into ½-inch slices.

Over a hot grill, a gas flame, or under the broiler, roast the peppers until the skin is blackened and blistered all over. Place the peppers in a plastic or brown paper bag, close the top, and set aside until cool. When the peppers are cool enough to handle, peel off the skin and discard. Slice in half and remove the seeds. Cut into fine julienne.

In a sauté pan set over a medium-high flame, heat the mustard oil. Add the spinach and toss for about 20 seconds. Add the roasted peppers and onions and heat through. Add the vinegar and remove from the heat. Season with salt and pepper.

Plantains

To prepare the plantains, heat the canola oil to 350 degrees. Peel the ripe plantains and cut into 2-inch chunks. Fry the chunks in the hot oil until golden brown, about 5 minutes on each side. Remove from the oil and drain on a paper towel.

Service and Garnish

Divide the salad among ten serving plates. Arrange the fried plantains around the salad. Carefully cut the empanadas in half with a sharp knife and position on top of the salad. Garnish with the orange curls.

Plantains

3 large, ripe yellow plantains
Canola oil for frying

Special Equipment

20 drinking straws
3-inch round pastry cutter
Deep cast-iron skillet

Wine Recommendation

Château Sociando-Mallet Haut Médoc 1989 (Bordeaux), or another full-bodied, tannic red wine.

Crispy Potato and Turnip Galettes with Foie Gras and Wild Mushrooms

Chef Raymond Blanc is among those who believe the nutritional composition of foie gras earns it the designation of a nutritional "super food." The restorative properties of this hearty autumnal dish make it hard to disagree. Crisp potatoes, sweet turnips, and earthy mushrooms provide the flavor backdrop for the succulent seared liver.

YIELD: 4 APPETIZER SERVINGS

Mushroom Sauce

1 tablespoon vegetable oil

4 ounces button mushrooms, finely chopped

6 shallots, peeled and finely chopped

1 tablespoon unsalted butter

⅛ cup sherry vinegar

⅛ cup ruby port

⅛ cup dry Madeira

1 teaspoon Amontillado sherry (optional)

Pinch dried cèpe powder (optional)

1 cup veal stock

½ cup light chicken stock, or water

2 tablespoons heavy cream

1 sprig thyme

1 strip orange zest

2 tablespoons water

Galettes

1 pound potatoes (see Chef Notes)

4 ounces small turnips

Coarse salt

White pepper, freshly ground

6 tablespoons unsalted butter, melted, plus extra for coating pan

Mushroom Sauce

Heat the oil in a sauté pan and cook the mushrooms until they begin to color. Set aside. In another sauté pan, sweat the shallots in the butter and cook until they turn a rust color. Deglaze the shallot pan with the sherry vinegar and allow the vinegar to evaporate completely. Add the port, Madeira, sautéed mushrooms, sherry, and cèpe powder, if using. Reduce the mixture by two-thirds, skimming occasionally. Add the veal stock and chicken stock or water, and stir in the heavy cream. Add the thyme and the orange zest and bring to a boil. Skim and force the sauce through a fine chinois into a small saucepan. Adjust the seasoning and stir in about 2 tablespoons of water to prevent a skin from forming on the sauce.

Galettes

Preheat the oven to 300 degrees. Wash, peel, and finely grate the potatoes. Rinse in a colander and squeeze out as much water as possible. Wash, peel, and grate the turnips

and combine with the grated potatoes in a mixing bowl. Season with salt and pepper and add the melted butter, making sure to coat all the vegetables. Brush the bottom of a large nonstick pan, set over medium-high heat, with melted butter. Place the ring mold in the pan and drop a small amount of the potato mixture into the ring mold to a thickness of ⅛ to ¼ inch. Gently pat the mixture down with your fingertips and cook for about 1 minute, until the bottom begins to crisp. Remove the ring mold and carefully flip the galette and cook until crisp and golden brown. Prepare a total of 12 galettes using this method. Cool the galettes on a wire rack and dry them in the oven for 5 minutes.

Garnish

Preheat the oven to 350 degrees. Place the shallots in a small ovenproof saucepan with the water. Add 1 tablespoon of the butter, sugar, and a pinch of salt. Cook the shallots in the oven, covered, for 20 minutes. Move

Garnish

12 shallots, peeled

6 tablespoons water

2 tablespoons unsalted butter

Pinch sugar

Coarse salt

½ cup fresh wild mushrooms, such as chanterelles, black trumpets, or hen of the woods, cleaned and trimmed

½ teaspoon fresh lemon juice, or to taste

4 to 5 tarragon leaves, chopped

1 small bunch chervil

¼ black truffle, sliced (optional)

saucepan to stovetop. Continue to cook the shallots over a high heat and reduce the liquid until the shallots caramelize. Set aside. Make sure all the mushrooms are the same size, cutting any large ones into smaller pieces. Heat the remaining butter in a sauté pan and add the mushrooms, lemon juice, a pinch of salt, and tarragon, and cook for 1 minute. Set aside. Reserve the chervil and truffle until service.

Foie Gras

Season the foie gras slices with salt and pepper. Sear the foie gras in a smoking hot pan for 10 seconds on each side. Let rest in a 200-degree oven for 10 minutes (see Chef Notes). Remove.

Service and Garnish

Warm the foie gras, galettes, shallots, and mushrooms in the oven for 1 minute. Drain the foie gras on paper towels and cut each slice into four slivers. Arrange a galette in the center of each of four serving plates, top with two slivers of foie gras. Top with another galette, two more slivers of foie gras, and a third galette. In a saucepan, combine the mushroom sauce, caramelized shallots, and truffles, if using. Pour the sauce around the galettes, allowing 3 shallots per plate. Garnish with the black truffle and a sprig of chervil.

Chef Notes

Use potatoes with a high starch content, such as Russet or Yukon Gold. If you use a lower-starch potato, such as new potatoes, do not rinse, simply squeeze the excess water from the grated potato. Resting the foie gras will allow it to cook gently to medium rare and will prevent overcooking.

Foie Gras

8 ounces foie gras, cut into 4 slices, each about 2 ounces
Coarse salt
Black pepper, freshly ground

Special Equipment

Fine chinois
3-inch round ring mold

Wine Recommendation

Château Le Barradis 1990 (Monbazillac), or another intensely fruity, rich sweet wine. Or for a different effect, Château Beychevelle 1986 (St.-Julien), or another silky, medium-full bodied red wine.

Salt-Crusted Foie Gras with Cèpes and Verjus

Throughout Europe, a crust of salt is used to bake various meats and seafood, from the black sea bass of the Ligurian coast to the Norman lamb of Mont Saint Michel. Thierry Rautureau uses this same technique to roast a whole foie gras. The salt crust seals in the juices and the flavor, without making the liver overly salty. The presentation can be dramatic, especially if the whole liver is brought to the table before it is sliced. The earthy flavors of the cèpe garnish draw out the flavor of the foie gras, and the verjus sauce provides a welcome counterpoint to the richness of the liver.

Verjus Sauce

2 cups verjus

3 sprigs fresh thyme

3 shallots, sliced

½ clove garlic, sliced

3 cups veal stock

3 tablespoons cold butter, or 2
    tablespoons rendered foie gras fat

Coarse salt

Black pepper, freshly ground

Foie Gras

3 pounds coarse sea salt

1 foie gras, about 1½ pounds, separated
    into 2 lobes and cleaned of all
    surface imperfections

Cèpes

1 tablespoon butter

1 tablespoon hazelnut or walnut oil

½ pound fresh cèpes, sliced lengthwise

2 shallots, minced

1 clove garlic, minced

1 teaspoon fresh thyme, chopped

Coarse salt

Black pepper, freshly ground

1 tablespoon chopped chives

Garnish

Brioche toasts

Edible flowers, such as bachelor's
    buttons or cornflowers
    (see Chef Notes)

Wine Recommendation

Guy Amiot Chassagne-Montrachet Les
Champs Gain 1994 (Burgundy), or
another concentrated Chardonnay.

Verjus Sauce

In a medium saucepan, place the verjus, thyme, shallots, and garlic and reduce over medium heat to a glaze. Add the stock and continue reducing until only 1 cup remains. Finish by whisking in the butter or foie gras fat and season with salt and pepper. Strain and set aside.

Foie Gras

Preheat the oven to 400 degrees. Fill a large sauté pan with the salt and heat over a moderately high flame until very hot. At the same time, heat an ovenproof sauté pan until hot but not scalding. Add one of the foie gras lobes to the empty hot pan, and sear it quickly on all sides, being careful not to burn it. Remove the lobe from the pan and set aside, reserving the rendered fat. Proceed the same way with the remaining lobe, reserving the rendered fat. Wipe the pan clean. Pour half the hot salt into the clean foie gras pan, lay the lobes on the salt, and cover with the remaining hot salt. Set the sauté pan in the preheated oven. Roast for 4 to 5 minutes then remove the smaller lobe and check for doneness by inserting a metal blade or sharp skewer to make sure that the interior of the lobe is warmed. If the blade feels cold, the liver is not ready. If it is hot, the foie gras will be overcooked. Roast the large lobe for approximately 5 minutes

more, testing for doneness before removing from the oven, and set aside.

Cèpes

While the foie gras is roasting, heat a medium sauté pan and add the butter and oil. When the mixture is hazelnut-colored, add the cèpes. Sauté until three-fourths done, 3 to 5 minutes, then add the shallots, garlic, and thyme, and the salt and pepper to taste. Add the chopped chives just before you remove the pan from the heat.

Service and Garnish

Remove the roasted lobes from the salt. Using a pastry brush, carefully brush off most of the salt and slice into ½-inch slices. Divide the cèpes evenly among the serving plates, and place two slices of the foie gras over the mushrooms. Drizzle the verjus sauce around the liver and arrange the brioche toasts around the plate. Decorate with the edible flowers.

Chef Notes

You can save the sea salt, which absorbs plenty of the flavorful fat from the foie gras, and use it eight to ten more times to prepare this dish. Bachelor's buttons and cornflowers are two types of edible flowers that make an attractive garnish for this dish. Other edible flowers may be substituted.

Tandoori Foie Gras with Turmeric Chili Potatoes, Mint Chutney, and Preserved Lime Pickle

An Indian tandoor is a tall, cylindrical oven with a rounded top made out of clay and brick. A smokey fire heats the oven to temperatures above 600 degrees. Meats marinated in yogurt and spices, and chewy flat breads are mainstays of tandoori cooking, a technique popular throughout India. The high heat imparts a distinctive smokey flavor and the rapid cooking keeps meats juicy and tender. Grant MacPherson, who was exposed to traditional Indian cooking while working in Singapore, adapts the tandoori technique for foie gras. The liver is marinated in yogurt and spices, skewered, seared in a tandoor, and finished in a conventional oven. Lime pickle and mint chutney are traditional tandoori condiments.

Lime Pickle

8 pounds whole limes, washed and
 dried, bases trimmed
 (see Chef Notes)
½ pound kosher salt
2 cups vinegar
½ pound garlic, sliced
½ pound ginger, thinly sliced
2 cups mustard oil
½ cup sesame oil
3 ounces sesame seeds, pounded
7 ounces mustard seeds, pounded

Mint Chutney

¼ pound fresh mint, finely chopped
2 ounces fresh coriander, finely
 chopped
4 cloves garlic, finely chopped
1 piece fresh ginger, ¼-inch long, finely
 chopped
6 to 8 green chilies, seeded and finely
 chopped
2 teaspoons fresh lemon juice
½ teaspoon sugar
¼ teaspoon coarse salt
¼ cup yogurt

Lime Pickle

Place the limes in a large nonreactive glass, ceramic, or stainless steel container with a tight-fitting lid. Add the salt and vinegar and mix well. Cover tightly and set aside for 45 days, turning the limes every 3 to 4 days. After this maturation period, remove the limes from the vinegar mixture and cut into 8 slices. Place the limes back in the pickling liquid and add the remaining ingredients. Mix well, cover tightly, and let marinate for 7 days.

Mint Chutney

In the bowl of a food processor, combine the mint, coriander, garlic, ginger, and green chilies. Process the mixture until it becomes a fine paste. Add the lemon juice and sugar and the salt to taste. Add the yogurt and blend thoroughly. Adjust the seasoning if necessary. For a more refined condiment, pass the chutney through a fine sieve.

Tandoori Foie Gras

Fire up the tandoor oven, if using one. In a large bowl, combine the yogurt, roasted besan, mustard oil, chili powder, garlic paste, ginger paste, tandoori coloring (if using), garam masala, lemon juice, and salt. Add the foie gras and marinate, refrigerated, overnight, or at room temperature for 2 hours, then freeze for 2 hours. Preheat a conventional oven to 200 degrees. Skewer the whole lobe of foie gras and grill in a moderately hot tandoor oven for 2 to 3 minutes. Remove the foie gras from the tandoor, take out the skewer, and let rest for 10 minutes. Place the foie gras in a roasting pan and cook in the conventional oven for 10 minutes. If a tandoor oven is not available, roast the foie gras in a conventional oven at 450 degrees for 13 to 15 minutes, until done.

Tandoori Foie Gras

½ cup yogurt

1 tablespoon besan, roasted
   (see Chef Notes)

1 teaspoon mustard oil

1 teaspoon chili powder

½ teaspoon garlic paste
   (see Chef Notes)

½ teaspoon ginger paste
   (see Chef Notes)

Tandoori coloring (optional,
   see Chef Notes)

Pinch garam masala (see Chef Notes)

2 teaspoons lemon juice

2 teaspoons coarse salt

1 large lobe foie gras, about 1 pound

Turmeric Chili Potatoes

2 medium Russet potatoes, about
   1 pound, peeled and cut into large
   dice

2 tablespoons ghee or butter
   (see Chef Notes)

1 tablespoon ginger, finely minced

1 green chili, seeded and chopped

1 teaspoon coarse salt

2 tablespoon fresh lemon juice

Pinch turmeric

3 tablespoons fresh coriander, chopped

Turmeric Chili Potatoes

Place the potatoes in a saucepan and cover with salted water. Bring to a boil and cook until tender, about 10 to 15 minutes. Set aside. Melt the ghee or butter in a large sauté pan set over medium heat. Add the ginger and green chili and sauté for 2 minutes. Add the salt and lemon juice and sauté for another minute. Add the turmeric and sauté for another 30 seconds. Add the reserved potatoes and the coriander. Using the back of a wooden spoon, smash the potatoes while combining all the ingredients. Adjust the seasoning, if necessary, and remove from the heat.

Garnish

In a sauté pan, heat 1 inch of oil to 350 degrees. Add the mint or curry leaves and fry until crisp. Remove from the oil and drain on paper towels. Add the pappadum strips to the oil and fry until they just begin to darken. Remove the pappadum from the oil and, while still very hot, curl around a chopstick or the handle of a wooden spoon. Allow the curls to drain on paper towels.

Service

Divide the potatoes evenly among four serving plates. Slice the foie gras into ½-inch thick slices and place two to three slices on each plate, on top of the potatoes. Spoon the mint chutney around each plate. Garnish with fried mint leaves, pappadum curls, and lime pickle.

Chef Notes

The lime pickle and mint chutney recipes will produce more than is needed for this dish. They can be used as condiments for various other dishes. Commercially prepared lime pickle can also be purchased. Besan, also known as gram flour, is a flour made from ground, dried chickpeas. To roast, spread the besan on a baking sheet and place in a preheated 300-degree oven for 7 to 10 minutes, watching carefully that it doesn't burn. Garlic paste and ginger paste are available in small tubes. Purées may be substituted. Garam masala is a blend of up to twelve spices that may include black pepper, cinnamon, cloves, coriander, cumin, cardamom, dried fennel, mace, and nutmeg. Tandoori coloring is a powdered substance that is added to marinades to give tandoori cooked foods their distinctive orange color. Ghee is a form of clarified butter that is aged to produce a complex flavor. Regular clarified butter can be substituted. Curry leaves are the delicate small leaves of the curry bush. All of these ingredients can be purchased in Indian markets and specialty food stores.

Garnish

Oil for frying

8 mint or curry leaves
 (see Chef Notes)

4 slices pappadum, about 1-inch wide
 (see Chef Notes)

Special Equipment

Skewers

Wine Recommendation

Fritz Haag Goldkapsul, Brauneberger Juffer Riesling Spätlese 1993 (Germany), or another white wine with moderate sweetness. Or for a different approach, Krug Clos de Mésnil 1990 (Champagne), or another vintage Champagne.

Foie Gras Sausages with Puy Lentils and Walnut-Mustard Vinaigrette

The ratio of meat to fat determines the success of a sausage. Fat adds flavor, softens the texture, and contributes to the juiciness of the finished links. Foie gras is a luscious alternative to other forms of fat used in sausage making. For his duck and foie gras sausages, Tim Rodgers uses chunks of foie gras in the sausage filling. As the sausages cook, the foie gras renders its fat, making them deliciously succulent.

YIELD: 20 MAIN COURSE SERVINGS

Smoked Foie Gras and Duck Sausages

4 pounds foie gras, cut into 1-inch dice

1¼ ounces salt

½ cup plus 2 tablespoons Armagnac

1¼ teaspoons white pepper, freshly ground

1¼ teaspoons TCM (see Chef Notes)

1¼ pounds duck meat

2 tablespoons salt

½ tablespoon dextrose (see Chef Notes)

¼ teaspoon dry mustard

⅛ ounce quatre épices

1 ounce shallots, minced and sautéed

1 pound pork jowl or kidney fat

¼ pound ice

1½ ounces nonfat dry milk powder, about 1 cup

1 tablespoon chives, chopped

1½ tablespoon chervil, chopped

Beef middle casings (see Chef Notes)

Smoked Foie Gras and Duck Sausages

Place the foie gras in a large bowl and add the salt, Armagnac, pepper, and 1¼ teaspoons of the TCM. Let the mixture marinate, refrigerated, for 24 hours. Combine the duck meat with the remaining TCM, salt, dextrose, dry mustard, quatre épices, and shallots, and chill the mixture well. Grind the duck mixture in a meat grinder fitted with a ⅛-inch plate. Clean the grinder and grind the fat. Process the ground duck mixture with the ice in a chilled food processor until the mixture reaches 40 degrees on an instant-read thermometer. Add the ground fat and continue to process until the mixture reaches 45 degrees. Add the nonfat dry milk powder and process until the mixture reaches 58 degrees. To test the texture and seasoning, poach a small spoonful of the filling in simmering water. Add the foie gras, chives, and chervil and fold into the duck mixture, making sure all of the foie gras pieces are evenly coated. Stuff the filling into beef middle casings using a sausage horn attached to a grinder. Smoke the sausages in a smoker, heated to 160 degrees, for 1 hour.

Heat a pot of water to 170 degrees. Poach the sausages until they reach an internal temperature of 155 degrees, then shock in ice water until the temperature is lowered to 60 degrees. Store under refrigeration for up to one week, or freeze for up to 1 month.

Foie Gras and Veal Sausages

Place the foie gras in a large bowl, add the salt, white pepper, Madeira, and TCM and let marinate, refrigerated, for 24 hours. Combine the veal with the salt, dextrose, quatre épices, coriander, and lemon zest. Refrigerate for at least 1 hour. Grind the veal in a meat grinder using a ⅛-inch plate. Clean the meat grinder then grind the fat using the same plate. In a food processor fitted with a chilled blade, process the ground veal with the ice until the mixture reaches 40 degrees. Add the ground fat and continue to process until the mixture reaches 45 degrees. Add the nonfat dry milk powder and continue to process until the mixture reaches a temperature of 58 degrees. To test the texture and seasoning, poach a small spoonful of the filling in simmering water. Fold in the foie gras,

Foie Gras and Veal Sausages

3½ pounds foie gras, cut into 1-inch cubes

1⅓ ounce salt

1½ teaspoon white pepper, freshly ground

6 ounces Madeira

1 teaspoon TCM (see Chef Notes)

1¼ pound veal trim

2 tablespoons salt

1½ teaspoons dextrose (see Chef Notes)

1½ teaspoons quatre épices

1½ teaspoon ground coriander

1 teaspoon lemon zest, finely grated

1 pound pork jowl or kidney fat

1½ ounces nonfat dry milk powder, about 1 cup

¾ pound ice

½ pound duck confit, cut into small dice (see page 276)

3 tablespoons fines herbes, chopped (see Chef Notes)

1 tablespoon tarragon, chopped

Beef middle casings (see Chef Notes)

Walnut-Mustard Vinaigrette

2 tablespoons champagne vinegar

1½ teaspoons brown mustard

1 small shallot, minced

¼ cup plus 1 tablespoon canola oil

1 tablespoon walnut oil

2 teaspoons fresh parsley, chopped

1 teaspoon chives, minced

Coarse salt

Black pepper, freshly ground

duck confit, fines herbes, and tarragon, making sure all the pieces of foie gras are coated evenly in the emulsion. Stuff the mixture into beef middle casings using a sausage horn attached to a meat grinder. Heat a large pot of water to 170 degrees. Poach the sausages until they reach an internal temperature of 155 degrees. Shock the sausages in ice water to lower the internal temperature to 60 degrees. Store under refrigeration for up to 1 week or freeze for up to 1 month.

Walnut-Mustard Vinaigrette

Combine the vinegar, mustard, and shallot. Gradually whisk in the oils to create an emulsion. Add the parsley and chives and season with salt and pepper.

Lentils

Bring a pot of salted water to a simmer and cook the lentils for 25 to 30 minutes until they are tender; drain and set aside. Heat the vegetable oil in a large sauté pan set over medium-high heat and sauté the vegetables until they are tender, about 5 minutes. Place the vinaigrette in a saucepan set over low heat, and cook until it is just warmed through. In a large bowl combine the lentils, sautéed vegetables, and warm vinaigrette. The mixture should be assembled as close to service time as possible because the lentils will toughen if left in contact with the vinaigrette for an extended period.

Service and Garnish

Preheat the oven to 250 degrees. Heat a sauté pan over medium-high heat and sear the sausages until lightly browned, about 3 minutes on each side. Place the sausages in the oven and warm for about 5 minutes, or until just heated through. Serve on a bed of lentils garnished with steamed baby carrots, bay leaves, and coarse-grained mustard.

Chef Notes

TCM is a curing agent made from sodium chloride and sodium nitrite. Other curing agents, such as curing salt and saltpeter, can be substituted in proportion to the amount of meat called for in the recipe. If the sausages will be used immediately, the curing agent is not necessary. Dextrose is a type of sugar used in sausage making that is less sweet and more easily dissolvable than sucrose. Both are available from sausage-making suppliers or specialty spice purveyors. If using natural casing, soak for 30 minutes in tepid water accidulated with 1 or 2 tablespoons of vinegar. Rinse well in cold water before stuffing. Jowl or kidney fat is the best fat for this recipe. The temperatures referred to throughout the recipe are important to ensure success. Use an instant-read thermometer to accurately determine the temperature at the stages indicated. Puy lentils are a small, green, flavorful lentil from France. Fines herbes is a dried herb mixture from France. The combination of herbs varies depending on the producer.

Lentils

Coarse salt

1 pound green puy lentils

1 tablespoon vegetable oil

2 carrots, cut into small dice

½ pound celeriac, cut into small dice

½ pound leeks, cut into small dice

Walnut-mustard vinaigrette
(from above)

Garnish

Steamed baby carrots

Coarse-grained mustard

Bay leaves

Special Equipment

Meat grinder with sausage stuffing
attachment

Instant-read thermometer

Wine Recommendation

Argiano Brunello di Montalcino Riserva 1990 (Tuscany), or another full-bodied, big red wine with elegant spice and tannins.

Whole-Roasted Foie Gras
with Fifty-Clove Garlic Confit

André Daguin is considered the culinary ambassador for his native Gascony, a region in southwest France renowned for its foie gras. This wintry dish stems from the Gascon tradition of pairing poultry with another regional specialty—garlic. By roasting it whole, the foie gras attains a firm texture and intense flavor. The pungency of the garlic is mellowed by slowly confiting the cloves in duck fat.

Roasted Foie Gras

1 foie gras, about 1½ pounds, cleaned of any surface imperfections

Sea salt

White pepper, freshly ground

Garlic Confit and Purée

1 pound rendered duck fat (see page 108)

50 cloves garlic, peeled

Coarse salt

White pepper, freshly ground

Pinch thyme

¼ teaspoon quatre épices

¼ cup heavy cream

Garnish

1 tablespoon unsalted butter

12 baby carrots, steamed until tender

Pinch sugar

Sprigs of fresh thyme

Coarse sea salt

White pepper, freshly cracked

Wine Recommendation

Château de Belingard 1990 (Côtes de Bergerac), or another light, fruity red wine from Southwest France, such as a Buzet or Côtes de Frontonnais.

Roasted Foie Gras

Preheat the oven to 375 degrees. Season the foie gras generously with sea salt and white pepper. Place the foie gras in a small roasting pan or ovenproof sauté pan that is only slightly larger than the liver itself. Roast for 25 to 30 minutes, until the liver has browned and the flesh is firm to the touch.

Garlic Confit and Purée

In a medium saucepan, combine the duck fat, garlic cloves, salt, pepper, thyme, and quatre épices. Bring to a gentle simmer and cook very slowly, making sure the garlic does not brown, until soft, about 1 hour. Remove approximately 30 cloves and purée them in a food processor. Return the purée to a small saucepan, combine with the heavy cream, and cook over low heat for 5 minutes. Remove from heat, strain, and keep warm. Reserve the remaining whole garlic cloves, covered.

Service and Garnish

In a sauté pan, warm the butter and toss with the steamed baby carrots and sugar until heated through. Place the garlic purée in the center of a serving platter. Carefully place the foie gras on the purée and arrange the carrots and reserved garlic cloves around the liver. Garnish with fresh thyme, sea salt, and cracked white pepper. If desired, portions can be sliced and individually plated from the serving platter.

Peasant-Style Potted Foie Gras with Hungarian Duck Crackling Biscuits

YIELD: 8 TO 10 APPETIZER SERVINGS

Peasant-Style Foie Gras

1¼ pounds rendered duck fat
(see page 108)

3 onions, coarsely chopped

6 cloves garlic, chopped

Coarse salt

Black pepper, freshly cracked

1 whole foie gras, about 1½ pounds,
cleaned of any visible surface
imperfections

Duck Crackling Biscuits

½ cup duck cracklings
(see pages 160 or 166)

½ cup rendered duck fat
(see page 108)

2½ cups all-purpose flour

1 teaspoon white vinegar

1 teaspoon black pepper, cracked, or
caraway seeds, plus additional
cracked black pepper to taste

½ cup plus 2 tablespoons lukewarm
milk

1 teaspoon sugar

½ teaspoon coarse salt

1 package (1 tablespoon) dry yeast

1 egg

1 egg yolk

Garnish

Black peppercorns, freshly cracked

Fresh herbs

Special Equipment

2-inch round cutter (see Chef Notes)

Wine Recommendation

Standing Stone Gewürztraminer 1996
(Finger Lakes), or another crisp, dry
Gewürztraminer.

Foie gras plays an important role in the culinary history of Eastern Europe, particularly Hungary. This traditional recipe is from the Ukraine, near the Hungarian border, where Daňo Hutnik grew up on a farm. Every family in town kept a few geese reserved for special occasions. Daňo remembers helping his mother make a mixture of pumpkin-seed oil and corn to fatten their birds. Daňo continues his family's tradition, preparing duck foie gras with shmaltz—smothered onions and duck fat cooked together— that diners spoon onto freshly baked crackling biscuits.

Peasant-Style Foie Gras

Preheat the oven to 300 degrees. In a large sauté pan, melt the duck fat and add the onions and garlic. Season with salt and pepper, and cook until the onions are translucent, 8 to 10 minutes. Transfer the onion mixture to a 10-inch baking dish. Season the whole foie gras with salt and pepper, and place in the center of the pan, within the onion mixture, making sure the onion mixture covers at least half of the liver. Bake until the liver feels firm, approximately 1 hour and 15 minutes. Remove from the oven and cool to room temperature.

Duck Crackling Biscuits

In a large mixing bowl, combine the duck cracklings, rendered duck fat, ¾ cup of the flour, the vinegar, and 1 teaspoon cracked pepper or caraway seeds. Gently form the dough into a square, cover with plastic wrap, and let rest in the refrigerator for 30 minutes. In the bowl of an electric mixer, place ½ cup lukewarm milk. Stir in the sugar and salt. Sprinkle the yeast over the surface and let stand for 5 minutes. Add the remaining flour and the whole egg. Mix with a dough hook until a ball is formed in the bowl. Cover with a dish towel and let rest 15 minutes in a warm spot. Cut the dough in half and roll each half into 2 squares, making sure that they are slightly larger than the square with the duck cracklings. Remove the duck crackling dough from the refrigerator and sandwich it between the two larger squares

of dough. Pinch the two larger squares together to seal. Roll out this dough until it is ½-inch thick, as though making puff pastry. Fold in half. Rewrap the dough and let rest in the refrigerator for 30 minutes. Repeat this process 2 additional times.

Preheat the oven to 375 degrees. Make an egg wash with the egg yolk and the remaining 2 tablespoons milk. Roll the dough to an even 1-inch thickness. Brush with the egg wash, season with cracked black pepper, and score in a crosshatch pattern with a sharp knife. Cut into 2-inch circles. Place on parchment-lined baking sheet and let rest in a warm place for 30 minutes, or until risen. Bake until golden brown, about 45 minutes.

Service and Garnish

Loosen the foie gras by running a flexible spatula around the edge of the baking dish. Lift out the foie gras and serve a ½-inch slice on a plate surrounded with duck fat, onions, and 1 or 2 biscuits. Garnish with freshly cracked black pepper and fresh herbs. This dish can also be served in the baking dish, with a platter of biscuits on the side.

Chef Notes

A 1½-inch round cutter will yield more biscuits, if desired. The foie gras can be made a day in advance, wrapped, and kept in the refrigerator. Let the dish warm to room temperature so the fat and onions are softened before serving.

Roasted Poblano Chilies Filled with Black Bean Purée and Grilled Foie Gras

YIELD: 4 MAIN COURSE SERVINGS

Roasted Poblano Chilies

4 fresh poblano chilies

Black Bean Purée

2 cups dried black beans, soaked
   overnight in water

8 cups chicken stock

Coarse salt

Black pepper, freshly ground

Foie Gras and Sauce

8 ounces foie gras, cut into 4 slices,
   each about 2 ounces and ½-inch
   thick

Coarse salt

Black pepper, freshly ground

1 ounce fresh ginger, peeled and cut
   into fine julienne

¼ cup sherry vinegar

½ cup heavy cream

4 teaspoons parsley, chopped

Garnish

Red bell pepper diamonds

4 teaspoons tomato concassée

Special Equipment

Cast iron grill pan

Wine Recommendation

Chalk Hill, Estate Vineyard, Botrytised
Sémillon 1994 (Sonoma), or another
sweet, dessert wine. Or, for a different
approach, Joseph Phelps Insignia 1993
(Napa), or another spicy red wine.

One of the reasons for the popularity of foie gras among today's chefs is its adaptability to almost any cooking style. The subtle flavor of the liver accepts accents from a variety of cuisines. Foie gras also adds a luxurious element to even the simplest regional dishes. In this preparation, Vincent Guérithault incorporates foie gras into an American Southwest classic. The recipe also offers a geographical pun, as foie gras comes from the southwest of France.

Roasted Poblano Chilies

Over a hot grill, a gas flame, or under the broiler, roast the chilies, turning frequently until the skin is blackened and blistered all over. Place the peppers in a plastic or brown paper bag, close the top, and set aside until cool. When the peppers are cool enough to handle, peel off and discard the skin, being sure to keep the peppers whole and intact. Leaving some of the blackened skin attached will produce a more rustic presentation. Slice an opening in the pepper lengthwise and remove the inner ribs and seeds, again being sure to keep the pepper whole. Set aside.

Black Bean Purée

Drain the soaked beans. Combine the stock and soaked beans in a medium saucepan and set over medium heat. Simmer for about one hour, until the beans are tender. Strain, reserving the stock, and purée the beans in a food processor or blender until smooth. If the beans are too dry to purée, add some of the reserved stock. Season with salt and pepper.

Foie Gras and Sauce

Place a cast iron grill pan over a high flame. Season the foie gras with salt and pepper. Sear the foie gras slices in the hot, dry pan for 30 seconds per side, rotating the slices once to produce attractive grill marks. Set the foie gras aside, keeping it warm. Transfer any fat that rendered out of the foie gras to a sauté pan and set over high heat. Fry the ginger in the foie gras fat until crisp. Remove the ginger and set aside on a paper towel to drain. Add the vinegar to the same pan with the fat. Add the cream and cook over medium heat until the mixture has thickened to a sauce, about 10 minutes. Taste for seasoning. Add the parsley just before serving.

Service and Garnish

Fill each roasted pepper with the warm bean purée. Lean the foie gras against the pepper and garnish with sauce, red pepper cutouts, and a sprinkle of concassée tomato. Top with the fried ginger.

Fresh Corn Tamales with Seared Foie Gras, Sesame Pineapple Mole, Pineapple Relish, and Lime Crema

According to Stephan Pyles, traditional Mexican tamales are stuffed or served with a wide array of ingredients. Adding foie gras is a natural evolution of his unique brand of Southwestern cuisine, a tempting blend of flavors and techniques from Europe, Mexico, and Central America. One of the classic sauces of the Mexican repertoire, mole is a blend of aromatics, nuts, seeds, and often chocolate, with an intense and complex flavor. The addition of pineapple in this mole adds a luscious sweetness that complements the rich foie gras.

YIELD: 8 MAIN COURSE SERVINGS

Pineapple Mole

3 corn tortillas

3 cloves garlic, chopped

2 ancho chilies, seeded

1 small onion, chopped

1 stalk celery, chopped

1 carrot, peeled and chopped

1 serrano chili, seeded and chopped

¼ cup sesame seeds

¼ cup sliced almonds

2 tablespoons pine nuts

4½ cups chicken stock

6 ounces dried pineapple

1 medium yellow tomato, cored and chopped

½ fresh pineapple, peeled and chopped

¼ cup sherry

¼ cup dry white wine

3 tablespoons golden raisins

1 cinnamon stick

1 teaspoon chili powder

½ teaspoon cumin

1 ounce white chocolate, chopped

¼ teaspoon ground allspice

Pinch ground coriander

Pinch ground cloves

Pinch ground nutmeg

Pinch ground aniseed

½ cup vegetable oil

Coarse salt

Pineapple Mole

Preheat the oven to 350 degrees. Combine the tortillas, garlic, ancho chilies, onion, celery, carrot, serrano chili, sesame seeds, almonds, and pine nuts on a baking sheet and toast in the oven until the tortillas are crisp and dark, about 20 to 30 minutes. Remove from the oven and break the tortillas into pieces. Meanwhile, in a large saucepan, combine the stock, dried pineapple, tomato, fresh pineapple, sherry, white wine, raisins, cinnamon stick, chili powder, and cumin, and bring to a boil. Reduce the heat and simmer for 10 minutes. Remove from the heat. Add the toasted tortilla and nut mixture. Remove the cinnamon stick. Add the white chocolate, allspice, coriander, cloves, nutmeg, and aniseed. Transfer this mixture to a blender. Purée in batches until smooth, about 2 minutes per batch. Place the vegetable oil in another large saucepan and heat until lightly smoking. Add the puréed mole mixture and fry for 15 minutes, until thickened, stirring frequently. Remove from the

heat, strain through a fine chinois, and season with salt to taste.

Pineapple Relish

In a small saucepan, combine the vinegar and brown sugar. Bring the mixture to a boil and reduce to ½ cup, 10 to 15 minutes. Reserve. Heat the olive oil in a medium sauté pan over high heat until lightly smoking. Add the corn and sauté for 2 minutes until tender. Add the pineapple, red pepper, and sugar-vinegar mixture, and remove from the heat. Stir in the basil and season with salt. Let cool to room temperature and refrigerate.

Lime Crema

Combine the sour cream, lime juice, and water, and mix well. The texture should be creamy but thin enough to drip off a spoon. Reserve.

Corn Tamales

Place the corn in the work bowl of a food processor and process for 3 minutes, until

Pineapple Relish

½ cup white wine vinegar or
    champagne vinegar

½ cup light brown sugar

1 tablespoon olive oil

¾ cup corn kernels, about 1 ear,
    steamed for 1 minute

½ fresh pineapple, peeled and cut into
    ¼-inch cubes

1 small red bell pepper, seeded and
    finely diced

2 tablespoons basil leaves, thinly
    shredded

Coarse salt

Lime Crema

¼ cup sour cream

1 teaspoon lime juice

2 teaspoons water

smooth. Transfer to a baking pan and bake in the oven for 1½ hours, or until the corn is dry, stirring every 15 minutes. Remove from the oven, transfer to a bowl, and refrigerate until completely cool. Place the masa harina in the bowl of an electric mixer. On low speed, using the paddle attachment, slowly add the hot water in a constant stream until the dough forms a ball. Continue to mix on medium-high speed for 5 minutes. Remove the dough from the bowl, wrap in plastic, and allow to cool completely in the refrigerator, about 1 to 2 hours. Return the dough (masa) to the bowl of the mixer and beat with the paddle for 5 minutes on high speed. Slowly add the shortening, 2 tablespoons at a time. Continue to beat until smooth and light, about 5 minutes. Scrape the sides of the bowl and reduce to low speed, continuing to beat. In a small mixing bowl, combine the stock, salt, and baking powder. Slowly add the stock mixture to the masa in a constant stream. Combine thoroughly. Beat on high speed for 5 minutes. Add the cooled corn mixture and maple syrup, then season with salt to taste. Soften the banana leaves over an open flame for 10 seconds on each side, being careful not to burn the leaf. Cut the leaves into a total of eight even pieces. Place one portion of the dough on each piece of banana leaf. Fold the banana leaf over the filling to form a tight packet and tie securely with strips of corn husk. Place the tamales in a conventional steamer or in a strainer or vegetable basket set in a saucepan with about 1 inch of water, making sure the folds of the tamales are on the bottom so they do not open while steaming. Cover the steamer with a tight-fitting lid. It is important that little or no steam escapes while cooking. Steam for 45 to 50 minutes; the water should always be lightly boiling. The tamales are done when the dough comes away easily from the husk. Reserve and keep warm.

Foie Gras

Season the foie gras slices with salt. Heat a large sauté pan over high heat for 5 minutes. Add the sliced foie gras to the pan and brown on each side, 30 to 45 seconds per side. Remove the foie gras from the pan and drain on paper towel.

Service and Garnish

Place a wrapped tamale on each of eight serving plates. Slice an opening into the top of the tamale with a knife and put a slice of foie gras on each tamale. Top with the pineapple relish and divide the mole evenly among the plates around the tamales. Garnish with lime crema and toasted pumpkin seeds. Serve hot.

Chef Notes

If you are planning to cook and serve this dish immediately, prepare the mole while the tamales are steaming and cover to keep warm until serving. Otherwise, the mole can be made in advance and reheated gently over a very low heat.

Corn Tamales

8 cups corn kernels, approximately 12 ears, raw
1¾ cup masa harina
1¾ cup water, very hot
½ cup plus 2 tablespoons cold vegetable shortening
¼ cup cold chicken stock
1½ teaspoons coarse salt, plus additional to taste
1 teaspoon baking powder
⅓ cup maple syrup
2 large banana leaves
Corn husk strips

Foie Gras

16 ounces foie gras, cut into 8 slices, each about 2 ounces and ½-inch thick
Coarse salt

Garnish

Toasted pumpkin seeds

Special Equipment

Steamer with tight-fitting lid

Wine Recommendation

Warre Tawny Port Reserve 1968 (Portugal), or Knudsen Erath Late-Harvest White Riesling Willamette Valley 1994 (Oregon), or another wine with moderate sweetness.

White Truffle and Foie Gras Baked Potato

This preparation epitomizes the ability of foie gras to transform even the humblest of ingredients. In Sottha Khunn's version of a stuffed baked potato, foie gras and white truffles are combined to create a luxurious and elegant dish. In 1997, prior to the opening of Le Cirque 2000, Sottha served this dish on a tasting tour through Europe, to introduce Europeans to American products and ingredients. He feels the combination of rare and common ingredients demonstrates the way in which American "meat and potatoes" cuisine has matured, rivaling the classic cuisines of the world.

Baked Potato

4 large baking potatoes, preferably
    Russet or Yukon Gold

4 ounces unsalted butter

¼ cup white truffle oil

Coarse salt

Black pepper, freshly ground

2 medium white truffles, 1 ounce each

Foie Gras

12 ounces foie gras, cut into 4 slices,
    each about 3 ounces and ¾-inch
    thick

Coarse salt

Black pepper, freshly ground

Special Equipment

Japanese mandoline or truffle slicer

Rock salt

Wine Recommendation

Krug Grand Cuvée Non-Vintage
(Champagne), or another full-bodied
Champagne.

Baked Potato

Preheat the oven to 350 degrees. Wash and dry the potatoes and bake on a rack for 45 minutes, or until cooked through. Slit the potatoes lengthwise and scoop out the insides with a spoon, being careful to keep the potatoes intact. Cover the skins with aluminum foil to keep warm. Mash the potato flesh with a fork, incorporating the butter and truffle oil, and season with salt and pepper to taste. Using a Japanese mandoline or truffle slicer, thinly slice the truffles. Reserve the slices for service, but chop the ends and any extra scraps very finely and add to the potato mixture. Cover the mixture and keep warm.

Foie Gras

Heat a sauté pan over a medium-high flame. Season the foie gras with salt and pepper and sear in the hot pan until both sides are brown, about 30 to 45 seconds per side. Pat the slices dry on paper towel. Reserve the foie gras fat in the pan.

Service

Mound a generous amount of rock salt in the center of each of four serving plates. Fill the potato-skin shells with the mashed potato mixture and place them in the center of the plates, using the rock salt as a base. Top with a slice of seared foie gras and cover with white truffle slices. Season with salt and pepper, and drizzle with the reserved rendered foie gras fat around and on top.

Foie Gras–Filled Pasta with Black Truffle Emulsion and Mascarpone Cream

By cooking the pasta and poaching the foie gras in the same consommé, and then incorporating it into a rich black truffle emulsion, Laurent Gras ties this elegant appetizer together seamlessly. The sweet, fresh taste of the mascarpone cream, with a subtle lemony tang, accents the strong, earthy flavors of the foie gras and black truffle. Because the stuffed pasta is steamed to order, it can be prepared several hours in advance and held until service.

YIELD: 4 APPETIZER SERVINGS

Foie Gras–Filled Pasta

3½ cups chicken stock

20 pieces Venetian schiaffoni, maniche giganti, or other large tubular pasta

1 small lobe foie gras, about ¾ pound, in one piece

Fleur de sel

Black pepper, freshly ground

Black Truffle Sauce

1 cup chicken stock

2 tablespoons butter, chilled

4 ounces duck fat, chilled

Fleur de sel

Black pepper, freshly ground

1½ ounce black truffle, chopped

1 tablespoon truffle juice

Mascarpone Cream

1 tablespoon butter

2 tablespoons flour

½ cup milk

½ cup heavy cream

2 ounces mascarpone cheese

Lemon juice, freshly squeezed, from about ½ lemon

Fine sea salt

4 drops Tabasco sauce, or to taste

Garnish

½ ounce black truffle, finely sliced

Special Equipment

Steamer with basket

Wine Recommendation

Frédéric Lornet Arbois Vin de Paille 1992 (Jura), or another medium-bodied white wine.

Foie Gras–Filled Pasta

Bring the chicken stock to a boil, add the pasta and cook for about 7 minutes, until al dente. Remove the pasta from the chicken stock with a slotted spoon and shock in ice water for a few seconds. Drain pasta and pat dry. Bring the stock back up to a boil and plunge the foie gras into the boiling stock, turn down the heat to a simmer, and poach for 5 minutes. Remove the foie gras with a slotted spoon and drain. Cut the foie gras into 20 pieces, making sure each piece will fit inside the pasta. Season the foie gras with fleur de sel and black pepper. Stuff each piece of pasta with a piece of foie gras and set aside.

Black Truffle Sauce

In a saucepan set over medium-high heat, reduce the chicken stock by half, about 20 to 30 minutes. Whisk in 1 tablespoon of the butter and the duck fat to form an emulsion. Season with fleur de sel and black pepper, strain through a fine mesh sieve, and reserve. In a small sauté pan set over low heat, melt the remaining tablespoon of butter. Add the chopped truffle and cook slowly, for 6 minutes. Add the truffle juice and reduce the

mixture by half. Add this truffle mixture to the reserved sauce.

Mascarpone Cream

In a small saucepan set over low heat, melt the butter. Add the flour and cook slowly to form a light roux. Remove from the heat and transfer the mixture to a bowl to cool. In another saucepan, bring the milk and the heavy cream to a boil. Whisk in the roux and simmer until the sauce has thickened. Add the mascarpone cheese and season with lemon juice, sea salt, and Tabasco. Bring the sauce back up to a simmer, strain through a fine mesh sieve, and set aside. The recipe will produce extra sauce, which can be saved for another use.

Service and Garnish

Arrange the stuffed pasta in the basket of a steamer in a single layer and set over simmering water. Steam for 3 minutes, or until the pasta and foie gras are warmed through. Place 5 stuffed pasta tubes on each of four serving plates. Top with the truffle sauce, then drizzle with the mascarpone cream. Garnish with sliced black truffle.

Poached Foie Gras with Parsley Bow Ties

Alain Ducasse is celebrated around the world for his deceptively simple preparations. This elegant dish, typical of his style, combines uncomplicated elements such as homemade pasta with elegant touches such as reduction sauces. The poached foie gras has a silken texture that virtually coats the fresh pasta, which is itself tender and light.

YIELD: 6 MAIN COURSE SERVINGS

Parsley Bow Ties

1½ cups all-purpose flour, plus additional for working the dough

1 cup high-gluten or bread flour

4 eggs

½ bunch flat-leaved parsley, cleaned and dried

Port Reduction

1 bottle ruby port (750 ml)

⅔ cup sherry vinegar

Poached Foie Gras

2 tablespoons duck fat

4 pounds duck bones, coarsely chopped

4 shallots, minced

5 cloves garlic, peeled

2 quarts chicken stock

1 whole foie gras, about 1½ pounds

Garnish

Fleur de sel

Black pepper, freshly cracked

Flat-leaved parsley

Special Equipment

Pasta machine

1½-inch circle cutter

Wine Recommendation

Château Trotanoy 1993 (Pomerol), or another intense, dark, rich red wine, such as a Zinfandel from California.

Parsley Bow Ties

Combine the flours and mound on a clean counter. Make a well, add the eggs, and mix to form a stiff dough. Knead the dough until smooth and elastic, 8 to 10 minutes. Wrap in plastic and refrigerate for 3 hours.

Divide the dough into 3 equal portions. Using a pasta machine, work the dough down to the second-from-last thinness. Lay out the dough on a very lightly floured surface. Over one half the length of the dough, arrange one-third of the parsley leaves. Carefully fold over the remaining half of the dough to envelop the parsley. Roll the top sheet of pasta with a floured rolling pin to press the dough together. Run this pasta, with the parsley sandwiched inside, through the pasta machine until you have reached the thinnest setting. The parsley will have broken down and spread into the dough in an attractive pattern. Gently dust the pasta dough with flour, cover with a clean dish towel, and set aside. Repeat until all of the dough has been processed.

On a floured surface, cut the pasta dough into 1½-inch-diameter circles using a metal cutter. To form the bow ties, pinch opposite sides of the pasta circles between your thumb and forefinger. Repeat until all of the pasta is shaped. Layer the bow ties in single layers on sheets of waxed paper and store, covered, in an airtight container in the refrigerator until ready to use.

Port Reduction

Combine the port and vinegar in a small nonreactive saucepan set over medium heat. Bring to a boil and reduce to a thick glaze, about 1½ hours.

Poached Foie Gras and Garnish

Heat the duck fat in a wide, deep saucepan or stock pot. Add the duck bones and sauté until dark brown. Add the shallots and garlic and continue cooking until browned. Pour off all of the fat. Add the stock and bring to a simmer. Set the cover ajar, reduce the heat, and continue simmering for 3 hours. Pass the finished poaching liquid through a fine mesh strainer into a clean pot. Return to the heat.

Transfer about 1½ cups of the poaching liquid into a small saucepan and set over medium-high heat. Reduce until only ¼ cup remains, about 45 minutes. Reserve.

Place the whole foie gras in the large pot of simmering poaching liquid. Turn the liver over once or twice with a large spatula to ensure gentle, even cooking. The foie gras will take about 20 minutes to poach. When it feels warm and supple to the touch, carefully remove it from the poaching liquid. Keep warm. Keep the poaching liquid simmering.

Brush off any excess flour from the pasta and place it into the simmering poaching liquid. After 2 minutes, remove the pasta with a wire sieve, drain well, and place in a warmed mixing bowl. Add a spoonful or two of the reserved reduced poaching liquid and some of the fat floating on the top of the foie gras poaching liquid. Toss and divide the pasta evenly among six warmed serving plates. Cut the foie gras into six equal portions and place on top of the pasta. Spoon the port reduction onto the plate and sprinkle with fleur de sel and cracked black pepper. Garnish with parsley.

Soupe aux Truffes Elysée V.G.E.

Paul Bocuse created this dish in 1976 for the then-president of France, Valéry Giscard d'Estaing (V.G.E.). Each soup is cooked individually under a puff pastry crown. The pastry seals in the heady aroma of the black truffles and the other ingredients so the diner experiences an intense, concentrated perfume when the trapped steam is released. Foie gras adds a subtle richness to the forceful truffles and a silken quality to the consommé.

Double Consommé

3 pounds veal bones

2 carrots, peeled and coarsely chopped

1 onion, peeled and coarsely chopped

1 stalk celery, peeled and coarsely chopped

2 to 3 quarts veal stock

1 pound very lean ground beef

8 egg whites

2 cups leek greens, sliced

½ cup celery leaves, sliced

½ cup parsley, coarsely chopped

Soupe aux Truffes

5 cups double consommé (from above)

Coarse salt

Black pepper, freshly ground

1 tablespoon butter

3 ounces mirepoix of carrots, onions, celery, and mushrooms, cut into brunoise

3 ounces black truffles, thinly sliced

7 ounces foie gras, cut into ½-inch cubes

3½ ounces poached chicken breast, finely chopped

4 tablespoons vermouth

6 ounces puff pastry

2 egg yolks, lightly beaten

Special Equipment

Cheesecloth

4 ovenproof bowls

4-inch round cutter

Wine Recommendation

J.-F. Coche-Dury Meursault Les Rougeots 1995 (Burgundy), or another white Burgundy that is dense, full-flavored, and has hints of oak and balanced acidity.

Double Consommé

Preheat the oven to 450 degrees. Place the veal bones in a large roasting pan and roast until brown, about 1 hour. Add the carrots, onion, and celery, and roast for an additional 30 minutes. Transfer the roasted ingredients to a small stock pot and cover with the stock. Bring to a boil, skim off any scum that rises to the surface, turn down the heat, and simmer, covered, for 2 hours. Remove from the heat, strain, and chill overnight. Remove any fat that has coagulated on the surface. In a clean stock pot, combine the ground beef, egg whites, leek greens, celery leaves, and parsley. Add the chilled stock, set over medium-high heat, and bring to a boil, stirring constantly to avoid sticking. Once the stock reaches a boil, reduce the heat to a simmer and stop stirring. Let simmer 1 hour. Turn off the heat and let sit for 30 minutes. Using a ladle, push back the "raft" that has formed on top of the stock and ladle the consommé through several layers of cheesecloth into another pot. Blot the surface with a paper towel to remove any fat.

Soupe aux Truffes

Preheat the oven to 350 degrees. Bring the consommé to a simmer. Adjust the seasoning with salt and pepper. In a sauté pan, melt the butter. Add the mirepoix and cook the vegetables until they begin to sweat. Divide the truffles, foie gras, mirepoix, and chicken breast meat among four bowls. Divide the vermouth and hot consommé among the bowls. Roll out the pastry to ¼-inch thick. Cut out four circles using the 4-inch round cutter. Score the top. Place a puff pastry disk over each bowl and press the dough to the bowl to seal well. Brush the top of the pastry with egg yolk. Place the bowls on a sheet pan and bake for 20 to 30 minutes, until the pastry is fully puffed and golden brown.

Service

Immediately after the soup is removed from the oven it should be brought to the table with the pastry crust intact so the diner can fully experience the fragrant aromas that are released when the crust is pierced.

Foie Gras Butter

1 cup foie gras mousse (see page 114)

⅓ cup unsalted butter, at room
    temperature

Squash and Apple Soup

3 tablespoons butter

2 medium onions, chopped

½ cup calvados

6 cups light chicken stock, plus 1 cup
    extra to adjust consistency

2 medium Idaho potatoes, peeled and
    chopped

4 whole star anise

1 bay leaf

1 vanilla bean, 2 inches long, split

6 delicata squash, seeded and chopped

3 Granny Smith apples, peeled and
    chopped

Coarse salt

Black pepper, freshly ground

⅓ cup foie gras butter (from above)

Foie Gras Tortellini

24 wonton wrappers, cut into 1½-inch
    circles

⅔ cup foie gras butter (from above)

1 egg, beaten

Chestnut Cream

⅓ cup unsweetened chestnut purée,
    canned or fresh

¼ cup crème fraîche, plus more
    if necessary

Garnish

4 ounces foie gras, diced

¼ cup pumpkin seeds

1 delicata squash, cut into 8 half-moon
    shapes

4 lady apples, sliced lengthwise

Toasted pumpkin seed oil
    (see Chef Notes)

8 sage leaves

16 whole star anise

Wine Recommendation

S.A. Huët Vouvray Moelleux Clos du
Bourg Premier Trie 1995 (Alsace), or
another full-bodied, moderately sweet
white wine.

Delicata Squash and Granny Smith Apple Soup with Foie Gras Tortellini, Toasted Pumpkin Seeds, and Chestnut Cream

Don Pintabona uses foie gras butter, which is essentially an enriched mousse, to act as a liaison to bind and thicken the squash and apple soup. Foie gras butter is also used as the filling for the tortellini to create an intense flavor that explodes in the mouth. The toasted pumpkin seed oil, a traditional Austrian condiment, accents the autumnal character of this satisfying soup.

Foie Gras Butter

Place the foie gras mousse and butter in the bowl of a food processor. Process until thoroughly combined. Refrigerate.

Squash and Apple Soup

In a stock pot, melt the butter over low heat. Add the onions and cook, stirring, until the onions are translucent, about 10 minutes. Add the calvados and cook until the mixture is almost dry. Add the stock, potatoes, star anise, bay leaf, and vanilla bean, and simmer over medium heat for 10 minutes. Add the squash and apples, and simmer until soft. Remove the bay leaf, star anise, and vanilla bean, and purée the soup in batches, in a food processor or blender, until smooth. Adjust the consistency with more stock, if necessary. Strain the soup through a coarse sieve or china cap and season with salt and pepper. Chill until needed.

Foie Gras Tortellini

Place a teaspoon of the foie gras butter in the center of the wonton wrapper. Fold the wrapper over the butter to make tortellini. Seal the edges with the beaten egg. Repeat this process to create 16 to 24 tortellini. Reserve tortellini and leftover foie gras butter until service.

Chestnut Cream

Combine the chestnut purée and the crème fraîche. The mixture should have the consistency of honey. Make adjustments as needed.

Garnish

Preheat the oven to 400 degrees. In a very hot sauté pan, cook the diced foie gras for about 30 seconds. Toast the pumpkin seeds in the oven for 2 to 3 minutes. Bring a large pot of water to a boil and blanch the squash for 1 minute. Place the lady apples on a sheet pan, cut side down, and roast until soft, about 10 to 15 minutes. Reserve the pumpkin seed oil, sage, and star anise until service.

Service and Garnish

Bring the soup to a boil and remove from the heat. Whisk in ⅔ cup foie gras butter. Place the tortellini in boiling water and cook for 2 minutes. Ladle the hot soup into eight bowls. Add 2 to 3 tortellini to each bowl. Place a dollop of chestnut cream in the center of each bowl, and drizzle the pumpkin seed oil around it. Gently arrange the toasted pumpkin seeds, 1 sage leaf, a piece of squash, 2 star anise, and half a lady apple in each bowl.

Chef Notes

If delicata squash are unavailable, substitute 3 pounds of butternut squash, peeled and dried, and omit the potatoes. Extra foie gras tortellini and foie gras butter can be frozen and saved for another use. For the tortellini, fresh pasta dough (see page 240) can be substituted for the wonton wrappers and the shape can be altered as desired.

Surf and Turf of Sautéed Foie Gras and Tomelo Bay Abalone with Meyer Lemon Sauce

YIELD: 8 MAIN COURSE SERVINGS

Texture plays an important role in the composition of any dish. When sliced thick and seared, foie gras has a crisp outer layer and a molten, creamy interior. Thomas Keller contrasts these textures with a fried julienne of fresh abalone, similarly crisp on the outside, but pleasantly chewy on the inside. Both have a seductive, subtle flavor that is enlivened by the sweetly acidic Meyer lemon sauce. The result is a contemporary surf and turf.

Meyer Lemon Sauce

2 quarts duck stock

6 Meyer lemons (see Chef Notes)

2 tablespoons Banyuls vinegar
(see Chef Notes)

1 teaspoon sugar

Coarse salt

Black pepper, freshly ground

Abalone

Flour for dredging

Coarse salt

Black pepper, freshly ground

2 fresh abalones, 4 to 6 ounces each,
cleaned, trimmed, and cut into fine
julienne (see Chef Notes)

½ cup canola oil

1 tablespoon parsley, chopped

Foie Gras

1½ pounds foie gras cut into 8 slices,
each about 2 to 3 ounces and
¾-inch thick

Coarse salt

Black pepper, freshly ground

Garnish

8 brioche rounds, 3 inches in diameter,
brushed with olive oil and lightly
toasted

1 Meyer lemon, segmented

8 sprigs chervil

Gray sea salt

Black pepper, freshly ground

Wine Recommendation

Newton Vineyards Chardonnay
Unfiltered 1993 (Napa), or another
white wine with intense fruit and
subtle oak undertones.

Meyer Lemon Sauce

In a medium saucepan, bring the stock to a boil and add the whole lemons. Reduce the heat and simmer for 30 minutes. Remove and discard the lemons. Reduce the stock until only 1 cup remains and the reduction has the consistency of a rich sauce, about 1 to 1½ hours. In a small bowl, mix the vinegar, sugar, salt, and pepper. Stir this mixture into the sauce. Adjust the seasoning if necessary. Strain through a chinois. Set aside and keep warm.

Abalone

In a small bowl, generously season the flour with salt and pepper. Add the abalone to the seasoned flour and toss to coat. Transfer to a sieve and continue tossing, allowing the excess flour to fall away. In a sauté pan, heat the oil until just before it reaches the smoking point. Pan fry the abalone until light golden brown, about 20 seconds. Drain on paper towels, toss with the chopped parsley, and set aside in a warm place.

Foie Gras, Service, and Garnish

Using a paring knife, score both sides of each slice of foie gras in a diamond pattern, less than ⅛-inch deep. Heat a sauté pan over moderately high heat. Season the foie gras with salt and pepper and sear the slices on both sides until they are brown and crisp, about 30 seconds per side. To serve, ladle 1 ounce of sauce onto the center of each plate, place a toasted brioche round in the sauce, and lay a slice of foie gras on top. Top with a small handful of fried abalone and lay a Meyer lemon segment on top. Garnish with a chervil sprig and a sprinkling of gray sea salt and black pepper.

Chef Notes

Although wild abalone are preferable to farm-raised, they are increasingly hard to find. To clean, cut the abalone out of their shell, trim off the black edge (for aesthetics), then slice horizontally into about fifteen to twenty slices before cutting them into fine julienne. Meyer lemons are a sweet variety of lemon; regular lemons can be substituted. Banyuls vinegar is a red wine vinegar from the Banyuls region of France. If unavailable, any other French red or white wine vinegar can be used.

Seared Foie Gras with Diver-Caught Sea Scallops, Crispy Artichokes, and Black Truffle Julienne

There is a distinct similarity between the texture of seared foie gras, with its crisp outer layer and molten interior, and the texture of fresh diver-caught sea scallops, sautéed to golden brown on the outside and tender and sweet on the inside. Eric Ripert pairs these ingredients with artichoke bottoms crisped in foie gras fat and a generous helping of black truffles to create this delectable appetizer.

Truffle Sauce

8 tablespoons butter

¼ pound foie gras

½ cup truffle juice

½ cup shrimp stock

1 small black truffle, finely chopped

Garnish

2 quarts water acidulated with the juice of 2 lemons

4 artichoke bottoms, trimmed

3 tablespoons balsamic vinegar

2 large black truffles, about 1½ ounces each, 1 chopped and 1 cut into fine julienne

Foie Gras and Scallops

4 large diver-caught sea scallops

Coarse salt

Black pepper, freshly ground

2 tablespoons vegetable oil

½ pound foie gras, cut into 4 slices, each about 2 ounces and ½-inch thick

Wine Recommendation

Domaine Leroy Clos de Vouget 1994 (Burgundy), or another full-bodied spicy white wine.

Truffle Sauce

Combine the butter and foie gras in a food processor and purée until smooth and well blended. In a small saucepan, combine the truffle juice and shrimp stock and bring to a simmer. With a wire whisk, whip in the butter and foie gras mixture to emulsify. Pass through a fine mesh sieve into a clean saucepan. Bring back to a gentle simmer and add the chopped truffle. Do not boil or the sauce will break. Keep warm.

Garnish

Bring the 2 quarts of acidulated water to a boil in a large saucepan. Add the artichoke bottoms and cook until tender, about 30 minutes. Drain and shock in ice water to stop the cooking. Cut two of the artichoke bottoms into long strips, about ¼-inch wide (bâtonnets), and the remaining two into small dice. Set aside until service.

Foie Gras and Scallops

Season the scallops with salt and pepper. Heat a small sauté pan over medium-high heat and add the vegetable oil. Add the scallops and sear on both sides to caramelize, leaving the center rare. Remove from the pan and keep warm. Drain the oil from the pan, and return to a medium-high flame. Season the foie gras with salt and pepper and sear until brown, about 30 seconds on each side. Remove and keep warm. Pour all but a tablespoon of the foie gras fat out of the pan. Set the pan back over the heat.

Service

Add the artichoke bâtonnets and dice to the hot foie gras fat and brown. Deglaze the pan with the balsamic vinegar and add this mixture to the truffle sauce. Arrange the artichokes on four serving plates, top with a seared scallop, and lay a medallion of foie gras on top. Spoon the sauce around the plate and garnish with the chopped and julienned truffle.

Foie Gras

14 ounces foie gras, cut into 4 slices,
    each about 3½ ounces and ½-inch
    thick
Coarse salt
Black pepper, freshly ground
¼ cup Sauternes

Turnips

2 teaspoons unsalted butter
2 teaspoons sugar
8 baby turnips of equal size
½ cup duck or chicken stock
Coarse salt
Black pepper, freshly ground

Filling

2 teaspoons unsalted butter
½ pound small chanterelle mushrooms
Coarse salt
Black pepper, freshly ground
12 almonds, fresh or blanched
    (see Chef Notes)
1 small shallot, finely minced

Papillote

1 small head Savoy or green cabbage,
    cored and trimmed of darker
    outside leaves
Coarse salt
Black pepper, freshly ground
8 fresh langoustines, Santa Barbara
    shrimp, or other large-sized shrimp,
    peeled and cleaned
8 sprigs chervil
¼ cup duck or chicken stock

Wine Recommendation

Trimbach Gewürztaminer Vendage
Tardive 1990 (Alsace), or another
white wine with some sweetness and
lively acidity.

Papillote of Foie Gras, Langoustines, Chanterelles, and Fresh Almonds in Sauternes Jus

Hubert Keller prepares this dish during the early summer months, when fresh almonds and yellow chanterelles are both in season. Fresh almonds are the tender, ripe nut of the almond tree before it is dried and roasted to produce the almond with which we are more familiar. Fresh almonds are pale and soft, with a very subtle flavor and delicate, almost ephemeral quality. Though difficult to find, they have become popular among chefs in France and California, which are both reputed for their almond groves. The gentle steaming of this dish serves to preserve the flavors and textures in their most natural state.

Foie Gras

Season the foie gras slices with salt and pepper, and set in a shallow dish. Sprinkle with the Sauternes, cover with plastic wrap, and refrigerate for about 1 hour.

Turnips

In a saucepan large enough to accommodate the turnips in a single layer, combine the butter, sugar, and turnips. Add the stock, season with salt and pepper, and bring to a simmer. Cover and cook for about 12 to 15 minutes, or until the turnips are tender and golden and coated with a syrupy liquid. Set aside.

Filling

In a sauté pan, heat the butter over high heat. Sauté the chanterelles, tossing occasionally, for 2 minutes. Season with salt and pepper and add the almonds and shallot. Cook for 2 minutes longer, transfer the filling to a platter, and set aside.

Papillote

Separate the leaves from the cabbage and cut out the thick stem in the center of each leaf. Fill a large saucepan with salted water and bring to a boil. Plunge the leaves into the boiling water and blanch for about 5 minutes, until the leaves are limp and flexible, but not mushy. Drain and shock the leaves in a large bowl of ice water. Drain and pat dry.

Preheat the oven to 425 degrees. Heat a nonstick sauté pan over very high heat. Remove the foie gras from the Sauternes, reserving the Sauternes. Sear the foie gras for 30 seconds on each side. Reserve. Fold four 12-inch-square sheets of aluminum foil in half. On the lower part of each piece of foil, place 2 leaves of cabbage and season with salt and pepper. Lay a piece of the seared foie gras on top of the cabbage. Spoon 2 or 3 tablespoons of the filling on top. Add 2 langoustines per papillote. Split each turnip in half and divide them, along with the chervil sprigs, among the four papillotes. Top each papillote with 1 tablespoon of the reserved Sauternes and 1 tablespoon of stock. Close the papillotes by folding the edges all around the envelope.

Service

Place the papillotes on a sheet pan and bake in the preheated oven until they puff up, about 7 minutes. Remove them from the oven and immediately place one on each of four hot serving plates. Cut a small **X** on top of each to ease opening, and serve immediately, allowing diners to open their own papillotes at the table.

Chef Notes

If substituting blanched almonds, reblanch them for a minute or two in boiling water to soften them before using.

Chaud-Froid of Pan-Seared Rouget and Torchon of Foie Gras with Japanese Seaweed Aspic, Salad of Grilled Cèpes, and Citrus Zest

Based on the classic French dish rouget à la moelle *(red mullet with marrow), Craig Shelton has created this unusual combination that combines seemingly disparate elements of land and sea. Craig uses the seaweed aspic as a bridge to bring the dish together. The juxtaposition of the hot rouget and the cold foie gras adds another contrast to this entrée.*

YIELD: 4 MAIN COURSE SERVINGS

Torchon

1 large lobe foie gras, about 1 pound, cleaned for low-heat cooking (see page 93)

¼ cup Sauternes

3 tablespoons brandy

1 teaspoon quatre épices

½ teaspoon Sichuan peppercorns, lightly toasted and finely ground in a coffee mill

2 cups chicken stock, or enough to cover torchon

2 sheets dried nori, untoasted

Seaweed Aspic

2 cups water

1 cup fresh hyashi wakame or Japanese seaweed salad, tightly packed (see Chef Notes)

Torchon

Place the cleaned foie gras in a small bowl and sprinkle with the Sauternes and brandy. Season with the quatre épices and Sichuan pepper. Let marinate for 6 hours. Wet a countertop or table with a damp cloth and lay down a large piece of plastic wrap (about 18 inches). The dampness should keep the plastic wrap flat, with no wrinkles. Arrange the foie gras at one end of the plastic wrap. Roll up the foie gras in the plastic wrap to form a very tight sausage (in a manner similar to making a compound butter), pinching both ends and twisting them tightly in opposite directions like a candy. Poke holes in the plastic wrap with the tip of a paring knife to release air, then twist the torchon again to get it as tightly rolled as possible. Tie both ends with butcher's twine, or knot the plastic wrap to seal. Let rest 4 to 6 hours.

Bring the stock to a boil, making sure there is enough to immerse the torchon com-

pletely. Have a large bowl of ice water at the ready. Immerse the torchon in the rapidly boiling stock for 5 minutes or until you see it begin to release some fat. Shock the torchon in the ice water, then immediately hang it up vertically in the refrigerator so that it maintains its cylindrical shape. (If you put the foie gras on a plate, it will flatten on one side.) Refrigerate for at least 24 hours.

The next day, prepare the nori. Lay the 2 sheets of nori on the counter, side by side with the shiny side down, overlapping the sheets by ½ inch. Dab the seam with water to seal the sheets together. Unwrap the torchon and lay the foie gras at the bottom edge of the nori. Roll up the foie gras in the nori so that the torchon is completely wrapped in the seaweed. Trim off any excess nori and seal once again by dabbing water along the seam. Keep refrigerated until service. For best results, let rest in the refrigerator for one full day.

Fennel Salad

2 tablespoons orange juice

¼ cup olive oil

1 teaspoon shallots, minced

1 teaspoon chives, minced

Zest of 1 orange, finely minced

Coarse salt

Black pepper, freshly ground

1 large bulb fennel, shaved into
   paper-thin strips

1 cup mâche, lightly packed

1 cup frisée, lightly packed

3 tablespoons black truffle, cut into
   fine brunoise (optional)

2 tomatoes, peeled, seeded, and cut
   into ⅛-inch dice

Seaweed Aspic

In a small saucepan, combine the water and hyashi wakame or seaweed salad. Set over medium heat, cover, and bring to a boil. Immediately remove from heat, and strain through a fine seive. Cover and let cool to room temperature. The mixture will start to gel. Pour ¼ cup of the mixture onto each of four serving plates. If the mixture has become too stiff to pour, warm it slightly. Cover the plates with plastic wrap, making sure it does not touch the aspic. Refrigerate the plates until service.

Fennel Salad

To make the dressing, in a small mixing bowl, combine the orange juice, olive oil, shallots, chives, and orange zest. In another mixing bowl, combine all the rest of the ingredients except the tomatoes.

Grilled Cèpes

Slice the cèpes into ¼-inch slices. Season the slices with salt and pepper, then brush with olive oil. Grill the cèpes briefly on both sides. Set aside in a cool place until ready to serve.

Pan-Seared Rouget

Heat the olive oil in a sauté pan over medium-high heat. Season the rouget fillets with the thyme, salt, and pepper. Sear the fillets, skin side down, in batches, until the skin is crispy and browned. Cook on the skin side only so that the fish emerges medium rare.

Service

Arrange the grilled cèpes in a small circle over the aspic. Dress the fennel salad to taste, mixing carefully. Add the tomatoes. Divide the salad among the four serving plates on which you have already arranged the cèpes. Remove the torchon from the plastic wrap. Using a sharp knife that has been slightly warmed in hot water, slice the foie gras torchon into 16 equal slices. Place two fillets of rouget on top of each salad, then top with four slices of the torchon. Serve immediately.

Chef Notes

Hyashi wakame is the principal ingredient in Japanese seaweed salad, which is usually pre-seasoned with sesame oil and red pepper flakes. It can be found in Asian grocery stores or health food stores.

Grilled Cèpes

8 to 10 cèpes (porcini)
Coarse salt
Black pepper, freshly ground
2 tablespoons olive oil

Pan-Seared Rouget

Olive oil for sautéing
4 large rougets (red mullet), scaled but
    not skinned, cut into 8 fillets
2 tablespoons fresh thyme leaves
Coarse salt
Black pepper, freshly ground

Special Equipment

Butcher's twine

Wine Recommendation

Château Rayas Châteauneuf-du-Pape Blanc 1989 (Rhône), or another white Châteauneuf-du-Pape.

Foie Gras and Monkfish with Wild Mushrooms, Root Vegetables, and Truffle Vinaigrette

With a medley of root vegetables, sautéed medallions of monkfish, and black truffles, Rick Moonen turns slices of seared foie gras into a hearty main course. Cooking the beets in vinegared water preserves their color and texture and provides a bracing complement to the richness of the foie gras.

YIELD: 4 MAIN COURSE SERVINGS

Braised Cipolline

2 tablespoons unsalted butter

1 tablespoon sugar

4 large cipolline onions, blanched and peeled

½ cup chicken stock, or more as needed

Pinch coarse salt

Beets

3 cups water

3 tablespoons sugar

3 tablespoons white vinegar

1 teaspoon salt

1 golden beet, peeled and thinly sliced

1 red beet, peeled and thinly sliced

Boiled Potatoes

1 small baking potato, peeled and cut into thin rounds

1 tablespoon olive oil

Coarse salt

Port Reduction

1 cup ruby port

Braised Cipolline

Place the butter, sugar, and onions in a small saucepan over medium-high heat and sauté for 1 to 2 minutes to coat with the butter. Add the stock and salt. Cover tightly, reduce the heat, and simmer until the onions are tender, about 40 minutes. If the stock evaporates during that time, add more. When the onions are done, they should have turned a golden caramel color. Remove from the heat and set aside.

Beets

In a large saucepan, combine the water, sugar, vinegar, and salt. Set over high heat and bring to a boil. Lower the heat to a steady simmer. Add the golden beets and simmer until tender, about 40 minutes. Be careful not to overcook or they will fall apart. With a slotted spoon, remove the beets and reserve the cooking liquid. Place in a small mixing bowl, toss with a spoonful or two of the cooking liquid, and set aside. Using the same cooking liquid, cook the red beets in the same manner.

Boiled Potatoes

Blanch the potato slices in salted boiling water until tender, about 2 or 3 minutes. Remove from the water and drain. Toss with the olive oil and salt. Set aside.

Port Reduction

In a small, nonreactive saucepan, reduce the port over medium heat until only ¼ cup remains, about 30 minutes. It should have a thick, syrupy consistency.

Truffle Vinaigrette

Place the chicken stock in a small saucepan and set over high heat. Add the truffles, cover, and remove from the heat. Place the shallots in a small bowl and cover with about ½ cup of the hot stock mixture. Allow both the truffles and the shallots to steep, covered,

Truffle Vinaigrette

2 cups chicken stock

2 large black truffles

1 shallot, minced

3 tablespoons olive oil

2 tablespoons sherry vinegar

1 tablespoon truffle oil

Coarse salt

Black pepper, freshly ground

Monkfish and Foie Gras

1 pound monkfish, cut into
    8 medallions, 2 ounces each

½ pound foie gras, cut into 4 slices,
    each about 2 ounces and ¼-inch
    thick

Coarse salt

Black pepper, freshly ground

2 tablespoons clarified butter

for at least 1 hour. After they have steeped, remove the truffles from the stock. Slice very thinly and place in a small bowl. Toss with 1 tablespoon of the olive oil and set aside until service. Return the truffled stock to the heat and reduce by half, about 30 minutes.

To finish the truffle vinaigrette, add the sherry vinegar, remaining olive oil, and the truffle oil to the shallot and stock mixture and mix well. Adjust the seasoning with salt and pepper.

Monkfish and Foie Gras

Preheat the oven to 450 degrees. Season the monkfish medallions and sliced foie gras with salt and pepper. Heat a large sauté pan over high heat. Add the clarified butter. Sear the monkfish on both sides until browned and set the pan in the oven. Roast the monkfish until cooked through, about 5 to 8 minutes. Meanwhile, heat another pan over high heat. Sear the foie gras for 40 seconds on each side and remove from the pan. Set aside and keep warm.

Sautéed Mushrooms

While the monkfish and foie gras are cooking, heat a sauté pan over medium-high heat. Add the butter and mushrooms and sauté gently until tender, 4 to 5 minutes. Season with salt and pepper.

Service and Garnish

In a small saucepan, gently heat the truffle vinaigrette. Toss the beets, potatoes, and sliced truffles in the vinaigrette and arrange on four serving plates. Place two medallions of seared monkfish and one slice of foie gras in the center of each plate. Garnish with the braised cipolline, sautéed mushrooms, and greens. Drizzle the port reduction and some of the truffle vinaigrette around each plate.

Sautéed Mushrooms

3 tablespoons unsalted butter

6 ounces assorted mushrooms, such as oyster, shiitake, pousseron, and others

Coarse salt

Black pepper, freshly ground

Garnish

Corn shoots and other seasonal greens

Wine Recommendation

Erath Vineyards Willamette Valley Pinot Noir 1992 (Oregon), or another Pinot Noir from Oregon or Burgundy.

Medallions of Ahi Tuna and Seared Foie Gras with Pinot Noir Sauce

Pinot Noir Sauce

3 tablespoons unsalted butter

¼ pound shallots, sliced

4 portobello mushrooms, stems only, chopped (reserve caps for grilling)

3 white peppercorns

3 coriander seeds

1 bay leaf

2 tablespoons sugar

¼ cup red wine vinegar

1½ cups Pinot Noir

2 cups veal stock

Crispy Potato Cakes

2 large Russet potatoes

10 chives, chopped

2 egg whites

2 teaspoons coarse salt

2 tablespoons potato starch

Peanut oil for frying

Grilled Mushrooms

1 clove garlic, minced

1 shallot, minced

2 teaspoons fresh herbs

1 tablespoon balsamic vinegar

¼ cup olive oil

4 portobello mushroom caps (reserved from above)

Coarse salt

Black pepper, freshly ground

Tuna, Foie Gras, and Spinach

1½ pounds sushi-grade ahi tuna, cut into 6 steaks, about 4 ounces each

Vegetable oil for grilling

1 foie gras, 1½ pounds, cut into 6 cubes, about 4 ounces each

Coarse salt

Black pepper, freshly ground

½ pound spinach, cleaned

1 tablespoon olive oil

Special Equipment

2-inch-square mold

Wine Recommendation

King Estate Pinot Noir Reserve 1994 (Oregon), or another American Pinot Noir.

Tournedoes Rossini, a favorite of the famed composer, is comprised of filet mignon topped with foie gras and served with a sauce bordelaise (Bordeaux wine, bone marrow, and truffles). As chef of a seafood and fish restaurant, George Morrone created this interpretation as a noncarnivorous twist on an Old World classic, substituting tuna loin for filet and Pinot Noir for Bordeaux. This hearty seafood entrée easily stands up to a full-bodied red wine, a pairing that has become increasingly popular.

Pinot Noir Sauce

Melt the butter in a large saucepan over medium heat. Add the shallots and sauté until translucent, about 10 minutes. Add the mushrooms and cook until they have released all their liquid, 7 to 10 minutes. Add the peppercorns, coriander seeds, bay leaf, and sugar, and continue cooking until caramelized, an additional 3 minutes. Add the red wine vinegar and reduce until the mixture is dry, about 5 minutes. Add the Pinot Noir and reduce by three-forths, about 30 minutes. Add the veal stock and simmer until the mixture takes on the consistency of a light sauce, about 1 hour. Strain through a chinois and reserve.

Crispy Potato Cakes

Preheat the oven to 375 degrees. Bake the potatoes for 30 minutes or until they are barely tender. Let cool slightly, then peel and grate. Add the chives, egg whites, salt, and potato starch. Mold the potatoes into six cakes using a 2-inch-square mold; the cakes should be roughly ¾-inch thick. Heat the peanut oil in a large sauté pan and fry the potato cakes until golden brown on both sides, about 3 minutes per side. Set aside.

Grilled Mushrooms

Combine the garlic, shallot, herbs, balsamic vinegar, and olive oil. Marinate the mushroom caps in this mixture for at least 2 hours. Remove the mushrooms from the marinade. Season with salt and pepper, and grill until tender, about 3 or 4 minutes per side. Dice the grilled mushrooms into ½-inch cubes.

Tuna, Foie Gras, and Spinach

Place the potato cakes in a medium-hot oven to heat through. Brush the tuna with oil. Season the tuna and the foie gras with salt and pepper. On a very hot grill, sear the tuna on both sides. In a very hot sauté pan, sear the cubed foie gras on all sides until brown. In another pan, sauté the spinach in the olive oil and let drain on a paper towel. In another sauté pan, heat the Pinot Noir sauce and the diced portobello mushrooms. Place a potato cake in the center of each of six dinner plates with a small pile of sautéed spinach on top of each cake. On top of the spinach, place one tuna steak and one cubed foie gras steak. Spoon the Pinot Noir sauce with the chopped mushrooms around the plate.

Chef Notes

Fresh herbs such as thyme, marjoram, parsley, and rosemary work well in this preparation.

Pot-au-Feu Royale

Duck Consommé

1 tablespoon vegetable oil

2 duck legs

4 medium white mushrooms, cleaned
and sliced in half

2 cloves garlic, peeled

1 small onion, peeled and cut in half

1 celery stalk, cut into 1-inch pieces

1 large carrot, cut into ½-inch dice

Coarse salt

Black pepper, freshly ground

4 stems parsley

2 sprigs thyme

1 bay leaf

Pot-au-Feu

2 quarts duck consommé (from above)

Coarse salt

Black pepper, freshly cracked

12 baby carrots, peeled, stems trimmed

12 baby turnips, peeled, stems trimmed

½ cup fresh cranberry beans, rinsed
and picked over

8 spring onion bulbs, cleaned and split
in half

8 yellow wax beans, cut into 1-inch
pieces

1 celery stalk, peeled and sliced into
¼-inch pieces

¼ pound fresh woodear mushrooms,
cleaned and cut into small pieces
(see Chef Notes)

½ pound foie gras, cut into 4 slices, each
about 2 ounces and 1-inch thick

Garnish

Small bunch chives, cut into 2-inch
pieces

Special Equipment

Fine-mesh strainer

Cheesecloth

Wine Recommendation

Michel Niellon Chevalier-Montrachet
1995 (Burgundy), or another
concentrated, full-bodied Chardonnay
from Burgundy or California.

*Although pot-au-feu has its roots in country cooking, Daniel Boulud's regal multicourse version
incorporates baby vegetables, wild mushrooms, and foie gras to increase the level of sophistication. The
pot-au-feu Daniel remembers from his childhood consisted of more modest meats, such as beef, sausage,
and capon—foie gras was reserved for special occasions. In this pot-au-feu royale, the foie gras is
essentially poached, a method of preparation that Daniel favors because of the subtle flavor
and creamy texture it gives to the liver.*

Duck Consommé

In a 3-quart saucepan set over a high flame,
heat the oil. When hot, add the duck legs and
brown lightly on all sides. Add the mushrooms, garlic, onion, celery, and carrot to
the pan and season lightly with salt and pepper. Lower the heat and stir. When the onion
and celery are translucent, about 8 minutes,
add 2½ quarts of water to cover. Bring to a
boil, add the parsley, thyme, and bay leaf,
and simmer gently for 45 minutes, skimming
regularly to remove the fat from the top of
the broth. Using a small ladle, pass the broth
through a fine-mesh strainer lined with a
double layer of cheesecloth, being careful
not to disturb the sediment at the bottom.
Remove the legs and discard the vegetables
and herbs. The meat from the legs can be
removed from the bone, shredded, and used
in another recipe. When cool, the consommé
should be reserved in the refrigerator or
frozen until ready to use.

Pot-au-Feu

Place 1 quart of duck consommé into each
of two 2-quart saucepans and bring both to
a slow boil. Adjust the seasoning. Add the
carrots, turnips, and cranberry beans to one
pot and cook for 5 minutes. Add the onion
bulbs, yellow wax beans, celery, and mushrooms to the same pot and cook for an
additional 10 to 12 minutes. When the vegetables are nearly tender, score the foie gras
slices, season with salt and cracked pepper,
and plunge into the second pot of boiling
consommé. Simmer for 2 to 3 minutes, or
until warm in the center.

Service and Garnish

Place one slice of foie gras into each of four
warm, deep serving bowls. Divide the hot
consommé with the vegetables among the
bowls and sprinkle with the chives.

Chef Notes

Fresh woodear mushrooms work well in this
dish because they retain a pleasingly chewy
texture during the cooking process. They are
typically available in the fall, but trumpet
mushrooms can be substituted in the off season. Don't use the dried Asian variety of
woodear mushrooms, which tend to have a
slightly rubbery consistency when rehydrated.

Cumin-Crusted Foie Gras with Crispy Sweetbreads, Napa Cabbage, Ramps, Morels, and Red Wine Emulsion

YIELD: 4 APPETIZER SERVINGS

The combination of earthy flavors in this appetizer by Charlie Trotter evokes the flora and fauna of the forest in early spring when fresh ramps—actually wild leeks—and morels sprout from the forest floor in the height of their season. The rich texture and subtle flavor of sweetbreads provides a perfect complement to the seared foie gras.

Basil Oil

3 cups fresh basil, packed lightly

Coarse salt

2 cups grapeseed oil

1 cup olive oil

Veal Stock

10 pounds beef and veal bones

2 tablespoons grapeseed oil

2 carrots, coarsely chopped

2 stalks celery, coarsely chopped

1 yellow onion, coarsley chopped

1 leek, cleaned and coarsely chopped

1 bulb garlic, cut in half

½ cup tomato concassé

4 cups dry red wine

Red Wine Emulsion

2 tablespoons grapeseed oil

1 Spanish onion, coarsely chopped

1 carrot, coarsely chopped

1 stalk celery, coarsely chopped

1 Granny Smith apple, coarsely chopped

2 cloves garlic

1 bottle red Burgundy (750 ml)

2 cups port

1 cup chicken stock

3 tablespoons butter

Coarse salt

Black pepper, freshly ground

Basil Oil

Blanch the basil in boiling salted water for 15 seconds. Immediately shock in ice water and drain. Coarsely chop the basil and squeeze out the excess water. Place the basil in the bowl of a blender or food processor. Add the oils and purée for 3 minutes, or until the mixture is bright green. Pour the mixture into a container, cover, and refrigerate for 24 hours. Strain the oil and refrigerate for one more day; store in a clean bottle in a cool, dry place for up to 1 month.

Veal Stock

Preheat the oven to 450 degrees. Place the bones in a roasting pan and roast for 2 hours, until dark brown. Heat the oil in a large stockpot. Add the carrots, celery, onion, leek, and garlic and cook until caramelized. Add the tomato concassé and cook for an additional 5 minutes. Deglaze the stockpot with the wine and reduce until ¼ cup remains. Add the browned bones to the stockpot and cover with cold water. Bring to a boil, reduce the heat to medium, and let simmer for 8 hours. Strain the stock through a fine-mesh sieve into a saucepan. Simmer the stock over medium heat until it coats the back of a spoon, about 45 minutes.

Red Wine Emulsion

Heat the oil in a medium saucepan. Add the onion, carrot, celery, apple, and garlic and cook until the vegetables are caramelized. Add the Burgundy and the port and simmer over medium heat for 2 hours. Strain into a small saucepan and add the chicken stock. Continue to simmer over medium heat for 1 hour more, until you have ½ cup of liquid. Whisk in the butter and season to taste with salt and pepper.

Napa Cabbage and Ramps

Heat the butter in a sauté pan. Add the cabbage and cook until it begins to wilt. Season with salt and pepper. Push the cabbage to one side of the pan and add the ramps to the pan. Cook until the ramps are heated through, about 1 minute.

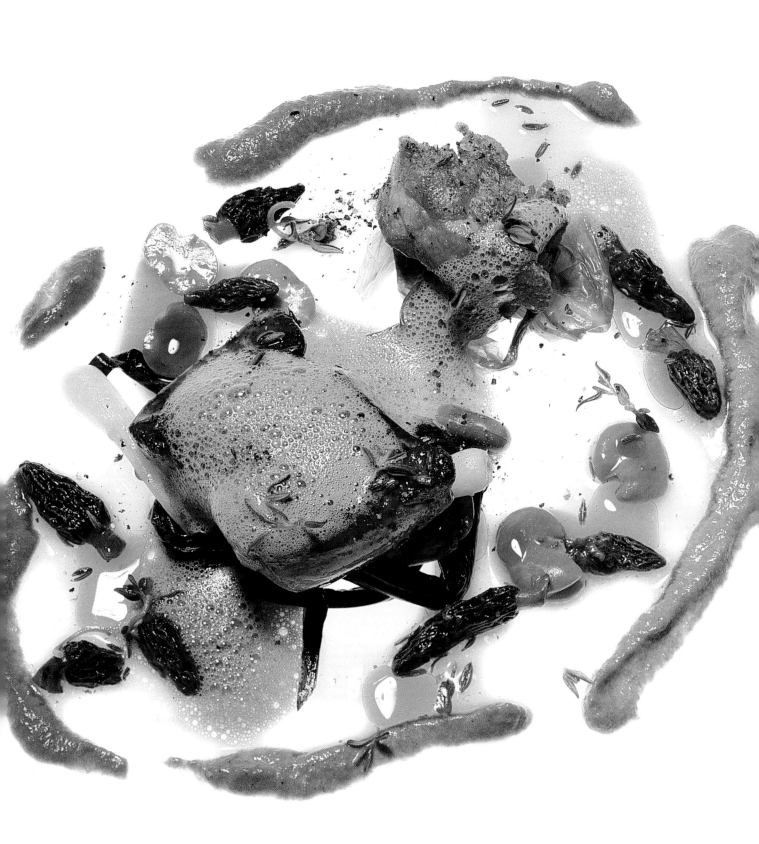

Napa Cabbage and Ramps

1 tablespoon butter

1½ cups shredded Napa cabbage

Coarse salt

Black pepper, freshly ground

8 ramps, cleaned

Morel Purée

2 cups tiny morels

2 tablespoons extra-virgin olive oil

1 cup water

Coarse salt

Black pepper, freshly ground

½ cup chicken stock, if necessary

Crispy Sweetbreads

1 large calf's sweetbread,
    about 4 ounces

2 lemons

Coarse salt

Black pepper, freshly ground

3 tablespoons all-purpose flour

3 tablespoons grapeseed oil

Morel Purée

Preheat the oven to 350 degrees. Place the morels in a small roasting pan. Add the olive oil, water, and salt and pepper to taste. Cover the pan and roast the morels for 30 minutes. Place half of the morels in the bowl of a blender or food processor, along with any of the juices that have accumulated in the pan. Reserve the remaining morels for garnish. Process until smooth. If necessary, add the chicken stock to create a smooth, even purée. Adjust the seasoning and keep warm.

Crispy Sweetbreads

Soak the sweetbreads in salted water acidulated with the juice of two lemons for 1 to 2 hours, changing the water twice during the process. Drain and place in a pot of cold salted water. Bring to a boil and cook for 3 minutes. Drain, and plunge the sweetbread into ice water. Remove any cartilage, tough ducts, or membrane that remains. Place the sweetbread on a plate and place another plate on top. Weight the top plate and refrigerate for about 2 hours. During this time the sweetbread should release most of its water and develop a firm texture. Break the sweetbread into four even-sized nuggets. Season the nuggets with salt and pepper and lightly dust with the flour. Heat the oil in a sauté pan set over high heat. Add the sweetbread pieces and sauté until golden brown and crisp, 1 to 1½ minutes per side. Season with salt to taste.

Cumin-Crusted Foie Gras

Season the foie gras with salt and pepper and sprinkle lightly with the cumin. Heat a sauté pan over high heat, add the foie gras, and cook for about 45 seconds per side.

Service and Garnish

Just before service, place the red wine reduction in a small saucepan and warm over low heat. Create an emulsion from the reduction using a hand blender. The mixture should remain frothy.

Divide the Napa cabbage among each of four serving plates, placing it in a mound on the right side of each plate. Place a sweetbread nugget on top of the mound. Arrange two ramps on the left side of each plate in a circle. Place a piece of foie gras over the ramps. Garnish the plates with the reserved morels and the fava beans. Spoon the morel purée in a wide ring around each of the plates. Spoon some of the red wine emulsion over the foie gras and around the plate. Drizzle the veal stock reduction and the basil oil around the foie gras and the sweetbreads. Top with freshly ground black pepper and thyme leaves.

Cumin-Crusted Foie Gras

4 pieces foie gras, each about 2 ounces
Coarse salt
Black pepper, freshly ground
2 teaspoons cumin seeds, toasted and
    coarsely ground

Garnish

Baby morels (reserved from above)
¾ cup fava beans, blanched and cleaned
Black pepper, freshly ground
8 sprigs young thyme, leaves picked
    and reserved

Wine Recommendation

J. L. Grippat St.-Joseph Vignes de l'Hospice 1996 (Rhône), or another light-style Syrah to complement the spice in the dish without overpowering it.

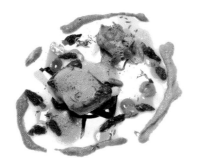

Lavender Oil

½ cup extra-virgin olive oil

¼ cup fresh lavender

Cranberry Compote

¼ cup sugar

⅓ cup water

1 cup dry Riesling

½ lemon, diced with the rind

½ lime, diced with the rind

½ orange, diced with the rind

1 cup fresh cranberries

½ teaspoon coarse salt

Roasted Shallots

¼ cup extra-virgin olive oil

12 shallots, peeled

Foie Gras Mashed Potatoes

3 large Yukon Gold potatoes, about
  1½ pounds, peeled and diced

6 ounces foie gras, cut into small cubes

⅓ cup heavy cream

1 tablespoon unsalted butter

1 tablespoon white truffle oil

Coarse salt

Black pepper, freshly ground

Quail

4 whole quail, cleaned, back and breast
  bones removed

Coarse salt

Black pepper, freshly ground

3 tablespoons unsalted butter, melted

Garnish

4 sprigs chervil

Special Equipment

Fine-mesh strainer or cheesecloth

Pastry brush

Vegetable mill

Wine Recommendation

Dehlinger Pinot Noir Russian River
Valley 1995 (California), or a similar
light-bodied red wine.

Roasted Quail Stuffed with Foie Gras Mashed Potatoes, with Roasted Shallots, Cranberry Compote, and Lavender Oil

Bradley Ogden uses foie gras to enrich and flavor the mashed potato stuffing for his roasted quail. As the quail cooks, the foie gras renders its fat into the stuffing, virtually basting the bird from within. The cranberry and roasted shallot garnish give the dish a wintry character.

Lavender Oil

In a small saucepan, combine the lavender and oil and heat to 150 degrees. Place in the refrigerator overnight. The next day, pass the mixture through a fine-mesh strainer or several layers of cheesecloth. Discard the lavender and reserve the flavored oil.

Cranberry Compote

In a medium stainless steel saucepan, combine the sugar and water. Set over high heat and bring to a boil. Reduce the heat to medium, brushing the sides of the pan every 3 to 4 minutes with a wet pastry brush to prevent crystallization. When the sugar becomes lightly caramelized, add the Riesling and diced fruits. Stir and let cook for about 10 minutes. Add the cranberries and salt. Cook just until the cranberries start to burst. Half the cranberries should remain whole. Cool immediately by pouring the mixture into a cold bowl and setting it in the refrigerator.

Roasted Shallots

Preheat the oven to 375 degrees. Set an ovenproof sauté pan over high heat and add the olive oil. Add the shallots and sauté until they begin to caramelize. Transfer the shallots to the oven and roast them, turning occasionally, until they are nicely caramelized, about 12 minutes.

Foie Gras Mashed Potatoes

Preheat the oven to 350 degrees. Boil the diced potatoes in salted water until tender, about 15 to 20 minutes. Strain and place the potato pieces on a half sheet pan. Set the potatoes in the oven for 10 minutes to dry out. Pass the potatoes through a vegetable mill. Remove about ¼ cup of potato and set aside.

Heat a medium sauté pan over high heat and sear the foie gras until brown. Add the cream and butter to the pan, bring to a quick boil, and remove from the heat. Fold the foie gras mixture into the milled potatoes and mix well. Add the truffle oil and season to taste with salt and pepper. Adjust the consistency of the stuffing with the reserved potato. The stuffing should be stiff enough to hold its shape.

Quail

Preheat the oven to 425 degrees. Fill the cavity of each quail with the mashed potato mixture. Season the outside of the quails with salt and pepper and brush with melted butter. Roast in a preheated oven for 10 to 12 minutes, just until the flesh is pink and the birds have browned.

Service and Garnish

Warm the cranberry compote slightly and divide evenly in the center of each of four serving plates. Place the roasted quail over the compote. Divide the shallots among the plates, placing them around the quail. Drizzle the lavender oil over the quail and outside the ring of cranberry compote. Garnish with the chervil sprigs.

Foie Gras Pithiviers

Filling

½ pound pork fat, skin removed, cut into 1-inch dice

1 pork tenderloin, about ½ pound, cleaned and cut into 1-inch dice

¾ pound duck breast, cut into 1-inch dice

Pinch sugar

2 teaspoons coarse salt

½ teaspoon black pepper, freshly ground

5 juniper berries, ground

1 egg

1 cup heavy cream

1 ounce black truffle, minced

1 teaspoon fresh sage, minced

Pithiviers

1 sheet puff pastry, 10 by 20 inches

1 pound foie gras, cut into 6 slices, each about 2½ ounces and ½-inch thick

1 egg, lightly beaten

Red Wine Sauce

5 tablespoons butter

1 small onion, chopped

1 small carrot, chopped

1 pound assorted bones and trimmings, duck, chicken, quail, or other game

1 bouquet garni

½ cup red wine vinegar

2 cups demi glace

3 cups chicken stock

2½ cups red wine

Coarse salt

Black pepper, freshly ground

Garnish

Fresh herbs

Special Equipment

Meat grinder with medium blade

5- and 3-inch round cookie cutters

1 small glass bowl, 4 inches wide

Fine chinois

Wine Recommendation

Turley Zinfandel Napa Valley Hayne Vineyard 1996 (Napa), or another red wine with pronounced spice.

The French town of Pithiviers is known for a traditional dessert made of a disk of puff pastry filled with sweet almond cream. Outside Pithiviers the term has come to mean anything sandwiched between two pieces of puff pastry. This variation by Roland Passot incorporates slices of foie gras in a pork and duck forcemeat. Like a savory turnover, Roland's Pithiviers makes a rich and satisfying entrée.

Filling

In a large bowl, combine the pork fat, pork tenderloin, duck meat, and sugar. Add the salt, pepper, and ground juniper. Cover and refrigerate 3 to 4 hours. Pass this mixture through a meat grinder fitted with a medium blade. Add the egg, heavy cream, truffle, sage, and mix well.

Pithiviers

On a lightly floured surface, roll out the puff pastry to about ⅛-inch thick. Using the cookie cutters, cut out six 5-inch circles and six 3-inch circles. Flour the glass bowl and line it with one of the larger pastry circles. Spread ½ cup of filling over the pastry circle inside the bowl. Place a slice of foie gras in the center and top with more filling to create an even, semicircular surface. Top with a smaller circle of pastry and pinch the edges together to seal. Flip the bowls onto a baking sheet to unmold the pithiviers. Repeat to form a total of six pithiviers. Brush the tops of the pithiviers with the lightly beaten egg. Using the tip of a sharp knife, start at the top of each dome and make a gentle, curved incision toward the edge of the dome. Repeat, creating a pinwheel design on each dome. Cover the tray and refrigerate the pithiviers for 10 minutes. Preheat the oven to 450 degrees. Place the tray in the oven and turn down the oven to 350 degrees. Bake for 45 minutes, until golden brown.

Red Wine Sauce

Heat 2 tablespoons of the butter in a large saucepan over high heat. Add the onion, carrot, and trimmings and sauté until nicely browned, about 15 minutes. Add the bouquet garni and continue cooking for an additional 5 minutes. Add the vinegar and reduce until dry. Add the demi glace, chicken stock, and red wine. Bring to a boil, skim off any scum that rises to the surface, reduce the heat, cover, and simmer for about 3 hours, skimming frequently. Pass through a fine chinois into a clean saucepan. Reduce the sauce over low heat to the consistency of a light syrup, about 20 minutes. Whisk in the remaining butter, adjust the seasoning with salt and pepper, and set aside.

Service and Garnish

Spoon the sauce onto six warmed serving plates and place a pithiviers on each plate on top of the sauce. Garnish with sprigs of fresh herbs.

Chinese Spiced Duck Breast with Seared Foie Gras, Caramelized Mango, and Asian Vegetables

Known for his beautifully constructed presentations and tantalizing flavor combinations, New York City chef Alfred Portale reunites foie gras with duck in this Asian-inspired entrée. Both the duck and the sauce are seasoned with Chinese five-spice powder—a fragrant blend of cinnamon, clove, fennel, star anise, and Szechwan peppercorns. The Asian vegetables and caramelized mango garnish enlivens both the flavor and presentation of the finished dish.

Duck Sauce

2 tablespoons canola oil

1 scallion, chopped

2 large garlic cloves, peeled and crushed

1 tablespoon chopped fresh ginger

1 cup dark chicken or duck stock

½ cup water

1 dried shiitake mushroom

1 tablespoon mushroom soy sauce or regular soy sauce

1½ teaspoons hoisin sauce

½ teaspoon Chinese chili paste with garlic

Pinch Chinese five-spice powder

Coarse salt

Chinese Spiced Duck Breast

4 Muscovy duck breasts, about 10 ounces each

2 teaspoons Chinese five-spice powder

Coarse salt

Black pepper, freshly ground

2 scallions, finely sliced

1 piece ginger, 3 inches long, peeled and sliced

¼ cup cilantro, chopped

Duck Sauce

In a medium saucepan, heat the oil over medium heat. Add the scallion, garlic, and ginger and cook, stirring frequently, for 3 minutes, until the mixture is softened and fragrant. Add the remaining ingredients except the salt, and bring to a boil over high heat. Reduce the heat to low and simmer for 30 minutes, or until the liquid reduces to about 1 cup. Add salt, if necessary, and strain into a small bowl.

Chinese Spiced Duck Breast

Trim away any excess skin and fat from the duck. Using a sharp knife, score the skin lightly in a crosshatch pattern, being careful not to pierce the flesh. Season the duck breasts on both sides with the five-spice powder, salt, and pepper. Spread the remaining ingredients equally over the breasts. Cover and refrigerate for at least 6 hours, but not more than 24 hours.

Season the duck breasts with additional coarse salt, and place in a cold, nonstick sauté pan. Place the pan over medium heat and cook until the skin is browned and crisp, about 10 minutes. Turn the breasts and cook for 3 minutes, to medium rare. Transfer to a plate and lightly tent with aluminum foil. Let rest 5 minutes.

Asian Vegetables

Bring a large pot of lightly salted water to a boil. Add the bok choy and cook until just tender but still firm, 4 to 5 minutes. Remove the bok choy from the pot and shock in a bowl of ice water. Bring the water back to a boil, add the snow peas, and cook for 1 minute, until they are bright green. Remove the snow peas and shock in the ice water. When cool, remove the vegetables from the ice water, dry, and set aside.

In a sauté pan, heat 1 tablespoon of the vegetable oil. Add the mushroom caps and cook for 3 minutes. Turn the caps and cook for another 2 minutes, until tender. Season with salt and pepper and set aside.

Asian Vegetables

4 baby bok choy, about 4 ounces each,
    bottoms trimmed so they will stand
    on the plate when cooked

16 snow peas, trimmed

2 tablespoons vegetable oil

16 mushroom caps

Coarse salt

White pepper, freshly ground

½ small head Napa cabbage

Caramelized Mango

2 tablespoons butter

2 teaspoons canola oil

2 tablespoons sugar

2 ripe mangos, peeled, pitted, and cut
    in half

Pinch coarse salt

Cut the cabbage into quarters, leaving the core intact. Heat the remaining oil in the sauté pan, over high heat until very hot. Add the cabbage pieces, cut side down, and cook until the cut side is golden brown, about 3 minutes. Turn and cook for 3 more minutes, until the other cut side is golden brown. Season with salt and pepper.

Caramelized Mango

Heat the butter and oil in a sauté pan set over low heat. Add the sugar and cook until the sugar begins to caramelize, about 6 minutes. Season the mango halves with salt and add to the sauté pan. Cook until caramelized, about 5 minutes. Remove from the pan and keep warm.

Foie Gras

Score the foie gras and season with salt and pepper. Set a sauté pan over high heat. Sear the foie gras slices for 1 minute on each side. Keep warm.

Service and Garnish

Spoon 2 tablespoons of duck sauce in the middle of four warmed serving plates. Slice the duck breasts into ¼-inch-thick slices. Place a sliced duck breast over the sauce, fanning the slices. Stand the bok choy above the duck breast and arrange the leaves to create a petal effect. Place a piece of foie gras and a piece of mango on each duck breast. Place 4 snow peas and 4 mushroom caps on each plate and garnish with scallions and cilantro.

Foie Gras

12 ounces foie gras, cut into 4 slices, each about 3 ounces and ½-inch thick
Coarse salt
Black pepper, freshly ground

Garnish

Scallions
Cilantro

Wine Recommendation

Bouchard Père & Fils Volnay Caillerets Ancienne Cuvée Carnot Domaine du Château de Beaune 1989 (Burgundy), or another premier red Burgundy.

Foie Gras and Sweet Onion Bread Pudding with Pecan-Crusted Duck Leg Confit, Wilted Spinach, and Andouille Salad

With its roots in French, Spanish, and African cooking, the cuisine of New Orleans is known for hearty dishes with robust flavors. One of the genre's most renowned practitioners is Emeril Lagasse, who, for this preparation, blends Cajun and Creole classics with French ingredients and techniques. Although bread pudding is usually served as a dessert, Emeril's savory version incorporates foie gras, which, as it melts, enriches the custard. The result is a comforting, stuffinglike pudding that is a perfect accompaniment to the pecan-crusted duck leg confit.

YIELD: 10 MAIN COURSE SERVINGS

Duck Confit

10 duck legs

1½ cups coarse salt

1 teaspoon black peppercorns

1 bunch fresh thyme

8 juniper berries

2 to 3 quarts rendered duck fat
(see page 108)

Bread Pudding

3 tablespoons unsalted butter

1 pound foie gras, cut into ½-inch
cubes

3 cups sliced onions

2 teaspoons coarse salt

¼ teaspoon cayenne pepper

½ teaspoon black pepper, freshly
ground

1 tablespoon garlic, chopped

7 large eggs

3 cups heavy cream

½ teaspoon Tabasco sauce

1½ teaspoons Worcestershire sauce

8 cups cubed white bread, without
crusts

½ cup Parmigiano-Reggiano cheese,
grated

Duck Confit

Rinse the duck legs under cold water and pat dry with paper towels. In a small bowl, combine the salt, peppercorns, thyme, and juniper. Holding 1 duck leg at a time over the bowl of salt, rub a generous amount of the salt and seasonings into the skin and flesh of the leg. Place in a half hotel pan or other nonreactive dish and repeat with the remaining legs. The salted legs can be layered 2 or 3 deep. All of the salt should be used. Any that is left over can be sprinkled on top. Refrigerate overnight. The following day, brush away any salt and spices from the duck legs and pat dry with paper towels. Heat the rendered fat in a heavy 6- or 8-quart saucepan over medium heat to between 220 and 230 degrees. Add the duck legs, making sure they are submerged in the fat, and cook until browned and tender, about 1 hour and 45 minutes. When the legs are nearly cooked, the meat will pull away from the leg bone. Remove from the heat and let cool at room temperature for 1 hour. Transfer the legs to a ceramic bowl, crock, or other nonreactive container. If not using immediately, strain the fat on top to cover. The confit will keep up to one year in the refrigerator. To use confit that has been stored in the refrigerator, gently heat the bowl in a pot of simmering water to melt the hardened fat.

Bread Pudding

Preheat the oven to 350 degrees. Grease a 2-quart rectangular glass baking dish with 1 tablespoon of the butter. Heat a large sauté pan over moderately high heat and sear the foie gras cubes in several batches, about 30 seconds per batch, stirring gently with a wooden spoon. Remove the cubes and drain them on a paper towel, leaving the fat in the pan. Add the remaining butter to the pan and sauté the onions until translucent, about 5 to 10 minutes, adding 1 teaspoon of the salt, ½ teaspoon of the cayenne pepper, and all the black pepper. Add the garlic and sauté for 1 minute longer. Remove this mixture from the heat and let cool.

In a large mixing bowl, whisk the eggs for 30 seconds. Add the heavy cream, the remaining salt and cayenne pepper, the Tabasco sauce, and the Worcestershire sauce. Whisk this mixture until all ingredients are well blended. Stir in the onion mixture. Add the bread cubes and mix well. Fold in the seared foie gras. Pour the mixture into the buttered pan and sprinkle with the grated cheese. Bake in the preheated oven for 45 to 55 minutes, or until set. If the top begins to brown, cover with aluminum foil. Remove the pudding from the oven and let it rest for 5 minutes before serving.

Pecan-Crusted Duck Confit

2½ cups pecans, lightly toasted (see Chef Notes)

3¾ cups flour

Essence of Emeril (see Chef Notes)

Coarse salt

Black pepper, freshly ground

3 eggs beaten

¼ cup milk

10 legs duck confit (from above)

¼ cup olive oil

Wilted Spinach Salad

2½ cups andouille sausage, finely chopped (see Chef Notes)

¼ cup shallot, minced

2½ tablespoons garlic, minced

1½ cups onion, finely chopped

½ cup balsamic vinegar

1½ cups olive oil

Coarse salt

Black pepper, freshly ground

1 medium red onion, sliced thinly

10 cups fresh spinach, cleaned, stems removed, and firmly packed

Pecan-Crusted Duck Confit

Preheat the oven to 375 degrees. In a food processor, combine the pecans with 1½ cups of the flour. Pulse until the pecans are finely ground, being careful not to over-process the mixture to a paste. Season the mixture with the Essence of Emeril. In a shallow bowl, season the remaining flour with salt and pepper. In another shallow bowl, beat together the eggs and milk. Dredge the confit legs in the seasoned flour. Dip each leg in the egg wash, letting the excess drip off. Dredge the legs in the pecan mixture, coating each leg completely. Heat two ovenproof sauté pans, each large enough to hold five duck legs without crowding, over medium-high heat. Divide the olive oil among the two pans and heat. Lay the pecan-crusted legs into the hot oil, five per pan. Pan fry the legs for 3 minutes on the first side, flip, and remove the pan from the heat. Place the pans in the preheated oven and cook the duck legs for an additional 6 minutes. Remove from the pan, drain on paper towel, and keep warm.

Wilted Spinach Salad

In a hot sauté pan, sear the andouille sausage for 1 minute, until the fat renders. Add the shallot, garlic, and chopped onion and sauté for 2 to 3 minutes more. Remove the pan from the heat and add the balsamic vinegar.

Pour the mixture into a medium mixing bowl and whisk in the olive oil. Season to taste with salt and pepper. Transfer to a small stainless steel container and set aside in a warm place. Reserve the red onion and spinach until service.

Service

Using a 2½-inch round metal cutter, cut circles out of the bread pudding. Place the spinach into a large mixing bowl and toss with the red onions and the warm vinaigrette. Season the salad with salt and pepper. Mound some salad onto one side of each of ten serving plates. Lay a duck confit leg on top of each salad and a round of bread pudding on the side.

Chef Notes

To toast the pecans, place the nuts on a sheet pan and set in a 350 degree oven for 10 minutes. Cool completely before using. Essence of Emeril is a proprietary spice blend available in grocery and gourmet stores. As a substitute, use any combination of sweet and hot spices to your taste. Andouille is a dense smoked sausage typical of Louisiana. It can be found in most specialty meat or charcuterie shops. Do not confuse Cajun andouille with French andouille, which is a tripe sausage typical of Lyons.

Special Equipment

2-quart rectangular glass baking dish, 8 by 12 inches

2½-inch round metal cutter

Wine Recommendation

Domaine Michel Lafarge Volnay 1993 (Burgundy), or another rich and elegant Chardonnay.

Foie Gras in Peking Duck Skins

Although ducks have been part of China's culinary tradition for thousands of years, foie gras has been produced in China only recently. In this dish, Lydia Shire borrows one element of the ancient ritual of Peking duck, the skin, and combines it with seared foie gras prepared in the European tradition. The scallion pancakes served on the side emphasize the cross-cultural nature of the dish.

Scallion Pancakes

2 cups all-purpose flour, plus extra
    flour for rolling

¾ cup boiling water

1 teaspoon coarse salt

2 tablespoons toasted sesame oil

1 bunch scallions, white and green
    parts, sliced into thin rounds

2 tablespoons peanut oil

Taro Purée

1 pound peeled taro

2 cloves garlic, peeled

Coarse salt

5 tablespoons unsalted butter, at room
    temperature

Black pepper, freshly ground

Taro Chips

1 piece taro, 6-inch long, peeled and
    cut in chunks

Peanut oil for deep frying

Coarse salt

Scallion Pancakes

Mix together the flour, water, and salt and knead until smooth, about 15 minutes. Cover with a damp cloth and let rest in the refrigerator for 15 minutes. Cut the dough into 12 small balls, each weighing approximately 1 ounce. Brush the top halves of two balls of dough with sesame oil. Press one ball down onto the other ball, oiled sides touching, to create a flattened double pancake with a layer of oil in between. Repeat until you have six sandwiches. Place the pancakes on a sheet pan or cutting board covered with wax paper, re-cover with a damp cloth, and let rest again for 15 minutes. On a very lightly floured board, roll out the first double pancake rapidly and evenly into an 8-inch round. Before giving the double pancake its last "roll," sprinkle 1 teaspoon sliced scallions on one side and roll out once so they stick to the pancake; turn over and repeat. Repeat the entire process until all six portions are completed. Heat a few drops of peanut oil in a nonstick or a well-seasoned heavy-bottomed sauté pan, and place one double pancake in the pan, cooking 1 to 1½ minutes on each side. It should color and puff slightly. Remove from the pan and immediately sep-

arate the two pancakes. Repeat until you have 12 thin pancakes. Wrap well in plastic wrap and reserve at room temperature.

Taro Purée

In a small saucepan, combine the taro with the garlic and salt. Add enough water just to cover the taro. Cover the saucepan and bring to a simmer. Remove the cover and continue to cook until tender, about 45 minutes. Drain well, and place the cooked taro and the butter into the bowl of a food processor. Purée. Season with additional salt and freshly ground pepper to taste. Remove the purée to a bowl, cover, and reserve for final preparation.

Taro Chips

With a sharp potato peeler, peel off strips of taro, approximately ½-inch wide. Fill a large frying pan with peanut oil, about 1 inch deep. Heat the oil to 325 to 350 degrees, and fry the taro strips in batches until golden and crisp. If the oil temperature rises above this temperature, the taro will turn black when fried. Drain on paper towels, and salt lightly. Keep in a slightly warm place until ready to use.

Dipping Sauce

¾ cup soy sauce

¼ cup rice wine vinegar

2 tablespoons ginger, finely chopped

1 tablespoon garlic, finely chopped

½ teaspoon toasted sesame oil

¼ teaspoon chili oil

3 tablespoons scallions, thinly sliced

2 tablespoons fresh cilantro, chopped

Salad

3 scallions, white and green parts, cut
    into julienne

½ cup daikon, cut into julienne

4 radishes, sliced into thin rounds

½ cup cilantro sprigs

Coarse salt

Black pepper, freshly ground

Juice of 1 lime

2 tablespoons light olive oil

1 tablespoon mirin

1 tablespoon rice wine vinegar

Peking Duck

1 whole Peking duck (see Chef Notes)

4 additional Peking duck legs

Dipping Sauce

In a medium mixing bowl, whisk together
the soy sauce, rice wine vinegar, ginger,
garlic, sesame oil, and chili oil. Stir in the
scallions and cilantro. Reserve to prepare the
foie gras and for garnish.

Salad

Mix the scallions, daikon, radishes, and
cilantro in a bowl and toss with salt and pepper. Just before serving, add the lime juice,
olive oil, mirin, and rice wine vinegar to the
bowl. Toss well to combine.

Peking Duck

Twenty minutes before serving, preheat the
oven to 300 degrees. Reheat the duck and
duck legs for 10 minutes to recrisp the skin.
Carefully remove the skin from the duck and
slice into twelve pieces, approximately 1
inch by 3 inches. Separate the legs from the
whole duck. Keep warm.

Foie Gras

Marinate the foie gras slices in the dipping
sauce for 1 minute. Remove and pat dry. In a
very hot pan, sauté the slices for about 30
seconds on each side. Keep warm.

Service and Garnish

Warm the taro purée over a double boiler. Reheat the pancakes in the oven for 1 minute, remove, and fold each into quarters. Place a handful of salad in the center of each of six serving plates. Lay a slice of duck skin and a duck leg on top of the salad. Arrange a piece of seared foie gras beside the duck leg. Drizzle with hoisin sauce. Finish the plate with 2 folded pancakes and a spoonful of the warm taro purée. Garnish with taro chips, a spoon of reserved dipping sauce, scallion brush, lemongrass, and seasonal fresh Asian herbs.

Chef Notes

All the elements except the duck and the foie gras can be prepared in advance. Order a whole Peking duck from your favorite Chinese restaurant that you can pick up or have delivered an hour or so before service. The meat is delicious the next day and won't go to waste. Alternately, you can substitute the crisp duck skin garnish in Gray Kunz's recipe (page 136).

Foie Gras

1⅛ pounds foie gras, cut into 6 slices, each about 3 ounces and ½-inch thick

½ cup dipping sauce (from above)

Garnish

Hoisin sauce

6 scallions, sliced into brushes

Fresh lemongrass

Asian herbs

Wine Recommendation

Trimbach Clos St. Hune Riesling 1993 (Alsace), or another Alsatian white wine.

Soft Yellow Corn Pancakes with Barbecued Duck, Foie Gras, and Habanero-Star Anise Sauce

At his popular Southwestern restaurants, Bobby Flay reserves foie gras for special occasions such as New Year's Eve. This popular dish reflects Bobby's affinity for bold, flavorful cooking, redolent of strong spices and hot peppers. He sears the smaller lobe of the foie gras whole, slices it into medallions, and along with the succulent barbecued duck, fills freshly griddled corn pancakes. The spicy acidity of habanero chiles counteracts the richness of the filling.

YIELD: 4 MAIN COURSE SERVINGS

Barbecue Sauce

3 tablespoons unsalted butter

1 small red onion, finely diced

2 cloves garlic, finely minced

7 plum tomatoes, coarsely diced

¼ cup tomato ketchup

2 tablespoons Dijon mustard

2 tablespoons dark brown sugar

1 tablespoon honey

1 teaspoon cayenne pepper

1 tablespoon ancho chili powder

1 teaspoon pasilla chili powder

1 tablespoon paprika

1 tablespoon Worcestershire sauce

Barbecued Duck

3 duck legs, skin removed

½ cup barbecue sauce (from above)

2 tablespoon cilantro, coarsely chopped

3 cups duck stock

Coarse salt

Black pepper, freshly ground

Mustard Oil

½ cup grapeseed oil

1 teaspoon powdered mustard

½ teaspoon ground turmeric

Barbecue Sauce

In a large sauté pan set over medium heat, melt the butter. Add the onion and garlic and cook until soft. Add the remaining ingredients and simmer for about 15 minutes, until the tomatoes turn into a liquid. Purée the mixture in a food processor until smooth, pour into a bowl, and set aside.

Barbecued Duck

Preheat the oven to 300 degrees. Slather the duck legs with the barbecue sauce and place them in a baking pan. Sprinkle the cilantro around the pan. Pour the stock around them. Cover the pan with aluminum foil and place in the oven to cook for 1½ hours. Remove the cover, turn over the duck, and continue cooking for an additional 1½ hours, until the meat falls off the bone and has browned. Remove the duck meat and reserve the cooking liquid. Shred the meat and discard the bones. Transfer the shredded meat to a sauté pan. Add one-fourth of the cooking liq-

uid and heat until simmering. Season with salt and pepper to taste. Remove from the heat and set aside.

Mustard Oil

In a small saucepan combine the oil, mustard, and turmeric. Heat to a gentle simmer and cook for 5 minutes. Remove from the heat and cool. Line a funnel with a coffee filter and place on top of a jar. Pour the flavored oil into the filter and let sit until all of the oil has passed through.

Habanero Sauce

Place all the ingredients in a small saucepan, set over medium heat, bring to a simmer, and reduce until only 1 cup of the mixture remains. Strain through a fine sieve and season with salt and pepper to taste.

Yellow Corn Pancakes

In a medium bowl combine the cornmeal, flour, baking powder, and salt. In a separate

Habanero Sauce

3 cups duck stock

¼ cup apple juice

2 tablespoons dark brown sugar

2 whole star anise

1 cinnamon stick

1 habanero pepper, coarsely chopped

1 tablespoon fennel seed, toasted

Coarse salt

Black pepper, freshly ground

Yellow Corn Pancakes

½ cup yellow cornmeal

½ cup all-purpose flour

1 teaspoon baking powder

Pinch coarse salt

1 large egg, beaten

1 cup plus 2 tablespoons milk

2 tablespoons honey

2 tablespoons unsalted butter, melted,
   plus extra for greasing the pan

bowl, combine the egg, milk, honey, and melted butter. Add this second mixture to the dry ingredients and mix well. Heat a griddle or cast-iron skillet over high heat, and brush with melted butter. Drop the batter by spoonfuls, and swirl the pan to make a thin, even 6-inch pancake. Cook until the pancake just begins to brown and the edges begin to pull up, about 1 minute. Flip and cook the other side until set, about 10 seconds. Repeat the process to make four pancakes. Stack the pancakes on a plate and wrap with aluminum foil to keep warm.

Foie Gras

Just before service, generously season the foie gras lobes with salt and pepper. Set a heavy sauté pan over medium-high heat and heat until the pan is almost smoking. Sear each lobe of the foie gras for approximately 1 minute on each side, until deep brown in color. Remove from the pan and set on paper towels to drain.

Service and Garnish

To serve, place one of the warm yellow corn pancakes, pale yellow side down, in the middle of each of four serving plates. Mound 2 tablespoons of barbecued duck on one side of each pancake. Slice each lobe of foie gras on the diagonal into seven or eight even pieces. Fan out three to four pieces of foie gras around the duck mixture on each plate. Fold the other half of the pancake over the filling to form a taco. Place another spoonful of duck on top of the folded pancake. Spoon the warm habanero sauce around the plate, drizzle with the mustard oil, and garnish with the diced red pepper and chopped herbs.

Chef Notes

The sauce recipes will produce more than you need for just four portions. Leftovers can be stored in airtight containers in the refrigerator for two weeks. The barbecue sauce is also delicious on pork. The pancake recipe will also produce more than needed; the batter will keep, refrigerated, for a day or two.

Foie Gras

2 small lobes foie gras, whole, about 1 pound total
Coarse salt
Black pepper, freshly ground

Garnish

Red pepper, finely diced
Cilantro, finely chopped
Chives, finely chopped

Special Equipment

Funnel
Coffee filter
Griddle or cast-iron skillet

Wine Recommendation

ZD Winery Chardonnay 1995 (Napa), or another full-bodied Chardonnay with balanced fruit and oak to stand up to the spicy flavors of the dish.

Roasted Crépinette of Squab and Foie Gras in Braised Cabbage

Derived from the French word for caul fat, crépine, *the crépinette is a classic preparation for game that involves wrapping a forcemeat or filling with caul fat and shaping it into a compact package. As the crépinette roasts, the caul fat bastes the filling and the transparent membrane, which actually serves to maintain the shape, disappears. Alsatian-born chef Jean Joho wraps a tender squab around a nugget of seasoned foie gras and sliced black truffle, envelopes the squab in savoy cabbage, and holds it all together with caul. Served with knefla, a tender homemade Alsatian noodle similar to German spaetzle, and braised chestnuts, this dish offers the hearty taste of traditional Alsatian cooking.*

YIELD: 2 MAIN COURSE SERVINGS

Crépinettes

2 small squab, ¾ to 1 pound each

Coarse salt

Black pepper, freshly ground

1 tablespoon port

2 pieces caul fat, rinsed well under cold running water

4 to 5 Savoy cabbage leaves, blanched, thick veins removed

2 medallions foie gras, each about 2½ ounces and ½-inch thick

1 ounce black truffle, thinly sliced

Braised Chestnuts

½ pound whole chestnuts in the shell

2 tablespoons onion, chopped

2 tablespoons celery, chopped

1 bay leaf

1 cup beef or chicken stock

Coarse salt

Black pepper, freshly ground

2 teaspoons butter

Crépinettes

Debone the squab, keeping the skin intact, and place in a nonreactive bowl. Season the squab well with salt and pepper, add the port, and marinate at room temperature for 2 hours. Preheat the oven to 400 degrees. To prepare the crépinette, lay out a piece of the caul fat on the work surface. Arrange one or two leaves of the blanched cabbage on top of the caul. Lay the boned squab on top of the cabbage, skin side down. Arrange one medallion of foie gras and half the black truffle on the breast. Gather up the caul, cabbage, and squab to form a tight ball. Twist the caul together on the bottom to form a compact package. Trim off any excess caul. Lay a piece of plastic wrap over the top and gather the ends. Continue twisting and tightening the plastic wrap to shape the crépinette into a ball. Repeat with the remaining squab. Refrigerate until service.

Braised Chestnuts

Using a small, sharp paring knife, make a slit on one side of each chestnut shell. Place the slit chestnuts in a pot, cover with cold water, bring to a boil, and boil for 1 minute. Remove a couple of chestnuts at a time from the water and peel off the outer shell. Using a paring knife, scrape the bitter inner skin off each nut.

Place the peeled chestnuts into another pot with the onion, celery, and bay leaf. Add enough stock to cover the chestnuts by about 1 inch, adding water if necessary. Bring to a boil, then simmer slowly, partially covered for about 40 minutes, until the chestnuts are tender but still whole. Take care not to cook too hard or the chestnuts may fall apart. Drain and reserve the chestnuts and liquid. Place the liquid in a large sauté pan and reduce until it becomes syrupy, 30 to 40 minutes. Adjust the seasoning with salt and pepper. Add the cooked chestnuts, coating them in the syrup, and keep warm. Reserve the butter until service.

Black Truffle Sauce

Heat 1 tablespoon of the butter in a saucepan over medium-low heat. Briefly sauté the

Black Truffle Sauce

4 tablespoons butter

3 tablespoons black truffle, finely diced

Coarse salt

Black pepper, freshly ground

3 tablespoons Madeira

2 cups demi-glace

Alsatian Knefla

1 large egg, beaten

⅔ cup all-purpose flour

⅔ cup sour cream

1 teaspoon chives, finely chopped

½ teaspoon coarse salt

Black pepper, freshly ground

1 tablespoon butter

truffles, seasoning with a little salt and pepper. Remove the truffles from the pan and reserve. Return the pan to the heat and deglaze with 2 tablespoons of the Madeira. Add the demi-glace and simmer for 5 minutes. Return the truffles to the sauce and remove from the heat. Add the remaining butter and Madeira while stirring. Adjust seasoning before serving.

Alsatian Knefla

Bring a large pot of salted water to a boil. In a bowl, combine the egg, flour, sour cream, chives, salt, and pepper, mixing until thickened. Holding a potato ricer fitted with a coarse disk over the boiling water, pass the knefla batter through the ricer to form rough noodle shapes. Cook until they rise to the top, about 2 minutes. Gently remove the knefla from the water with a slotted spoon, drain, and cool slightly. Melt the butter in a sauté pan, add the knefla, and cook for 3 to 4 minutes, making sure to coat all of the knefla in the butter. Keep warm.

Service and Garnish

Preheat the oven to 400 degrees. Remove the plastic wrap from the crépinettes, place them in a roasting pan, and roast for 15 to 20 minutes, depending on the size of the squab, to an internal temperature of 120 degrees. Reheat the chestnuts in the reduced chestnut syrup and add the butter. Reheat the knefla in a sauté pan. Warm the black truffle sauce. Cut the crépinettes in half vertically. Place each squab crépinette on a dinner plate. Arrange the knefla and chestnuts around the squab and spoon the black truffle sauce onto the plate. Garnish with the baby carrots.

Garnish

Steamed baby carrots, sliced on the bias

Special Equipment

Potato ricer fitted with a coarse disk

Wine Recommendation

Joseph Drouhin Echézeaux Côte de Beaune 1990 (Burgundy), or another soft, medium-bodied red Burgundy.

Coffee Barbecue Sauce

2 tablespoons vegetable oil

¼ cup coffee beans

½ medium onion, chopped

½ cup chopped garlic

¼ cup chopped fresh coriander

1 serrano chili

1 teaspoon ground cumin

1 teaspoon chili powder

1 teaspoon red pepper flakes

Zest of 1 lemon

1 cup ketchup

¼ cup red wine vinegar

¼ cup dark brown sugar

Juice of 1 lemon

Coarse salt

Black pepper, freshly ground

2 cups tomato purée

Onion-Pistachio Marmalade

2 tablespoons olive oil

1 large onion, diced

3 tablespoons sugar

3 tablespoons red wine

6 tablespoons red wine vinegar

½ teaspoon coarse salt

¼ teaspoon black pepper, freshly
   cracked

½ cup pistachios, shelled

⅓ teaspoon cayenne pepper

2 teaspoons dark molasses or honey

Corn Bread

Unsalted butter

6 tablespoons cornmeal

½ cup all-purpose flour

¼ teaspoon baking powder

¼ cup sugar

3 tablespoons unsalted butter, at room
   temperature

½ teaspoon coarse salt

1 teaspoon black pepper, freshly
   ground

1 egg

1 egg white

½ cup milk

2 tablespoons honey

Coffee-Barbecued Squab with Foie Gras Corn Bread Torte and Onion-Pistachio Marmalade

David Burke playfully reinterprets traditional American cooking in this homage to the Southern classics of barbecue, corn bread, and pickled vegetables. Squab stands in for chicken, foie gras for bacon, and onions and pistachios for cauliflower and cucumbers, resulting in an elegant and hearty dish. The diced foie gras binds and flavors the torte filling, creating a rich accompaniment to the opulent flavors on the plate.

Coffee Barbecue Sauce

In a large saucepan, heat the oil over medium heat. Add the coffee beans, onion, garlic, coriander, serrano chili, cumin, chili powder, red pepper flakes, and lemon zest and cook for 2 minutes. Add the ketchup, vinegar, brown sugar, and lemon juice, and cook, stirring occasionally, until the mixture reduces by half, 20 to 30 minutes. Season with salt and pepper and stir in the tomato purée. Cover and simmer over low heat for 2 to 3 hours, stirring occasionally. Strain and reserve.

Onion-Pistachio Marmalade

Preheat the oven to 350 degrees. In a saucepan, heat the olive oil over medium heat. Add the onion and sauté, stirring, for 2 minutes, until the onion is translucent. Reduce the heat, add the sugar, and continue cooking, stirring, until the onion is glazed and begins to brown, 8 to 10 minutes. Add the wine, vinegar, salt, and pepper, and cook until the mixture has thickened. Remove from the heat. Toast the pistachio nuts in the oven for 5 minutes in a dry pan. In a small bowl, combine the toasted pistachios, cayenne pepper, and molasses or honey until all the nuts are well coated. Spoon into a pie plate or other small, shallow baking dish, and bake 10 to 15 minutes, until the pistachio mixture is crisp and dry. Mix the pistachios into the onion mixture and keep warm.

Corn Bread

Preheat the oven to 400 degrees. Butter a standard loaf pan. In a medium bowl, combine the cornmeal, flour, and baking powder. Set aside. In another bowl, combine the sugar, butter, salt, and pepper, and cream until light and fluffy. In a third bowl, beat together the egg, egg white, and milk, and gradually add to the butter mixture. Add the dry ingredients to this batter, continuing to mix. When the ingredients are combined, stir in the honey. Spoon the corn bread mixture into the greased pan and bake for 20 to 30 minutes, until a skewer inserted in the center comes out clean. The corn bread should only be about 1½ inches high.

Barbecued Squab

Season each of the squab halves with salt and pepper, brush generously with the coffee barbecue sauce, and marinate for 30 minutes. Preheat a grill or broiler, and cook squab for 5 minutes on each side, until browned, slightly crisp, and medium rare. Set aside four squab halves. From the remaining four halves, carefully remove the breast meat from the bone, keeping it in one piece, and shred the leg meat. Set aside.

Barbecued Squab

4 squab, cleaned and split in half

Coarse salt

Black pepper, freshly ground

1 cup coffee barbecue sauce
   (from above)

Foie Gras and Corn Bread Torte

4 ounces ground chicken

1 egg

Coarse salt

Black pepper, freshly ground

½ cup cream

½ pound foie gras, diced

Meat of 4 barbecued squab legs,
   shredded (reserved from above)

1 loaf corn bread (from above)

Foie Gras and Corn Bread Torte

Preheat the oven to 350 degrees. Place the ground chicken in the bowl of a food processor fitted with a metal blade. Add the egg, salt, and pepper and purée. Continue to process and slowly add the cream. Place the chicken mixture in a bowl and add the foie gras and the shredded squab meat. Adjust the seasoning. Using a 3-inch round cutter, cut two cylinders of corn bread out of the loaf. Slice each cylinder of cornbread crosswise into four disks of equal thickness. Place four 3-inch metal rings on a greased baking sheet. Lay one disk of corn bread on the bottom of each ring. Divide the foie gras mixture equally among the four rings on top of the corn bread. Top with the remaining corn bread disks to make four sandwiches or tortes. Gently press down the top layer of corn bread with your finger tips to even out the filling. Bake the tortes for 6 to 8 minutes, until the tops begin to brown. Turn and bake another 6 to 8 minutes.

Service and Garnish

Melt the butter in a sauté pan, and sauté the corn kernels for 2 minutes. Season with salt and pepper. Remove the corn from the heat and mix in the chives. Heat the coffee barbecue sauce. Thinly slice the reserved squab breasts on the bias. Place a torte in the center of each of four dinner plates. Place a whole squab half on top of the torte and drape the slices of breast meat on top. Spoon the barbecue sauce over the squab and garnish each plate with onion-pistachio marmalade and sautéed corn.

Chef Notes

The coffee barbecue sauce recipe will make more than you need for four servings. It can be stored, covered, in the refrigerator for up to two weeks.

Garnish

2 tablespoons unsalted butter

1 cup raw corn kernels, about 1 large ear of corn

Coarse salt

Black pepper, freshly ground

2 teaspoons chopped chives

Special Equipment

Grill (optional)

3-inch round cutter

4 round metal rings, 3-inches in diameter, about 1-inch deep

Wine Recommendation

Byron Pinot Noir 1995 (Santa Barbara), or another American Pinot Noir.

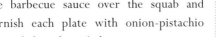

Wood Pigeon Reduction

12 wood pigeons, about 3 pounds

½ carrot, chopped

1 shallot, sliced

¼ cup white wine

1½ cups chicken stock

2 black peppercorns

1 juniper berry

Parmesan Crowns

6 ounces Parmigiano-Reggiano cheese,
    freshly grated

2 tablespoons all-purpose flour

Foie Gras "Butter"

1 tablespoon rendered foie gras fat

1 small shallot, minced

3 ounces foie gras

1 teaspoon dry white vermouth

Wood Pigeon Mousse

¼ pound boneless chicken breast

2 wood pigeons, fully boned

2 ounces foie gras

½ cup heavy cream

6 ice cubes

2 egg whites

1½ teaspoons coarse salt

½ teaspoon black pepper, freshly
    ground

Wood Pigeon

12 wood pigeon breasts
    (reserved from above)

1 teaspoon fresh sage, chopped

1 teaspoon fresh rosemary, chopped

Coarse salt

Black pepper, freshly ground

¼ cup Marsala

Wood pigeon mousse (from above)

2 tablespoons olive oil

2 cloves garlic, unpeeled

1 shallot, peeled and sliced

2 sage leaves

½ cup wood pigeon reduction (from
    above)

Foie Gras–Stuffed Wood Pigeon and Risotto Montecato in a Crispy Artichoke and Parmesan Crown

Roberto Donna is a native of Piemonte, a lush region of Italy where game is plentiful and foie gras, prevalent. Roberto uses foie gras to adorn each component of this dish. Although risotto is traditionally mounted (montecato in Italian) with butter and Parmesan cheese before being served, he uses foie gras instead in this recipe to achieve a rich, velvety texture. Foie gras is also used to bind the wood pigeon stuffing.

Wood Pigeon Reduction

Preheat the oven to 425 degrees. Remove the breasts from the wood pigeons and reserve. In a small roasting pan, place the bones and roast for about 15 minutes, until brown. Add the carrot and shallot and continue roasting for another 10 minutes. Transfer to a small saucepan and deglaze the roasting pan with the wine. Add the deglazing mixture to the saucepan with the remaining ingredients. Bring to a boil, reduce the heat, and simmer for 45 minutes. Strain into another saucepan, bring back to a boil, and reduce to ½ cup. Reserve.

Parmesan Crowns

Preheat the oven to 400 degrees. In a mixing bowl, combine the cheese and flour. On a nonstick baking pan or a silicone mat sprinkle the mixture to form 6 rectangular strips, 2 inches wide and 9 inches long. Bake until the strips turn a golden color, and remove from the oven. While warm and pliable, wrap each strip around a wine bottle to form rings. When cool and hardened, carefully remove from the bottle and reserve.

Foie Gras "Butter"

Heat a small sauté pan over medium heat. Add the foie gras fat and minced shallot, and

sauté until translucent. Let cool. Place the sautéed shallots along with the remaining ingredients in a blender and blend for 2 minutes until the mixture is smooth. Keep refrigerated.

Wood Pigeon Mousse

Place the chicken breast, boned wood pigeon meat, and foie gras in a blender and purée. Blend in the cream, ice, egg whites, salt, and pepper, and continue puréeing until smooth. Transfer this mixture to a bowl sitting over ice and mix thoroughly with a spatula to remove any air bubbles.

Wood Pigeon

Season the wood pigeon breasts with the sage, rosemary, salt, pepper, and Marsala, and let marinate for 2 hours. Place between two sheets of plastic wrap and gently pound with a rubber mallet to flatten. Using a teaspoon, place a spoonful of mousse in the center of six of the pounded breasts. Top each with another breast to make a sandwich. Secure the seams with toothpicks to make a cylinder shape. Refrigerate and reserve the remaining ingredients until service.

Artichokes

4 artichokes, with stems

2 quarts water, acidulated with the
    juice of 2 lemons

1 quart grapeseed oil

Risotto

3 tablespoons unsalted butter

½ onion, finely chopped

½ teaspoon rosemary, chopped

½ teaspoon sage, chopped

½ teaspoon thyme, chopped

1 pound Carnaroli superfino rice
    (see Chef Notes)

1 cup Prosecco or dry white wine

2 quarts chicken stock, simmering

2 ounces Parmigiano-Reggiano cheese,
    freshly grated

4 ounces foie gras "butter" (from
    above), cut into chunks

Coarse salt

Black pepper, freshly ground

Artichokes

Clean the artichokes, removing the chokes, while keeping the stems intact. Thinly slice each one lengthwise on a mandoline, placing the slices immediately into acidulated water. In a large sauté pan, heat the oil to 350 degrees. Drain the artichoke slices and dry on a paper towel. Fry in small batches until crisp, 3 to 5 minutes. Place on another towel and keep warm.

Risotto

Place the butter in a large saucepan set over medium heat. Add the onion, rosemary, sage, and thyme. When the onion is translucent, add the rice and stir for 2 minutes. Add the Prosecco and let it reduce completely. Add the simmering stock one ladleful at a time, stirring after each addition until the stock is absorbed before adding more. After 15 minutes, remove from the heat and beat in the grated cheese and foie gras butter until well blended. Adjust the seasoning with salt and pepper.

Service

Preheat the oven to 375 degrees. Heat the olive oil in a medium ovenproof sauté pan and brown the stuffed wood pigeon breast on all sides. Add the garlic, shallot, sage, and half of the wood pigeon reduction, and adjust the seasoning with salt and pepper. Place the pan in the preheated oven and roast the wood pigeon for 12 to 15 minutes, until cooked through to an interior temperature of about 135 degrees on an instant-read thermometer, and remove from the pan. Deglaze the pan with the remaining wood pigeon reduction, strain through a chinois, and reserve to sauce the dish. Let the wood pigeon rest for 5 minutes in a warm place. Remove the toothpicks. Cut each stuffed wood pigeon breast in half.

Place a Parmesan crown in the center of each of six serving plates. Fill the crown with risotto and top with the wood pigeon breast. Crown the top with artichokes and spoon the wood pigeon sauce around the dish.

Chef Notes
Carnaroli superfino rice is a long-grain, high-starch rice imported from Italy. If it is unavailable, Arborio rice can be substituted.

Special Equipment
Teflon baking pan or silicon mat
Toothpicks
Mandoline
Wine bottle (optional)

Wine Recommendation
Bruno Giacosa Arneis 1994 (Piedmont), or another full-bodied fruity Arneis from a reputable producer. Or, for a different approach, Angelo Gaja Barbaresco Costa Russi 1993 (Piedmont), or another light, fruity Barbaresco.

Kyoto Beef Rolls

¼ cup mirin

1 teaspoon salt

1 tablespoon light soy sauce

1 teaspoon ginger, minced

½ teaspoon sansho (see Chef Notes)

½ teaspoon garlic, minced

1 pound foie gras, cut into ¼-inch
cubes

¼ pound Kobe beef, thinly sliced into
24 thin pieces, 3 inches wide
(see Chef Notes)

Ponzu Sauce

½ cup dashi (see page 130)

½ cup light soy sauce

½ cup mirin

2 tablespoons sugar

1 teaspoon lemon zest, grated

½ teaspoon cornstarch

1 tablespoon fresh lemon juice

Millefeuille

Peanut oil for frying

4 ounces fresh shiitake mushrooms

12 bean curd skins or dried tofu skins,
3 by 4 inches each (see Chef Notes)

4 ounces daikon, cut into fine julienne

1 small carrot, cut into fine julienne

4 scallions, cut into fine julienne

4 shiso leaves

Sansho (optional)

Special Equipment

Grill or grill pan

Wine Recommendation

Meerlust Rubicon Stellenbosch 1986
(South Africa), or another medium-
bodied red wine that is not too fruity.

Tofu Skin Millefeuille with Foie Gras–Filled Kyoto Beef Rolls and Ponzu-Sansho Pepper Sauce

According to Toni Robertson, an appetizer must be like the opening words of a great novel—tantalizing, provocative, and alluring. This dish tantalizes with a hauntingly rich combination of Kobe beef and foie gras. Robertson balances cold and hot, soft and crisp, light and dark, all on the same plate. Her own background and expertise, her Asian roots, American upbringing, and classical training inform the East-meets-West philosophy that makes this appetizer delicious.

Kyoto Beef Rolls

In a large bowl, combine the mirin, salt, soy sauce, ginger, sansho, and garlic. Add the foie gras to the mixture, cover, and marinate overnight in the refrigerator. Divide the foie gras evenly among the 24 Kobe beef slices, and create 3-inch-long rolls. Cover with plastic wrap and refrigerate until service.

Ponzu Sauce

In a saucepan, combine the dashi, soy sauce, mirin, sugar, and lemon zest and bring to a boil. Dissolve the cornstarch into the lemon juice, and slowly add to the dashi mixture simmering until the sauce has thickened. Remove from heat and keep warm.

Millefeuille

Place an inch of peanut oil in a frying pan and heat to approximately 350 degrees. Fry the shiitake mushrooms until crisp. Drain the excess oil on paper towels and reserve. In the same pan, fry the bean curd skins one at a time, keeping them flat, until crisp. Drain the excess oil on paper towels. Reserve the remaining ingredients until service.

Service and Garnish

On a hot grill or in a grill pan, grill the beef rolls for about 4 minutes, ensuring all sides are brown and that the foie gras remains pink inside. Place a fried bean curd skin in the center of four serving plates. Place 3 beef rolls on the skin, side by side. Drizzle warm Ponzu sauce over the beef rolls, sprinkle with shiitake mushrooms, and top with the julienned vegetables. Repeat the layering process once more and finish by topping each with a crisp skin. Garnish each millefeuille with the remaining mushrooms, julienned vegetables, and a shiso leaf. Drizzle the remaining Ponzu sauce around the plate and sprinkle with more sansho pepper, if desired.

Chef Notes

Sansho is a peppery Japanese spice made from the ground pod of the prickly ash. It is used to balance the richness of fatty foods. To help slice the Kobe beef thinly, it can be chilled to just below freezing and sliced on a mandoline. Alternately, top quality, prime aged beef can be substituted for Kobe beef. Dried bean curd or tofu skins are usually sold in the size specified, or they can be cut to size before cooking.

Roasted Prime Rib, Braised Short Rib, and Poached Foie Gras in Consommé with Marrow and Roasted Garlic

In this satisfying dish, Tom Colicchio uses three distinct cooking techniques: poaching, roasting, and braising. Each technique is best suited to the cut of meat to which it is applied, and the result of serving them all together is a subtle, satisfying contrast between textures and flavors. The rich marrow and foie gras are delicately poached in order to maintain their integrity and delicateness. The tender prime rib is roasted rare to capture its true flavor. The hearty short ribs are braised slowly until they are succulent and tender. A rich consommé ties the whole dish together.

YIELD: 6 MAIN COURSE SERVINGS

Beef Stock

5 pounds beef bones

5 pounds veal bones

8 gallons water

½ cup tomato paste

1 large carrot

3 celery ribs

1 large onion

2 leeks

1 bunch fresh thyme

1 bay leaf

Roasted Garlic

12 shallots, unpeeled

12 cloves garlic, unpeeled

1 tablespoon olive oil

Coarse salt

Black pepper, freshly ground

Braised Short Ribs

2 tablespoons peanut oil

6 short ribs, bone in, about 4 ounces
   each

1 medium carrot

1 rib celery

1 medium onion

1 leek, washed, tops trimmed

1 sprig thyme

1 bay leaf

1 cup red wine

Beef stock to cover, about 2 quarts
   (from above)

Beef Stock

Roast the beef and veal bones in a 500-degree oven until brown, 1½ to 2 hours, turning frequently to avoid burning. Transfer the bones to an 8-gallon stock pot, cover with half the water, and bring to a boil. Let boil for 5 minutes, skimming the scum that rises to the top. Discard the water and return the bones to the pot. Add the remaining water and the tomato paste. Bring to a boil. Reduce to a simmer and cook about 5 hours, skimming the stock every 20 minutes. Add the carrot, celery, onion, leeks, thyme, and bay leaf and continue cooking for another hour. Strain the stock, discarding the vegetables and the bones.

Roasted Garlic

Preheat the oven to 275 degrees. Place the shallots and garlic in a roasting pan. Drizzle with olive oil. Season with salt and pepper. Roast until the shallots and garlic are soft, 45 minutes to 1 hour. Cool, peel, and reserve.

Braised Short Ribs

Preheat the oven to 275 degrees. In a heavy roasting pan, heat the peanut oil over medium heat. Add the short ribs and brown on all sides. Add the carrot, celery, onion, leek, thyme, bay leaf, and wine, and just enough stock to cover the ribs and vegetables. Cover with foil and place in the oven for 1½ hours. The meat should be well cooked and almost falling off the bone. If the meat is not tender, return the roasting pan to the oven to cook for another 15 minutes. Let the meat cool in the stock and then refrigerate. When cold, remove the meat from the stock and slice lengthwise in strips off the bone. Reserve until service. Bring the liquid and other ingredients in the pan to a boil. Strain and reserve liquid for consommé.

Poached Foie Gras

In a medium pot, bring the stock to a gentle simmer. Place the foie gras in the stock and cook for 15 minutes, or until slightly firm to

Poached Foie Gras

4 quarts beef stock (from above)

1 lobe foie gras, 12 ounces cleaned

Consommé

Braising liquid (reserved from
    beef ribs)

Poaching liquid (reserved from
    foie gras)

Beef stock (from above)

12 egg whites

1 small carrot, minced

1 small onion, minced

1 small leek, minced

1 rib celery, minced

Roasted Prime Rib

1 double-cut prime rib on the bone,
    about 1½ pounds

Coarse salt

Black pepper, freshly ground

the touch and cooked through. Remove the foie gras, being careful to keep the lobe intact, wrap well, and cool. Reserve the liquid for the consommé.

Consommé

In a large pot, combine the reserved braising liquid, poaching liquid, and all the unused beef stock. Bring to a boil and reduce by two-thirds. Cool to room temperature, transfer to a smaller pot, and skim off any fat that rises to the top. Beat together the egg whites and the minced carrot, onion, leek, and celery. Whisk this mixture into the cooled stock. Place the pot over medium heat. Stir occasionally to keep the whites

from sticking to the bottom. When a "raft" starts to form on top of the stock, reduce the heat to barely a simmer and cook for 20 minutes. When finished, push back the raft and carefully ladle the consommé through a china cap lined with several layers of cheesecloth into another pot. Discard the raft.

Roasted Prime Rib

Preheat the oven to 400 degrees. Season the prime rib with salt and pepper. In a large pan, sear the rib on both sides. Finish by roasting in the oven for 10 to 15 minutes for medium rare, or until desired doneness. Let rest for 10 minutes at room temperature before slicing into ¼-inch slices.

Marrow

Remove the marrow bones from the soaking water and cover with kosher salt. Let stand for 1 hour. Push the salted marrow out through the bones with a small spoon or a blunt knife. Place the milk in a small saucepan and bring to a gentle simmer. Poach the marrow in the milk until soft, about 5 minutes. Reserve the marrow and the bones.

Service and Garnish

Reheat the shallots and garlic in a 350-degree oven until warmed, about 10 minutes. In a saucepan, gently reheat the foie gras in a small amount of the consommé. In another saucepan, heat the braised beef in a small amount of the consommé. Heat the remaining consommé. When reheated, slice the foie gras into six 2-ounce slices. Place a slice of foie gras, a slice of roasted prime rib, a braised short rib, and a marrow bone in each of six bowls. Fill the marrow bones evenly with the poached marrow. Divide the shallots and garlic among the bowls. Pour hot consommé over and garnish with baby mustard greens, coarse salt, cracked black pepper, and blanched flowering chives.

Chef Notes

The marrow bones must be soaked in ice water for three days, refrigerated, in advance of serving. Be sure to change the water daily. The stock and roasted garlic can be made several days in advance and reserved.

Marrow

6 marrow bones, soaked
   (see Chef Notes)
Kosher salt
2 cups milk

Garnish

Baby mustard greens
Coarse salt
Black pepper, freshly cracked
Flowering chives, blanched

Wine Recommendation

Argyle Pinot Noir Reserve 1995 (Willamette Valley), or another rich, spicy Pinot Noir from California, Oregon, or Burgundy. Alternatively, Château des Jacques Moulin-à-Vent 1994 (Beaujolais), or another medium-bodied red wine.

Seared Venison with Sautéed Foie Gras, Pickled Fennel Relish, and Herbed Potato Chips

The juxtaposition of classic ingredients and innovative combinations, not to mention daring presentations, sets Charlie Palmer's creative American cooking apart. In this dish he makes a natural pairing of game and seared foie gras, but contrasts it with a bracing fennel relish. By using the rendered foie gras fat to season the potato side dish, he brings all of the flavors together. The translucent herbed potato chip has become one of Charlie's signature garnishes.

Herbed Potato Chips

¼ cup clarified butter
1 large Idaho potato
10 chive points, each 2 inches long
10 tarragon leaves
10 chervil sprigs
Coarse salt

Pickled Fennel Relish

4 strips lemon zest
1½ cups water
¾ cup white wine
¾ cup white wine vinegar
6 tablespoons honey
6 black peppercorns
4 whole cloves
3 star anise
2 tablespoons coarse salt
3 fresh fennel bulbs

Crisp Potatoes

4 large Idaho potatoes
2 tablespoons olive oil

Herbed Potato Chips

Preheat the oven to 275 degrees. Brush a heavy, nonstick sheet pan with half the clarified butter. Make sure the sheet pan is perfectly flat, otherwise the potato chips will pull apart while baking. Peel the potato, rinse under cold running water, and pat dry. Using a mandoline, thinly slice half of the potato lengthwise, discarding the curved ends. You should have nine to ten slices of even size. Place each slice on the baking sheet, making sure they are not touching. Arrange a piece of each herb on each potato slice, making sure to leave a border of potato around the circumference of the slice. Quickly slice the remaining potato half, keeping the curved ends. Dry the slices slightly, and place them evenly over the herb-topped slices. Press each potato "sandwich" together to seal the edges, brush with the remaining clarified butter, and season to taste with the salt. Bake for 30 to 35 minutes, until golden brown, turning the sheet pan once or twice to ensure even baking.

Pickled Fennel Relish

In a medium nonreactive saucepan, combine the lemon zest, water, wine, vinegar, honey, peppercorns, cloves, star anise, and 2 tablespoons coarse salt to make the pickling mixture. Set over high heat and bring to a boil. Boil for 3 minutes, stirring occasionally. Remove from the heat. Strain into a clean, nonreactive saucepan, discarding the solids.

Wash the fennel bulbs and trim off the tops. Using a mandoline, slice the whole fennel lengthwise very thinly. Set the pickling mixture over medium-high heat and bring to a boil. Add the thinly sliced fennel and remove the mixture from the flame. Allow the fennel to macerate for 45 minutes. Drain and set the fennel aside.

Crisp Potatoes

Preheat the oven to 325 degrees. Wash and dry the potatoes. Pierce each potato with a fork and generously brush the skins with the olive oil. Place the potatoes in the preheated oven and bake for 35 minutes or until just

Balsamic Glaze

4 cups veal stock

1¼ cups balsamic vinegar

Foie Gras and Venison

12 ounces foie gras, cut into 6 slices,
each about 2 ounces and ¾-inch
thick

Coarse salt

Black pepper, freshly ground

12 venison medallions, 3 ounces each

2 tablespoons vegetable oil

Garnish

Fresh chervil

¼ cup fennel seed, toasted

Special Equipment

Nonstick sheet pan

Mandoline

Wine Recommendation

Iron Horse Cabernet Sauvignon
Alexander Valley Cuvée Joy 1994
(Napa), or another California Cabernet
Sauvignon.

tender when pierced with the tip of a sharp knife. Remove from the oven and allow to cool. Trim off and discard the ends. Cut the potatoes crosswise into 3 equal pieces. Set aside.

Balsamic Glaze

In a medium nonreactive saucepan, combine the stock and balsamic vinegar. Set over medium-high heat and bring to a boil. Lower the heat and simmer for about 1 hour, until the mixture has reduced to 1½ cups. Set aside.

Foie Gras

Lay the foie gras slices flat and, with the tip of a knife, cut a crosshatch design, ⅛-inch deep, across the top of each piece. Season with salt and pepper. Cover and refrigerate until ready to cook. Reserve the venison and vegetable oil until service.

Service and Garnish

Heat two large sauté pans over medium-high heat. Season the venison with salt and pepper. Place the vegetable oil in one pan and add the venison. Sear the venison for 45 seconds. Turn and reduce the heat to medium. Sear for an additional 3 minutes. Remove from the heat, but leave in the pan. At the same time, place the foie gras, scored-side down, into the other pan and immediately lower the heat to medium. Using your fingertips, gently push the foie gras into the pan so that it immediately begins to render its fat. Sear the foie gras for 30 seconds or until it begins to caramelize. Turn and brown the other side for 30 seconds or until crisped. Remove the foie gras from the pan and keep warm, reserving the rendered fat in the pan.

Return the sauté pan with the rendered fat to medium heat. Add the potato pieces and fry for 1½ minutes per side, until golden and crisp. Season with salt and pepper. Remove from the pan and drain on a paper towel.

Return the balsamic glaze to low heat. Place two crisp potato pieces in the center of each of six warm serving plates. Set a foie gras medallion on top of the potatoes and two slices of venison next to the potatoes. Arrange the pickled fennel around the edge of the plate. Garnish with the herbed potato chip and fresh chervil. Sprinkle the fennel seeds over the plate and drizzle the balsamic glaze around the plate.

Chef Notes

Everything up to the cooking of the foie gras and venison can be prepared up to 1 day in advance.

Chef Biographies

Israel Aharoni
Owner of the Golden Apple Restaurant in Tel Aviv—named the best restaurant in Israel in 1998 by GaultMillau—and Ying Yang, a popular Chinese restaurant also in Tel Aviv, Israel Aharoni is the foremost food authority in Israel, and is one of few Israeli chefs to achieve international acclaim. He has written 11 cookbooks and pens a cooking column for a national newspaper. Aharoni studied in Holland and Taipei, and continually travels worldwide in pursuit of culinary inspiration.

Martin Berasategui
Martin Berasategui's eponymous restaurant in Lasarte-Oris is the proud holder of two Michelin stars, and the chef has been honored as the best in the country. After beginning his career at his mother's restaurant, Bodegón Alejandro in San Sebastián, Berasategui spent many years honing his culinary skills throughout France and Spain. He worked in the kitchens of renowned French chefs Didier Oudiil and Alain Ducasse prior to opening Martin Berasategui in 1993. He also oversees the restaurant in the Guggenheim Museum in Bilbao.

Raymond Blanc
Located in England's bucolic Oxford countryside, Le Manoir aux Quat' Saisons debuted in 1984, and has since become one of the premier country-house hotels and restaurants in the world. Raymond Blanc's cuisine focuses on seasonal produce—the property boasts a prolific garden with over 90 varieties of herbs and vegetables. In 1991 Raymond Blanc established Le Manoir Ecole de Cuisine, a cooking school that operates out of the restaurant's kitchen, the only one of its kind. Blanc opened a more casual restaurant, Le Petit Blanc, in 1996. He has written several cookbooks based on his culinary philosophy of freshness and strong flavors. The restaurant has garnered two stars from the esteemed Michelin Guide.

Paul Bocuse
Considered the ambassador of French cuisine, Paul Bocuse is the descendent of a long line of chefs. Bocuse worked throughout France before fulfilling his dream to purchase the restaurant once owned by his grandfather in his native Collognes. In 1965, the restaurant Paul Bocuse earned three Michelin stars for the chef's innovative *Nouvelle Cuisine*. Bocuse also presides over a prestigious international cooking competition, Le Bocuse d'Or, held annually in Lyons. In 1982 he opened Le Pavillon de France, with Roger Vergé and Gaston Lenôtre, at Walt Disney World's Epcot Center, where he continues his mission to promote French cuisine worldwide.

Daniel Boulud
Daniel Boulud developed his *cuisine du marché* cooking style while training with Roger Vergé and Michel Guérard in his native France. In 1982 Boulud came to New York to assume the position of executive chef of Le Régence at the Plaza Athénée, and in 1986 he was named the executive chef of Le Cirque. During his tenure, the food at Le Cirque was lauded as among the best in the country. Boulud's solo venture, Daniel, opened in 1993, and quickly received four stars from *The New York Times.* In 1997 he and his pastry chef, François Payard, opened a pastry shop and bistro named Payard. In 1998 Chef Boulud converted the original Daniel to Café Boulud (named for his grandfather's restaurant) and relocated Daniel to a grand new home in the site of the former Le Cirque.

Frank Brigtsen
A native of New Orleans, Frank Brigtsen began his culinary career as an apprentice to superstar Cajun chef Paul Prudhomme at the legendary Commander's Palace. When Prudhomme opened K-Paul's Louisiana Kitchen, Brigtsen worked his way through the ranks, eventually becoming executive chef. Brigtsen's opened in 1986, and in 1994 Brigtsen was named Chef of the Year by *New Orleans* magazine. In 1997 Chef Brigsten received the title of Best Chef: Southeast by the James Beard Foundation.

David Burke
Trained at The Culinary Institute of America, David Burke cooked his way through France before returning to the United States to become executive chef of the celebrated River Cafe in Brooklyn. At Park Avenue Cafe, opened in Manhattan in 1991, Burke's menu caused a sensation with its whimsical creativity and artful presentation. His success stretched to Chicago with the opening of a second Park Avenue Cafe and Mrs. Park's Tavern in 1995. Chef Burke is often thought of as the quintessential American chef.

Tom Colicchio
Raised in New Jersey, Tom Colicchio began cooking at the age of 17. His impressive resume includes stints at renowned New York City restaurants including the Quilted Giraffe, Gotham Bar & Grill, Rakel, and Mondrian, where Colicchio was named one of *Food & Wine* magazine's Best New Chefs in America. In 1994 Colicchio opened Gramercy Tavern with award-winning restaurateur Danny Meyer.

André Daguin
An eleventh-generation chef, André Daguin has spent his career exploring the limits of his native Gascon cuisine. While chef and owner of the Michelin two-star Hôtel de France in Auch, Daguin was responsible for

revitalizing the duck industry in his region by creating a cuisine utilizing *magret de canard*. Daguin has been influential in imploring scientists to explore the effect of foie gras on health, noting that the Gascons tend to live long, healthy lives despite their high-fat diet. He currently serves as the president of France's society of hoteliers and restaurateurs.

Ariane Daguin

An internationally celebrated restaurant, the Michelin two-star Hôtel de France, was the culinary training ground for Ariane Daguin. There, her father, André Daguin (see above) had her deboning ducks before the age of ten. Describing herself as a "foie-gras missionary," in 1984 Daguin opened the New Jersey–based D'Artagnan, a game and foie gras supplier. Today she supplies foie gras and other luxury products to fine chefs across the country.

Christian Delouvrier

Born in Bologne-Sur-Gess in Gascony and trained at the École Hotelière in Toulouse, Christian Delouvrier has worked at L'Archestrate in Paris, Saint Amable in Montréal, King's Inn Hotel in the Bahamas, and the highly regarded Maurice in New York City. In 1991 Delouvrier opened Les Célébrités and Café Botanica at the Essex House/Hotel Nikko, where he developed his signature cooking style that he calls *cuisine de terroir*. In 1998 Delouvrier was tapped to take over the kitchen of Lespinasse, where after just three months, he received a glowing four-star review from *The New York Times.*

Traci Des Jardins

Early in life, Traci Des Jardins knew she was destined for a career in the kitchen. After working with Joachim Splichal in Los Angeles, she apprenticed with the legendary Troigros family in France. Des Jardins worked at Montrachet in New York and then journeyed to France for stints at Lucas Carton, Arpège, and Louis XV. Returning to California, Des Jardins became chef de cuisine at Patina in Los Angeles and later helped open Elka in San Francisco. In 1994 Des Jardins was named executive chef at Rubicon in San Francisco. In 1997 she left to open her own restaurant, Jardinière, garnering critical acclaim.

Rocco DiSpirito

After graduating from The Culinary Institute of America, Rocco DiSpirito continued his training at the Hôtel Prince de Galles in Paris. DiSpirito returned to work at the Peninsula Hotel in New York City and later, Aujourd'Hui in Boston. After *stages* with various top New York chefs, DiSpirito was hired at the four-star Lespinasse, where he became sous chef to Gray Kunz. DiSpirito opened Union Pacific in New York in 1997 to a shower of praise.

Roberto Donna

As a child in Torino, Roberto Donna was fascinated by the chefs at the local restaurants. By the time he was in his late teens, he was head chef at Scudodi Savoia, one of Torino's finest restaurants. Donna arrived in Washington, D.C. in 1980 where he worked at Romeo and Juliet before opening his first restaurant, Galileo, in 1984. Donna is influential in promoting authentic Italian food and wine and was given the Insegna del Ristorante Italian, which designates Galileo as one of the 20 best Italian restaurants in the world. Donna's D.C. culinary empire includes 11 restaurants and an Italian bakery. In 1996 Chef Donna was named Best Chef: Mid Atlantic by the James Beard Foundation.

Alain Ducasse

A reverence for ingredients guides Alain Ducasse, who grew up on a foie gras farm in southwest France. Ducasse worked with Michel Guérard, Gaston Lenôtre, Roger Vergé, and Alain Chapel, whom he credits as his most influential mentor. In 1979 Ducasse became the chef at the Hôtel Juana in Juan-les-Pins. In 1987 he was named executive chef of Louis XV in Monte Carlo, where he became the youngest chef ever to receive three stars from Michelin. In 1996 he took over Joël Robuchon's acclaimed restaurant in Paris, transforming it to Restaurant Alain Ducasse. Chef Ducasse is one of only two chefs in history to possess a total of six Michelin stars.

Todd English

After graduating from The Culinary Institute of America, Todd English worked at various restaurants in the United States before deciding to explore the cuisine of northern Italy. It was there that he found his culinary niche. Settling in Boston, English opened the Mediterranean-accented Olives in 1989, which was named Best New Restaurant by *Boston Magazine*. His second restaurant, Figs, opened in 1992. English has since opened outposts in Charleston, Massachusetts; Las Vegas, Nevada; Westport, Connecticut; and Israel. He is the recipient of two James Beard Foundation Awards and is the author of two cookbooks.

Bobby Flay

Prompted by his first employer, Joe Allen, native New Yorker Bobby Flay attended The French Culinary Institute. Flay trained with Jonathan Waxman and moved on to become the chef at Miracle Grill, where he developed his flair for creative, flavorful Southwestern cuisine. Flay opened the critically acclaimed Mesa Grill, a southwestern-style restaurant, in 1991 and Bolo, with a Spanish-influenced menu, in 1994. Flay was the recipient of the 1993 James Beard Foundation Rising Star Chef Award.

Susanna Foo
Raised in Taiwan, Susanna Foo came to the United States with a B.A. in history to earn an M.A. in Library Science. Her plans changed in 1979 when she and her husband were asked to run Hu-nan, a restaurant owned by the Foo family. Foo took charge of the kitchen. Encouraged by the favorable response to her cooking, Foo attended The Culinary Institute of America. In 1987 she opened Susanna Foo Chinese Cuisine in Philadelphia. Since then, Foo has received the Award of Excellence from Les Dames d'Escoffier and a James Beard Foundation Award.

Pierre Gagnaire
Often described as a cerebral chef, Pierre Gagnaire offers diners at his eponymous Paris restaurant a veritable lesson in food composition. Gagnaire's success began while he was a *stagiare* with Jean Vignard in Lyons, where he was voted the top apprentice in the Rhône region. After stints at Maxim's and Lucas Carton, Gagnaire took over his family's restaurant, earning his first Michelin star. In 1990, he opened his first solo venture in Saint-Etienne, where he garnered three Michelin stars. In 1996 he relocated Gagnaire to Paris, where he has reestablished his three-star rating.

Laurent Gras
A recent addition to the culinary landscape in the New World, Laurent Gras cooked at some of the most renowned restaurants in France before taking over the kitchen of Peacock Alley in New York's Waldorf-Astoria hotel. Gras's career began at the Hotel Juana under the tutelage of Alain Ducasse, who became his mentor. After stints at Restaurant Guy Savoy, Lucas Carton, and Restaurant Maison Blanche, Gras returned to Ducasse's kitchen as chef de cuisine of the venerable Louis XV. At Peacock Alley, Gras has received raves for masterfully simple preparations.

Christopher Gross
When Christopher Gross took a cooking job at the age of 14 in Phoenix, he never thought it would lead to a career. But Gross's interest in food led him to Paris, where he worked at Chez Albert. He continued his training at L'Orangerie and the Century Plaza Hotel in Los Angeles. Returning to Phoenix, Gross opened Le Relais, where he was named one of America's Best New Chefs by *Food & Wine* magazine. Gross opened Christopher's and Christopher's Bistro in 1990. In 1998, he moved across the street to open Christopher's Fermier, a popular brasserie.

Vincent Guérithault
Vincent Guérithault began his culinary career as an apprentice at the Michelin three-star L'Oustau de Baumanière in the south of France. In Paris he worked at Maxim's and the legendary catering shop Fauchon. Guérithault found his home in Phoenix as chef of Oaxaca, where he began an innovative combination of French techniques with Southwestern ingredients. In 1986 he opened Vincent Guérithault on Camelback, where he was the first chef ever to receive a Citation of Excellence from the International Food and Wine Society. He received a James Beard Foundation Award in 1993.

Marc Haeberlin
When Marc Haeberlin took over for his father, Paul, and assumed the helm of the kitchen at the venerable restaurant Auberge de l'Ill, situated on a riverbank in the tiny Alsatian village of Ilhaeusern, he was faced with the challenge of maintaining the restaurant's three-star Michelin rating. Haeberlin's contemporary culinary spirit adds a spin to classic dishes, while his flawless renditions of regional favorites continue to garner raves.

Daňo Hutnik
Born in the Ukraine, Daňo Hutnik was a ballet dancer in Vienna for fifteen years before pursuing a culinary career. After studying in Paris and at the California Culinary Academy, Hutnik went on to work in varied establishments including the San Ysidro Ranch in Santa Barbara, and SeaGrill in Manhattan's Rockefeller Center. Hutnik and his wife, artist Karen Gilman, settled in Ithaca, New York, to open Daňo on Cayuga in 1990, acclaimed as a haven of fine food in upstate New York.

Jean Joho
After cooking in Germany, Switzerland, Italy, and France, Jean Joho worked at the Michelin three-star Auberge de l'Ill with Paul Haeberlin in his native Alsace. Joho came to Chicago to direct the reopening of Maxim's de Paris. After the closing of Maxim's, Joho was asked by the Lettuce Entertain You group to open Everest in 1987, which the *Chicago Tribune* gave a four-star rating. In 1995 Joho opened his second restaurant, Brasserie Jo, which won a James Beard Foundation Award for best new restaurant in 1996.

Hubert Keller
After graduating from the École Hotelière in Strasbourg, Hubert Keller trained with

culinary giants Paul Bocuse, Gaston Lenôtre, and Roger Vergé. Keller maintained his tie to Vergé, heading his kitchens at La Cuisine du Soleil in San Paolo, Brazil, and Sutter 200 in San Francisco. In 1986 Keller became co-owner of Fleur de Lys in San Francisco, where he receives raves for his Mediterranean-accented French cuisine. In 1997 he received a James Beard Foundation Award.

Thomas Keller
Considered a "modern classicist" for his understated cuisine, Thomas Keller began his cooking career in a restaurant managed by his mother. He worked at La Reserve and restaurant Raphael in New York City before traveling to France to apprentice at Taillevent, Guy Savoy, and Pré Catalan. In 1990 he was named executive chef of Checkers Hotel in Los Angeles. Keller opened the French Laundry in Yountville, California, in 1994. In 1997 he received the James Beard Foundation's Outstanding Chef Award.

Matthew Kenney
While growing up on the coast of Maine, Matthew Kenney developed a love of fresh, seasonal food. In New York, Kenney worked with David Ruggerio at La Caravelle while attending The French Culinary Institute. Kenney began to make a name for himself as the chef of Banana Cafe. In 1993 he opened Matthew's, where his elegant Morrocan-inspired cuisine earned him the distinction of being named one of the Best New Chefs of 1994 by *Food & Wine* magazine.

Sottha Khunn
Cambodian-born Sottha Khunn trained with French masters Alain Senderens and Pierre and Jean Troisgros before he was lured to the United States to become

Daniel Boulud's sous chef at Le Régence. In 1986 Khunn joined Boulud at Le Cirque as his sous chef. Le Cirque 2000 opened in 1997 with Khunn at the helm as executive chef. Under his direction the restaurant received four stars from *The New York Times.*

Gray Kunz
Classically trained in Switzerland, Gray Kunz worked with Frédy Girardet at his legendary restaurant in Crissier near Lausanne before becoming executive chef at the Hong Kong Regent's famed restaurant, Plume. Kunz became a master at blending the flavors of the Far East with French cuisine. Kunz opened Lespinasse in New York's St. Regis Hotel in 1991, where he received a four-star rating from *The New York Times.* Kunz was honored Best Chef: New York by the James Beard Foundation in 1995. In 1998 Kunz left Lespinasse to complete a book project and pursue the opening of his own restaurant.

Emeril Lagasse
Emeril Lagasse worked in various fine restaurants in New York, Boston, and Philadelphia before taking the position as executive chef at the legendary Commander's Palace in New Orleans. In 1990 Lagasse left to open his own restaurant, Emeril's, which was named Restaurant of the Year by *Esquire* magazine in 1991. He opened NOLA in 1994, his Las Vegas venture, Emeril's New Orleans Fish House, in 1996, and an Emeril's in Orlando in 1999. Today Lagasse's popular TV shows, *Essence of Emeril* and *Emeril Live,* have made him one of the most popular food personalities in the country.

Susur Lee
Hong Kong–born Susur Lee received his classical training as an apprentice at Hong

Kong's renowned Peninsula Hotel. Combining his native knowledge of Asian ingredients and techniques with European sensibility allowed Lee to develop his own unique cognitive style of cooking. After moving to Toronto, Lee worked at the Westbury Hotel, Le Trou, and Peter Pan before opening Lotus, a small French-Asian restaurant, named the best restaurant in Canada by GaultMillau. In 1998 Lee moved to Singapore to consult for the Tung Lok Group, which operates House of Mao and Club Chinoise. In 1999 *Food & Wine* magazine listed Lee as one of the chefs to watch in the new millenium.

Grant MacPherson
Grant MacPherson began his career as a culinary apprentice at the Niagara Rainbow Center and continued to perfect his skills throughout Canada. MacPherson ventured to far-off corners of the world—Sydney, Kuala Lumpur, and the Big Island of Hawaii—where he assisted with the opening of world-class hotels for the Ritz-Carlton and the Regent hotel companies. MacPherson recently left his post as executive chef of Raffles Hotel in Singapore to become executive chef of the lavish Bellagio Hotel in Las Vegas.

Waldy Malouf
A graduate of The Culinary Institute of America, Waldy Malouf has worked in many of New York's top kitchens, including the Four Seasons, La Côte Basque, the St. Regis Hotel, and La Cremaillère in Banksville, New York. As executive chef of the Hudson River Club in Manhattan, Malouf developed his signature style, which focuses on the richness and bounty of New York's Hudson River Valley. In 1996 Malouf became the executive chef and director of the Rainbow Room, the quintessential New York restaurant atop

Rockefeller Center. His latest venture, Beacon, opened in New York in 1999.

Laurent Manrique

The inspiration for Laurent Manrique's cooking is the cuisine from the Gascon region of France, where he was born. Manrique worked in many top French kitchens, including Relais de l'Armagnac, Restaurant Le Toit de Passey, and the Michelin three-star restaurant Taillevent. Manrique traveled to New York to become chef de cuisine at Peacock Alley in the Waldorf-Astoria Hotel in 1992. In 1997 Manrique opened Gertrude's in New York City. In 1999 Manrique relocated to San Francisco where he assumed the position of executive chef of the Campton Place Hotel.

Nicole Manrique

As president of "The Happy Gastronomes of Gascony," Nicole Manrique is a true connoisseur of the cuisine of foie gras country, the southwestern region of France. Manrique lives on a working farm in Roques and is a professor at the College Samatan. Her son, Laurent Manrique (see above), credits her with being his most important culinary influence.

Nobu Matsuhisa

Born and raised in Tokyo, Nobu Matsuhisa received rigorous training as a sushi chef before he realized his dream of traversing the globe. His travels led him to Peru and Alaska, where he opened sushi bars. Challenged by unfamiliar regional ingredients, Matsuhisa developed his innovative, interpretive Japanese style of cooking. He opened Matsuhisa in Los Angeles in 1987 to instant critical acclaim, followed by Nobu in New York in 1994, Nobu in London in 1997, and Matsuhisa in Aspen in 1997. In 1998 he opened a restaurant in his native Japan, with additional openings slated for 1999.

Marc Meneau

Raised in Saint-Père-sous-Vézelay, Marc Meneau has developed a personal cuisine redolent of the *terroir* of the rich Burgundy region that is home to his restaurant L'Espérance. Among his mentors, he counts the celebrated chef of Maxim's, Alex Humbert. His overriding culinary philosophy, "freshness doesn't have a price," inspires his cooking and informs his role as one of France's most celebrated chefs. Meneau received his first star from the Michelin inspectors in 1972. After moving his restaurant to a renovated mill in his home town in 1975, he received a second star. His third star was awarded in 1983, the same year he was cited as France's Chef of the Year.

Michael Mina

While still attending high school, Michael Mina worked full time at a French restaurant in his home town of Ellensberg, Washington. After graduating from The Culinary Institute of America, Mina trained with George Morrone at the Hotel Bel-Air in Los Angeles and with Charles Palmer in New York. Mina was the opening chef de cuisine at Aqua in San Francisco, was promoted to executive chef in 1995, and in 1998 received four stars from the *San Francisco Chronicle*. Mina is also executive chef of Charles Nob Hill and an additional Aqua outpost in the Bellagio Hotel in Las Vegas. He also received the 1997 James Beard Foundation Rising Star Chef Award.

Rick Moonen

A fascination with the chemistry of cooking motivated Rick Moonen to attend The Culinary Institute of America. After graduation, he came to New York to work in the respected kitchens of La Côte Basque, Le Cirque, and Le Relais before taking charge as executive chef of The Water Club. In 1994 Moonen became executive chef of Oceana, where he has garnered critical acclaim for his inventive seafood preparations.

George Morrone

After apprenticing at a bakery in his native New Jersey, George Morrone attended The Culinary Institute of America. Following graduation, Morrone trained with Charles Palmer in New York and Bradley Ogden in San Francisco before becoming executive chef of the prestigious Hotel Bel-Air in Los Angeles. In 1991 Morrone opened Aqua, an exclusively seafood restaurant that earned a four-star rating. Morrone continued his relationship with Bradley Ogden by becoming the chef of Ogden's One Market in San Francisco, which opened in 1993. In 1999 Morrone became chef of Fifth Floor in San Francisco.

Eberhard Mueller

Formally trained in Germany and Switzerland, Eberhard Mueller credits his work alongside Alain Senderens as the true origin of his cooking career. In New York, Mueller worked at Windows on the World before becoming the executive chef of Le Bernardin, where his innovative seafood preparations earned him four stars from *The New York Times*. In 1995 he became executive chef of New York's famed French restaurant, Lutèce.

Wayne Nish

Trained as an architect, Wayne Nish did not succumb to his desire to cook until he was in his thirties. After studying at the New York Restaurant School, Nish apprenticed at the Quilted Giraffe in New York, where he was able to explore his creative style. In

1988 Nish became executive chef of La Colombe d'Or. In 1990 he and Joseph Scalice opened March, which received four stars from *Forbes* magazine.

Patrick O'Connell

While studying theater at Catholic University, Patrick O'Connell supported himself by working as a cook and a waiter. A year of travel in Europe convinced him to abandon the life of the stage for a culinary career. He began by establishing a catering business in Washington, Virginia. His success encouraged him to open the Inn at Little Washington in 1978, hailed by many critics as the best country inn in America. O'Connell has received numerous awards, including several from the James Beard Foundation.

Bradley Ogden

An honors graduate from The Culinary Institute of America, Bradley Ogden was named chef of the American Restaurant in Kansas City in 1979. In 1983 Ogden earned a reputation for innovative American cuisine at the Campton Place Hotel in San Francisco. In 1989 Ogden opened the Lark Creek Inn in Larkspur, California, and in 1993 he opened One Market in San Francisco. He has received numerous honors including the James Beard Foundation Best Chef: California award.

Jean-Louis Palladin

Raised in Gascony, Jean-Louis Palladin was exposed at an early age to the fundamentals of classical cooking. He worked at the famed Hôtel de Paris and the Plaza Athénée before returning to his home town to open La Table des Cordeliers, where he became the youngest chef ever to receive two Michelin stars. Palladin came to Washington, D.C., to open Jean-Louis at the

Watergate in 1979, for many years considered one of the finest restaurants in the country. He received the James Beard Foundation Outstanding Chef Award in 1993, and opened Napa, in Las Vegas, in 1996. In 1999 he opened a second restaurant, Palladin, in New York City.

Charles Palmer

After graduating from The Culinary Institute of America, Charles Palmer trained with Jean-Jacques Rachou at La Côte Basque in New York. He left to run the kitchen of the Waccabuc Country Club in Westchester, New York, and was later hired as executive chef of the River Cafe in Brooklyn. Palmer's New York restaurant empire began with the opening of Aureole in 1988. His other restaurants include Alva, the Lenox Room, and Astra. In 1999 he opened a second Aureole outpost in Las Vegas. He is also part owner of Egg Farm Dairy in Peekskill, New York, and he oversees an organic food cooperative in Amagansett, New York. Chef Palmer is the recipient of the 1998 James Beard Foundation Award for Best Chef: New York.

Roland Passot

After his apprenticeship to Pierre Orsi in Lyons, Roland Passot was invited to work in the kitchen of Jean Banchet at Le Français in Wheeling, Illinois. Passot went on to become executive chef of Le Castel in San Francisco and to open the French Room at the Adolphus Hotel in Dallas. Passot returned to San Francisco in 1988 to open his own restaurant, La Folie, where his California-accented French cuisine continues to win raves.

Jacques Pépin

A culinary legend, Jacques Pépin began his cooking career in France at his parents'

restaurant, Le Pelican. After training at the Grand Hôtel de L'Europe, Maurice, and the Plaza Athénée, Pépin worked as a private chef for three French heads of state. In New York, he worked at the historic Pavillon, was director of research and development for Howard Johnson's, and developed the concept for La Potagerie. Author of numerous cookbooks and host of many TV shows, Pépin now also serves as dean of special programs at New York's French Culinary Institute. He has been honored as a recipient of the James Beard Foundation Lifetime Achievement Award.

Don Pintabona

With a voracious appetite for sampling new cuisines, Don Pintabona took an extensive tasting tour of Europe after graduating from The Culinary Institute of America. He worked for Michelin three-star chef Georges Blanc in Vonnas, France, and as sous chef at Gentille Alouette in Osaka, Japan. In New York, Pintabona worked for Charles Palmer and Daniel Boulud before being approached by restaurateur Drew Nieporent and actor Robert De Niro to open Tribeca Grill in 1990.

Alfred Portale

Since 1984, Alfred Portale has been impressing diners with his visually stunning and flavorful food at New York's quintessential contemporary restaurant, Gotham Bar and Grill. After attending The Culinary Institute of America, graduating first in his class, he completed *stages* in renowned kitchens, such as that of three-star Michelin chef Michel Guérard at Eugénie-Les-Bains. Portale's former profession as a jeweler adds to his precise, architectural sense of food presentation. Gotham Bar and Grill has received four three-star reviews from *The New York Times*. Portale has authored a cookbook and been named Best Chef: New York by the James Beard Foundation.

Stephan Pyles

A fifth-generation Texan, Stephan Pyles began cooking at his parents' truck-stop café. A trip to France after his college graduation cemented his interest in food. Pyles opened Routh Street Café in 1983, where he created a "new Texas hill country cuisine" that incorporates varied flavors, from barbecue to Cajun to Mexican. He has been named Best Chef: Southwest by the James Beard Foundation, has authored several cookbooks, and hosts a PBS television series on Texas hill country cooking. After closing Routh Street Café, Pyles opened Star Canyon in 1994 and Aquanox in 1998.

Patricia Quintana

The first lady of Mexican cuisine, Patricia Quintana travels worldwide to promote the food of her native land, and is considered one of the foremost experts on Mexican cooking. Her culinary career began over 25 years ago when she traveled to France and Switzerland to study under French masters Paul Bocuse, Gaston Lenôtre, Alain Chapel, and the Troigros brothers. Quintana later established a cooking school in Mexico City, which inspired her to learn more about the exciting regional cuisines of Mexico. Since then Quintana has written nine books on the subject, and is published extensively in the United States and Mexico.

Thierry Rautureau

The son of farmers from the Muscadet region of France, Thierry Rautureau began cooking with the seasonal ingredients that surrounded him. He apprenticed to a local chef at the age of 14 and continued to work in classical French kitchens for six years before heading to the United States. Drawn to the lifestyle of the Pacific Northwest, Rautureau bought Seattle's Rover's in 1987, where he has been lauded as the best chef of the Pacific Northwest by *Pacific Northwest* magazine. In 1998 Rautureau received the James Beard Foundation Award for Best Chef: Northwest.

Michel Richard

After working at Gaston Lenôtre's world-renowned pastry shops, Michel Richard opened his own pastry shop in the La Fonda Hotel in Santa Fe, and later in Los Angeles. Richard opened Citrus restaurant in 1987, which was named best restaurant in America by *Travelers* magazine and for which he received the James Beard Foundation award for Best Chef: California. His success as the originator of "California Bistro" cuisine spread across the country with Bistro Bar in Los Angeles, Bistro M in San Francisco, and Citronelle restaurants in both Washington, D.C. and Santa Barbara. Today Richard is concentrating his efforts on the Washington, D.C. Citronelle.

Eric Ripert

Eric Ripert's deep appreciation for food began with his childhood in Andorra. After his apprenticeship at the historic La Tour d'Argent in Paris, Ripert went on to work for Joël Robuchon. Lured to the United States to be sous chef for Jean-Louis Palladin in Washington, D.C., he later relocated to New York to become the chef de cuisine at Le Bernardin. In 1994 Ripert was named executive chef of Le Bernardin, which was awarded four stars by *The New York Times* in 1995 and was picked the best restaurant in America by *GQ* magazine. In 1998 Ripert was named Best Chef: New York by the James Beard Foundation.

Toni Robertson

Preparing traditional dishes in her native Burma was Toni Robertson's first exposure to the kitchen. Robertson began to work in grand hotels around the globe, such as The Ritz-Carlton Chicago, the Four Seasons Beverly Hills, and the Grand Wailea in Maui. As executive chef of the Palace Hotel in Sun City, South Africa, Robertson turned the hotel into the culinary capital of the region. After a return to Asia, to the Pan Pacific Hotel in Singapore as Asia's first female executive chef, her culinary globe-trotting brought her back to the United States as executive chef of the acclaimed Sonoma Mission Inn.

Tim Rodgers

As a certified Culinary Hospitality Educator and a team leader for curriculum and instruction at The Culinary Institute of America, Tim Rodgers is influential in shaping the direction of culinary education in the United States. Rodgers had a successful career in top kitchens before becoming an instructor at his alma mater. He has appeared in the public television series *Cooking Secrets of the CIA* and has won gold and silver medals at the New York Food Show and the Salon of Culinary Arts.

Douglas Rodriguez

A graduate of Johnson and Wales University, Douglas Rodriguez is credited with elevating Latin food to new gastronomic heights. He created a sensation at Yuca in Miami, where he developed a unique cooking style that reflected his Cuban roots. In 1994 he opened Patria in New York City, where he impressed diners with his Nuevo Latino cuisine. Rodriguez won the James Beard

Foundation's Rising Star Chef Award in 1996 and has authored two cookbooks. He is now the Chef of Unico in New York City.

Alain Rondelli

While pursuing a degree in engineering, Alain Rondelli took a job at La Manoir in Paris, where he realized his true vocation. Rondelli worked at the Michelin three-star L'Espérance with Marc Meneau and went on to become the chef at Mas de Chastelas in St. Tropez. In 1990 Rondelli came to the United States to become executive chef of the venerable San Francisco restaurant Ernie's, where he developed his personal culinary style that highlights individual ingredients. In 1993 he opened Alain Rondelli in San Francisco, earning a four-star review. In 1998 he closed his namesake restaurant to pursue other projects, including the development of a specialty-food product line.

Anne Rosenzweig

Trained as an anthropologist, Anne Rosenzweig developed an interest in food through her studies of different cultures. She began her culinary career as an apprentice in several New York restaurants and was a member of the team that reopened the famed '21' Club. Rosenzweig's Arcadia opened in 1985, serving American food with urban flair. The Lobster Club, named for a signature dish, opened in 1995. In 1998, Rosenzweig closed Arcadia to work on a project for Joseph Baum & Michael Whiteman Co.

Alain Sailhac

A native of France, Alain Sailhac built his reputation in New York, where he was the sous chef at the Plaza Hotel and the chef at Manoir. He was executive chef at Le Cygne in the late 1960s, where he earned four stars from *The New York Times.* Le Cirque secured its legendary reputation during the nine years Sailhac served as its executive chef. He later went on to run the kitchens of the '21' Club, the Plaza Hotel, and the Regency. In 1991, Sailhac became the dean of culinary studies at The French Culinary Institute. He has been inducted into the James Beard Foundation's "Who's Who" of Food and Beverage in the United States.

Arun Sampathavivat

Thai literature was the original passion of Arun Sampathavivat, a native of Trang, a southern province of Thailand. After working as a consultant on Asian affairs, Sampathavivat joined with a group of investors to open Arun's, a Thai restaurant in Chicago. The plans with the investors failed to materialize, yet Sampathavivat forged ahead, teaching himself how to transform the exotic and aromatic cuisine of his homeland into elegant fine dining. Among many accolades, Arun's was named the best restaurant in Chicago by *Gourmet* magazine.

Julian Serrano

A native of Madrid, Julian Serrano received his formal culinary training at the Escuela Gastromomie on Spain's Costa del Sol before working in some of the most celebrated restaurants in Europe. Serrano found his mentor in Masa Kobiashi when he was hired as the sous chef at Masa's in San Francisco. In 1987, Serrano became executive chef of Masa's, which received an Award of Excellence from *Wine Spectator* magazine, four stars from the *Mobil Travel Guide,* and the highest rating in the *Zagat Guide.* In 1998 Serrano left Masa's to open Picasso in the Bellagio Hotel in Las Vegas, and, in the same year, he was named Best Chef: California by the James Beard Foundation.

Jamie Shannon

Growing up on the Jersey Shore, Jamie Shannon developed a love for seafood, traditional methods of cooking, fresh ingredients, and American cuisine. After graduating from The Culinary Institute of America he relocated to New Orleans, where he worked through the ranks at the historic Commander's Palace. As executive chef of the restaurant since 1990, Shannon continues to use traditional methods and seasonal ingredients to create his unique blend of Creole and American cuisines. Under his toque, Commander's Palace had been awarded Best Restaurant: Southeast by the James Beard Foundation.

Craig Shelton

Craig Shelton trained with Joël Robuchon, Paul Haeberlin, and Gaston Lenôtre in France, and was sous chef to David Bouley in New York. Since he took over the stoves at the Ryland Inn—a farmhouse set in Whitehouse, New Jersey, where he raises much of his own produce—Shelton has received four stars from the *Star Ledger,* and the first "extraordinary" rating from *The New York Times.* The Ryland Inn has been named the top restaurant in New Jersey by *Gourmet* magazine's readers' poll.

Lydia Shire

A native of Brookline, Massachusetts, Lydia Shire traveled across the pond to attend Le Cordon Bleu Cooking School in London. After graduation she returned to Boston to work at such notable restaurants at Maison Robert, Harvest, Cafe Plaza at the Copley Plaza Hotel, Parker's, and Seasons Restaurant. In 1986 Shire left Boston to open the Four Seasons Hotel in Beverly Hills, becoming the first female executive chef of a luxury hotel in America. She returned to Boston to open the celebrated Biba in 1989, followed by Pignoli in 1994.

Shire has received a James Beard Foundation Award for Best Chef: Northeast.

Nancy Silverton

While studying liberal arts at California State University, Nancy Silverton took a job as a vegetarian cook in her dormitory, and subsequently went on to study at Le Cordon Bleu in London, and Ecole Lenôtre in France. After working in the pastry department at Michael's in Santa Monica, Silverton became the head pastry chef at Spago. In 1989 Silverton opened La Brea Bakery and Campanile with her husband, becoming one of the United States' foremost authorities on bread baking. She has received the James Beard Foundation Award for Outstanding Pastry Chef, written several cookbooks, and operates what many consider the finest commercial bakery in the country.

André Soltner

Owner and chef of the legendary Lutèce in New York from 1961 to 1995, André Soltner is one of the most highly regarded chefs in the world. Soltner grew up in the small Alsatian town of Thann and began his apprenticeship at the age of 15. By his mid-twenties, he was executive chef of Chez Hansi in Paris. Since its inception, Lutèce has received almost every honor imaginable, including a Mobil five-star award. Soltner was one of the first French chefs outside the Republic to receive the coveted Meilleur Ouvrier de France. Soltner is now a dean at The French Culinary Institute and has recently received several "lifetime achievement" awards.

Hiro Sone

The École Technique Hotelière Tsuji in Osaka provided Hiro Sone with rigorous training in French, Japanese, Chinese, and Italian cuisine. He worked at La Colomba and Madame Toki in Tokyo before becoming sous chef at the Tokyo branch of Spago, and later chef at the Los Angeles Spago. In 1988, Sone and his wife opened Terra, a wine-country restaurant in St. Helena, California, where he was named one of America's Best New Chefs by *Food & Wine* magazine. Rissa Oriental Cafe, also in St. Helena, opened in 1990.

Roger Souvereyns

A native of Belgium, Roger Souvereyns began his culinary career as a *commis* in a restaurant in Liège at the age of 14. During his 40-year career as a chef, he has also operated restaurants in Anvers (Sir Anthony Van Dijck) and Liège (Le Clou Doré). But in 1983, Souvereyns divested himself of his enterprises to concentrate on the restoration of an early eighteenth-century farm. With several acres of magnificent gardens providing much of the produce for the kitchen, this farm, Scholteshof, has become one of the premier restaurants of Europe, earning a near perfect 19 out of 20 from GaultMillau. In 1995, GaultMillau selected Souvereyns as "Chef of the Year" for all of Europe.

Susan Spicer

When a friend requested Susan Spicer's assistance with the preparations of her catering business, she was thrilled at the opportunity to cook professionally. This start led to a position at the Louis XVI restaurant in New Orleans. After an apprenticeship with Roland Durand in Paris, Spicer became chef of the Bistro at the Maison de Ville in New Orleans. In 1990 she opened Bayona, where her "New-World Cooking" has won her awards from GaultMillau, the James Beard Foundation, and *New Orleans* magazine. She has recently opened Spice, a gourmet retail shop and cooking school.

Joachim Splichal

Raised in Germany, Joachim Splichal completed his culinary training in France, working at La Bonne Auberge, L'Oasis, and Chantecler Restaurant. Splichal came to the United States to work at the Regency Club in Los Angeles and then at the Seventh Avenue Bistro. In 1989 Splichal opened Patina, the first restaurant of his budding Los Angeles-based enterprise that today includes Pinot Bistro, Cafe Pinot, and Patina Catering. Patina is consistently rated as the highest-scoring restaurant in the GaultMillau guide, and Splichal has received the award of Best Chef: California from the James Beard Foundation.

Allen Susser

Drawn to the warmth and tropical flavors of Miami, Allen Susser, a native New Yorker, earned his bachelor's degree in hospitality from Florida International University. After working at Le Bristol Hôtel in France and Le Cirque in New York, Susser returned to Miami to take charge of the kitchen at the Turnberry Island Resort. In 1986 Susser opened Chef Allen's, where his "New-World Cuisine" has earned him the reputation as one of Miami's top chefs. Susser has authored several books on the subject of "New-World Cuisine" and has received a James Beard Foundation Award.

Bill Telepan

During high school Bill Telepan worked at a small restaurant in his New Jersey neighborhood. When given the chance, Telepan astounded the owners, and diners, with his flair for interpreting classic dishes. After graduating from The Culinary Institute of America, Telepan worked with Alfred Portale at Gotham Bar and Grill. Stints in France with Alain Chapel, and in New York with Gilbert LeCoze and Daniel Boulud prepared him to become sous chef at

Gotham. Telepan opened Ansonia in 1996, and in 1998 moved on to JUdson Grill, where he continues to receive rave reviews.

Charlie Trotter

At his eponymous restaurant in Chicago, Charlie Trotter has achieved the status of one of the country's top chefs and restaurateurs. Among its countless accolades and awards, the restaurant has received the Grand Award from the *Wine Spectator;* five stars from *Mobil Travel Guide;* and five diamonds from AAA. Trotter was named Best Chef: Midwest, by the James Beard Foundation in 1992, and has been inducted into the Who's Who of Food and Beverage in America. Trotter hosts a TV show and has authored a series of extraordinary cookbooks.

Norman Van Aken

When Norman Van Aken came to Key West from his native Illinois, he was instantly entranced by the Caribbean and Spanish influences in the food. He was named chef of Sinclair's at the Jupiter Beach Hilton, and later became well known on the South Beach dining scene, opening Louie's Backyard, Mira, and A Mano. His first solo venture, Norman's, opened in 1995 and was named Best New Restaurant in Miami by *South Florida* magazine, and the number one restaurant in South Florida by *Gourmet* magazine in 1996 and 1997. Van Aken won the Robert Mondavi Culinary Award of Excellence, and The James Beard Foundation's Best Chef: Southeast award.

Roger Vergé

Roger Vergé has earned the status of a culinary legend. In 1969, Vergé opened Le Moulin de Mougins, which instantly became one of the premier dining destinations in France, along with his second restaurant, L'Amandier. Vergé's desire to pass on his vast knowledge led him to found L'Ecole du Moulin, which has become a training ground for fine chefs across the globe. Vergé collaborated with Paul Bocuse and Gaston Lenôtre to establish Le Pavillon de France at Walt Disney World's Epcot Center, a project designed to familiarize Americans with French cuisine.

Jean-Georges Vongerichten

Known as "the palate" to his family in Alsace, Jean-George Vongerichten's love for food paved the way for his future career. He trained with Michelin three-star chefs Paul Haeberlin, Paul Bocuse, and Louis Outhier before being named executive chef of the Oriental Hotel in Bangkok. In New York, Vongerichten was the chef of Lafayette, which earned four stars in 1988. Jo Jo, his first solo venture, opened in 1991, Vong opened in 1993, and the critically acclaimed Jean-Georges, which opened in 1997, brought him back to the four-star galaxy. Vongerichten is the recipient of two James Beard Foundation Awards—in 1996, Best Chef: New York, and in 1998, Outstanding Chef.

Jasper White

Jasper White worked at various restaurants in San Francisco, Seattle, and Montana before he settled in Boston, where he was executive chef at some of the city's finest hotels—the Parker House, the Bostonian, and Copley Plaza. In 1983 White opened Jasper's, where he became known for his regional New England cuisine. Jasper's earned the "Best of Boston" title from *Boston Magazine* for eleven years, and White was named Best Chef: Northeast by the James Beard Foundation in 1991. White closed Jasper's in 1995 to become executive chef and director of operations of Legal Sea Foods, a world-renowned seafood company. White is the author of *Jasper White's Cooking from New England* and *Lobster at Home.*

Alan Wong

Committed to cultivating Hawaiian regional cuisine, Alan Wong's cooking highlights Hawaiian ingredients while utilizing French techniques and Asian accents. After graduating from the culinary program at Kapiolani Community College, Wong apprenticed at the Greenbrier in West Virginia and worked at Lutèce in New York. Wong returned to Hawaii to become executive chef of Canoe Boat House and Le Soleil at the Launa Maui Bay Hotel. In 1995 he opened Alan Wong's in Honolulu. He was named Best Chef: Pacific Rim in 1998 by the James Beard Foundation.

Foie Gras Glossary

Foie gras is produced and consumed all over the world. In order to ensure a common understanding of the terminology used throughout this book, we have compiled this glossary of foie gras, duck, and goose terms. In some instances, particularly in France, commercial foie gras terms are defined by law. In others, common practice dictates their meaning.

Alsace [al-ZAS]

A northeastern region of France, situated between the Vosges Mountains and the Rhine River, where primarily goose foie gras is produced and consumed. Strasbourg, a major city in Alsace, is the reputed birthplace of the chilled pâté de foie gras. Today goose foie gras production is centered in this region.

Bile

A bitter, alkaline, green secretion produced by the liver. During the processing of foie gras, the bile sac is often ruptured, causing a greenish discoloration on the liver. Though edible, the bile may add a bitter taste to the foie gras and, therefore, any discoloration should be removed with a sharp paring knife prior to cooking.

Bloc [blok]

A commercially produced, canned foie gras product consisting of large pieces of foie gras compressed into a block. By French law, at least 30 percent of the total weight of the product must consist of solid foie gras pieces. Truffles may also be added.

Bocale [boh-KAL]

French for "bottle." Foie gras prepared *en bocale* is preserved in glass jars in a process similar to home canning. Prepared in this way, foie gras can be kept for up to ten years, the flavor maturing as it ages. See recipe, page 106.

Brioche [bree-OHSH]

An egg-and-butter-enriched French bread, brioche is often served with foie gras. The richness of the bread complements the richness of the liver.

Canard [kah-NAR]

French for "duck." Young ducklings for roasting are sometimes referred to as *caneton.*

Confit [kohn-FEE]

A traditional Gascon method of preserving meat—usually the tougher parts of duck, goose, or pork—that involves curing the meat with salt and spices and cooking it slowly in its own fat. The cooked confit is then stored in crocks and covered with the fat to protect it from exposure to air. Whole foie gras can also be cooked in this way, as can certain vegetables and garlic. See recipes, pages 108, 226, and 276.

Connective tissue

The two lobes that comprise a whole foie gras (or any fowl liver, for that matter) are joined by a series of nerves, veins, and proteinous connective membrane and tissue. Any dangling, detectable tissues should be removed when cleaning a liver for either hot or cold preparations.

Conserve [kohn-SERV]

French for "processed." When French foie gras products are designated *en conserve,* they are simply being distinguished as preserved products rather than fresh.

Cracklings

Strips of duck or goose skin rendered of all fat and fried until crisp. In French, cracklings are known as *frittons.* See recipes, pages 136, 156, 160, and 166.

Crop

A pouch in the esophagus of birds used primarily to store food prior to digesting. Also called a craw.

Cru [krew]

French for "raw." In some French foie gras-producing regions, raw foie gras is considered a delicacy. Although it poses no potential health risks, some chefs prefer to cure the raw foie gras in salt before serving it. See recipe, page 142.

Cure

Some foie gras preparations involve curing the liver in a mixture of salt and spices. Because heat is not applied, cured foie gras retains all of its fat. There is no need to cook the foie gras once it is cured. See recipe, page 104.

Deveining

For low-heat preparations, such as steaming or baking, that will be served chilled (for example, a terrine), it is important to remove any visible veins or other discoloration and blemishes from the liver. For best results, it is imperative to keep the liver as intact as possible. See Cleaning Foie Gras, page 91.

Duck (or goose) liver

A non-fattened duck or goose liver is similar to a chicken liver, only slightly larger. The phrase duck (or goose) liver is sometimes used as a translation for foie gras, although the meaning is ambiguous. An ordinary duck liver typically weighs approximately three ounces; a whole foie gras can exceed two pounds. For clarity, the French sometimes use the term *foie maigre,* literally "thin liver," to denote ordinary duck and goose livers. In English, the terms should not be used interchangeably.

Entier [ahn-TYAY]

French for "whole." Foie gras entier refers to a product, usually canned, that is made from an entire foie gras without the addition of any other meat or liver. See recipe, page 106.

Fat

Distinctions are made between foie gras fat and duck (or goose) fat because foie gras fat has a slightly different flavor. Foie gras fat refers to the fat that renders out of the foie gras during cooking; duck or goose fat is rendered from the skin and carcass of the bird. Foie gras fat is slightly milder tasting and lighter than plain duck or goose fat. It is high in monosaturated fat, which leads some nutritionists to believe it may help reduce blood-serum cholesterol. See nutrition information, page 84.

Fegato grasso [FAY-gah-to GRAH-soh]

Italian for "foie gras."

Foie gras [fwah GRAH]

Literally, "fat liver," foie gras refers to the fattened liver of a force-fed duck or goose. By French law, a duck foie gras must be larger than 250 grams (about 9 ounces) and a goose foie gras must be larger than 400 grams (about 14 ounces). The size of an ideal liver is a matter of preference depending to some extent on the method by which the liver will be prepared. In general, larger livers render more fat and have a more subtle flavor. American chefs tend to prefer larger livers than do French chefs.

Force-feeding

Known as *gavage* in French, force-feeding (or hand-feeding) is the process by which the duck or goose livers are fattened. The period of force-feeding extends anywhere from 15 to 32 days, depending on the species of bird and the technique used. A feed of corn or a mixture of corn and other grains is traditional. Feeding takes place anywhere from two to five times a day. A premeasured amount of feed is coaxed down the esophagus of the birds to the crop, where it remains until digested. The birds are readied for feeding by a process called *prégavage,* whereby they are slowly fed increasing amounts of food.

Fresh

Fresh foie gras has only been available commercially in the United States since the mid-1980s. Until then, only processed foie gras products imported from France were available. Fresh foie gras is highly perishable and has a flavor and texture unmatched by any canned product. It is sold refrigerated in vacuum packs at specialty gourmet shops, by wholesale meat distributors, and by mail order. There is no substitute for fresh foie gras, which should be prepared within two weeks of purchase. French producers have recently received USDA approval to begin exporting fresh foie gras to the United States. Although fresh foie gras can be frozen, moisture is drawn out and the cell walls deteriorate, diminishing the smooth creaminess of the product.

Frittons [free-TOHN]

French for "cracklings" (see **Cracklings**).

Gascony

A region of southwest France that comprises the departments of Gers and Landes and that is known as the principal foie gras-producing region of the world. The majority of Gascon foie gras is produced from the mulard duck.

Gavage [ga-VAHJ]

The French term for the force-feeding process (see **Force-feeding**).

Goose foie gras

Although goose foie gras was once more popular than duck foie gras, over the last 20 years, duck production has increased more than tenfold. The geese used for foie gras production are all of the genus *Ancer.* In France, the largest breeds are known as Toulouse or Strasbourg geese, while the smaller breeds are sometimes referred to as grey geese.

Grade

In the United States, foie gras is graded by the producer into three categories, A, B, and C, depending on size, shape, firmness, and appearance. See details, page 89.

Grilling

Popular in Israel, grilled foie gras now appears on menus around the word. The high-heat technique is appropriate for medallions or cubes of foie gras. When grilling foie gras it is important to cut the liver thick enough so that it does not disintegrate. Particular attention should be paid to flare-ups on the coals that result from the melting fat. Alternately, a cast iron grill can be used to produce an attractive, "grilled" look. See recipes, pages 190 and 230.

Kaved avaz [kah-VED AV-ahz]

Hebrew for "goose liver."

Lobe

Foie gras consists of two lobes: the anterior lobe, which is roughly two-thirds the total weight of the liver; and the posterior lobe, which accounts for the remaining third. When using the liver whole, such as when roasting or poaching, the lobes should be left attached. When slicing the liver into medallions, however, the lobes should be separated.

Magret [mah-GRAY]
The specific term used to designate the breast of a foie gras duck. Magret can be used for sautéing, grilling, smoking, and curing.

Marché au gras [mar-SHAY oh GRAH]
Literally "fat market," this is the term used to designate the regional foie gras markets of southwest France, the largest of which is held Monday mornings in the town of Samatan. Both the livers and the ducks are sold. Other markets are held in Montfort-en-Chalosse, Pomarez, Gimont, Thiviers-en-Périgord, and elsewhere.

Marinating
To infuse the liver with flavor, many recipes call for marinating or macerating the foie gras in alcohol (Armagnac, port, brandy, or Sauternes) and seasonings before cooking. The liver should not be marinated for more than two days or the texture may break down.

Medallion
The term used to designate a slice of foie gras, usually ½ to ¾ inch thick and anywhere from 2 to 5 ounces in weight. Medallions are often cut on the bias to increase the surface area of the slices. See High-Heat Cooking, page 92.

Mi-cuit [mee-KWEE]
A French term meaning "half-cooked," *mi-cuit* is a commercial term used in France for a particular type of foie gras processing. *Mi-cuit* foie gras is akin to a commercially prepared terrine. It is the processed product closest to fresh foie gras. *Mi-cuit* products tend not to have extended shelf lives and are usually sold refrigerated in vacuum packs. *Mi-cuit* may also be referred to as *semi-conserve*.

Milk bath
Traditional recipes often suggest soaking foie gras in salted milk for several hours before working with it. This technique was devised to draw out any residual blood within the liver. Due to modern processing techniques this procedure is no longer necessary.

Mousse [moos]
A generic term for any whipped foie gras product, mousses are usually made by marinating the foie gras to flavor it and gently cooking it, either in steam or in a bain marie. Once cooled, the liver is passed through a fine sieve and any fat rendered off during the cooking process is whipped back in. See recipe, page 114.

Mulard [moo-LAHR or moo-LAHRD]
Sometimes spelled "moulard" or "mullard," this is the name of the hybrid duck preferred today for foie gras production. The mulard is a cross between a Pekin female and a Muscovy male. The resulting mule (hence "mulard") is a hardy, disease-resistant breed that produces a large foie gras and a flavorful, tender magret.

Muscovy
Also known as "Barbary," the Muscovy duck is a wild duck sometimes used for foie gras production. Muscovy foie gras tends to render more fat and have a flatter shape. Muscovy males are bred with Pekin females to produce the mulard offspring.

Nerve
Threadlike membranes that connect and run through the two lobes of the liver. Any detectable nerves should be removed during cleaning.

Oie [wah]
French for "goose."

Parfait [pahr-FAY]
A French term for a processed mousse of foie gras that contains other liver and duck or goose meat in addition to the foie gras. By law, the percentage of foie gras included must be indicated on the label.

Pâté de foie gras [pah-TAY duh FWAH GRAH]
A generic term for a smooth, often spreadable preparation of foie gras which usually includes other liver (duck or goose) and meat (duck, goose, or pork). Pâtés vary in texture from coarse to very fine. They are often molded into shapes or crocks and served chilled or at room temperature. See illustrations, pages 34, 35, and 36.

Peeling
Some chefs will recommend peeling away the outer membrane of the liver before preparing the foie gras. This membrane is very fine and, if not peeled, is virtually undetectable once the liver is cooked. In addition, peeling can cause the liver to break apart when it comes into contact with heat. As a rule, peeling foie gras is not advised.

Pekin [pee-KIHN]
The maternal breed of the mulard duck that is crossed with a Muscovy male. The famous Long Island ducks are of the Pekin species.

Poaching
Poaching has become a popular method for preparing foie gras. The gentle heat allows the liver to retain most of its fat. By adding aromatics to the poaching liquid, the liver can be infused with a variety of flavors. See recipes, pages 146, 150, 240, and 262.

Render

The process of melting animal fat to separate it from skin, meat, or bones. Rendered fat is usually passed through several layers of cheesecloth or a fine sieve to remove any solid particles. Rendered duck fat has a high smoking point and adds a delicious flavor to foods. Rendered fat is essential to prepare confit. See techniques, page 108.

Roasting

Foie gras is traditionally roasted whole. The dry-heat cooking intensifies the flavor of the liver, resulting in a firmer, meatier texture. See recipes, pages 140, 216, 218, 226, and 228.

Shipoudim [ship-oo-DEEM]

Hebrew for "skewers," this is the term applied to the way foie gras is grilled on skewers and served with pita and mezze in Israel.

Steaming

Steaming has become a popular way to prepare foie gras. Whole livers are generally preferred to smaller pieces for steaming. By setting the liver over an aromatic broth, the liver can be infused with a variety of flavors. See recipe, page 148.

Terrine [tuh-REEN]

Named for the rectangular mold in which it is usually prepared, a terrine is a specific foie gras preparation that involves gently marinating the liver, pressing it into a ceramic or enameled mold, heating it delicately in a water bath, weighing it down to compact the liver, and chilling it to allow the flavors to mature. See recipes, pages 110, 112, 114, 118, 120, 124, 126, and 140.

Torchon [tohr-SHAWN]

A traditional technique of cooking foie gras in which the cleaned liver is wrapped tightly with a dish towel (*torchon* in French) and shaped into a sausage. The torchon is gently poached in a court bouillon (aromatic broth) and chilled prior to serving. See recipes, pages 122, 130, and 252.

Truffée [troo-FAY]

Literally, "truffled." Foie gras is often prepared with black truffles. By law, processed French foie gras which bears the description *truffée* must contain truffles equal to at least three percent by weight.

Veins

The main arteries and capillaries that carry blood into and out of the liver. For purely aesthetic reasons, when preparing terrines and pâtés, the veins should be removed. The veins in the large lobe form an inverted Y. In the smaller lobe, a central vein is easy to remove. For hot preparations or those that require a whole liver, the veins should be left intact. See Low-Heat Cooking, page 93.

Culinary Glossary

The recipes in this book come from 82 chefs working in kitchens around the world. Although each recipe has been tested and edited to conform to a standardized style, we have compiled this second glossary of culinary terms, ingredients, and techniques in order to avoid any ambiguity in the execution of the dishes.

Abalone

A deep-water shellfish prized for its subtle flavor and dense texture. Although wild abalone are preferred to farm-raised, they are becoming increasingly difficult to find. Dried abalone are prized in Chinese cooking, but should not be substituted for fresh abalone.

Achiote oil

Deep red in color, achiote oil is a condiment used in Latin American cooking. It can either be purchased or prepared at home. Simmer 1 teaspoon of achiote, also known as annatto seed, in ½ cup vegetable or grapeseed oil in a sauté pan until the oil is hot, but not smoking. Remove from the pan and let the seeds steep in the oil until the pan is cool. Pass the oil through a fine mesh strainer or several layers of cheesecloth. Store in the refrigerator for up to two months.

Andouille [an-DOO-ee]

There are several types of andouille available. In Louisiana, the term *andouille* refers to a dense, smoked pork sausage used primarily in Cajun and Creole cooking. It should not be confused with French andouille, which is a white tripe sausage typical of Lyon, France.

Armagnac [ar-mahn-YAK]

Armagnac is double-distilled brandy from the Gascon region of France, an area known for foie gras. Armagnac is often used in foie gras preparations to add a distinct regional flavor.

Bain marie [behn mar-EE]

To slow the cooking process, many foie gras preparations require a bain marie, or water bath. To create one, lay a cloth towel or several sheets of paper towel in the center of a large baking or roasting pan. Set the foie gras cooking vessel on top and fill the pan with warm water at least halfway up the side.

Ballotine

A boneless tied roll of meat, fish, or fowl that is roasted or braised.

Bamboo leaves

Available fresh or dried, bamboo leaves are used to wrap foods for cooking (similar to the way corn husks are used to make tamales) or as a garnish. They can be purchased in Asian markets. Dried leaves should be reconstituted in hot water before using.

Banana leaves

Like bamboo leaves (see above) banana leaves are available fresh or dried and are used for cooking and presentation. They are available in Asian and Caribbean markets.

Blanching

The process of quickly cooking vegetables or other ingredients in a boiling liquid for a minute or two. Often the blanched ingredients will be shocked in an ice bath to cease the cooking process immediately.

Bonito [boh-nee-toh] flakes

These flavorful fish flakes are made by drying, smoking, and fermenting the bonito fish. They provide the principle flavor to Japanese dashi. Bonito flakes will keep indefinitely. They are available in Japanese markets.

Bouquet garni

A classic seasoning of fresh herbs—which often includes parsley, thyme, and bay leaf—tied together with string. Technically, if the herbs are wrapped in cheesecloth, the bundle is known as a **sachet.**

Bread crumbs

Bread crumbs are either fresh or dried. Fresh crumbs are made by placing fresh bread (with or without the crust) in a food processor fitted with a metal chopping blade and blending until fine. Dried bread crumbs are made by allowing bread to dry out in a very low oven and processing as for fresh bread crumbs. For Japanese **panko,** the crusts are removed and the bread is dehydrated completely before being processed into large, almost flake-like crumbs. For toasted bread crumbs, increase the oven temperature and allow the bread to brown while drying. To produce fine bread crumbs, pass the ground crumbs through a fine tamis or sieve.

Brunoise

A fine dice, no more than ¹⁄₁₆-inch square.

Caramelize

The process by which sugar, whether added to or occurring naturally in food, reaches 320 degrees and begins to brown, taking on a pleasant, toasted flavor.

Caul fat

The thin, fatty, membranous abdominal lining from pigs or cattle that is used to shape and flavor forcemeats, pâtés, and other classic preparations.

Cèpe [sep] powder

Cèpe powder is made from dried, ground boletus mushrooms (also known as cèpes or porcini). It is available from specialty mushroom purveyors.

Cheesecloth

Cheesecloth is used to finely strain stocks, sauces, and other liquids. When used in a torchon preparation, the fabric's porous quality allows the cooking liquid to flavor the torchon while retaining a sausage-like shape. The highest-quality cheesecloth is available from cheese-making suppliers. For a finer cloth, you can also use what is known in the industry as butter muslin.

Chestnut purée

Imported chestnut purée is available canned or jarred from Italy or France. To make it fresh, score ¼ pound chestnuts with an **X** and place them in boiling water for 5 minutes. Remove from the water, allow to cool, peel, and return to the boiling water for 30 to 40 minutes, until tender. Purée in a food processor until smooth and store refrigerated until needed.

Chiffonade

A very fine julienne or shredding, as for leafy greens and herbs.

Chili peppers

Chili peppers are available in myriad varieties, each with its own distinct flavor and degree of hotness. Among the most common are jalapeño, scotch bonnet (and the similar, but distinct, habanero), and ancho. Chipotle peppers are actually smoked jalapeños. Dried peppers usually have a more concentrated flavor than fresh peppers, and are generally reconstituted by soaking in hot water before using. Roasting peppers—by heating them over an open flame or roasting them in a hot oven and removing the blackened skin—actually sweetens the peppers somewhat. Most of the heat is contained in the seeds of the pepper, which can be removed. To ensure the best results, try to use the peppers specified in each recipe.

China cap

A conically-shaped metal colander, the china cap holds a large capacity and drains quickly. The smaller **chinois,** with a fabric mesh, provides a finer sieve.

Chinese five-spice powder

A classic seasoning used in Chinese cooking, five-spice powder is a blend of ground cinnamon, Szechuan peppercorns, star anise, black pepper, and clove in equal proportions. It is available wherever spices are sold.

Consommé

A consommé is made by clarifying an enriched stock or demi glace. To clarify 2½ quarts of stock, combine 1½ pounds very lean ground beef, 2 leeks, white part only, cleaned and chopped, 2 stalks celery, cleaned and chopped, and 6 egg whites. Place the chilled stock in a 5-quart stock pot and whisk in the meat mixture. Set the stock pot over medium-high heat and stir until a "raft" of meat and vegetables begins to form. Stop stirring and bring to a boil. Turn down the heat to a simmer, and cook for 1 hour. Turn off the heat and cool slightly. Gently push back the raft with a ladle, being careful not to break it, and ladle the consommé into a fine-mesh strainer lined with several layers of cheesecloth. Degrease the consommé with a sheet of paper towel.

Corn husks

Fresh corn husks are dried and packaged for sale in Hispanic markets. They are primarily used to make tamales. Dried husks must be reconstituted by soaking in hot water for 30 minutes before being used.

Country ham

Country ham is a specialty of the southern United States, especially Virginia. The hams are dry-cured in salt and sugar and smoked over hardwood before being air dried for up to 12 months. Most country hams are very salty and should be soaked in several changes of water for a day or two before using.

Demi glace

Although many people use the phrase *demi glace* to refer to brown veal stock, it actually refers to a veal stock that has been reduced by half to concentrate the flavor. A demi glace will be dark, rich, and heavily gelatinous.

Edible flowers

Edible flowers add both a visual and a flavor element to dishes. Among the most popular are nasturtiums, chive blossoms, roses, violets, lavender, squash blossoms, and pansies. Be sure to order flowers that are not treated with pesticides. As a rule, most flowers sold by florists have been treated in some way. Be sure to ask before using decorative flowers for cooking.

Eggs

Unless otherwise specified, eggs (from chickens) should be size large. Duck eggs may be substituted for chicken eggs to produce a richer texture and slightly more pronounced flavor. Because duck eggs are larger than chicken eggs, they should be substituted in a ratio of 2 to 3. Quail eggs, which are much smaller than chicken eggs, are used primarily as garnish.

Emulsion

An emulsion is a physical state in which a fat is dispersed in a liquid, usually through a medium known as an emulsifier. Mayonnaise is a classic emulsion in which the oil is dispersed in vinegar or lemon juice with the help of egg yolks. When sauces are finished or "mounted" with butter, a temporary emulsion is formed that produces a rich, silky texture. As a rule, the fat needs to be slowly but rapidly beaten into the liquid for the emulsion to work properly.

Fish sauce
Known as *nam plah* in Thailand and *nuoc nam* in Vietnam, fish sauce is a staple in Southeast Asian cooking. It is made from the run off of salted and fermented anchovies and other small fish. The Thai version is slightly milder. Some bottles feature a picture of a squid on the label, but the condiment does not contain squid. It will keep indefinitely without refrigeration. Fish sauce can be purchased in most Asian markets.

Fleur de sel
An imported French sea salt from Brittany, fleur de sel is considered the finest (and most expensive) salt available. It has a distinctly deep, briny flavor that is more pronounced than most other sea salts. The large granules of this off-white salt also add texture. Fleur de sel is available in gourmet stores.

Galangal
Similar to ginger, galangal is a rhizome with a sweet and hot flavor. It is available fresh, frozen, and bottled in brine in Asian markets and specialty produce stores.

Galantine
Similar to a **ballotine,** with the exception that a galantine is poached and served cold.

Garam masala
A traditional Indian blend of up to 12 species that may include black pepper, cinnamon, cloves, coriander, cumin, cardamom, dried fennel, mace, and nutmeg. It is available in Indian markets.

Gelatin
Available both in powdered and sheet form, gelatin is made from beef and veal bones, cartilage, and skin. All gelatin should be dissolved in cold water before being used. Powdered gelatin (one envelope contains about ¼ ounce, enough to gel 2 cups of liquid) should be dissolved for 5 minutes. Sheet gelatin (four sheets equal one envelope of powdered gelatin) should be soaked for about 15 minutes and squeezed out before being used.

Ghee
Ghee is a special type of clarified butter used in Indian cooking. To prepare it, place 1 pound unsalted, cultured butter in a small, deep saucepan and melt over low heat. Simmer for 10 to 15 minutes, until the butter stops making a crackling noise, which indicates that all of the moisture has evaporated. Skim the froth off the top of the melted butter and continue simmering until the milk solids on the bottom of the pan begin to turn dark brown. Let cool and pour off the ghee into a container, leaving the browned milk solids behind in the pan. Ghee will keep refrigerated for up to one year. Regular clarified butter can be substituted, although the resulting dish will have less depth of flavor.

Glace [glahs]
Further reduced than demi glace, glace or glace de viande is reduced by at least three-quarters from the original liquid, and sometimes as much as seven-eighths or until almost dry.

Greens
To achieve a complexity of visual and flavor elements, chefs use a variety of greens. Lately, mizuna and tatsoi have become very popular. Mesclun is a generic mixture of baby lettuces and greens that is used for salads and garnish. Microgreens, sprouts germinated in dirt rather than water, are now available in hundreds of varieties. They provide a delicate, attractive, and flavorful alternative to mesclun. Other greens, such as pea shoots, mustard greens, broccoli rabe, and dandelion greens, should be used as specified in each recipe.

Green tomato
The phrase "green tomato" is often confusing. Tomatillos from Central America are sometimes referred to as green tomatoes, although they are only a relative of our more familiar, red tomato. In the southern United States, "green tomato" usually refers to unripened red tomatoes picked form the vine while still hard and sour. They are pickled, fried, and used to make jams. A relative newcomer, the sweet green tomato is fully ripe and ready to eat while still green. Be sure not to confuse the variety of green tomato called for in the recipe.

Grills
Unless specified otherwise, whenever grilling is required, an open-fire grill is preferred. The flavor incorporated into foods, created by fat drippings burning in the fire, is an important element of a grilled preparation. When grilling foie gras, be sure to have a spray bottle of water nearby. The flare ups can be serious. Cast iron stovetop grill pans are useful for grilling small vegetables and delicate fish, although the affect is mostly visual and does not contribute to the overall flavor of the foods.

Infuse
The process of steeping a flavoring agent in a liquid to impart the flavor to the liquid, such as when making flavored oils or teas.

Julienne
A classic French cut, whereby the ingredients are sliced thinly and cut into matchstick-sized pieces. Very fine julienne, or shredding, such as for leafy greens and basil, is called **chiffonade.**

Jus
A light, unthickened pan gravy made by degreasing a roasting pan, deglazing with wine, and reducing to concentrate flavors.

Kobe [koh-bay] **beef**
A highly prized and expensive type of beef produced in Kobe, Japan, for which the cattle are fed a special diet that includes beer, and are massaged daily. The resulting meat is highly marbelized, rendering it tender and rich. Although there really is no substitute for Kobe beef, aged prime beef will produce the closest results.

Kombu [komboo]
Known in English as "kelp," kombu is a large, dark green seaweed used to make Japanese dashi. Dried kombu often has a white bloom that should not be rinsed before using. It is sold in healthfood stores and Japanese markets.

Lemongrass
This traditional aromatic and citrusy Thai flavoring resembles a long, woody scallion. Lemongrass is generally steeped in a liquid to extract its flavor or crushed into curry pastes.

Liquid smoke
A flavoring available from some specialty gourmet or spice stores, liquid smoke is a distillation of hickory wood. Used sparingly, it imparts the distinct flavor of smoke obtained by prolonged hardwood smoking.

Maple syrup
Maple syrup is the reduced sap of the maple tree. It is available in several grades based on color that range from Fancy (or Grade AA), which is the lightest and most delicate, to Grade C, the darkest and most robust.

Masa harina
Made from hominy, a special corn that is soaked in lime water and dried, masa harina, literally "dough flour," is used to make tamales and tortillas. Lime water is a mixture of water and the mineral lime, not the fruit.

Meyer lemon
A sweet, low-acid lemon grown in California.

Mirepoix
A classic combination of equal parts onion, carrot, celery, and sometimes leek, used to flavor soups, stews, sauces, braises, and other dishes.

Mirin
A sweet Japanese rice wine used for cooking. "Naturally brewed," a designation indicated on the label assuring that the mirin contains no additives or flavor enhancers, is considered the best quality. Mirin is available from Japanese markets and gourmet stores.

Miso
This fermented soy bean paste is produced in a variety of colors and styles, ranging from the mild-tasting white miso to the deeply flavored dark red. It is available in Japanese markets and healthfood stores.

Mustard oil
A flavored oil with a bright yellow color, mustard oil can be purchased in specialty gourmet markets. Do not confuse it with the clear, painfully hot mustard oil used to create delicacies such as the mustard fruits of Cremona, Italy. Mustard oil can also be made by toasting 1 tablespoon of mustard seeds in a saucepan until they pop. Add 1 cup grapeseed oil to the pan and cook until the mixture reaches a boil. Pass the flavored oil through a coffee filter into a jar and store in the refrigerator for up to one month.

Nori
Also called *laver,* nori is a mild seaweed traditionally used for wrapping sushi. It is available in thin sheets approximately 8-inches square, either toasted (*yaki-nori*) or untoasted. It should be stored airtight in the freezer. It is available in Asian grocery stores or healthfood stores.

Oils
Whenever a recipe calls for a particular type of oil, it has been specified by the chef. Unrefined oils, such as extra-virgin olive oil, walnut oil, or pistachio oil, should be used fresh and stored in the refrigerator to prevent oxidation. Grapeseed oil is often called for in recipes for flavored oils because of its light, neutral flavor.

Panko
Large, white, untoasted Japanese bread crumbs available in Japanese markets and gourmet stores.

Parmigiano-Reggiano
There is no substitute for the flavor of authentic Parmigiano-Reggiano cheese from the Emilia-Romagna region of Italy, which should be used whenever parmesan is called for.

Pepper
Black or white pepper is specified in each recipe and should be freshly ground whenever used. The best black peppercorns are considered the Tellicherry peppercorns from India.

Pink peppercorns
Not related to black or white pepper, pink peppercorns are actually the dried buds of

the Baies rose plant, which is cultivated in Madagascar.

Pistachio oil
Used in Indian cooking, pistachio oil is available from Asian and Indian markets, as well as from French importers of nut oils.

Poaching
Poaching is defined as cooking gently in barely simmering water at a temperature of approximately 160 to 180 degrees.

Pomegranate syrup
Available from Middle Eastern markets, pomegranate syrup is the reduced juice of pomegranates with a measure of added sugar. When fresh pomegranate juice is unavailable, the syrup can be diluted and substituted in order to achieve the desired flavor and consistency required for the recipe.

Port
A sweet, fortified wine from the Oporto region of Portugal, port is available in four general styles: ruby, tawny, vintage, or late-bottled vintage. White ports are also produced, although they are extremely difficult to find in the United States. Most recipes call for ruby port. Although finer ports may be substituted, by the time they are cooked, reduced, seasoned, or otherwise manipulated, the flavor nuances of the higher-quality ports are lost.

Quatre épices [KAT-ruh ay-PEACE]
Literally "four spices," quatre épices is a traditional seasoning used in France for pâtés and terrines. The four spices vary, but usually include pepper, nutmeg, cinnamon, and cloves. Quatre épices was traditionally used both as a flavor enhancer and as a

preservative since cloves possess an antiseptic quality.

Ras el hanout
Ras el hanout is a proprietary Moroccan spice blend that may contain up to 50 different spices. Every spice purveyor has his or her own secret recipe. It may be purchased in most Middle Eastern markets. Though no two blends are alike, it is important to make sure the ras el hanout is fresh.

Rice wine
A sweet, white, low-alcohol wine produced by fermenting rice. The most common varieties are sake and **mirin.**

Ring molds
Increasingly popular among chefs, ring molds, circular bands of metal or PVC plastic pipes, are available in varying sizes and depths. They are used to shape food for cooking and presentation.

Roasting
Roasting is a method of dry-heat cooking in which hot air circulates around the ingredients in the oven.

Sachet
A classic seasoning of fresh herbs, often including parsley, thyme, and bay leaf, wrapped and tied in cheesecloth.

Salt
A variety of types of salt are now on the market. For seasoning, coarse kosher salt is recommended for it's purity of flavor and large, easy-to-sprinkle and measure granules. For garnishes and more sophisticated preparations, specialty sea salts such as **sel gris** or **fleur de sel** are often preferred by chefs. Crystallized rock salt also makes an attractive presentation.

Saltpeter
Also called curing salt, saltpeter is actually potassium nitrate. It acts as a preservative and is used in some chilled foie gras preparations to help the liver maintain a desirable pinkish color. Saltpeter can be purchased at drug stores and specialty sausage-making suppliers. It may be omitted from most recipes without any significant consequence to flavor.

Sansho
A peppery Japanese spice made from the ground pod of the prickly ash. Sansho is available in Japanese markets and specialty Asian grocery stores.

Saucepans
In general, saucepans should be the highest quality to ensure even heating and accurate temperature control. As a size guideline, consider a small saucepan to be 1 to 2 quarts, a medium saucepan to be 3 to 4 quarts, and a large saucepan to be 5 quarts and larger. I have been very partial to the All-Clad brand.

Sauté
Sauter is French for "jump," and to sauté means to cook quickly over high heat in a small amount of fat while quickly moving the ingredients around the pan.

Sauté pans
Because of the high heat necessary to sear foie gras and sauté other ingredients, it is important to use the highest quality sauté pans. Some chefs prefer cast iron pans because they attain a higher heat than stainless steel. Regardless of which type of pan you use, size is important. A pan that is too small will not allow ingredients to sear or brown properly. As a guideline, consider a small sauté pan to be 8 inches in diameter

or smaller, a medium sauté pan to be 9 to 12 inches, and a large sauté pan to be anything larger than 12 inches. I have been very partial to the All-Clad brand.

Scoring

Scoring ingredients such as meats, vegetables, and seafood before cooking ensures even cooking and provides an attractive visual element. In the case of squid and other ingredients that have a tendency to toughen, scoring improves the texture. Foie gras is often scored to produce an attractive pattern when seared. To score foie gras, make shallow cuts, no more than a millimeter deep in a cross-hatch pattern on the surface of the liver.

Sea urchin

Both a French (*oursin*) and Japanese (*uni*) delicacy, fresh sea urchin is available from fine fish stores and Japanese markets.

Searing

Searing usually refers to browning meats or other ingredients over very high heat to color and flavor, but not actually cook, them. Because of the delicate texture of foie gras, however, searing is usually enough to cook the foie gras through. The change in color of seared meats results from a physical and chemical process known as *Maillard browning*, caused by the reaction of the sugar and protein in the meat.

Sel gris [sel-GREE]

Literally "grey salt," sel gris is a greyish sea salt harvested in Brittany. It is available in specialty gourmet stores. The more expensive fleur de sel is whiter in color and has a deep flavor.

Sel rose

Literally "pink salt," sel rose is an imported French curing agent consisting of sodium chloride, potassium nitrate, and cochineal natural coloring. It cannot be used as a substitute for other seasoning salts. Sel rose has a pinkish color that preserves the naturally pink color of foie gras. It is available from importers and specialty sausage-making suppliers. It may be omitted from most recipes without affecting the flavor of the finished dish.

Sheet pans

Sheet pans are the most common baking pans in professional kitchens. Made of aluminum, they are sized to fit into commercial ovens (18 × 26 inches). Half sheet pans (18 × 13 inches) are better suited to home ovens.

Shiso

A relative of basil and mint, shiso, which is also called perilla or Japanese basil, has a slight anise flavor. It is available at specialty Japanese stores.

Sticky rice

Sometimes called glutinous rice or sweet rice, sticky rice is used throughout Asia. The long-grain variety is preferred in Thailand, where it is known as *khao niew*. It can be purchased in Asian markets.

Stock

There is no substitute for homemade stock. If you do not have your own standard recipes, here are a few that you can adapt. In general, stocks are not salted until they are used in final recipes.

Dark Veal Stock

Preheat the oven to 500 degrees. Place 10 pounds of veal bones in a large roasting pan and roast until dark brown, about 1 to 1½ hours. Pour off any fat that has rendered. Add 4 onions, quartered, 1 head garlic, split in half, and 5 large carrots, peeled, and continue roasting until browned, an additional 30 minutes. Add one 6-ounce can of tomato paste and roast for an additional 10 minutes. Transfer to a tall 12-quart stock pot. Deglaze the roasting pan with 1½ cups red wine and pour into the stock pot. Cover with cold water and bring to a boil, skimming off any scum or foam that rises to the top. Add 3 ribs celery with leaves, 2 leeks, cleaned, 10 sprigs parsley, 2 bay leaves, 10 black peppercorns, 1 clove, and 4 juniper berries. Bring to a boil, reduce heat to a simmer, and cook for 12 hours. Add water to be sure the bones and vegetables are covered. Remove from the heat and strain through a fine-mesh sieve. Degrease the stock and cool quickly in a cold-water bath. Yields about 7 quarts. To make a **white veal stock,** follow the same directions but do not roast the veal bones or the vegetables prior to simmering.

Light Chicken Stock

In a large 12-quart stock pot place 5 chicken carcasses, rinsed well, or 2 whole stewing hens. Add 4 onions, quartered, 5 carrots, peeled, 3 ribs celery, 1 turnip, quartered, 10 parsley stems, 2 bay leaves, 6 white peppercorns, 2 cloves garlic, and 1 clove. Cover with cold water and bring to a boil. Skim off any scum or foam that rises to the top. Turn down the heat and simmer for 4½ hours, adding more water if the level falls below the bones and vegetables. Strain through a fine-mesh sieve and degrease. Cool quickly in a cold-water bath. Yields about 7 quarts. To make a **dark chicken stock,** roast the bones with the onions and carrots at 400 degrees for 1 to 1½ hours, or until browned before proceeding with the recipe.

Duck Stock

Preheat the oven to 400 degrees. In a large roasting pan place 4 duck carcasses, about 8 pounds of bones, trimmed of any visible fat and roast for 1 to 1½ hours until browned. Pour off the rendered fat and add

4 onions, 5 carrots, and 4 cloves garlic, roughly cut. Return to the oven and roast an additional 30 minutes. Transfer the roasted ingredients to a 12-quart stock pot. Deglaze the roasting pan with 1 cup Madeira and add to the stock pot. Also add 2 leeks, cleaned, 4 stalks celery with leaves, 8 black peppercorns, 2 bay leaves, 4 juniper berries, and 1 clove. Cover the ingredients with cold water, set over high heat, and bring to a boil, skimming off any scum or foam that rises to the top. Turn down the heat and simmer for 6 hours, adding more water if the level falls below the bones and vegetables. Remove from the heat, strain through a fine-mesh sieve, degrease, and cool in a cold-water bath. Yields about 7 quarts.

Fish Stock
In a 6-quart stock pot, sauté 2 diced onions in 4 tablespoons butter until translucent. Add 2 ribs celery, with leaves, chopped, and continue sautéing for 2 minutes. Add 5 pounds fresh fish bones, preferably not from oily fish such as salmon or bluefish, cleaned of any gills, heads, or impurities. Sauté for an additional 5 minutes to draw out the flavor. Add 2 cups dry white wine, 2½ quarts cold water, 10 parsley stems, 1 bay leaf, 5 white peppercorns, and 2 sprigs fresh thyme, and bring to a boil. Reduce the heat to a simmer and cook for 40 minutes to produce a lightly flavored stock. Strain through a fine-mesh sieve. Degrease, cool, and refrigerate or freeze until needed.

Shrimp or Lobster Stock
Sauté 2 diced onions in ¼ pound sweet butter until translucent. Add 2 ribs of celery, with leaves, chopped, and continue sautéing for 2 minutes. Add the shells and heads of 5 pounds shrimp or 5 lobsters and cook for 10 to 15 minutes, mashing with the back of a spoon or a potato masher, to draw out all the flavor from the shells. Add

2 cups dry white wine, 2½ quarts cold water, 10 parsley stems, 1 bay leaf, 5 white peppercorns, and 2 sprigs fresh thyme, and bring to a boil. Reduce the heat and simmer for 45 minutes. Strain through a fine mesh sieve. Degrease, cool, and refrigerate or freeze until needed.

Tamarind
Available in a variety of forms, tamarind is a sour fruit used as a flavoring in both sweet and savory dishes throughout Asia. The reddish-brown flesh of the ripened fruit is sometimes dried with the seeds (which need to be removed before the pulp is used). Seeded tamarind is also dried and compressed into dense cakes. Tamarind is sometimes sold powdered or as stiff, concentrated paste. All tamarind must be reconstituted in hot water before being used. After soaking for 15 minutes, the pulp should be squeezed and kneaded to moisten and disperse the fruit in the water. Straining removes the seeds and any tough fibers.

Tangerine peels, dried
Dried tangerine peels are an essential Chinese ingredient that can be purchased at Chinese herb shops. They can also be prepared by drying out tangerine peels (with the white pith) in an oven with the pilot light on for 24 hours or in a food dehydrator.

Terrines and molds
The size, shape, and construction of the terrine or mold will affect the quantity and cooking time of the recipe. Most chefs prefer using enameled cast iron or ceramic terrines when cooking foie gras. The standard rectangular enameled cast iron terrine by Le Creuset holds 6 cups, which requires approximately two whole Grade A foie gras to fill. Smaller terrines in

different shapes and sizes (for example, a 3-cup oval to hold one liver) are available from a number of manufacturers. Be sure to select a terrine appropriate for the size of the dish you are preparing—if it is too large, the liver will cook too quickly, if it is too small, the rendered fat will overflow.

Ti leaves
A staple of Hawaiian and Polynesian cooking, ti leaves are used to wrap and flavor foods for cooking. They are sometimes available fresh from florists, but be sure they are not treated with pesticides. Before using them for cooking, fresh ti leaves should be rinsed in cold water and dried. Dried ti leaves should be reconstituted in hot water before using.

Toasting
Most spices, nuts, and seeds should be toasted before incorporating them into a recipe in order to enhance their flavor. Place them on a dry sheet pan and set in a preheated 350-degree oven for 8 to 10 minutes until they release their oils and you can detect a slightly toasted aroma.

Tomato concassé
A fine **brunoise** of peeled, seeded tomato used as a flavoring agent or garnish.

Truffle
The truffle traditionally called for in foie gras recipes is the prized black Périgord truffle (*Tuber melanosporum*). These truffles should be carefully peeled with a sharp paring knife and are best when gently cooked to release their flavor. They are available fresh from early December to late February. The more expensive white truffles of Italy's Piedmont region (*T. magnatum*), on the other hand, do not have to be peeled, just cleaned, and are rarely cooked.

Instead, white truffles are freshly shaved on top of a prepared dish just prior to service. They are available from September to December. Canned truffles and other processed truffle products are available year round.

Truffle juice

Truffle juice is imported from France in small jars or tins. A by-product of preserving truffles, truffle juice is a thin, truffle-flavored liquid with the consistency of soup. It is available from specialty truffle importers.

Truffle oil

Commercially produced truffle oils vary in quality, ranging from those that contain a simple, manufactured essence of truffle to those that have been intensely infused with fresh truffles. To prepare your own truffle oil, gently steep truffles in a fine but mild olive or more neutral oil (such as grapeseed). Heat to just below a simmer for several minutes and store in an airtight jar with the truffle, for one week before using.

Verjus

A traditional Medieval sour condiment that predates vinegar, verjus has recently regained popularity. It is made from the juice of unripened grapes, and is increasingly available in specialty gourmet stores.

Vinegar

It is important to use the vinegar specified in each recipe to produce the best flavors. The quality of balsamic vinegars varies tremendously. Use the best that you can afford—usually the vinegars that are aged longer, at least seven years, are of higher quality. Those labeled "aceto balsamico tradizionale di Modena" are the best on the market and command a very high price. Other vinegars, such as sherry, white wine, red wine, and cider vinegar are generally less acidic than plain white vinegar and provide a more subtle flavor. Some specialty vinegars, such as melfor (from Alsace) or cane (from New Orleans), provide a distinct regional taste. When rice wine vinegar is required for a recipe, use the unflavored variety.

Wakame [wah-kah-may]

A green, ribbonlike seaweed grown off the coast of Japan in the Pacific waters, wakame is available fresh and dried. Fresh hiyashi wakame is the principle ingredient in the common seaweed salad (*sunomono*) dressed with hot pepper flakes and sesame oil and served in Japanese restaurants. When boiled in liquid, fresh hiyashi wakame has strong gelatinlike properties, similar to agar agar. Dried wakame can be reconstituted in warm water, but it loses its gelling properties.

Wasabe [wah-sah-bee]

It is impossible to compare fresh wasabe and wasabe paste, the former offering a more complex flavor and a delicate texture. The price of fresh wasabe, however, can be prohibitive. When available, fresh wasabe, actually the root of a plant that grows in the mountains of Japan and is now being cultivated in Oregon, should be peeled and finely grated. Dried wasabe should be purchased in small amounts and mixed with water to form a paste.

Sources

FOIE GRAS AND DUCK PRODUCTS

Hudson Valley Foie Gras
80 Brooks Rd.
Ferndale, NY 12734
Phone: (914) 292-2500
Tollfree: (877) BUY-FOIE
Fax: (914) 292-3009
Website: www.foiegras.net
Will ship mulard foie gras and duck
products directly or provide a list of local
distributors.

Sonoma Foie Gras
P.O. Box 2007
Sonoma, CA 95476
Phone: (707) 938-1229
Tollfree: (800) 427-4559
Fax: (707) 938-0496
www.sonomafoiegras.com
Producer of fresh muscovy foie gras.

D'Artagnan
280 Wilson Ave.
Newark, NJ 07105
Phone: (973) 344-0565
Tollfree: (800) D'ARTAGNAN
Fax: (973) 465-1870
Website: www.dartagnan.com
Ships both domestic and imported foie
gras.

SPECIALTY MEATS AND GAME

Calhoun's Ham House
211 S. East St.
Culpeper, VA 22701
Phone: (540) 825-8319
Tollfree: (877) 825-8319
Fax: (540) 825-6708
Website: www.calhounhams.com
Some of the best country ham produced
in the country.

D'Artagnan
Wide selection of domestic and imported
game and prepared products. See above.

Niman Ranch
1025 East 12th Street
Oakland, CA 94606
Phone: (510) 808-0330
Fax: (510) 808-0339
Website: www.nimanranch.com
The finest quality beef, lamb, and pork,
raised with ecological respect.

Polarica
105 Quint St.
San Francisco, CA 94124
Phone: (415) 647-1300
Tollfree: (800) 426-3872
Fax: (415) 647-6826
Website: www.polarica.com
Fresh foie gras and game distributors.

Salumeria Biellese
376 Eighth Ave.
New York, NY 10001
Phone: (212) 736-7376
Fax: (212) 736-7376
Classic Italian and French style sausages,
plus custom orders.

FISH AND SEAFOOD

Browne Trading Company
260 Commercial Street
Portland, ME 04101
Phone: (207) 766-2402
Tollfree: (800) 944-7848
Fax: (207) 766-2404
Website: www.brownetrading.com
Premium fresh seafood, caviar, and related
products.

Ducktrap River Fish Farm
RR #2, Box 378
Lincolnville, ME 04849
Phone: (207) 763-4141
Tollfree: (800) 828-3825
Fax: (207) 763-4235
Website: www.ducktrap.com
All natural smoked seafood products.

Caviarteria
502 Park Ave.
New York, NY 10021
Phone: (718) 482-8480
Tollfree: (800) 4-CAVIAR
Fax: (718) 482-8985
Website: www.caviarteria.com
Wide variety of caviars.

Legal Seafoods Market
5 Cambridge Center
Cambridge, MA 02139
Phone: (617) 783-8084
Tollfree: (800) 343-5804
Fax: (617) 254-5809
Website: www.legalseafoods.com
Primarily lobster and fresh fish based on
availability.

Perona Farms
350 Andover-Sparta Rd.
Andover, NJ 07821
Phone: (973) 729-7878
Tollfree: (800) 762-8569
Fax: (973) 729-1097
Website: www.peronafarms.com
Smoked salmon and other speciality
products.

Petrossian
182 W. 58th St.
New York, NY
Phone: (212) 245-0303
Tollfree: (800) 828-9241
Fax: (212) 337-0007
Website: www.petrossian.com
A celebrated name for caviar, smoked fish, foie gras, and other imported products from France.

Seafood.com
430 Marrett Rd.
Lexington, MA 02421
Phone: (781) 861-1760
Fax: (781) 861-3823
Website: www.seafood.com
Gathers online seafood purchasing sites on one homepage.

HERBS, SPICES, AND CONDIMENTS
Kalustyan's
123 Lexington Ave.
New York, NY 10016
Phone: (212) 685-3451
Fax: (212) 683-8458
Website: www.kalustyans.com
Outstanding selection of spices and specialty ingredients from Asia, Middle East, and elsewhere.

Penzey's Spices
W19362 Apollo Dr.
Muskego, WI 53150
Phone: (414) 679-7207
Fax: (414) 679-7878
Website: www.penzeys.com
Impressive selection of the finest and freshest spices available.

SPECIALTY PRODUCE
Brooks Tropicals
P.O. Box 900160
Homestead, FL 33090
Phone: (305) 247-3544
Tollfree: (800) 327-4833
Fax: (305) 242-7393
Website: www.brookstropicals.com
Extensive selection of tropical fruits.

The Chef's Garden
9009 Huron Avery Rd.
Huron, OH 44839
Phone: (419) 433-4947
Tollfree: (800) 289-4644
Fax: (419) 433-2403
Specialty produce, including a wide array of microgreens.

Freida's Rare and Exotic Foods
P.O. Box 58488
Los Angeles, CA 90058
Phone: (714) 826-6100
Tollfree: (800) 241-1771
Fax: (714) 816-0203
Website: www.freidas.com
Impressive selection of fruits, vegetables, and other specialty produce.

Indian Rock Produce
Box 317
530 California Rd.
Quakertown, PA 18951
Phone: (215) 536-9600
Tollfree: (800) 882-0512
Fax: (215) 529-9447
Finest quality produce.

Royal Hawaiian Sea Farms
P.O. Box 3167 Kailua-Kona, HI 96745
Phone & Fax: (808) 329-5468
Email: limu@ilhawaii.com
The freshest seaweed shipped direct from the source.

TRUFFLES AND TRUFFLE PRODUCTS
Gourmand
2869 Towerview Rd.
Herndon, VA 20171
Phone: (703) 708-0000
Tollfree: (800) 627-7272
Fax: (703) 708-9393
Website: www.gourmand.com
Superb for truffles and all types of specialty imported products.

Urbani
29-24 40th Ave.
Long Island City, NY 11101
Phone: (718) 392-5050
Tollfree: (800) 281-2330
Fax: (718) 392-1704
Website: www.urbani.com
Leading truffle distributor in the world.

MUSHROOMS
D'Artagnan
Extensive selection sold under the Aux Délices des Bois label. See previous page.

Fresh and Wild
P.O. Box 2981
Vancouver, WA 98668
Phone: (360) 737-3652
Tollfree: (800) 222-5578
Fax: (360) 737-3657
A wide variety of wild and cultivated mushrooms shipped directly.

Mr. Mushroom
www.mushroom.com
Online catalog of specialty mushrooms.

SPECIALTY GROCERIES
Balducci's
424 Sixth Ave.
New York, NY
Phone: (212) 260-0400
Tollfree: (800) 225-3822
Fax: (212) 982-4591
Website: www.balduccis.com
Top quality groceries, meats, and
prepared foods with an emphasis on
Italian products.

Dean & DeLuca
560 Broadway
New York, NY 10012
Phone: (212) 431-1691
Tollfree: (800) 221-7714
Fax: (212) 334-6183
Website: www.dean-deluca.com
Everything under the sun, including
extraordinary cheese, condiments, and
cookware.

Zingerman's
422 Detroit St.
Ann Arbor, MI 48104
Phone: (734) 769-1625
Tollfree: (888) 636-8162
Fax: (734) 769-1260
Website: www.zingermans.com
Specialty groceries, condiments, spices,
and prepared foods shipped direct.

**The King Arthur Flour Baker's
Catalogue**
P,.O. Box 876
Norwich, VT 05055
Tollfree: (800) 827-6836
Fax: (802) 649-5359
Website: www.kingarthurflour.com
Exotic flours, baking equipment, and
other supplies.

Gourmet Market
www.gourmetmarket.com
Tollfree: (800) 913-9247
Online source for hard-to-find groceries.

DAIRY PRODUCTS
Egg Farm Dairy
2 John Walsh Blvd.
Peekskill, NY 10566
Phone: (914) 734-7343
Tollfree: (800) CREAMERY
Fax: (914) 734-9287
Website: www.eggfarmdairy.com
Cultured butter, organically produced
milk, and other products.

COOKWARE
Bridge Kitchenware
214 E. 52nd St.
New York, NY 10022
Phone: (212) 688-4220
Tollfree: (800) 274-3435
Fax: (212) 758-5387
Website: www.bridgekitchenware.com
If they don't have it, it isn't available.

Chef's Catalog
3215 Commercial Ave.
Northbrook, IL 60062
Phone: (972) 401-6300
Tollfree: (800) 825-8255
Fax: (972) 401-6306
Website: www.chefscatalog.com
Extensive selection of high-end
professional and home cookware.

**New England Cheesemaking Supply
Company**
P.O. Box 85
Ashfield, MA 01330
Phone: (413) 628-3808
Fax: (413) 528-4061
Website: www.chesemaking.com
Finest quality cheesecloth and butter
muslin.

GENERAL FOOD WEBSITES
www.digitalchef.com
www.epicurious.com
www.foodtv.com
www.gourmetspot.com
www.starchefs.com

Index